The Origins of Arab Nationalism

List of Contributors

Lisa Anderson is Associate Professor of Political Science and Director of the Middle East Institute, Columbia Unviersity.
Beth Baron is Assistant Professor of History at City College of the City University of New York.
C. Ernest Dawn is Professor Emeritus of History at the University of Illinois.
Mahmoud Haddad is Assistant Professor of History at Columbia University.
M. Şükrü Hanioğlu is Associate Professor of Near Eastern Studies at Princeton University.
James Jankowski is Professor of History at the University of Colorado.
Rashid Khalidi is Associate Professor of Modern Middle East History and Director of the Center for Middle Eastern Studies at the University of Chicago.
Muhammad Muslih is Assistant Professor of History at C.W. Post College.
William Ochsenwald is Professor of History at Virginia Polytechnic Institute.
Samir Seikaly is Professor of History at the American University of Beirut.
Reeva S. Simon is Staff Associate at the Middle East Institute, Columbia University.
Ahmed Tarabein is Professor of History at al-Ain University, United Arab Emirates.
Mary C. Wilson is Associate Professor of History at the University of Massachusetts, Amherst.

The Origins of
Arab Nationalism

Edited by
Rashid Khalidi, Lisa Anderson,
Muhammad Muslih, and Reeva S. Simon

Columbia University Press   NEW YORK

Note on Transcription

In the transliteration of Arabic and Turkish words, personal names, and place names, we have been sparing in the use of diacritical marks and have used them only when it was absolutely essential. Otherwise commonly accepted English forms are used, especially for Arabic and Turkish place names. In titles of books and articles and in quotations, we kept the transliteration of the original sources intact. For words and names which have both Arabic and Turkish transcription forms, we have inserted the other form of transcription in parentheses.

Columbia University Press
New York   Chichester, West Sussex

Copyright © 1991 Columbia University Press
All Rights Reserved

Library of Congress Cataloging-in-Publication Data

The origins of Arab nationalism / edited by Rashid Khalidi . . . [et al.].
    p. cm.
    Includes bibliographical references and index.
    ISBN 978-0-231-07435-3 (pbk.)

    1. Nationalism—Arab countries—History. 2. Arab countries—Politics and government. I. Khalidi, Rashid.
DS63.6.075 1991
320.5'4'09174927—dc20   91-17101
                                                                  CIP

Casebound editions of Columbia University Press books are printed on permanent and durable acid-free paper.

Printed in the United States of America

Contents

The Origins of Arab Nationalism: Introduction   vii
Rashid Khalidi

Part 1. Issues in the Development of Early Arab Nationalism

1. The Origins of Arab Nationalism   3
   C. Ernest Dawn

2. The Young Turks and the Arabs Before the Revolution of 1908   31
   M. Şükrü Hanioğlu

3. Ottomanism and Arabism in Syria Before 1914: A Reassessment   50
   Rashid Khalidi

Part 2. Syria and Iraq

4. Shukri al-ʿAsali: A Case Study of a Political Activist   73
   Samir Seikaly

5. ʿAbd al-Hamid al-Zahrawi: The Career and Thought of an Arab Nationalist   97
   Ahmed Tarabein

6. Iraq Before World War I: A Case of Anti-European Arab Ottomanism   120
   Mahmoud Haddad

7. The Education of an Iraqi Ottoman Army Officer   151
   Reeva S. Simon

8. The Rise of Local Nationalism in the Arab East   167
   Muhammad Muslih

Part 3. The Hijaz

9. Ironic Origins: Arab Nationalism in the Hijaz,
   1882–1914   189
   William Ochsenwald

10. The Hashemites, the Arab Revolt, and Arab
    Nationalism   204
    Mary C. Wilson

Part 4. Northeast Africa

11. The Development of Nationalist Sentiment in Libya,
    1908–1922   225
    Lisa Anderson

12. Egypt and Early Arab Nationalism, 1908–1922   243
    James Jankowski

13. Mothers, Morality, and Nationalism in Pre-1919
    Egypt   271
    Beth Baron

    Glossary   289
    Bibliography   291
    Index   313

The Origins of Arab Nationalism: Introduction

Rashid Khalidi

For most of this century, Arab nationalism has been regarded as the leading ideology in the Arab world. Recently, there has been skepticism about ascribing such importance to Arab nationalism, both in the present and in retrospect. This change was a reflection of its decline as a political force, the growing significance of nation-state nationalism, and the reemergence of Islamic ideologies in the Middle East. As a result, some scholars nowadays argue that even if not dead, Arab nationalism is a spent force.[1]

Whether this will prove to be true or not will be settled by future historians. The logic of *raison d'état* rather than *raison de la nation* would certainly appear to be dominant in the Arab world today,[2] while religion has become a formidable challenger to all other ideologies. However, Arab nationalism, which can be summarized as the idea that the Arabs are a people linked by special bonds of language and history (and, many would add, religion), and that their political organization should in some way reflect this reality, still has force throughout the Arabic-speaking world. Its corollary is that the Arab states form a system that should function with a high degree of cohesion. Although this system has never worked as its partisans might have wished it to, its continued existence (as revealed for example during Arab summit meetings and in the functioning of the Arab League) is evidence that the bonds of Arabism are still important today.

The rise and apparent decline of Arab nationalism as a political force in the Arab world has influenced the study of its early years: the period before the British and French mandates began in the *mashriq*, or Arab East. This period encompasses the earliest roots of the modern ideology of Arabism in the late nineteenth century, the crucial second Ottoman constitutional period from 1908 to 1914, the events of World War I, and the brief interlude of King Faysal's (Faisal's) Arab government in Damascus from 1918 until 1920. Although much research has been done on this subject by several generations of historians, there remain many controversies between scholars with different approaches.

This book is a response to these controversies, and to the continuing relevance of Arab nationalism, and brings together several of these differing perspectives, although it does not cover all parts of the Arab world or all aspects of the subject. It grew out of informal discussions initiated by Lisa Anderson, Muhammad Muslih, and Reeva Simon, whose individual research on the Maghrib (Maghreb), Palestine, and Iraq approached the question of pre-World War I Arabism from different historic and geographic perspectives. In November 1986, the Middle East Institute of Columbia University, under the directorship of Richard Bulliet, sponsored an international conference, whose goal was to broaden the political and geographic scope of inquiry. The present volume includes revised versions of most papers presented at the conference, with two additional essays. The essays were revised by their authors in light of discussion during the conference, and we would like to acknowledge here the contributions of those who participated, particularly L. Carl Brown, Leila Fawaz, J. C. Hurewitz, Hasan Kayali, Philip Khoury, Martin Kramer, Suleiman Musa, Salim Nasr, Abdul Karim Rafeq, Bassam Tibi, and the late R. Bayly Winder. The editors would also like to acknowledge the special assistance of Mahmoud Haddad, and of Kate Wittenberg of Columbia University Press in the preparation of this book. The essays are complemented by a glossary and bibliography specially prepared for this publication, so as to make it more useful to students and researchers alike.

Among the problems concerning early Arab nationalism central to the conference and addressed in many essays are the changing conceptual boundaries and political implications of the notion itself. The term *Arabism* was first made current by C. Ernest Dawn, who used it to describe early Arab nationalism and contrasted it with *Ottomanism*, the ideology prevalent in the late Ottoman period. It has since been pointed out that there were several diverse way stations between Ottomanism and Arabism, and that the two ideologies were by no means mutually exclusive. Thus, Arabists could also be believers in the Ottomanist ideal, and before World War I most were. In this, there was a clear difference before 1914 between the majority of Arabists, whose emphasis on Arab identity was linked to continued loyalty to the Ottoman Empire, and the tiny minority of extreme Arab nationalists who called for secession from the empire. Dawn himself has noted that since his first seminal articles on the subject appeared nearly thirty years ago,[3] he has come to recognize the fluidity of opinions possible between the poles of his "ideal types" of Ottomanism and Arabism.

We also asked ourselves which sources can best be used for study of this subject. There are many difficulties inherent in the use of foreign diplomatic sources, as Lisa Anderson noted during discussions at the conference, pointing out that foreign observers often see what they want in local autonomy movements. C. Ernest Dawn and Martin Kramer questioned some uses of the local press, in particular by modern historians of what Kramer called the "Beirut school": scholars at the American University of Beirut who have utilized the Arabic-language press extensively in their work.[4] Casting doubt on the reliability of the press as a source, they pointed to censorship, self-censorship, and the vexing issue of how representative the press actually is: as Dawn noted, it is difficult to infer what people are thinking from newspaper articles. Samir Seikaly and Rashid Khalidi argued that identical problems exist with other sources, whose utility depends on the careful checking of one type of source against another. They added that while the press has flaws as a source, it has the advantage of having been a vehicle for the expression of ideas among key sectors of the politicized elite, whose views are often hard to discern otherwise.

Several other questions that arose at the conference form the backdrop of the essays in this volume. The first is the extent to which Turkish nationalism contributed to the evolution of Arab nationalism. How much was the Committee of Union and Progress (CUP), which dominated Ottoman politics for the decade after 1908, influenced by Turkish nationalism? What in turn was the impact of the so-called "Turkification" policies it pursued in the Arab provinces of the empire? How were these things perceived by Arab elites? C. Ernest Dawn argues that the Turkish nationalism of the CUP has been overemphasized and that the party's ideology remained basically Ottomanist, reformist, and Islamic until 1918. M. Şükrü Hanioğlu, utilizing his discoveries of the private papers of several secretaries of the CUP's secret Central Committee, suggests, however, that the CUP was a more intensely Turkish nationalist organization from an earlier date than many historians have suspected. The language used in their secret correspondence by key leaders and founders of the CUP identified them without question as Turkish nationalists, for whom the term Ottomanist had a very narrow meaning.

Recent research on Arab-Turkish relations during the three Ottoman parliaments elected before World War I shows that it is important to distinguish between imperial law and local practice where "Turkification" was concerned.[5] Often all this process amounted to was the replacement of incumbent officials for political reasons. Thus in 1908–1909 many of Sultan ʿAbdülhamid II's Arab appointees in Syria and Libya were replaced by reliable CUP members, mainly Turks. This was the first of several waves of administrative changes that took place as the CUP solidified its hold over the empire's administration, alienating many Arab notables in the process. The intense negative reaction to these changes was based in part on the fact that the CUP's inner circle was made up entirely of Turks. As a result, many in the empire came to identify it, rightly or wrongly, with Turkish nationalism. William Ochsenwald notes that in many respects the CUP's policies were not dissimilar to those of ʿAbdülhamid, although the Sultan had been less effective, more reliant on religion as an ideological support (the avowedly secular CUP could not credibly claim to be motivated by religion in its policies) and better able to rely on high-ranking Arab officials, many of whom were Damascenes. Throughout the Arab provinces, therefore, demands for decentralization and reform were in fact a response not to "Turkification" per se, but rather to a new variety of centralization, which in practice meant domination by a stronger central government controlled by the CUP, whose leadership was largely Turkish.

These observations raise the related problem of the extent to which early Arab nationalism was a response to a combination of Turkish nationalism and CUP-inspired centralization, or to the empire's decline under the pressure of the imperialist European powers. In the Arab periphery of the empire, which was vulnerable to European designs, this external pressure was often the main concern of the populace, whose attitude toward the state, and their self-definition, were largely determined by how well it defended them against external dangers. At the same time, as analyses of the cases of Libya, the Hijaz (Hejaz) and Iraq demonstrate, there were great variations between different regions on the empire's periphery.

Thus, Lisa Anderson stresses that in Libya during this period the primary preoccupation was Italian ambition in the north and French designs in the south, rather than centralization or "Turkification." The empire was seen as a vital shield against the European powers, and there was thus little growth of Arabism before 1914. In the Hijaz, by contrast, opposition to centralization, rather than nationalism per se, was the primary concern during this period, according to William Ochsenwald. This view is supported by Mary C. Wilson, who argues that the Hashemites were initially little influenced by the relatively developed Arabism of the urban elites in the Fertile Crescent.

In Iraq, Mahmoud Haddad discerns a pattern of opposition to foreign, and in particular British, expansion. Significantly, he finds this more important than any anticentralization tendency. Opposition to the CUP arose essentially because it was perceived as being insufficiently active in defense of Iraq against foreign powers, and it was even accused of complicity in facilitating foreign penetration. In the face of European ambitions, certain Arab political forces thus embraced both Arabism and Ottomanism. This pattern is also noted in Syria by Ahmed Tarabein and Samir Seikaly, whose studies of the leading Arabists Shaykh ʿAbd al-Hamid al-Zahrawi (Abdülhamid el-Zehravi) and Shukri al-ʿAsali reveal them to be deeply concerned about European ambitions, and show that they faulted the CUP for failing to resist them. They and others point out the significance of differences within regions, such as those between Beirut and Damascus in *bilad al-sham*.

A final issue emerges from several papers: the religious tone that pervaded the writings of many of the political ideologies of the day. Some scholars have thus stressed that an Islamic focus of identity, such as Ottomanism, or the Hashemites' Islamic-based Hijazi regional patriotism, was stronger during these years than the largely secular appeal of Arab nationalism. Others argue that the CUP's perceived secularism and favoring of Turkish nationalism robbed Ottomanism of much of its Islamic content, at least for the politicized elite, pushing many of them toward Arabism. Moreover, Arabism was by no means entirely secular, of course, but included both Islamic and secular elements, depending on the individual who espoused it and his background. Religious influences were apparent in the writings of some leading Arabists, and in the Arabist newspapers and journals they edited, while such influences played little or no role in the thinking of others.

The initial essay in part 1, by C. Ernest Dawn, sums up the conclusions of his pioneering research over more than three decades, adding to it a wealth of new material. Dawn here provides perhaps the most convincing clarification of a question that has long vexed historians of Arab nationalism: what was the impact of the nineteenth-century literary *nahda*, or renaissance, on Arab nationalism, and in particular the contribution of the mainly Lebanese Christians who played such a large part in this literary revival? Dawn conclusively shows that Muslim Turks and Arabs played the primary role in forming a nationalist self-view in the Middle East, pointing particularly to the role of Islamic modernists who became Arab nationalists. Dawn then goes on to dispute conclusions reached by other researchers since the publication of his seminal *From Ottomanism to Arabism*. He introduces a variety of new data, much of it from Turkish and Ottoman sources, to show that Arabism was not a response to "Turkification," and that it remained a minority tendency in Syria and the Arab world generally until 1918.

Dawn's essay is followed by that of M. Şükrü Hanioğlu, whose recent research in the Albanian State Archives and elsewhere has unearthed the private papers of two secretaries of the secret Central Committee of the CUP, Ishak Sükûti and Bahaeddin Sakir Bey. Comparing their correspondence with data culled from the better-known Ottoman and European diplomatic archives, Hanioğlu reveals that these and other CUP leaders had a strongly nationalist orientation. This Turkish nationalism developed well before the 1908 revolution and combined with a profound attitude of superiority to Arabs and other nationalities in the empire to contribute to later conflicts between the Arabists and the CUP.

Rashid Khalidi's essay builds on those of Dawn and Hanioğlu to argue the necessity for a reassessment of the relative balance between Ottomanism and Arabism in Syria before 1914. Stressing the new findings on the Turkish-Arab relations of young Turkish historians like Hanioğlu and Hasan Kayali, Khalidi reaffirms the impact of CUP policies that were perceived by many Arabs as being motivated by Turkish nationalism in spurring the growth of Arabism. He notes that the importance of Beirut, Palestine, and other coastal areas (and of centers like Cairo and Istanbul) have been underestimated by historians who have focused on Damascus and who ignore elements of the cultural, economic, and political unity of the entire region before 1914. Khalidi carries further his previous work on the vital roles of the Ottoman parliament and of the Arabic-language press in the growth of Arabism, arguing that they deserve more attention in study of this period. He concludes with suggestions for further refinements in our definitions of the terms Arabism and Ottomanism, and of the nature of the political elite in *bilad al-sham* before World War I.

In part 2, Samir Seikaly and Ahmed Tarabein offer studies of Shukri al-ʿAsali and Shaykh ʿAbd al-Hamid al-Zahrawi. Members of the Ottoman parliament and prominent journalists, both played leading roles in the Arabist movement, both appeared to have come to terms with the CUP in 1913, and both ended their lives on the gallows after being convicted of treason by a military court-martial in Damascus in 1916. These essays show that in spite of such similarities, the two were quite different in a number of respects: al-Zahrawi, who received religious training from reformist *salafi* teachers, represents the Islamic modernist trend in Arabism, while al-ʿAsali, the product of state schools and a career in the state bureaucracy, personified the more secularist tendency. These portraits refine considerably our view of two major actors in the politics of the period.

Mahmoud Haddad examines the development of Arabism in Iraq before 1914. The first issue to unify Arab deputies in the

Ottoman parliament emerged from Iraq in 1909: the British Lynch Brothers concession for Mesopotamian river navigation. Haddad finds that agitation over this concession, as well as a later controversy over the sale of government land to foreigners, fit a pattern of opposition to external encroachment by specific social forces in Iraq based on local patriotism. He shows that the Ottoman authorities' weakness in resisting foreign encroachment (which at times they even facilitated) was the basis of Iraqi complaints about the CUP-dominated government, rather than the latter's ideology per se. The resulting stimulation of local patriotism in turn contributed to the growth of Arabism in Iraq.

Reeva Simon focuses on the expansion of military education in Iraq as part of the formation of a new Ottoman officer corps in the late nineteenth century. In doing so, she assesses the constitution and influence of the officer corps itself, an institution of importance both in Ottoman and Iraqi mandatory politics, and lays stress on education, which has received insufficient attention in research on the late Ottoman period and on early Arab nationalism. Simon shows how the teaching of Turkish history and of the Turkish roots of the Ottoman state in Ottoman military schools came to have a political significance, particularly after the 1908 revolution. She also notes the importance of this training in forming bonds among Iraqi army officers that continued long afterward.

There is an interesting contrast between the two papers on Iraq: one focuses on Iraqis in Iraq, most of them notables, merchants, and landowners, while the other deals with Iraqi officers in the Ottoman army in Istanbul, most of them from relatively humble backgrounds. Simon's paper is one of the few in this collection to deal with the careers of the individuals from the lower social classes and their role in politics, surely a topic that deserves more attention.

Muhammad Muslih deals with the emergence of nation-state nationalisms alongside Arab nationalism during the rule of King Faysal's Arab government in Damascus from 1918 until 1920. He analyzes this formative experience in the careers of leaders who later played important roles in the national movements of Syria, Iraq, and Palestine, showing how it laid the foundation for the development of territorially based nationalism in all three countries. He demonstrates that although the development of these separate nationalisms was a response to specific conditions created in the three countries by the European mandates, it was also a result of difficulties in reconciling the different interests of members of their elites which emerged in Damascus under Faysal. These included conflicts based on differing class origins and varying regional perspectives.

With the papers in part 3, we move to the Hijaz, site of the Arab revolt of 1916, and home of the Hashemite dynasty, which eventually came to rule two of the states carved by Britain and France from the Arab provinces of the Ottoman Empire. Here too there are a number of questions that have long been a source of controversy among historians, including the role of the Hashemites in the rise of Arab nationalism and the extent of the family's commitment to Arabism in the period before the revolt.

William Ochsenwald's essay shows how limited was the spread of Arab nationalism in the Hijaz before 1914. He demonstrates that religion and tribal links, rather than nationalism, were the bases of politics in the Hijaz. This was in large measure due to the limited growth in the Hijaz of secular education, of the professional groups it created, and of the press, all of which were essential ingredients in the spread of Arabism elsewhere. Ochsenwald illustrates this thesis with an analysis of the politics of the Hijaz from 1908 until 1914, showing that throughout his conflict with the central government in this period, Sharif Husayn's ideology was pragmatic with little trace of nationalism. He thus points out the irony in the fact that the Arab revolt and "Arab independence began in the non-nationalist Hijaz."

Mary C. Wilson applies similar arguments to the crucial period of the Arab revolt. She shows that "Arabism was not espoused by the Hashemites until it became of particular use to them." Only after their forces had crossed the boundaries of the Hijaz and moved toward Syria did the Hashemites begin to employ Arabism against the Ottoman state. Wilson contrasts the approach of Amir ʿAbdallah (Abdullah), whose focus was the Arabian peninsula, with that of his brother Faysal, leader of the Arab forces moving northward into Syria, who embraced Arabism as the vehicle for his appeal to the elites of Syria, where his own ambitions were directed. Although ʿAbdallah had been in touch with Arabist currents as a deputy in the Ottoman parliament in Istanbul, during the Arab revolt he confined himself to traditional tribal means of gathering support against the besieged Ottoman garrison at Medina, and against the Hashemites' main Arab rival, Ibn Sa'ud. When 'Abdallah moved into Transjordan in early 1921, he employed Arab nationalist rhetoric, as had Faysal during his northward march five years earlier, but unlike his younger brother, who found important Arab nationalist constituencies in Syria and later in Iraq, 'Abdallah learned that Transjordan was infertile soil for this ideology.

The final part of the book deals with regions that were influenced by Arab nationalism later than Syria, Iraq and the Hijaz. They are nevertheless areas of importance for early Arab nationalism—Libya as the focus of a conflict beginning in 1911 between Italian imperialism and the Ottoman state, and Egypt as the largest Arabic-speaking country and an influential center of Arabist publishing and thinking among émigré Syrians.

In the Libyan case, as Lisa Anderson shows, the growth of Arabist sentiment was prevented by specific circumstances, among which were: the existence of non-Arab Berber elements; strong links with Istanbul (and with CUP politicians in particular because many had spent time in exile in Libya); and the intense fear of European encroachment, which reinforced the Libyans' desire for close ties with the Ottoman Empire. She shows that Islamic loyalties linked to support for the empire tended to predominate in Libya through World War I. This was in part because of the important role played by the Ottomans in supporting Libyan resistance to European imperialism in what Professor Anderson calls a "'reverse Arab revolt'—a local revolt supported by the Ottomans to undermine the British position during the war." Thus, even after the collapse of the empire, Libyan identity was expressed primarily in Islamic rather than Arab terms.

In Egypt, Islamic components of identity, connected with a desire to retain links to the Ottoman Empire, were also important in the period before World War I, as was the territorial patriotism summed up in the slogan "Egypt for the Egyptians," which originated in what Schölch has called "the socio-political crisis [in Egypt] of 1878–1882."[6] Both tendencies were related to opposition to European domination of Egypt. The parallels with Libya's struggle with foreign control are obvious, and yet in the Egyptian case there was a more complex relationship between the various elements of identity. The specificity of the country was perhaps more strongly felt and more important politically than in Libya, while in both cases the link to the Ottoman Empire was largely a matter of pragmatic convenience, with Arabism playing a very small part in the thinking of most Egyptians until much later, as James Jankowski shows.[7]

Writing on women and nationalism in Egypt before 1919, Beth Baron points out that until the dissolution of the Ottoman Empire "most Egyptians still felt attached to the empire and favored Egyptian Ottomanism." In this circumstance, much of the involvement of women in Egyptian nationalist politics took the form of support for the Ottoman state, particularly when it was in distress, as during the Italian invasion of Libya. Upper-class women were prominent in these activities, and the fact that many of them were of Turkish origin and felt a deep kinship for the Ottoman elite increased this sentiment. But as Baron shows, for many women participation in nationalist struggles was a means to legitimize their increased emancipation as much as it was a result of their patriotic opposition to British occupation of their country. She explores women's involvement in nationalist politics, concluding that their efforts were "probably more important to their own development than to national struggle." These thirteen essays represent the frontier of scholarship on the origins of Arab nationalism, and on the society in which it emerged. At the same time, many of the questions they touch on remain open ones, and some of the gaps they have identified deserve further attention.

We still know very little about the intersection between Arab and Turkish nationalism, and between the end of the Ottoman and the beginning of the mandatory periods in the Arab *mashriq*. This gap presents a problem not just because it represents the convergence of so many different subjects and periods, which involves so many varied types of expertise, including facility in languages ranging from Ottoman to modern Turkish, and from Arabic to European, as well as familiarity with sources in all these languages. Historians of the Arab world must learn more about Ottoman and modern Turkish sources in order to deal better with the Ottoman aspect of modern Arab history, while Turkish historians in turn need to immerse themselves in the local sources of the Arab provinces and other outlying regions in order to get a better sense of the interaction between the center and this periphery in the late Ottoman period.

The regional variations in the development of Arab nationalism and local territorial nationalism also merit further attention. Fresh monographic work of quality is emerging, focusing on specific regions and treating nationalism and other trends that affected Egypt, Syria, Iraq, Libya, and the Hijaz over the past century. But many questions remain unanswered. For example, did the social background of those attracted to nationalism vary from country to country? What was the effect of Zionism, not just on Palestinian nationalism, but on Arab nationalism as a whole? Why were the impact of European ideas and the reaction to European imperialism apparently different from country to country? While this volume includes some efforts in the direction of such broadly based comparative work, there is a need for more, particularly in view of the current emphasis on the variations between the different Arab countries.

These lacunae reflect our inadequate grasp of the overall shape of social transformation in the Arab world since the nineteenth century and its relation to the political and ideological trends that have already been extensively examined. Here again, monographic work on specific countries has been done, while broader synthetic analysis addressing the region as a whole has been lacking. There seem to have been many common social trends in several Arab countries, as domination by traditional notables and the central state authorities gave way to an uneasy alliance between notables and middle-class elements in a tenuous relation to European colonial powers. This new elite was often replaced after independence by a lower-middle-class one based in part in the military. While the outlines of this pattern are generally accepted and aspects of it have been examined, a comprehensive treatment spanning more than a century and covering the region as a whole has been absent.

Although this volume could not address itself fully to such a broad research agenda including so many questions, it is an indication of the breadth of its approach that it shows clearly how much remains to be done in illuminating the origins and impact of early Arab nationalism.

Notes

1. To give a recent example, this is the main thesis in several essays in Tawfic Farah, ed., *Pan-Arabism and Arab Nationalism: The Continuing Debate* (Boulder, Colo.: 1987).
2. These terms are applied to nation-state nationalism and pan-Arab nationalism respectively by Walid Khalidi in his article "Thinking the Unthinkable," *Foreign Affairs* 56, no. 4 (July 1978): 695–713.
3. These articles were collected in C. Ernest Dawn, *From Ottomanism to Arabism*. Perhaps the most influential among them were the title essay, pp. 122–47, and "The Rise of Arabism in Syria," pp. 148–79.
4. Among the most notable of these scholars was the late Marwan R. Buheiry, whose untimely death interrupted a career marked by an exceptional sensitivity to the import and value of the local press. Several of his essays, collected in Lawrence I. Conrad, ed., *The Formation and Perception of the Modern Arab World: Studies by Marwan R. Buheiry*, use the press and other local sources, as do most of the papers in Marwan R. Buheiry, ed., *Intellectual Life in the Arab East, 1890–1939*.
5. At the conference, Hasan Kayali discussed recent research on this subject. His Ph.D. dissertation, "Arabs and Young Turks: Turkish-Arab Relations in the Second Constitutional Period of the Ottoman Empire (1908–1918)," was presented at Harvard University in May 1988.
6. This is the subtitle of Alexander Schölch's *Egypt for the Egyptians!*, the definitive study of this topic.
7. In addition to the article in this volume, see James Jankowski, "Ottomanism and Arabism in Egypt," pp. 226–59. See also Israel Gershoni and James P. Jankowski, *Egypt, Islam, and the Arabs*.

PART ONE

Issues in the Development of Arab Nationalism

ONE

The Origins of Arab Nationalism

C. Ernest Dawn

For years, the most prevalent explanation of the origins of Arab nationalism undoubtedly was that contact with the West revived latent Arab nationality, so long suppressed by Islam or the Turks, among Lebanese Christian Arabs, who then led their compatriots in the movement to base political and cultural life on nationality, not religion. In this view, the genesis of Arab nationalism was part of the Arab awakening by which the Arabs moved into the modern world of Western science and secularism. First popularized among Western observers and students by George Antonius, this version has retained its popularity—and perhaps the best statement of some of its elements has been given by Albert Hourani and Hisham Sharabi. The Muslims sought in Western culture the means of warding off Western power, but in so doing had an "uneasy feeling of being untrue to themselves." The Christians, on the other hand, did not feel that Christian Europe was alien.[1] The role of the Christians is further explained by Sharabi and Bassam Tibi in their use of the common notion that nationalism is a movement of the bourgeoisie. The Christian Arabs, they believe, were the only bourgeois element in Arab society at the time.[2]

The Christian explanation faces insurmountable difficulties. Its exponents present no persuasive evidence or argument on behalf of either the supposed sympathy of Christian Arabs and European Christians or the bourgeois nature of either the Christian Arabs or the Arab nationalists. The common argument given for this explanation is the activity of Western missionary schools, especially the American, which, it is claimed, first introduced Western ideas in the Arab world.[3] This argument evidently was made by some Arabs before 1914, for we find a prominent Syrian Arab nationalist intellectual, Muhammad Kurd ʿAli, rejecting it even then; and when Anis Nusuli made this argument in 1926, Kurd ʿAli again rejected it.[4] Kurd ʿAli insisted that the learned and educational institutions of the Egyptian state were by far the most important promoters of the Arab awakening, and though he gave some credit to the missionary schools (especially for their use of Arabic as the language of instruction in their early years), he joined the common Arab nationalist criticism of the missionary schools as weakening national feeling.[5] The missionary schools long confined their efforts to purely sectarian education, not modern secular learning. The learned and educational institutions of the Egyptian state, as Kurd ʿAli insisted, were by far the more important force in the introduction of Western thought. The Ottoman state schools were probably as important as the Egyptian institutions.[6] Among pre-1914 Syrian Arab nationalists, persons educated in Ottoman state schools (63 percent) were far more numerous than persons educated in either traditional or Western schools (20 percent and 17 percent, respectively). Moreover, Christians comprised only 6 percent of the pre-1914 Arabists while in 1926 they were 10 percent or 12 percent of the total Syrian population.[7] Hourani, whose treatment in *Arabic Thought* of the Christian Arabs' role in Arab nationalism was ambiguous, later wrote, "The Lebanese Christian movement was not a major factor."[8]

The process of forming a nationalist self-view among the Arabs began with the adaptation to Near Eastern conditions of the European concept of patria and patriotism. The evidence presently available indicates that Muslim Arabs and the Turks took the lead. Of the Arabs, Rifaʿah Rafiʿ al-Tahtawi was the most influential. Between 1834 and mid-century, in his account of his residence in Paris and in his poetry, Tahtawi expounded the ideas that the earth was comprised of countries with their own special characteristics, and that inhabitants of each such country had a peculiar relationship to and a special love for it. He rendered the French *patrie* by the Arabic *watan*, spoke of the love of the *watan* and, ultimately, of *wataniyya*, patriotism. Tahtawi's *watan* was Egypt, and the people of Egypt had been a distinctive entity since the time of the pharaohs.[9] During the same period, Ottoman Turkish intellectuals and statesmen were setting forth the concept that the Ottoman territories formed the Ottoman *vatan*, which the Ottoman people should love.[10]

The appeal of the European concept of patriotism to Egyptian and Ottoman intellectual bureaucrats resulted from their desire to overcome the perceived deprivation of the Islamic countries or the Ottoman Empire. They had direct contact with European civilization as a result of occupying positions of authority and responsibility in the governance of their polities. They were painfully aware that the European countries and the Christian Franks were far more advanced in civilization than the Muslim countries. They fervently wished to bring the Islamic countries up to the level of the West. Tahtawi, in describing the purpose of his book recording his sojourn in Paris, said, "I made it speak to stimulate the lands of Islam to investigate the foreign sciences, arts, and industries, for the perfection of that in the land of the Franks is a well-known certainty, and the truth deserves to be followed." They believed that the progress of Europe was the result of patriotism, the love of the French, for example, of their fatherland. Patriotism thus was a source of progress and strength, a means to overcome the gap between the lands of Islam and Europe.[11]

The perception of the Self as deprived relative to the Other often injures the self-view, and Arab and Turkish intellectuals and statesmen were no exception. Tahtawi followed his admission of the perfection in sciences, arts, and industries of the Franks with the exclamation, "By the Eternal God! During my stay in this country I was in pain because of its enjoyment of that [perfection] and its absence from the lands of Islam." The pain caused by the invidious comparison was eased, as is commonly the case, by noting some virtues possessed by the Self and lacking in the Other and by finding hope for the future of the Self in its past. The Muslims were still blessed with the perfect religion, while the Franks, Christian in name only, relied on reason alone. Moreover, in the past Muslims had been the teachers of the Franks in the natural sciences, as some of the Franks admitted. Thus, the Muslims should borrow the Western sciences from the Franks and hold fast to the true religion. In doing so, it was thought, the gap would soon be closed.

Such defensive reaffirmations of the self-view were, as far as it is possible to judge such matters, sincere personal expressions of grief for the present and hope for the future, of confidence in the worth of the authors and their fellow countrymen. At the same time, these ideas grew out of a division within the community. Ottoman and Egyptian advocates of Westernizing reform had rivals. The advocates were members of the government, but their opponents charged them with heresy and treason, of trafficking with the hostile alien, and countered with assertions of the adequacy of the community's inherited beliefs, laws, and institutions. Despite such opposition, the reformers retained power in Egypt and the empire and continued their policies. As the second half of the nineteenth century began, the adequacy of both government and opposition ideologies was put in doubt. By this time, the failures of Egypt and the Ottoman state in comparison to Europe were too obvious. One could question the efficacy of both the reforms and the inherited culture, but there seemed to be no escape from adopting the ways of the West. This perception increased the injury to the self-view, which could no longer be eased by ideas like Tahtawi's, which still composed the ideology of the establishment. Consequently, the opposition was able to advance an opposing self-view, the set of beliefs that later came to be known as Islamic modernism and revivalism. Perhaps the earliest exponents of the new view were the Young Ottomans, followers of Mustafa Reshid Pasha, the originator of the Tanzimat reforms that had been defended by thinkers like Tahtawi, who had fallen from power. Some of the crucial elements, whose similarity to earlier ideas is obvious, appeared in the Arabic works of Khayr al-Din al-Tunisi and Tahtawi in the late 1860s. The doctrine was given its fullest expression in Arabic by Jamal al-Din al-Afghani and Muhammad ʿAbduh from the 1880s onward.[12]

The obvious need to imitate the West intensified the injury to the Ottoman and Eastern self-view. The literature produced after the 1860s had an emotional intensity that was absent from the writings of Tahtawi. The government was attacked in the strongest terms for betraying Islam and the fatherland to the Christian West, which was depicted as a determined and unprincipled enemy. The starting point was a bitter lamentation for the lost power and glory that had once been Islam's but had now passed to the Christian West. Islam and the East had not always been in such a sad state. The glories, military and cultural, of the Islamic past were recalled, and the reputed debt of European civilization to Islam was emphasized. In fact, it was declared, the modernity of Europe was of Islamic origin, borrowed from the Muslims and used to advantage, while the Muslims deviated from the original true Islam and consequently suffered stagnation and decline. Immediate blame for this sad situation was assigned to the reforming governments, which had knuckled under to the Europeans by the piecemeal borrowing of Western practices, which could only produce hybrids, Levantines. The correct path was to eliminate the corruptions in the heritage and return to true pristine Islam, which would establish constitutional representative government, freedom, etc., which were of Islamic origin even though their current best manifestation was in the West. In this way, Islam would recover its lost power and glory.

The Muslim Arab reaction to the West that culminated in 'Abduh's Islamic modernism was shared by many Christian Arabs, including most of those commonly called the creators of secular Arab nationalism. Far from expressing feelings of kinship with the West, their writings share the Muslim defense of an injured self-view. Butrus al-Bustani, like many Eastern Christians, resented the perceived patronizing arrogance of Anglo-Saxon Protestant missionaries, and warned against borrowing Western blemishes and vices, as did Ahmad Faris al-Shidyaq and Adib Ishaq. Criticism of excessive "Frankification" became a commonplace of Christian Arab writers. Finally, none of them were Arab nationalists. Bustani, Shidyaq, and Ishaq were Ottoman patriots, as were later luminaries, such as Sulayman al-Bustani, Shibli Shumayyil, and Farah Antun.[13] Both Tibi and Sharabi at times acknowledge the Ottomanism of these intellectuals but cannot abandon belief in their Arabism. Both are ambiguous and inconsistent and provide few particulars, but they regard these Christian Arabs as the creators and propagators of a cultural Arab nationalism that outweighed their Ottomanism. There is no doubt that these Arabs did regard themselves as Arabs.[14]

Many, perhaps all, of the early Western-influenced intellectuals of the Ottoman territories and Egypt held overlapping self-views without any sense of contradiction. Bustani and, to a lesser extent, Ishaq did call themselves Arab and take pride in their Arab heritage. But so did Tahtawi. None of them, Christian or Muslim, attributed political consequences, or even ultimate cultural consequences, to Arabism. None expressed disloyalty to the Ottoman Empire, and the two Christians' political loyalties were decidedly Ottoman. Their cultural identities were also broader. Tahtawi was concerned with the revitalization of all Muslim lands; Bustani and Ishaq, like Shidyaq, fervently longed for the East's recovery of its lost glory. All talked about fatherland and patriotism, *watan* and *wataniyya*, but one person could have more than one *watan* and more than one nation (*umma*). Among some, the smaller *watan* sometimes seemed to be the most important center of loyalty. Tahtawi's Egyptianism has long been the subject of scholarly attention. Just as important was Bustani's Syrian patriotism. But, as already remarked, they did not subordinate the broader identities to the narrower. For some this was not true.

Arabism and regional patriotism were mingled and given predominance over Ottomanism by some in Syria and Lebanon. As early as 1868, Ibrahim al-Yaziji called for the Arabs to recover their lost ancient vitality and to throw off the yoke of the Turks.[15] He also participated in a secret society that worked for this goal in the late 1870s and posted a few placards calling for rebellion in Beirut. During the same period there was a similar movement among Lebanese and Damascene notables, mostly Muslim but possibly with some Christian participation. Though both movements soon disappeared, one spoke almost entirely for Christian Arabs and aimed at an independent Lebanon, while the other was predominantly Muslim Arabs and sought an autonomous Syria that would retain some ties with the Ottoman state.[16] Ibrahim al-Yaziji also spoke of Syria, and it is likely that ideas such as his contributed to the development of Lebanese and Syrian nationalism among the Christians of Lebanon, which had appeared by the end of the century.

By the first years of the twentieth century, Muslim Arabs had developed an Arab nationalist self-view that was to provide the nucleus of Arab nationalist ideology for the twentieth century. The new Arabism was an outgrowth of 'Abduh's Islamic modernism and revivalism. Islam was not intrinsically backward, the self-view held. The true Islam of the ancestors had bestowed rationality on mankind and created the essentials of modernity, which the West had borrowed. While Europe moved forward on the basis of these borrowings, the Muslims fell into error and corrupted and abandoned the true Islam. The cure for the present humiliation and abasement of the Muslims was to return to the true Islam of their ancestors. This done, the power and glory that Islam had lost to the Christian West would return to its rightful owners. That the true Islam was the Islam of their ancestors, and the ancestors were Arab, meant the revival of Arabism and the Arab culture and the restoration of the Arabs to their position of leadership among the Muslims. These ideas were developed by ʿAbduh's followers, Muhammad Rashid Rida and ʿAbd al-Rahman al-Kawakibi. The former hesitated on the brink and refrained from advocating political autonomy, but the latter called for the establishment of a dual Arab and Turkish Ottoman Empire with the Arabs exercising religious and cultural leadership.[17] This version of Islamic modernism was adopted by the earliest exponents of Arab nationalism. While there has not been any systematic study of their writings, enough is known about Mahmud Shukri al-Alusi, ʿAbd al-Hamid al-Zahrawi (see Ahmed Tarabein's essay in this volume), Muhammad Kurd ʿAli, and ʿAbd al-Ghani al-ʿUraysi to justify classifying them as Islamic modernists who had become Arab nationalists.[18]

Islamic modernism's relationship to Arabism has been variously interpreted. Sylvia G. Haim, perhaps the first scholar to investigate the subject, apparently does not derive Arab nationalist ideology from Islamic modernism. In her most recent study of the subject, she points to ʿAbduh's implicit "glorification of Arab Islam and depreciation of Ottoman Islam," and calls Kawakibi "the first true intellectual precursor of modern secular Pan-Arabism," but considers their chief influence to have been, like that of Afghani and others, to "increase skepticism concerning Islam" among Muslims. Her interpretation is similar to that of Elie Kedourie, who depicts Arab nationalism as having been created by the spread of European theological and political doctrines that weakened the hold of Islam and Christianity. He believes that Arab nationalism was established by military officers installed in power by the British after World War I and spread by them, the British, and Egypt's King Faruq (Farouk) and his entourage. Haim also believes that true Arab nationalism was an importation from the West at the time of World War I, and that there was no "serious attempt to define its meaning" until the late 1930s. In order to survive, according to Haim, the newly imported secular Arabism had to become "consonant with" Islam.[19]

In similar fashion, Sharabi and Tibi deny Islamic modernism's parentage of Arabism. The former distinguishes Islamic reformers (e.g., ʿAbduh) from Islamic secularists (e.g., Kawakibi) and regards the latter as having led the Arab nationalist movement from before 1914 until the end of the interwar period, when it collapsed in the face of the secular Arab nationalism that had been created by Lebanese Christians. The latter holds that Islamic modernism contributed to the formation of Arab nationalism, that Kawakibi was an "important pioneer of Arab nationalism," but that Arab nationalism was a secular movement, originating with the Lebanese Christians, "which was eventually to destroy the Islamic revitalism movement," even though Islam was not abandoned by the Arab nationalists.[20]

Those who deny Arabism's birth in Islamic modernism have not provided any specific identification of its ancestry. They write of Arab nationalism without Arab nationalists, of a movement without participants. In this, they unfortunately do not differ from most who have written about Arab nationalism. It has simply been assumed that Arab nationalism must have been imported from the West and is therefore secularist. There has been very little scholarly investigation of the writings of Arab nationalists, and the few who have been studied are late, virtually all post-1939, and there has been no demonstration that they were representative or influential.

There is convincing evidence that the prevailing ideology of Arab nationalists in the twentieth century was formed in the 1920s, at the latest, from Islamic modernist roots. It is impossible at present to determine first authorship and influences, but a number of Arab nationalist publications and authors can be identified. Among them are Amir Shakib Arslan, a postwar convert from Ottomanism to Arabism (but an Islamic modernist at all times), and two prewar Arabists, Muhammad Kurd ʿAli and Muhibb al-din al Khatib. In their publications, the Islamic modernism of Kawakibi, Tahir al-Jaza'iri, and Mahmud Shukri al-Alusi—who are the acknowledged masters—provides the basis for a conception of universal history that incorporates the Semitic wave theory as expressed in Breasted's *Ancient Times* and, among some, certain semi-Marxist ideas.[21] These ideas were incorporated in a number of history textbooks by ʿUmar Salih al-Barghuthi and Khalil Tuta (Tota),[22] Muhammad ʿIzzat Darwaza,[23] and Darwish al-Miqdadi,[24] which appeared in repeated editions in the 1920s and 1930s. By 1931 a more or less standard formulation of the Arab self-view had received statement in these text books. The authors were associated with leading nationalist politicians in the Fertile Crescent, and their books were adopted in the schools of Palestine, Syria, and Iraq. From the late 1920s on, there was a growing use of the same ideas by Egyptian politicians and organizations.[25] Finally, the same ideas appear in the ideology incorporated in Nasserist and Baʿthist school textbooks in Egypt, Syria, and Iraq.[26]

Arab nationalist ideology was a development from Islamic modernism, but some Christian Arabs participated in the Arab nationalist movement. Sharabi offers Najib ʿAzuri and Amin al-Rihani as Arab nationalists, presumably among those unspecified Christians who created the secular Arab nationalism that, according to Sharabi, eliminated Islamic modernism.[27] That either had any influence is yet to be demonstrated. ʿAzuri's curious career need not detain us.[28] Rihani was a prominent man of letters and an Arab nationalist. His book *Muluk al-ʿarab* (Kings of the Arabs; 1924–25) was praised while his sketch of Syrian history, *al-Nakbat* (The Calamities; 1928), was excoriated by Kurd ʿAli.[29] Rihani and his fellow Christian Arabists accepted the special place of Islam and Muhammad in the life of the Arab nation that had already been acknowledged by pre-1914 Christian Arabs.[30] The tradition had later expositors, notably Michel ʿAflaq.[31]

The earliest Arab nationalists disseminated their doctrines by means of publications, usually in Egypt, and by personal communication. With the Young Turk revolution and the restoration of Parliament and the easing of restrictions on the press and political activity, the Arabists entered politics. The degree to which and the reasons why Arabism won adherents remain subject to dispute. Few accept Antonius' view of seething Arab nationalism suppressed by Turkish barbarism. Zeine thinks that Arab nationalists were few in the nineteenth century and still a minority in 1914, but he gives no explicit evidence or argument.[32] In my view, Arab nationalism arose as the result of intra-Arab elite conflict, specifically (in the case of the territories later included in the Syrian Republic) being an opposition movement of Syrian notables directed primarily against rival Syrian notables who were satisfied with and occupied positions in the Ottoman government, an opposition that remained a minority until 1918.[33] Tibawi regards the Arabists as unimportant before the Young Turks period, probably still a minority in 1914.[34] Sharabi considers the pre-1914 nationalists to be an elite minority, as do Tibi, Khalidi, and Hourani, who explicitly accept this part of my work.[35] Zeine, Tibawi, Sharabi, Tibi, and Khalidi differ from my view in emphasizing Young Turk policy as a major cause of Arabism. They see Arabism arising as a reaction to the Turkish nationalism of the Committee of Union and Progress (CUP), which was manifested in the press and in laws requiring the sole use of Turkish in the administration, the courts, and the schools.[36] To this Khalidi adds Zionism. All believe that Arab nationalism was increasing in strength during the Young Turk period. Khalidi is ambiguous but seems to believe that Arabism was the majority movement by 1914.[37]

The belief that Arab nationalism was a rapidly growing movement in the Young Turk period and that CUP policy was the major cause stems from a tradition created by European diplomats (especially British) and Arab nationalists. Zeine and Khalidi have provided the most extensive documentation. The former's main source is the set of handbooks prepared by the British Foreign Office for use at the Paris Peace Conference. Khalidi has consulted the original sources in the contemporary British and French diplomatic reports and in the Arab nationalist literature, especially contemporary newspapers. The bias of the Arabists is self-evident. Most of both the British and French diplomats, contrary to their governments, favored supporting Arab separatism. The manifest bias of such testimony cannot be eliminated by repetition. Moreover, most of this testimony is limited to generalities; few particulars are given. When considering their claims about the extent of Arab anti-Ottoman sentiment, one should keep in mind the poor record of American journalists and other observers in predicting American elections and remember that the latter's technical competence for such judgments far exceeded that of the European diplomats. In short, the sources are highly suspect and are of no utility unless particulars are presented that can be examined in the light of other evidence.

In order to estimate the strength of Arab nationalism in 1914, one must identify Arab nationalists. I have done this in my work by identifying members of societies that were active before 1914 for Arab nationalist goals. Of the 126 persons identified, only 51 Syrians were subject to study because of the availability of biographical data.[38] Khalidi thinks this number is too low and cites: a French diplomatic document that said "at least" forty Arab officers at Constantinople were planning to create an Arab state extending from Egypt to Baghdad in case the empire collapsed; Amin Sa'id's assertion that 315 of 490 Arab officers in Istanbul in 1914 belonged to al-'Ahd; and Antonius' claim that al-Fatat had over two hundred members by 1914.[39] The French document's description of the Arab officers could apply to loyal Ottomanists as well as Arabists. But all three statements cannot be checked because no names are given. Darwaza, the only source who was a leading participant in the Arab nationalist movement from before 1914 through the interwar years, says of Sa'id's assertion, "He does not mention a source. So, it is likely that the number is exaggerated. Apparently, the number of members of the party had reached a not-insignificant number when the First World War broke out."[40] There is no need nowadays to discuss Antonius' deficiencies as a source. There is no way of knowing the total number of adherents of Arabism before World War I. But it is clear that the incidence of known activists was greater in Syria than in Lebanon, Palestine, or Iraq. Some notion of the number of followers may be provided by the telegrams of support sent to the First Arab Congress in Paris in 1913. The names of seventy-nine Syrians appear on those telegrams, of whom twelve were members of the societies.[41] It should not be assumed that these numbers reflect the importance of the Arabists in Ottoman Syria. The leaders were mostly notables with substantial followings of their own. They constituted a powerful political force.

Khalidi offers two other arguments for ascribing greater strength to the pre-1914 Arab nationalist movement. One is that Arabist newspapers greatly outnumbered Unionist papers. Although there has not been any thorough study of the press, this may well be true. But the press is a very poor index of political strength. In the United States since 1936, electoral success by presidential candidates and political parties has had a high inverse correlation with press support. Khalidi's other argument makes use of Arab activities in the Ottoman parliament.

(See Khalidi's discussion of this topic in his essay in this volume.)

Arab nationalists' participation in parliamentary politics may provide a measure for the extent of prewar Arabism. Khalidi broke new ground with an innovative investigation of parliamentary elections, and concludes that a majority of deputies from the Syrian provinces (including mandatory Syria, Lebanon, Palestine, and Transjordan) were Arab. His most recent statement is that of twenty-two Arab deputies from the Syrian provinces on the eve of elections in 1912, eighteen were members of the opposition, who joined the *Entente Liberale.* The opposition was sweeping the campaign, but the CUP cracked down, forced some of the Ententists to join the Unionists in the election, and managed the election by coercion. The result was that only six of the twenty-two Arabs elected during 1908 to 1912 were returned to Parliament. The implication is that, in free elections before 1912, Arabists won eighteen of twenty-two seats and most of these would have been won in 1912 if the elections had been free or if they had been willing to collaborate with the CUP.[42]

There are a number of problems. The only sources cited for the number of oppositionists are contemporary Arab anti-CUP newspapers; few names are listed. In Khalidi's discussion, oppositionists and Ententists are implicitly counted as Arabists, which is not necessarily true and in some cases is known to be false. Specific details are provided for only a few individuals. The electoral data that Khalidi uses is incomplete and contains errors, but it can be partially corrected by Ahmad and Rustow's study of the Young Turk parliaments.[43] Of the twenty-two Arab deputies that provide the basis for Khalidi's implication that eighteen Arab nationalists were elected before 1912 and defeated in 1912 by Unionist coercion, two had died before 1911, one had resigned, and one was a Turk who later was deputy from Antalya and much later a member of the Grand National Assembly. Considering those holding seats in 1912 and presumably possible candidates for reelection, there is no reason to believe that there was an anti-CUP or Arab nationalist landslide underway. A few uncertainties remain concerning the Arab membership of the Young Turk parliaments, but a highly probable account can be constructed. In 1912 there were twenty-three deputies, of whom two were Turks and one was Armenian.

Of the twenty Arab deputies, six were identifiable Arabists. These six and a non-Arab nationalist (Kamil al-Asʿad) entered the 1912 election as Ententists, but just before the balloting one of the Arabists and Asʿad shifted to the CUP. The two defectors won, but the remaining five Ententists—all Arab nationalists— were defeated. Of the twenty Arab deputies in 1912, five certainly, and possibly six or seven (including Asʿad and the defecting Arab nationalist), were reelected. But Khalidi's conclusion that only six of those elected before 1912 collaborated with the CUP is not justified. In the 1914 elections, held when the Unionists were in their strongest position thus far, five who had been deputies in 1912 were elected (one, possibly two, of whom had been reelected in 1912). Thus, the Syrian Arab members of Parliament in 1912 who were reelected in 1912 or 1914 under CUP auspices numbered nine, or possibly ten (not six), as compared to six Arab nationalists, five of whom refused to cooperate with the Unionists. Nothing further on the careers of the remaining five or six deputies is known; they played no significant role in Syrian political life after 1912. Nine, possibly ten, out of twenty Arab members of the 1912 parliament collaborated with the CUP in 1912 or 1914. Only six can be identified as Arab nationalists, of whom five campaigned against the Unionists. So, in the last reputedly free Ottoman parliament, the Arab nationalists were a minority—an important minority, but still a minority.

The minority status of the Syrian Arab nationalists in Parliament evidently conformed to their status among Syrian notables as a whole. Direct evidence is lacking, but indirect evidence is provided by the participants in the Arab nationalist government and movement in Syria during 1919–1920, when the General Syrian Congress (elected under the Ottoman electoral law) and a Syrian Cabinet proclaimed that the Syrian people were members of the Arab nation and societies espousing Arabism ruled political life. But these postwar Arab nationalist activities were dominated by newcomers to Arab nationalism. Of the members of these Arab nationalist bodies, 82 percent were not Arab nationalists before 1918, 85 percent before 1914. As the prewar Arabists were a minority in 1919–1920, they are not likely to have been a majority before 1914. The Arab national revolution in Syria was carried out by latecomers to Arabism. There are grounds for believing that the post-1918 Arab nationalists had been loyal Ottomanists before 1914 or 1918. The post-1918 nationalists had been more successful in holding state office than the pre-1914 Arabists (35 percent as compared to 16 percent). The same relation obtained for the fathers (73 percent as compared to 13 percent). Some evidence has long existed that the post-1918 nationalists had opposed the Arabists before the war or had served the Ottoman government until the war or even 1918.[44] Since then, the new evidence that has become available supports both propositions.[45] The prewar Arab movement in Syria was an opposition movement among the notables that remained a minority movement until the end of the war, when the majority, hitherto Ottomanist, converted to Arabism.

The postwar preponderance in Syria of newcomers to Arabism, many of whom held office or actively supported the CUP until 1914 or 1918, casts grave doubt on the Arab nationalist charge of anti-Arab bias on the part of the Young Turks, a policy that some consider to have been a major stimulus to the growth of Arabism. It is difficult to reconcile such a policy with the large number of officials among the post-1918 Arabists. The Young Turks dismissed many Arab officials, including two very prominent ones, but many other Arabs held office, including a secretary to the sultan and two grand viziers, an Iraqi and an Egyptian, who, in the words of Berkes, "was an ardent Islamist who wrote only in French and Arabic."[46] Some important Syrian Arab notables during the Young Turk period opposed the government on Arab nationalist grounds, but the evidence strongly indicates that the majority cooperated with and held office in the Unionist government in Syria and the Syrian Arab nationalist movement long thereafter.

Arab nationalism remained a minority opposition movement until the end of World War I. The majority of the Arab notables remained loyal Ottomanists. Nevertheless, the Arab nationalists carried out a significant campaign against the Unionists. It may be the case that the Young Turk period provided the Arab nationalists a greater opportunity than did ʿAbdülhamid's reign. Arabism was a visible movement before the Young Turk revolution, but there does seem to be a relative increase after 1908. It seems likely that the restoration of Parliament and the consequent flourishing of party activity and expansion of the press would have facilitated political debate and provided an opportunity for the Arabists to win recruits, as Khalidi has proposed, although the changes started in the Tanzimat. Another plausible source of Arabism's increase is an increase in the number of civil servants and military officers, teachers and journalists, as Khalidi suggests,[47] although once again the process started over half a century earlier. As of now, there is no conclusive evidence of how such supposed new elements divided between Ottomanists and Arabists, or of their social origins. That they entered politics in the following of established notables, when not of notable origins themselves, is the most likely reading of some difficult evidence.[48] The changes proposed by Hourani as causative factors in the development of Arab nationalism are of such vague or general character that their connection with that development is not readily discernible.[49]

The Arab nationalists attacked the Young Turk government with specific charges. One charge was that the Young Turks supported Zionism. The other was that the Young Turks were Turkish nationalists who initiated a policy of Turkification. It has been suggested that these charges arose from new developments or policy changes peculiar to the period that stimulated the growth of Arab nationalism. (See Rashid Khalidi's discussion of this topic in his essay in this volume.)

Increasingly visible Zionist activity in Palestine became a political issue in the Young Turk period. Arab nationalists kept up a continuous attack on the CUP with allegations that it was supporting Zionism. In fact, Arab nationalist concern was no different from Unionist. The center of anti-Zionist agitation was Palestine. Here, deputies and journalists, CUP and opposition, opposed Zionism.[50] Outside Palestine, Arab nationalists distinguished themselves in pointing to the Zionist peril. In Parliament, Arabist deputies from Damascus and Beirut joined the Palestinian deputies (who were Unionists), but other Syrian deputies took no active part.[51] In similar fashion, all newspapers in Palestine were constantly calling attention to the Zionist danger, but outside Palestine most Arab nationalist papers raised the question with attacks on the government while most pro-CUP papers ignored the question.[52] In fact, Unionist attitudes and policies toward Zionism were the same as those of the Ententists and the Arab nationalists. All of them welcomed Jewish immigrants (provided they brought money and expertise, settled in dispersion throughout the empire, and became

Ottoman nationals), and all engaged in virtually identical negotiations with the Zionists.[53] The Unionists, occupying the government through most of the period, were caught. Their attempts to limit Zionist activities were frustrated by the European powers.[54] With respect to Zionism, the Unionists were not guilty of the Arab nationalists' accusations, and the issue apparently had little effect on the Arab members of Parliament.

Contemporary European diplomatic reports and Arab nationalists charged the CUP with Turkish nationalism and with Turkification, specifically with enacting laws requiring the use of Turkish in the administration, the courts, and the schools. The charges have been widely accepted as true, and Arab nationalism has very frequently been seen as a reaction to these Young Turk innovations. Nevertheless, this interpretation is doubtful. In the first place, Arabist ideology, including a bitter anti-Turkism, was fully formulated long before the Young Turk revolution. In the second place, the Young Turks, according to present knowledge, were not guilty as charged.

While Turkism had its advocates before 1908, they were a decided minority and the ideology of the CUP before 1908 was Ottomanist, without any Turkish bias.[55] (See Hanioğlu's essay in this volume on this point.) The Unionists continued to be Ottomanists ideologically for a considerable time after 1908 while Arab nationalists were becoming increasingly outspoken. The most important Unionist ideologist, Ziya Gökalp, did not become an active advocate of Turkism until 1913 or so, and he remained a believer in Ottomanism until late in World War I.[56] The Turkists increased their following beginning in 1911–1912, but there is no reason to believe that they captured the minds of the majority. Turkism was vigorously opposed by Westernists and Islamists, both of whom remained Ottomanists. The Turkish Islamists, indeed, drew heavily from the slate of the Egyptian modernists (including their glorification of the Arabs). One of them, Sa'id Halim, a member of the Egyptian khedival family, was grand vizier during 1913–1916. While in office, he published articles attacking ethnicity and nationalism as causing the Islamic decline, singling out the Mongols—and the Turkists implicitly—as the chief villain among the nationalities who had corrupted the pure Islam of the ancestors, meaning, of course, the Arabs. A prominent Turkish intellectual, Ahmed Naim, wrote glorifying the "Arab race, which every Muslim is under obligation to love." In this view, "the Arab race has to be praised by everyone, above any race, even above our own race, for their Islamic zeal, for their racial affinity to Muhammad, for their language being the language of the Qur'an (Koran), and for the sake of our gratitude to them for having brought Islam."[57] It may well be that the debates of Islamists and Westernists, Ottomanists, Arabists, and Turkists occupied only a minority of the total population. These developments have seized the attention of observers and students so much that little attention has been paid to the writings of ʿulama', who were not themselves political activists. Fritz Steppat has shown that some of the leading ʿulama' in Syria and Egypt remained relatively unaffected by the new currents.[58] They, and perhaps a majority of the population, continued to measure the legitimacy of the Ottoman state on traditional Islamic grounds, as was the case of the amir of Mecca, al-Husayn ibn-ʿAli ibn-ʿAwn, the future leader of the Arab revolt.[59] During the war, as Cleveland has shown, traditional Islamic legitimacy and solidarity was the basis for appeals to the Arab populace for support by both Husayn and the Unionist government.[60] Talib Mushtaq, an Iraqi Arab bureaucrat-politician whose long career began in Ottoman times, said: "Were we really subjects of imperialism when Iraq was under Ottoman rule? Never! We were one nation, living under one flag. The bond of religion bound us in the firmest of ties. Islam united our hearts and our feelings, and made us one bloc, supporting each other, like a solid building."[61]

The reputation of the CUP as Turkifiers appears to be undeserved. On the basis of the evidence presently available, the Young Turk period was not marked by any changes in the language of administration, the courts, or education. Turkish had always been the official language and the language of administration. The constitution of 1876 explicitly stated this to be the case and made knowledge of Turkish a requirement for public office and membership in the Parliament.[62] An 1888 law specified the degree of competence in Turkish required for various offices.[63] "The Ottoman language was the language adopted for all business in all departments of government," according to Yusuf al-Hakim, a Syrian Arab official who served before and after the Young Turk revolution.[64] Presumably, Turkish was also the language of the *nizami* courts before 1908. The only provision in the law was Article 1825 of the *Mecelle*, which required the presence of a reliable interpreter to translate the statements of any individual who did not know the language employed by the court.[65] The practice, according to Heidborn, was that Turkish was used in the courts, with the necessary translators, but in the Arab provinces Arabic was permitted.[66] According to Yusuf al-Hakim, Arabic was the usual language of court proceedings in the Arabic provinces, but the translator was necessary as judges often did not know Arabic well and transactions with higher courts were in Turkish.[67]

Education was governed by an 1869 law that placed all schools under government supervision, a provision reaffirmed by the constitution. The law, by implication, required that instruction in the state schools be in Turkish except for the lower elementary schools for non-Muslims, where instruction was to be in the local language. In the upper primary, secondary, and advanced schools, where Turkish was the principal subject of study—and, by implication, the only language of instruction—Arabic, Persian, and (in schools for the non-Muslims) the local language were also to be taught. No state schools for non-Muslims were established, so in effect Turkish was the language of instruction in all the state schools.[68] The available evidence indicates that in the Arab provinces Turkish was the principal language of instruction in all state schools. Yusuf al-Hakim says that the lower and upper primary schools taught Arabic and Turkish "without their reaching a great stage" and that in the lower secondary schools all instruction was in Turkish.[69] The nonstate schools evidently were spared the application of the education law and the constitution until a decree of 1894 required them to teach Turkish, but compliance with this decree evidently was not universal.[70]

The Young Turks did not make any radical changes with respect to the language of administration, education, or justice. The CUP programs, periodically set forth in party resolutions from 1908 to 1913, simply reaffirmed existing law. Turkish was declared to be the language of the state and of all official correspondence and petitions. Private schools were to be under the supervision of the state. Turkish was to be taught in all schools, including primary, and Turkish was the required language of instruction in schools above the lower primary level, but without interfering with the teaching of the language, beliefs, and literature of any nationality. In primary schools, instruction was to be in the local language.⁷¹ Evidently, the CUP legislation concerning schools did not change any of the provisions of existing law with respect to language, nor did the legislation concerning justice affect the language of the courts.⁷²

The Arab nationalists were not reacting to Young Turk innovations. Instead, they were continuing a campaign against a system that was established long before the Young Turks. The campaign against the Turks begun by Rida and Kawakibi was joined by intellectuals who blended with Islamic modernism's apotheosis of Arabic some newer ideas, presumably of European origin, according to which a nation's vitality was inseparable from its language. Prominent among such writers was the Damascene Muhammad Kurd ʿAli. From the first volume of his monthly journal *al-Muqtabas*, he assigned a major portion of the blame for Arab and Islamic decline to the Turco-Tartars, especially the Ottomans. Their greatest sin was the imposition of the barbarous language of an uncivilized people on the Arabs.⁷³ Kurd ʿAli was just as angry with his Arab compatriots in Syria as he was with the Turks. He bitterly accused them of preferring the state schools and Turkish to Arab national schools and Arabic in order to gain government positions or for purposes of commerce.⁷⁴ He leveled similar charges against those who attended the foreign missionary schools, or who preferred a European language to Arabic for materialistic gain.⁷⁵ He was perhaps more critical of the missionary schools than the Ottoman schools.⁷⁶ Kurd ʿAli's attack on the Ottoman schools was just as much an attack on fellow Arabs as on ruling Turks.

Arab nationalist ideology, like its nineteenth-century predecessors, was an accompaniment of political competition among the advantaged elements of Arab society. From Tahtawi to Kurd ʿAli, the successive statements of the self-view legitimized the claims of specific parties to hold or to acquire power and refuted claims of competitors. It may be that in all societies, including Arab society, social or political cleavage is the antecedent and cause of ideological contradiction. There is an immediate ring of verisimilitude to the words of a fourteenth-century Arab poet, "Verily, half the people are enemies of the one who has charge of the government; this, if he is just," which were considered an apposite quotation by an Arab statesman whose long career began under Abdülhamid II.⁷⁷ In Arab society, as in many others, one can point to seemingly opportunistic changes in ideology and to conflicts between clan or faction that appear to extend over generations as the only constants in a flux of ideological variations. But it may be that dissent and opposition arise from a human inability to agree on the just or the good.

In seeking place and its rewards, the intellectuals and politicians were also volunteering to assume responsibility for the problems of their community and polity. One problem gripped them all. From Tahtawi's pain at the sight of the Franks in possession of values that were lacking in the Islamic lands to Kurd 'Ali's perception of his own people's "inferiority" and "sick ideas" in comparison to the Westerners,[78] experience of the West was wrenching. The resultant pain was eased and hope for the future was instilled by recalling the past glory of the Self in comparison to the present abasement of the Self and the past inferiority of the threatening Other. Return to the true Self of the glorious past was the remedy for this illness. And this subsequent governments set about doing, but each in turn was not successful in eliminating the possibility of the perceived deprivation of the Self in comparison with the threatening Other, and so did not eliminate the occasion for opposition and dissent. The Western problem remained the hub of politics, an insolvable problem that demanded solution. The impotence of the successive governments in the face of the universally perceived danger may well have caused some to oppose and dissent; it certainly could have legitimized opposition and dissent, whatever the cause.

The CUP government, like its predecessors, could not meet the requirement of its own ideology that clear progress be made in the contest with the West, the Ottoman Empire's threatening Other. The Young Turks were no more the promoters of Zionism than were their opposition, but the CUP as the ruling party could not escape blame for the increasing visibility of the Zionists. Consequently, when possible, Unionist partisans ignored Zionism while opponents kept it to the fore. The issue apparently had no great effect outside Palestine, but there the impact was inescapable. Palestine provides an example of a manifest political conversion over a concrete public issue in the case of journalist Najib Nassar, a longtime Unionist and eternal anti-Zionist. The government's failures with respect to this issue resulted in a change of allegiance.[79] Similar Young Turk failures in the wars with Italy and the Balkan states could not have increased confidence in the Unionists and Ottomanism. Contemporary diplomatic reports and later Arab nationalist accounts give great weight to these military failures in stimulating Arab dissent and opposition.[80]

Arab nationalism arose as an opposition movement in the Ottoman Empire. It was directed quite as much against Ottoman Arabs as against the Ottoman Turks themselves. The conflict was between elements of the Ottoman Arab elite who competed for office, a conflict of the sort that exists in every society and is the most likely starting point of politics everywhere. As in every society, the competitors offered themselves as the ones best qualified to realize the ideals of the society and ward off the dangers that threatened it. Throughout the nineteenth century, the contenders for office had to deal with the perceived inferiority of Islam or the East to the West. Various attempts to meet this problem had no satisfactory result. Arab nationalism arose out of the failure of its immediate predecessor and its ideological parent, Islamic modernist Ottomanism. The movement made progress before 1914, but it remained a minority movement until 1918, when the Arab revolt, the British agreement with the amir Husayn, and the British defeat of the Ottomans left the dominant faction of the Syrian and Iraqi Arab notables with no alternative to Arabism.

Notes

This paper owes much to research carried out when I was a fellow of the Institute for Advanced Studies of the Hebrew University of Jerusalem. I also thank the Regenstein Library of the University of Chicago and Bruce Craig. I, of course, am solely responsible for its contents.

1. Albert Hourani, *Arabic Thought*, p. 95 (quotation); and Hisham Sharabi, *Arab Intellectuals*, pp. 2–3, 8, 57, 59, 60.
2. Sharabi, *Arab Intellectuals*, pp. 2–3, 115, 128; and Bassam Tibi, *Arab Nationalism*, pp. 69–70, 71.
3. Sharabi, *Arab Intellectuals*, pp. 54–56; and Tibi, *Arab Nationalism*, pp. 74–75. Hourani's statement, though asserting the Christians' sympathy with the West, does not assign them and the missionary schools the same influence (Hourani, *Arabic Thought*, pp. 95–97, 245).
4. *al-Muqtabas*, 1 (1324/1906): 432–33; 2 (1325/1907): 620–21; 3 (1327/

1909): 109, 238, 503–8, 511–13; 6 (1329/1911): 52; 7 (1330/1912): 30–33, 54–56, 162–64. Anis Zakariya al-Nusuli, *Asbab al-nahda al-ʿarabiyya fil-qarn al-tasiʿ ʿashr* [Causes of the Arab awakening in the nineteenth century] (Beirut: Matbaʿa tabbara, 1345/1926); review of preceding by Muhammad Kurd ʿAli, *Majallat al majmaʿ al-ʿIlmi al-ʿarabi bi-dimashq* [Review of the Arab Scientific Academy in Damascus], 6 (1926): 381–82 (henceforth referred to as M.M.I.A.D.).

5. See also Muhammad ʿIzzat Darwaza, *Durus al-taʾrikh al-ʿarabi min aqdam al-azmina ila ilan* [Lessons in Arab history, from the earliest times until now], p. 299; Darwish al-Miqdadi, *Tarikh al-umma al-ʿarabiyya* [The history of the Arab nation], 2d ed. (Baghdad: 1350/1931), pp. 337, 494–95.
6. Ibrahim Abu-Lughod, *Arab Rediscovery*, pp. 28–65; and A. L. Tibawi, *A Modern History of Syria*, pp. 140–47, 194–95.
7. C. Ernest Dawn, *From Ottomanism to Arabism*, pp. 159–63, 177.
8. Albert Hourani, *Emergence of the Modern Middle East*, p. 204.
9. Dawn, *From Ottomanism to Arabism*, pp. 123–28; Abu-Lughod, *Arab Rediscovery*, pp. 77–78, 88–96, 108–9, 115–20, 125–26, 130–31, 137–40, 144–45, 153; Hourani, *Arabic Thought*, pp. 68–83; and Khaldun S. al-Husry, *Three Reformers*, pp. 11–31.
10. Niyazi Berkes, *Development of Secularism in Turkey*, p. 130; Bernard Lewis, *Emergence of Modern Turkey*, pp. 334–36.
11. For this and the following paragraph, see Dawn, *From Ottomanism to Arabism*, pp. 124–27; the quotation from Tahtawi is from *Kitab takhlis al-ibriz ila talkhis bariz* [The book of refining of gold in summarizing Paris] (Cairo, 1323H/1905), p. 4.
12. Dawn, *From Ottomanism to Arabism*, pp. 131–32, 133–36. To the works there cited add al-Husry, *Three Reformers*, pp. 19–23, 33–53; Khayr al-Din al-Tunisi, *The Surest Path: The Political Treatise of a Nineteenth-Century Muslim Statesman*, ed. and trans. Leon Carl Brown (Cambridge: 1967), pp. 73, 74–75, 79, 81–83, 88–89, 99, 107, 111–13, 130, 135–36, 138, 147, 160–61; and Hourani, *Arabic Thought*, pp. 91–94.
13. Dawn, *From Ottomanism to Arabism*, pp. 129–30, 141–42, 146; Butrus Abu-Manneh, "The Christians Between Ottomanism and Syrian Nationalism," pp. 287–304; Hourani, *Arabic Thought*, pp. 99–102, 195–96, 250–52, 253–59; and Donald M. Reid, *The Odyssey of Farah Antun*.
14. Sharabi, *Arab Intellectuals*, pp. 58–60, 64–65, 115; and Tibi, *Arab Nationalism*, pp. 76–79.
15. Dawn, *From Ottomanism to Arabism*, pp. 132, 140.
16. Zeine N. Zeine, *Emergence of Arab Nationalism*, pp. 59–67; Tibawi, *Modern History of Syria*, pp. 163–67; Fritz Steppat, "Eine Bewe-

gung unter den Notabeln Syriens," pp. 631–49; and Jacob M. Landau, "An Arab Anti-Turk Handbill, 1881," pp. 215–27.
17. Dawn, *From Ottomanism to Arabism*, pp. 135–40.
18. Elie Kedourie, *Arabic Political Memoirs*, pp. 125–28 (for Alusi and Zahrawi); Rashid Khalidi, "ʿAbd al-Ghani al-ʿUraysi and *al-Mufid*: The Press and Arab Nationalism before 1914," pp. 38–61; and Samir Seikaly, "Damascene Intellectual Life," pp. 125–53 (for Muhammad Kurd ʿAli and *al-Muqtabas*).
19. Sylvia G. Haim, ed., *Arab Nationalism: An Anthology* (Berkeley: University of California Press, 1962), pp. 10, 15, 16, 18–19, 21–22, 27, 35, 49, 53–61, 70 n. 148, 72 n. 156 (quotations, pp. 16, 21, 27, 35, 54); Kedourie, *Arabic Political Memoirs*, pp. 125, 136, 165–66, 168, 178; and Elie Kedourie, *The Chatham House Version*, pp. 206, 213–20, 287–90, 301–3, 306, 319–20, 324, 330, 333, 338, 342, 369, 378–79, 381.
20. Sharabi, *Arab Intellectuals*, pp. 64, 76–77, 91, 102–3, 107 n. 4, 108–9, 111–12, 118, 122, 123, 128, 131–32, 144; and Tibi, *Arab Nationalism*, pp. 50, 67–68, 70, 71, 90 (quotations, pp. 67, 68).
21. Luthruf Situdard, *Hadir al-ʿalam al-islami* [The contemporary Islamic world], ed. Shakib Arslan, trans. ʿAjaj Nuwayhid, 2 vols. (Cairo: Matbaʿal ʿIsa al-Babi al Halabi, 1343/1925); 2d ed., 4 vols. (1352/1933). Kurd ʿAli's works can be followed in the monthly *al-Muqtabas*, 1–8 (1324/1906–1334/1916), and M.M.I.A.D., 1 (1921), and the following: Muhibb al-Din al-Khatib, *Ittijah al-mawjat al-bashariyya fi-jazirat al-ʿarab* [The direction of the human waves in the Arabian Peninsula] (Cairo: 1344/1925); Jayms Hanri Birastid, *al-ʿUsur al-qadima wa huwa tamhid lidars al-tarikh al-qadim wa aʿmal al-insan al-awwal* [Ancient times, a preface to a study of ancient history and the first works of man], trans. Daud Qurban (Beirut: 1926; 2d ed., 1930).
22. ʿUmar Salih al-Barghuthi and Khalil Tuta (Tota), *Tarikh filastin* [The history of Palestine] (Jerusalem: 1923). The book was written for the Palestine schools but, according to A. L. Tibawi, was banned at the insistence of Sir Herbert Samuel. However, the educational system in Palestine described by Tibawi and by Humphrey Bowman permitted considerable freedom in the production and adoption of history textbooks to Arab officials and teachers, who were nationalists to a man. Abdul Latif Tibawi, *Arab Education in Mandatory Palestine: A Study of Three Decades of British Administration* (London: 1956), pp. 28–38, 95–97, 193–99; and Humphrey Ernest Bowman, *Middle-East Window* (London, New York, Toronto: 1942), pp. 310–14. For an ardent Arab nationalist who had a long and successful career in education, see Kedourie, *The Chatham House Version*, p. 341.

23. Muhammad 'Izzat Darwaza, *Mukhtasar tarikh al-'arab wal-islam* [An abridged history of the Arabs and of Islam], 2 vols. (Cairo: [1924?]; 2d ed. [1343H/1924–1344H/1925]; 3d ed. [1344/1925]. This was an elementary school textbook and was replaced by the author's *Durus al-tarikh al-'arabi min aqdam al-azmina ila al-an* [Lessons in Arab history from the earliest times until now]. Darwaza followed with other elementary school textbooks: *Durus al-tarikh al-qadim* [Lessons in ancient history] (Cairo: 1350/1931); 2d ed. (Jerusalem: 1355/1936).

    Darwaza's textbooks, in view of their favorable reviews, their number and many editions, and their author's prominent association with major Palestinian, Syrian, and Iraqi politicians throughout the interwar years, most likely were widely used in Palestine and Syria. According to Reeva Simon, some of them were used as teaching aids in the Iraqi schools. M.M.I.A.D., 4 (1924): 428–29; 11 (1931): 704; Reeva S. Simon, "The Teaching of History in Iraq Before the Rashid Ali Coup of 1941," *Middle Eastern Studies* 22 (1986): 42.

24. Darwish al-Miqdadi, *Tarikh al-umma al-'arabiyya* [The history of the Arab nation] (Baghdad: 1350/1931); 2d ed. (1351/1932); 3d ed. (1353/1934); 4th ed. (Baghdad: 1355/1936); rev. ed. (Baghdad: 1939). The fourth edition has not been accessible. Information concerning it has been provided by Dr. Reeva Simon.

    Miqdadi's textbook was an officially adopted text in the Iraqi intermediate schools. Its prime importance is attested to by two prominent Arab historians and educators who were students during the period, Nabih Amin Faris and Nicola Ziadeh. According to the former, Miqdadi's text "was selected as the text for the teaching of history in the secondary schools of Palestine, Syria, and Iraq, where it continued to be the standard text of Arab youth for several student generations." In the judgment of the latter it was "the first history to deal with Arab history on national grounds." Nabih Amin Faris, "The Arabs and Their History," *Middle East Journal* 8 (1954): 156–57; Nicola A. Ziadeh, "Recent Arabic Literature on Arabism," *Middle East Journal* 6 (1952): 471.

25. For an Iraqi politician's use of these ideas, see Khayri al-'Umari, *Yunis al-Sab'awi: sirat siyasi islami* [Yunis al-Sab'awi: The life of an Islamic politician] (Baghdad: 1978); and Khaldun S. al-Husry, "The Political Ideas of Yunis al Sab'awi," in Buheiry, ed., *Intellectual Life*, pp. 165–75. The most extensive treatment of early Egyptian pan-Arab thought is by Israel Gershoni, see his: "Arabization of Islam," pp. 22–57; "The Emergence of Pan-Nationalism in Egypt," pp. 59–94; and *The Emergence of Pan-Arabism in Egypt*. Important material is contained in Charles D. Smith, *Islam and the Search for*

Social Order in Egypt: A Biography of Muhammad Husayn Haykal (Albany: 1983); Richard P. Mitchell, *The Society of the Muslim Brothers*, Middle Eastern Monographs 9 (London: 1969); and James P. Jankowski, *Egypt's Young Rebels: "Young Egypt," 1933–52* (Stanford, Calif.: 1975).

26. For a thorough and systematic examination of Ba'thist and Nasserist ideology, see Olivier Carré, *La Légitimation islamique des socialismes arabes: analyse conceptuelle combinatoire de manuel scholaires égyptiens, syriens et irakiens* (Paris: 1979). See also, by the same author, *Enseignement islamique et idéal socialiste: analyse conceptuelle des manuels d'instruction musulmane en Egypte* (Beirut: 1974); and "L'Islam politique dans l'Orient arabe," *Futuribles*, no. 18 (November-December 1978): 747–63.
27. Sharabi, *Arab Intellectuals*, pp. 118–19.
28. Kedourie, *Arabic Political Memoirs*, pp. 111–21.
29. M.M.I.A.D., 5 (1925): 151–52; 8 (1928): 442–43.
30. Kedourie, *The Chatham House Version*, pp. 321–25, 339, 343–50; and Dawn, *From Ottomanism to Arabism*, pp. 142–43.
31. Hourani, *Arabic Thought*, pp. 310–11; Haim, *Arab Nationalism*, pp. 109–15, 167–71; for 'Aflaq, see especially Nora Salem Babikian, "A Partial Reconstruction of Michel 'Aflaq's Thought: The Role of Islam in the Formulation of Arab Nationalism," *Muslim World* 67 (1977): 280–94; also Spencer Lavan, "Four Christian Arab Nationalists," *Muslim World* 59 (1967): 117–19.
32. Zeine, *Emergence of Arab Nationalism*, pp. 52, 68–69, 83, 105, 149–50.
33. Dawn, *From Ottomanism to Arabism*, pp. 148–79.
34. Tibawi, *A Modern History of Syria*, pp. 167, 171, 201–2, 203–4.
35. Sharabi, *Arab Intellectuals*, pp. 88–89, 115, 116–17, 122, 123, 127; Tibi, *Arab Nationalism*, pp. 87–89; Khalidi, *British Policy*, pp. 202–3, 224–25, 239–40, 371–72; Khalidi, "Social Factors in the Rise of the Arab Movement in Syria," pp. 54, 62; and Hourani, *Emergence of the Modern Middle East*, pp. 201–2.
36. Zeine, *Emergence of Arab Nationalism*, pp. 83, 89–95, 100, 113–14; Tibawi, *Modern History of Syria*, pp. 201, 202; Sharabi, *Arab Intellectuals*, pp. 103, 107, 108, 123, 124; Tibi, *Arab Nationalism*, pp. 81–83; Khalidi, *British Policy*, pp. 217–31, 235, 241, 260, 271, 297.
37. Khalidi, *British Policy*, pp. 240, 272, and more strongly in "Social Factors," pp. 54, 56, 57–61, 62.
38. Dawn, *From Ottomanism to Arabism*, pp. 148–53.
39. Khalidi, "Social Factors," pp. 56–57, 57 n. 46, 69–70; there is another reference to the French diplomatic report in Khalidi, *British Policy*, p. 343.

40. Darwaza, *Hawla al-haraka al-ʿarabiyya al-haditha* [Regarding the modern Arab movement], 1:33.
41. Dawn, *From Ottomanism to Arabism*, p. 154.
42. Khalidi, "The 1912 Election Campaign," pp. 461–74; and Khalidi, *British Policy*, pp. 236–42.
43. Khalidi's list is in *British Policy*, between pp. 258 and 259; the only sources he gives for the reputed affiliations of the deputies are Arabic press reports ("The 1912 Election Campaign," pp. 461 n. 4, 463 nn. 8, 9). I have used Feroz Ahmad and Dankwart A. Rustow, "Ikinci Mesrutiyet Döneminde Meclisler: 1908–1918," *Güney-Dogu Avrupa Arastirmalari Dergisi*, 5 (1976): 279–83 (supplemented by information provided by the authors personally).
44. Dawn, *From Ottomanism to Arabism*, pp. 150–51, 157–58, 167, 169, 170, 175, 176 (appendix II), 178 (appendix VII), 179 (appendix IX).
45. For studies of two postwar converts from Ottomanism, see William L. Cleveland, *The Making of an Arab Nationalist*, and also his *Islam Against the West*. The fullest account of Arab participation in late Ottoman politics is in Philip S. Khoury, *Urban Notables and Arab Nationalism*, chapters. 3 and 4. See also: Ruth Roded, "Ottoman Service," pp. 81–82, 85, 92–94; Ruth Roded, "Social Patterns," pp. 158–69; and C. Ernest Dawn, "Ottoman Affinities," pp. 178–80.
46. Berkes, *Development of Secularism*, p. 349 n. 5.
47. Khalidi, "Social Factors," pp. 53–70.
48. Dawn, "Ottoman Affinities," pp. 172–87.
49. Hourani, *Emergence of the Modern Middle East*, pp. 205–6.
50. Neville J. Mandel, *Arabs and Zionism*, pp. 72–77, 85, 110–12, 128–30, 138–39, 174–85, 206, 216, 219, 226, 230; Yehoshua Porath, *The Palestinian-Arab National Movement*, 1:25–27, 30; and Khalidi, *British Policy*, pp. 226–28, 231, 297–98, 356–57.
51. Mandel, *Arabs and Zionism*, pp. 88–90, 100–101, 112–15; and Khalidi, *British Policy*, pp. 226–28.
52. Mandel, *Arabs and Zionism*, p. 130; and Porath, *The Palestinian-Arab Movement*, 1:30.
53. Mandel, *Arabs and Zionism*, pp. 102, 104–6, 115, 117, 141–72, 187–206, 208, 224–25.
54. Ibid., pp. 104–6, 115–19, 167–68.
55. Berkes, *Development of Secularism*, pp. 304–5, 317–18, 321–22, 328, 329; Lewis, *Emergence of Modern Turkey*, p. 349; and for material on the ideology of the Young Turks in Europe, see Ernest Edmonson Ramsaur, Jr., *The Young Turks*, pp. 23–25, 40–45, 67–70, 81–86, 90–93.
56. Uriel Heyd, *Foundations of Turkish Nationalism*, pp. 33–34, 71–74; and Berkes, *Development of Secularism*, pp. 332–33, 344–46, 373.
57. For the debates of the Young Turk period, see Berkes, *Development*

of Secularism, pp. 337–428; on the praise of the Arabs and the rejection of Turkism, see ibid., pp. 348–50, 353–55, 373–6; for the beginnings of these debates, see ibid., pp. 263–64, 297–99, and also David Kushner, *The Rise of Turkish Nationalism*, especially pp. 35–37, 61–80.

58. Fritz Steppat, "Khalifat, Dar al-Islam und die Loyalität der Araber zum osmanischen Reich bei hanafitichschen Juristen des 19. Jahrhunderts," *Actes, Ve Congres International d'Arabisants et d'Islamisants* (Brussels, c. 1970), pp. 443–62.
59. Dawn, *From Ottomanism to Arabism*, pp. 75–86.
60. William L. Cleveland, "The Role of Islam," pp. 84–101.
61. Talib Mushtaq, *Awraq ayyami, 1900–1958* [My diary, 1900–1958], p. 19.
62. Articles 18, 57, 68; English translation in Suna Kili, *Turkish Constitutional Developments and Assembly Debates on the Constitution of 1924 and 1961* (Istanbul: Robert College Research Center, 1971), pp. 151, 154, 155.
63. George Young, *Corps de droit Ottoman*, 1:20–21.
64. Yusuf al-Hakim, *Dhikrayat al-Hakim* [Memoirs of al-Hakim], 1:42.
65. Young, *Corps de droit Ottoman*, 6:442.
66. A. Hiedborn, *Manuel de droit public et administratif de l'Empire Ottoman* (Vienna and Leipzig: C. W. Stern, 1909), 1:2.398 n. 554.
67. Hakim, *Dhikrayat al-Hakim*, 1:114.
68. Young, *Corps de droit Ottoman*, 2:365–75; and Articles 15 and 16 of the constitution (Kili, *Turkish Constitutional Developments*, p. 151).
69. Hakim, *Dhikrayat al-Hakim*, 1:98–99, 106; Tibawi, *Modern History of Syria*, pp. 168–69, 170; Engin D. Akarli, "'Abdülhamid II's Attempts to Integrate Arabs into the Ottoman System," p. 80; 'Abd al-'Aziz Muhammad 'Awad, *al-Idara al-'uthmaniyya fi wilayat suriyya, 1864–1914* [The Ottoman administration in the province of Syria, 1864–1914] (Cairo: 1969), p. 262.
70. Kushner, *Rise of Turkish Nationalism*, pp. 91–95.
71. See the programs adopted by the annual CUP congresses and their implementation, *Revue de Monde Musulman* 6, no. 11 (November 1908): 515–16; 9, no. 9 (September 1909): 167; 10, no. 2 (February 1910): 250; 15, nos. 7–8 (July-August 1911), 142–143; 22 (March 1913): 155–56, and Tarik Z. Tunaya, *Türkiye'de Siyasî Partiler*, pp. 209, 211–12, 217–18 (Ronald Jennings has translated the relevant portions of these CUP programs for the author). A. L. Tibawi, *Islamic Education*, p. 67, evidently describing the Young Turk period, says that Turkish was the language of instruction from the upper elementary level (*ruzdiye*) on.
72. Turkey, *Düstur tertib-i sani*, 11 vols. (Istanbul, 1329/1911–28): 1:665–66, 790–91; 2:33–37, 77; 3:395, 467–68. See also the general sum-

maries of Young Turk policy and action in Stanford J. Shaw and Ezel Kural Shaw, *History of the Ottoman Empire and Modern Turkey* 2:275, 282–83, 285–87, 300. It is the only treatment that has extensively utilized Turkish legal and political documents (I owe the references to Turkish laws and CUP programs in Tunaya cited here and in n. 71 to this work). For Turkish legislation (July 10, 1908 to November 1, 1909), see Adrien Biliotti and Ahmed Sedad, *Legislation Ottomane depuis le retablissement de la constitution 24 Djemazi-ul-ahir 1326–10 Juillet 1324/1908* (Paris: 1912), vol. 1.
73. *al-Muqtabas*, 1 (1324/1906): 430, 493–94; 4 (1327/1909): 30–31, 110–11, 502; 6 (1329/1911): 51–2; 7 (1330/1912): 402.
74. *al-Muqtabas*, 5 (1328/1910): 512; 6 (1329/1911): 51–52, 7 (1330/1912): 30–31, 376.
75. *al-Muqtabas*, 1 (1906): 432–33; 4 (1327/1909): 237–38, 6 (1329/1911): 52; 7 (1330/1912): 34.
76. *al-Muqtabas*, 4 (1327/1909): 238–39; 5 (1328/1910): 512, 514–25; 6 (1329/1911): 52; 7 (1330/1912): 31, 55, 161–68.
77. Hakim, *Dhikrayat al-Hakim*, 1:136. The poet is identified as Ibn al-Wardi.
78. *al-Muqtabas*, 7 (1330/1912): 30.
79. Mandel, *Arabs and Zionism*, pp. 85, 110–12, 130, 179, 219.
80. Khalidi, *British Policy*, pp. 233–35, 264–65.

TWO

The Young Turks and the Arabs Before the Revolution of 1908

M. Şükrü Hanioğlu

Of the many secret groups of revolutionaries that had relations with the Young Turks before the 1908 revolution, the most important were the various Arab committees. Yet contrary to popular belief, these relations did not produce positive results. Influenced by the ideas of Turkish nationalism and Ottomanism, even before 1908, Young Turkish groups considered the Arab committees to be separatist organizations. (See C. Ernest Dawn, this volume, on this point.) In their publications, the Young Turks claimed that all ethnic groups of the Ottoman Empire were equal, that there was no difference between Arabs and Turks, and that it was normal for all groups to desire to develop their ethnic cultures.[1] But in the confidential correspondence of some of the important members of the Committee of Union and Progress (CUP) the opposite attitude can be seen through the use of such derogatory phrases for Arabs as "the dogs of the Turkish nation" in the private letters of two key members of the Central Committee of the CUP, Dr. Nâzım Bey, one of the reorganizers of the CUP in 1906, and Ishak Sükûti, one of its five founding members.[2]

The fact that they were of the same religion as the Arabs was not significant to the Young Turks. They saw themselves as bringing civilization to the tribal society of the Arabs and protecting it against Western imperialism. Indeed, when an Arabic-language newspaper claimed that "North Africa was conquered by the Arab Empire and lost to the imperialistic Western powers by the Sublime Porte," the Young Turks strongly objected.[3] Their response to Arab attitudes in general, however, can be summarized in two positions that emerged in the early years of the existence of the CUP—first, the Young Turks, whose aim was to save the decadent multinational Ottoman Empire, thought that even to have ideas of cultural autonomy was paramount to desiring separatism; and second, although Arabs were of the same religion as the Turks, the Young Turks viewed them as the most inferior ethnic group of the empire.

The overt activities of the Young Turks in the capital began in October 1895, following the Armenian troubles of that year.[4] In fact, the first official publication of the CUP appeared in December of that year. But earlier, a group called the Parti Constitutionnel en Turquie had begun to oppose the regime of Abdülhamid II. Its leader was Selim Faris (Salim Faris), an Ottoman citizen of Arab descent. Under his leadership a journal entitled *Hürriyet* (Liberty) had begun publication in London in 1895.[5] This journal elaborated the theses of liberal Ottoman intellectuals,[6] and also paid close attention to events in Syria.[7] Compared to the other opposition journals, *Hürriyet* contained a greater number of articles on Syria and the Arabs. After its first issues, the journal apparently felt constrained to explain its use of the Arabic notation of the script, which was different than that used in Turkish papers. It claimed that this was not because of an anti-Turkish tendency, but was a technical necessity.[8]

The Parti Constitutionnel en Turquie maintained relations with high-level Ottoman administrators, as well as with Arab opposition groups abroad, in preparation for a coup d'état. In its early activities and declarations, the CUP leadership attached much importance to these groups. The Ottoman government, meanwhile, paid close attention to the distribution of *Hürriyet* by British post offices,[9] which it interpreted as British support for Ottoman liberals who were using the Arab opposition groups to bring about a coup. The Ottoman authorities took strict measures to stop the distribution of the journal.[10] They paid the publishing house to terminate publication,[11] then filed a lawsuit against Faris and the *Hürriyet*.[12] When they discovered that the journal was being sent to the Ottoman Empire inside copies of *The Times* of London, they prohibited the distribution of that newspaper within the empire.¹³ After a strict investigation by the Ottoman intelligence services, the members of Faris' party in Istanbul were arrested¹⁴ and exiled to the African provinces of the empire.¹⁵ The Ottoman government also bought off two authors whose work appeared regularly in *Hürriyet*.¹⁶

Under the circumstances, Faris started negotiations with the Ottoman government for terminating the publication. In return for this concession, he obtained the privilege of controlling the distribution of drinking water in the city of Beirut.¹⁷ In addition, as part of this arrangement, he promised to become a loyal subject of the sultan and to withdraw from the opposition. Yet despite this bargain, Faris later went to France and tried to organize Arab groups there. However, because of strong objections by the Ottoman government and a lack of support from French authorities, he did not succeed.¹⁸

The Young Turks did not support Faris either, primarily because of his Arab origins. As Ahmad Riza, leader of the Central Committee for most of the period from 1895 to 1908, said in an editorial in the CUP's central organ *Meşveret*, "the journal *Hürriyet* is not a Turkish newspaper and for that reason cannot represent Ottoman society."¹⁹ When Faris decided to rejoin the opposition after his short honeymoon with the Ottoman government and published a Turkish-Arabic journal entitled *Khilafat*, the Young Turks attacked him more openly. One of their leaders insulted Faris and his journal in a private letter to Ishak Sükûti, saying: "This Arab dog doesn't even know what he is doing."²⁰ Immediately afterward, the official organs of the CUP declared that they had no relations with *Khilafat* or its editor, Selim Faris.²¹

At the same time the CUP began publishing *Mesveret*, an interesting conversation took place between an editor of a French newspaper and two Ottoman citizens of Arab descent, as related by the former:

Two persons came to visit us. They are the manager for the newspaper *Keşf-ül-nikab* and a member of the Turkish-Syrian Committee. These persons said very sad things about the suffering of the Ottoman citizens and [of] the poor people of Syria as well as relating their thoughts about the reforms that they desired for Syria. They added that they accepted France as a protector. The question for them was whether

France would let them remain in that difficult position or whether she would do the same as the British had done for the Armenians. "Will she show less interest in human rights in the Ottoman Empire than the Austro-Hungarian Empire? If the children of the great revolution leave us without any help it means we have to die."

Emir Arslan (Amir Amin Arslan, the leader of the Turkish-Syrian Committee) had received a warning a month earlier when Gabriel Hanotaux was minister of foreign affairs, advising him not to publish anything concerning the internal affairs of the Ottoman Empire, and threatening him with extradition:

"We have to explain to people, who think that civilization exists only in Western Europe, how Syrians have achieved a high intellectual level, and why they are rising against such a regime. We must remind you that these intellectuals are publishing thirteen newspapers in Egypt alone.

"Our party, which calls itself the Turkish-Syrian Committee, is the mediator between the Christian Armenian Committees and the Muslim Young Turkish party, which aims at the unity of the Ottoman Empire and tries to accomplish this by making reforms."

"Is this the old program of Midhat Pasa?"

"Yes, definitely."[22]

The Turkish-Syrian Committee that summarized its aim in these words was in fact an independent group, though it was mentioned as being a Young Turk group by the European press. Unlike Faris' party, however, it had very close relations with the CUP and was eventually absorbed by it. From 1890 on, there was an increase in the activities of Syrian Arab intellectual activists, some of them organized by Faris. But though their newspapers focused on the Arabs and the Arab lands, they themselves did not speak explicitly of Arab independence or autonomy.

At the same time, Habib Antony Salmoné, the publisher, in London, of the *Eastern and Western Review*,[23] established close relations with the other Arab members of the opposition in Europe. While researching a book on liberal movements in the empire, entitled *The Fall and Resurrection of Turkey*,[24] Salmoné conducted interviews with leaders of the Young Turks. In the book he presented four persons as the leaders of the reform movement and the Young Turks. Two of them were Ahmad Riza, the leader of the Paris branch of the CUP, and Murad Bey, the leader of the Geneva branch. The other two were Emir Emin Arslan (Amir Amin Arslan) and Halil Ganem (Khalil Ghanim), leading Arab members of the opposition whose roles were not as important as those of the first two, but who became founders of the Turkish-Syrian Committee.[25] Salmoné carried on his political activities until the beginning of 1897, when he ceased his involvement and petitioned the British to protect his family from the probable actions of the Ottoman government in Beirut.[26]

Earlier, in 1893, Emir Emin Arslan, who belonged to a prominent Arab Druze family from Lebanon, had come to Paris and had contacted Yusuf Elhac (Yusuf al-Hajj) and other opposition leaders there.[27] This arrival was related to the fact that Arslan's brother had been accused by the Ottoman authorities of disturbing the public order and of having been involved in various incidents, including the killing of an army captain.[28] While in Paris, Arslan led the Turkish-Syrian Committee and published its organ, *Keşf-ül-nikab* (*Kashf al-niqab*), in Arabic. The Ottoman government became very concerned about this new paper and its distribution in the Arab provinces of the empire.[29] For this reason, the Ottoman government made various attractive offers to Arslan, and after long negotiations he stopped publication of the newspaper.[30]

During this time, Halil Ganem, who had been a member of the first Ottoman parliament of 1877 as a deputy for Syria, was engaged in various activities in France. His articles on the political situation in the Ottoman Empire appeared in the *Journal des Debats*.[31] In 1893 he became publisher and editor of a short-lived Turkish-French journal called *Le Croissant-Hilâl*, most of whose articles were on Ottomanism.[32] This journal, too, silently disappeared from the scene after a bargain with the Ottoman authorities.[33]

Some time after these papers ceased publication, a defrocked Catholic priest, Alexis Kateb (Alexis Katib), began to publish the journal *El-Raca* (*al-Raja'*). Far more than the other two, this journal had the overt aim of blackmailing the Ottoman government, and indeed, Kateb had been accused by the CUP of harboring such motives. In fact, he was planning to turn it into an organ of French interests in the region. When Kateb wrote the book entitled *Oeuvre Patriotique de la Foi Chrétienne et de Pénétration Française en Syrie et dans tout l'Orient*,[34] this aim and his political inclinations became obvious, though his intentions can also be detected in his petitions to the French government requesting its support.[35]

In 1895, Arslan, Ganem, and Kateb, along with other Arab opposition leaders, agreed to establish an organized movement. A declaration was written by the editors of the various Arab newspapers published abroad and in Egypt that respectfully requested the sultan to recognize freedom of the press and thus to liberalize the regime.[36] Though respectful in tone, the declaration was taken by the government to reflect a separatist attitude because it was prepared by Arab editors and not by a group more representative of the citizens of the empire. In spite of its style, the declaration was identified by the authorities as an ill-intentioned publication.[37] Indeed, this move was probably a sign of the reorganization of the group rather than an attempt to influence the sultan. Emir Emin Arslan at this time also gave a public lecture in Paris on "Women in the East," supported by Shaykh Ebu Nazzara ('Abu Natharra) (the pen name of a Jewish journalist). Neither the Jewish Shaykh's help nor Arslan's speech pleased the Ottoman authorities, since both seemed to be evidence of the group's efforts to broaden its activities.[38]

Finally, in late 1895, the Turkish-Syrian Committee started to publish *La Jeune Turquie-Türkiya el-Fettat* under the leadership of Halil Ganem. This Arabic-French newspaper generated the suspicions of the Ottoman government, which issued threats against those involved.[39] Most important to us, however, is the presence of Halil Ganem among the main writers of *Meşveret*, the first official publication of the Committee of Union and Progress.

According to Ahmed Rıza Bey, Ganem's *Le Croissant-Hilal* could not be put in the same category with Faris' *Hürriyet*, because it could be considered the voice of "Turkish" and "Ottoman" public opinion. Rıza Bey later praised Ganem's new publication with these words: "There is an article on Islam by Halil Ganem Efendi in the newspaper *Türkiya-el-Fettat* which is published in Paris both in Arabic and French. This article does not sound like the ones written by self-seekers to fawn on the Sultan in some newspapers edited by priests and ordinary magazines that no one reads."[40]

The CUP's other leader, Murad Bey, commended the editorial

board of the newspaper, especially Arslan and Ganem, for being followers of Ottomanism.[41] There is something hard to explain here, however, because the newspapers Ahmad Riza Bey had criticized earlier had never actually claimed to be less Ottoman than this publication of the Turkish-Syrian Committee. Furthermore, these three people represented minorities among the Arabs of Syria: Arslan was Druze, while Kateb and Ganem were Catholics.

Nonetheless, the Turkish-Syrian Committee succeeded in joining the Union and Progress party (CUP). In 1896, speaking at a Young Turk banquet to celebrate the twentieth anniversary of the Ottoman constitution, Emin Arslan used the term "our party"—meaning the CUP, which was generally known as the Young Turk party.[42] Again, as seen from the foreign press, the Young Turk party's plans were made public through *Türkiya-el-Fettat* and the Arabs in the party were in agreement with the liberal Turks in the organization.[43] The presence of the signatures of three Turkish-Syrian committee leaders (Emir Emin Arslan, Halil Ganem, and their representative in London, Habib Antony Salmoné), along with the four main CUP leaders (Ahmed Rıza Bey, Colonel Şefik Bey, Mizancı Murad Bey, and Çürüksulu Ahmed Bey) on a petition sent in early 1897 to the British Foreign Office in the name of parties working for reforms in Turkey, confirms the cooperative attitude of the Arab leaders.[44]

The Young Turks and the Syrians appear to have merged their movements for two reasons. The first was that their union represented a halfway point between the "Young Syria" movement's dream of establishing a completely independent Syrian Republic[45] (which caused a reaction even among some Syrians who were close to the Young Turks) and the idea of Ottomanism envisaged by Ahmad Riza Bey. The second reason was the CUP's preference for Syria as its center instead of the Balkans; as we will see, the first military coup d'état these groups attempted was uncovered there.

From 1897 until his death in 1903, Ganem continued to play a role in the CUP and was the greatest supporter of Ahmed Rıza Bey in times of crisis. Had he lived until 1906, it might have been difficult for him to adjust to the changes in the organization. But none of his writings was related to Arab separatism; most addressed the general problems of the empire.[46]

Eventually, Salmoné left politics and Kateb became a French

agent. The only other member of importance, Emin Arslan, had been bargaining with the government in exchange for his leaving the opposition.[47] When attempts to pay him to return home failed, the authorities decided to entrust him with a post at an embassy. He was appointed consul-general in Brussels despite his continued publishing activity, which was considered "hostile" by the authorities.[48] Arslan appears not to have been an active organizer, nor was the voice of the Turkish-Syrian Committee heard from again. Instead, we see a gathering of Arab groups around Faris. Their contacts with the CUP were insignificant until its 1907 conference.

Although the Ottoman Ministry of Foreign Affairs considered this period a time of inactivity for the CUP in the Ottoman Empire,[49] it nevertheless witnessed a coup arranged by the CUP in the Syrian provinces. To date, the Balkan branches of the party have received the most scholarly attention. Obviously, the Balkan organization was important for the party's activities, but it was in Syria that most of its activities were concentrated between the years 1895 and 1897.

This activity became easier as a result of the absorption into the CUP of the Turkish-Syrian Committee in early 1897. In 1895, Dr. Şerafeddin Mağmumi, who had been given a temporary government appointment to keep him away from the capital, had visited all the headquarters in Syria and succeeded in founding important new branches, especially in Hama, Homs, Dayr al-Zawr, and Damascus.[50]

The spread of the party throughout Syria is clear from a perusal of CUP internal documents. We see a rapid increase in the party's activities in the area, which was visited by a number of its roving representatives.[51] At the same time, numerous reports were sent from Syria to headquarters, while many articles demanding political action in the region were published in its organs.[52] This obviously was a result of the popularity of the party among the personnel of the 5th Army based in Syria, whose commanders were made quite uneasy by the presence in its ranks of members of the opposition. The situation of this army, according to the opposition press, was of deep concern to the Palace. As one newspaper noted: "The names of all officers in the 5th Army were asked for in a telegraph in cipher from Istanbul. The information must have been insufficient for more information was requested. We wonder if the battalions that came from the 5th Army in the '93 revolution were remembered?"[53]

Reports about opposition activities piled up in offices of the government in Istanbul, which soon took action. Şem'azâde Ahmed Refik Paşa, who was in Damascus in mid-March 1897, presented to the government the information he had gathered in his investigations of the party, which, he reported, was very active in the Beirut and Damascus areas.[54] This information was extremely accurate; he had even succeeded in uncovering the names of the military members of the CUP. In the meantime, Edhem Paşa, who commanded Ottoman forces on the Greek frontier, informed the authorities about the organization of the Young Turks in Aleppo, information he had acquired from a Greek.[55]

During these investigations, the authorities realized that an opposition group other than the army was also playing a part in this alliance, and that it had extensive secret connections. According to one government document: "Unknown individuals succeeded in obtaining the Prime Minister's order to fire some civil servants in the capital and in the Administrative Council of the province of Hama. The members of the Geylani family working in court were also fired. We cannot understand how the Prime Minister let himself be used by these people."[56]

The CUP's penetration of the Syrian provinces had another dimension, namely its involvement in the differences between Sufi sects. In answers given by officials in the *vilayet* of Syria and by the 5th Army headquarters to questions asked by the authorities in Istanbul, it was reported: "There is no sign of any information of illegal organizations in Hama so far.... There has been an increase in the power and influence of the Rifai [Rifa'i] sect over various other sects through its uniting with members of other sects and gaining popularity among the public, including among top civil servants... Peace prevails in Christian-Muslim relations in the area."[57]

If there was such an organization involving members of the Sufi sects, the testimony of some of the civil servants who were later arrested for involvement in the plot in Hama suggests that the Kadiris (Qadiris) rather than the Rifa'i sect were behind it. The Syrian branch of the CUP also had considerable support from the *ulema* ('*ulama*') as well as CUP's Egyptian branch at this time. The characteristics and tone of letters and articles about Syria written by Saman Bey, who contributed to the central organ produced by CUP headquarters (and who was later to be director of the CUP's Barbary Coast branch), lent credence to this assertion.[58] In 1901, for example, a leading member of the *ulema*, Shaykh Abdülhamid el-Zehravi ('Abd al-Hamid al-Zahrawi) was arrested and imprisoned in Damascus for publishing the illegal newspaper *al-Munir* in Homs, where there was an important CUP branch.[59] (See Ahmed Tarabein's paper on al-Zahrawi, in this volume.) Moreover, when the *mutasarrıf* of Homs was dismissed by the *vali* (*wali*), most of those who wrote to protest this action were *ulema*.[60]

Also noticeable is the interest Syrian civil servants had in the CUP. The membership of many civil servants—including the director of the party's center in Aleppo, Osman Efendi; the secretary of the Aleppo administrative council, Halil Efendi; the vice public prosecutor of Hama, Vasfi Efendi; the town's chief secretary, Kadri Efendi; and the governor of Dayr el-Zor (Dayr al-Zawr)—confirms their involvement.[61] From a private letter written by a CUP member, we learn that Kazim Bey, the governor of Mosul, was also a member of the party.[62] Similarly, from a written complaint by the governor of Beirut, it is clear that Abdülkerim Bedran ('Abd al-Karim Badran), who was public prosecutor in that city, was also involved.[63] This broad range of officials from throughout Syria who were affiliated with the CUP demonstrates its popularity.[64]

In addition to the Sufi sect's *ulema* and officers, a fourth group appears in the organization of the party. These were the notables of the area and representatives of the leading families, as described in the messages sent to different branches from the center formed around Murad Bey in Geneva.[65] The presence on the arrest list of members of the two most important families in Hama—the Azimzâdes ('Azms) and Geylanizâdes (Kaylanis)—shows this. Both families were quite active in political matters. The Azimzâdes were involved in opposition movements and in organizing complaints to the government from the area.[66] The Geylanizâdes also made frequent political demands on the government.[67]

These conclusions are borne out by the dispatches of contemporary foreign diplomatic observers in the area, who pointed out that conflicts between top-level administrators and commanders led some of them to make contact with the Young Turks.[68] They also noted the activities and the political involvement of the Egyptians who came to Syria.[69] It is clear that in this way the party broadened its attempts to carry out its activities in the Syrian region.

The Palace, whose intelligence sources were remarkably wide, finally took action, realizing the seriousness of the situation. First, the governors of Hama and Damascus, who had been trying to resign because of these negative developments, were ordered to stay on and act responsibly.[70] This was obviously a warning to all civil servants involved. The investigations were accelerated as a matter of some urgency, because the party was distributing its regulations in Arabic as a means of expanding its activities in the region, an action that clearly alarmed the authorities. Then, after an investigation, the military commandant in Aleppo identified the officers who were involved in the movement.[71] Around the same time, a volunteer named Cudizâde Sabit Hoca, who was at the CUP Adana branch, was arrested.[72] Following this, the Palace immediately ordered the formation of a court-martial to try those under arrest.

An investigation in Beirut uncovered a recordbook that had been kept by the Beirut post office. An examination of this book disclosed the names of active members in Beirut (including Esad Bey, who was involved in the Ali Suavi incident, and other military officers) as well as those in Damascus.[73] Members who received illegal documents were identified and more arrests followed.[74] Afterward, a large group who had been making revolutionary plans, supported by military officers, was brought to light. Among them were shaykhs, leading civil servants, and officers.[75] It became clear through interrogations that their activities were widespread, and that they had been in contact with Armenian organizations and British representatives.[76]

Some of those convicted were exiled at once, and long terms of exile were given to officers in particular. In this way the largest local organization of the CUP was dismantled.[77] Foreign diplomatic reports called attention to the extensiveness of this organization.[78] However, even after these blows the party continued its activities in the region. The return of important civil servants to their former positions and the formation of secret groups by those who were sentenced to reside in Aleppo in the following years is a sign of this.[79] News about uneasiness and arrests in the 5th Army continued to appear in the foreign press.[80] German observers, including Goltz Pasha, who had been following developments in the military, pointed to the appeal of the Young Turks among military units in the area.[81] The eventual resumption of publications and other underground activities by the CUP, and the welcome the party later received in Aleppo, indicates that it was not totally uprooted in Syria.[82] But the rebirth of the CUP on a basis uniting the *ulema*, the notables, and the military with the hope of a new coup d'état was no longer even a dream, and the Syrian organization was reduced to being just another local branch of the CUP.

In addition to the activities of Arab committees that had relations with the Young Turks and CUP efforts in Syria, there were also activities in Northern Africa. In 1896 the Central Committee established the Berberistan (Barbary Coast) branch and sent some officers to North Africa to raise money. After the agreement between the Palace and the Central Committee in Contrexéville in 1897, the members of this branch resigned from the CUP. In 1901 another CUP representative was sent to Morocco and tried to make Young Turk propaganda there.[83] He visited the local newspapers, which wrote articles against the Ottoman sultan's regime.[84] He also succeeded in collecting some money. The Young Turks used the propaganda of "Muslim Brotherhood" for raising money in these areas.

In 1902 another Arab organization was formed with the interesting name of the Turkish Anarchist Committee. Despite its name, this was a purely Arab nationalist organization, and it worked for the separation of Yemen from the empire.[85] After the 1902 Congress of Ottoman Liberals, there were no further relations between the Young Turks and the Arab organizations abroad, which did not even participate in the congress. In 1907, when the Second Congress of Ottoman Liberals was held in Paris, the organizing committee asked an Arab group representing "the organization which publishes the journal *Khilafat*" to participate. But this does not imply the beginning of a close relationship between the Young Turks and the Arabs. Like the Arabs, representatives of the Jews who had settled in Egypt were also invited, and a delegation of them did attend the congress.

It is obvious that the Young Turks had strong nationalistic feelings even before the Young Turk revolution of 1908. Contrary to commonly held views, this policy did not begin after the Balkan wars of 1912–1913. In their early opposition years, they claimed that the Turks had certain rights because they were the majority in the empire, just as Austrians had rights in the Austro-Hungarian Empire or the Russians in the Russian Empire.[86] A number of prominent members of the CUP, moreover, authored articles that claimed that only Turks were real Ottomans or that the Ottoman language was Turkish.[87] Also, in the official organs of the CUP, Turks were described as an ethnically different group from Arabs or other Muslim groups in the empire, such as Albanians.[88] In a private letter, one of the founders of the CUP wrote that the Turks are relatives of the Hungarians by their ethnic origin and had no similarity to inferior Muslim groups such as the Arabs or Iranians.[89] This is an important point. The Young Turks were concerned about all separatist groups and criticized them sharply. But in their eyes, as we have seen, the Arabs were not only betraying the empire by establishing separatist organizations, they were also innately inferior.

For the period after 1908, very little information is available on the secret organization of the Central Committee of the CUP. In particular, it is not known how Central Committee members were elected. But it is a fact that there were no Arabs on this body after 1908. After the revolution, rival branches of the CUP were formed in some important Arab cities of the empire, such as Mosul, with important local leaders involved in the process.[90] But the second-class status of Arab members in the local CUPs and other branches (an issue that emerged in the Beirut branch of the CUP in 1911, discussed in Rashid Khalidi's paper, in this volume) can be inferred from remarks about Christians in an important confidential Central Committee circular written about 1897:

All correspondence [between the branches and the Central Committee] should be marked by secret numbers. Our great aim is union. For that reason you may allow Christians to become members of the Committee. But do not give the secret numbers of the Committee correspondence to them! Only show them the published materials of the Committee.[91]

In light of the attitudes of the many Young Turk leaders toward the Arabs, which we have explored, it is not a great surprise that after 1908 a conflict developed between Arab nationalists, who came to think of the Turks as oppressors, and the Young Turks, who thought Turks were the superior race in the Middle East and had the right to govern the Arabs.

Notes

1. Ahmed Riza, "Hükümetsizlik," *Meşveret*, no. 17 (August 23 108/ 1897):1.
2. From Dr. Nazim Bey to Ishak Sükûti, April 13, 1901, *Papers of Bahaeddin Sakir Bey*. Compare with Dr. Nazım Bey to Ishak Sükûti, n.d., *Arkivi Qëndror Shtetëror i Republikes Popullore Socialiste të Shqiperis* (hereafter cited as *Arkivi Qëndror*) [Central Archives of Albania], 19/106–5/916/1390.
3. To Schillingsfürst, Cairo, November 20, 1899 (pr. November 27, 1899, a.m.), no. 135, A. 12645, *Politisches Archiv des Auswërtägen Amtes*, (hereafter cited as *Auswärtiges Amt*) 732/3, die Jungturken, 198 (Bd. 1–2).
4. See M. Şükrü Hanioğlu, *Bir Siyasal ötrgüt Olarak Osmanli Ittihad ve Terakki Cemiyeti ve Jön Türklük* (1889–1902) [The Ottoman Committee of Union and Progress as a Political Organization and the Young turks, 1889–1902], pp. 184–88.
5. From Rüstem Pasha to Said Pasha, London, January 17, 1894/no. 620 19026, *Londra Büyükelçiligi Arşivi* [Archives of London Embassy], K. 295 (2) and from Rüstem Pasha to Süreyya Pasha, March 3, 1894, *Türk Inkılâp Tarihi Enstitüsü Arşivi* [Archives of Turkish Revolution, Ankara], 1c/no. 342, 344 from London Embassy to the Palace, *Basbakanlık Arşivi* (hereafter cited as *BBA*), [Prime Ministry Archives], *Hususi Maruzatı* 5 S 1311/no. 3119.
6. "Dersaadet Havadisi," *Hürriyet*, no. 8 (24 Ramadan 1312/1894):1; "Abdülhamid'in Hal'i Hakkında Rivayet-i Muhtelife," *Hürriyet*, no. 17 (July 3, 1895):1–2.
7. "Fransa Matbuatinin Suriye'deki Efkârı," *Hürriyet*, no. 1 (25 Rece 1311/1894):16; "Gavail-i Mündefi'a ve Gavail-i Gayr-i Mündefi'a," *Hürriyet* no. 2 (10 Saban 1311/1894):1–2.
8. "Hürriyet'in Hurûfatı," *Hürriyet*, no. 2 (10 Saban 1311/1894):9.
9. From General Post Office to Foreign Office, 243 V/7, August 7, 1895, *Public Record Office* (hereafter cited as PRO) Foreign Office (hereafter cited as FO), 78/5529; and from Lord Kimberley to Rüstem

Pasha, Foreign Office, March 28, 1894, *Londra Büyükelçiligi Arsivi*, K. 295 (2).
10. *BBA-BEO/Telgraf ve Posta Nezareti Giden*, 585–17/10, no. 1/43882, *BBA/BEO/Dahiliye Giden*, 94–3/43, 2966 (January 3, 1311/1895)/ 54657, *BBA-Irade-Hususı*, Cemaziy'ülevvel no. 37–779 (October 1313/ 1895).
11. *BBA-Yildiz Mütenevvı Günlük Marûzat*, 16 L 1311/no. 809–8464; from Thomas Sanderson to Antopulo Pasha, March 28 1895, PRO/ FO 78/4744.
12. Statement Against Sultan and Turkish Government in Turkish Paper *Hurriyet* Printed in England *L.O.O* 967 as to Prosecution of Printers, PRO/FO Registered Papers: 45:9741–A. 55743.
13. *BBA-BEO/Hariciye Reft* 183–5/39, 312 (April 23, 1312/1896)/58054, "Nouvelles de L'Etranger," *Le Temps*, May 10, 1896, p. 2.
14. *BBA-BEO/Zaptire Giden*, 662–21/13, 432, (October 26, 311/1895)/ 53427 and *BBA-BEO/Adliye Giden*, 23–1/23, 805, (December 3, 311/ 1895)/53617; "The Armenian Crisis: Details of the Scheme," *The Standard*, October 24, 1895.
15. "Avukat Acem Izzet Bey," *Osmanlı*, no. 44 (September 15, 1895):3.
16. From Antopulo Pasha to Tahsin Bey, October 5, 1896, *Londra Büyükelçiliği Arsivi*, K. 319 (2), *BBA-BEO/Hariciye Reft*, 184,5/40, 958, (September 4, 1313)/75540.
17. *BBA-Divan-i Hümayun Muhtelif ve Mütenevvi Defterler/Muharrerat-i Umumiye*, 84/135–217, Cemaziy'ülevvel 1315 (October 1897), and Count Goluchowski to Istanbul Embassy, October 7, 1897/no. 42 d (Pr. 17/X/97), *Haus-, Hof-u. Staatsarchiv*, PA XII 168 *Türkei Berichte* 1897 (VI-XII) (67382).
18. From Political Department to Barthou, Minister of Interior, January 7, 1898, *Affaires étrangères-Nouvelle Série-Turquie*, vol. 2 (1898) p. 9.
19. Ahmed Riza, "Osmanli Ittihad ve Terakki Cemiyeti ve Avrupa Matbuatı," *Mesveret*, no. 20 (October 8, 1896):2.
20. From Necmeddin Arif to Ishak Süküti, Paris, March 19, 1897, *Arkivi Qëndror*, 19/106–5//270/1711.
21. "Osmanlı," *Osmanlı*, no. 55 (March 1, 1900):8.
22. "Les evenements d'Orient: Interview de L'emir Arslan-Syriens, Armenians et Jeunes Turcs-Reformes pour tous," *L'Intransigeant*, November 29, 1895.
23. From Salmoné to Rüstem Pasha, Turkish Ambassador to England, May 3, 1892, *Londra Büyükelciliği Arsivi*, K. 277 (8).
24. H[abib] Antony Salomé, *The Fall and Resurrection of Turkey*, (London: n.p., 1896).
25. Ibid, pp. 248–51.
26. His petition of January 14, 1897, PRO/FO 78/4840.

27. From Esad Bey to the Palace, November 26, 1893, *Paris ve Viyana Sefaret-i Seniyesiyle Muhabereye Mahsus Defter, BBA-Yıldız Esas Evrakı*, 36/2585/148/XVI.
28. *BPA-Irade Hususi*, Cemaziy'ülahir, no. 49–1319 (November 1312/1894).
29. From Paris Embassy to the Foreign Ministry, no. 10950/160 and 9859/194, *Disisleri Bakanligi Hazine-i Evrak Arşivi* [The Archives of the Ottoman Foreign Ministry], Idari [Administrative]:198.
30. From Esad Bey to the Palace, October 30, 1893; from Ziya Bey to the Palace, October 27, 1894, *Paris ve Viyana Sefaret-i Seniyesiyle Muhaberata Mahsus Defter, BBA-Yıldız Esas Evrakı*, 36,2858/148/XVL, *Turk Inkılap Tarihi Enstitüsü Arşivi*, 82–18112. For the impact of the attitude of the French Government on this subject, see Emir Arslan's to the British Government, January 1895/no. 491, PRO/FO 78/4646.
31. Salmoné, *The Fall and Resurrection of Turkey*, p. 250.
32. Halil Ganem, "Hatt-i Hareketimaz," *Hilâl*, no. ? (December 1893):2.
33. *BBA-Y/Sadaret Hususi Maruzat*, 3 Ca 1311/no. 1536; 7 N 1311/no. 3143; 16 L 1311/no. 3606; 3 Za 1311/no. 3890; 25 Ca 1311/1879.
34. Alexis Kateb, *Ouvre Patriotique de la Foi Chrétienne et de Pénétration Française et Syrie et dans tout l'Orient*, (Paris, Imprimerie Charles Ronson, 1899).
35. From Alexis Kateb to the Prime Minister, Paris, January 24, 1899, and to the Foreign Ministry, January 22, 1899, *Affaires étrangères-Nouvelle Serie-Turquie*, vol. 3 (1899–1901).
36. *Memorandum Presente par la Presse Ottoman Libre à Sa Majeste Imperiale le Sultan Abdul-Hamid II, Paris Büyükelçiliği Arsivi*, D. 176.
37. *BBA-BEO/Hariciye Reft*, 183–5/39, 813 (July 16 311/1895)/49511.
38. From Ziya Pasha to Said Pasha, April 14, 1895/no 8797–158; *Paris Büyükelçiliği Arşivi*, D 176; and *BBA-Y/Sadaret Hususi Maruzat*, 16 Za 1312/no. 4320.
39. *BBA-Irade-Hususi*, Receb 1313 (December 1895)/no. 69; *BBA-BEO/Zaptiye Giden*, 662–21/13 (December 6, 1311/1895)/53773 and *BBA-BEO/Hariciye Reft*, 183–5/39, 1496 (December 7 1311/1895)/53790.
40. "Evrak-i Havadis: Türkiya-el-Fettat," *Ilave-i-Meşveret*, no. 7 (March 1, 1897):3.
41. "Teşekkür ve Memnuniyet," *Mizan*, no. 167 (March 12, 1896):2424.
42. "Banquet de la Jeune Turquie," *Mechveret Supplément Français*, no. 26 (January 1, 1897):7.
43. "Young Turkey Party's Plans," *New York Times*, May 3, 1896, p. 17.
44. Paris, January 26, 1897, PRO/FO, 78/4840.
45. "Suriye-el-Fettat," *Enin-i-Mazlum*, no. 6 (May 15, 1899):48.
46. "Halil Ganem," *Sura-yi Ümmet*, no. 34 (August 9, 1903):1–2; "Teessüf ve Ta'ziye," *Osmanlı*, no. 121 (September 1903):1.

47. *BBA-Irade-Hususi*, Cemaziy'evvel no. 84–545 (November 1315/1897), *BBA-BEO/Hariciye Reft*, 1155 (October 7, 1313/1897)/76875.
48. *BBA-Y/Saderet Hususi Maruzat*, 18 S 1318/no. 250.
49. *BBA-Y/Mutenevvi Maruzat*, 15 Ra 1314/no. 2222.
50. From Serafeddin Mağmumi to Ishak Sükûti, Paris, July 10, 1897, *Arkivi Qëndror*, 19/106–7/292/1950–2023–6.
51. M.A., "Suriye'den Mektub: 28 Subat 1311," *Ilave-i Meşveret*, no. 9 (April 1, 1897):3; M.A., "Suriyeden Mektub," *Ilave-i Meşveret*, no. 5 (February 1, 1897):3; M.A., "Suriye'den Mektub," *Meşveret*, no. 22 (November 8, 1896):6; "Sam'dan Mektub," *Ilave-i Meşveret*, no. 11 (May 13, 1897):3.
52. From Nuri Ahmed Bey to the Central Committee, Geneva, February 9, 1897, *Arkivi Qëndror*, 19/135/175/188.
53. "Cevab," *Mizan*, no. 179 (June 4, 1896):2520.
54. From Şem'azade Ahmed Refik Pasha to the Palace, March 17, 1313/1897/no. 27, *Memurin-i Muteferrikaya Mahsus Kayid Defteridir, BBA-Yildiz Esas Evraki*, 36/139–84/139, XX.
55. From Marshal Edhem Pasha to the Palace, June 27, 1313/1897/no. 86, *Alsonya Ordu-yu Humayun Umum Kumandanlığıyla Muhaberat Defteridir*, 2/49, *BBA-Yildiz Esas Evraki*, 36/139–40/139/XVIII.
56. "Havadis," *Mizan*, no. 173 (April 23, 1896):2472.
57. *BBA-BEO/VGG(2)*, Suriye Giden 352, 7, (March 27, 1313/1897)/69883; from 5th Army Headquarters to the Sublime Porte, March 28, 1313/1897.
58. Saman, "Suriye'den Mektub," *Ilave-i Meşveret*, no. 9 (April 1897):1.
59. Elie Kedourie, *Arabic Political Memoirs and Other Studies* (London: Frank Cass, 1974), p. 126.
60. A petition that was sent to the Sublime Porte, March 19, 1313/1897, no. 484–11860, *BBA-BEO/VGG(2)*, Suriye Giden: 352/69883.
61. *BBA-BEO/Dahiliye Giden*, 101/3/50, 50 (March 5, 1318/1902)/135853.
62. From Necmeddin Arif Bey to Ishak Sükûti, Paris, March 17, 1899, *Arkivi Qëndror*, 19/106–5/169/1691.
63. *BBA-BEO/VGG(2)*, Arabistan Telgrafi: 956, Suriye 98158/105, June 30, 1313/1897).
64. *BBA-BEO/Dahiliye Giden*, 101–3/50, 50 (March 5, 1318/1902)/135853 and from Adana Martial Law Commander to the Palace, March 29 1315/1899/no. 31; *Haleb ve Adan Fevkalade Kumandanlığı Vekaletine Mahsus Defterdir, BBA-Yıldız Esas Evrakı*, 19/39/139/XVIII.
65. "Acik Muhabere: Kastamoni-de (La . . .) Bey'e," *Mizan*, no. 24 (June 14, 1897):4.
66. *BBA-BEO/Hariciye Amed*, 155–3/11, 1275 (May 31, 1311/1895); from the vilayet of Beirut to the Palace, September 8, 1315/1899/no. 216, *Beyrut Vilayetiyle Muhaberata Mahsus Defter*, no. 27; *BBA Yıldız Esas Evrakı*, 36/24766/147/XVI; from Sevkat Bey, Governor of Hama

to the Palace, September 26, 1312/no. 711, *BBA-BEO/VGG(2), Arabistan Müteferrikasi*:211.
67. A petition was sent to the Sublime Porte, *BBA/BEO/VGG (2), Arabistan Müteferrikasi*:211, Hama, March 8, 1313/1897, no. 11.
68. To Hanotaux from Damascus Consulate General, December 18, 1897/no. 29, *Affaires étrangères Politique Interieure, (Syrie-Liban)-Dossier General II*. (July-December 1897):105, 116–67.
69. To Hanotaux from Beirut Consulate General, September 28, 1897/ no. 59 and no. 57; ibid, pp. 125, 131.
70. *BBA/VGG(2), Arabistan Vilayatı Giden:* 235, 15 (telegraph), April 24, 1313/ May 5, 1897, from Philip Currie to Foreign Office, Therapia, August 26 1897/no. 517–572 (conf.), PRO/FO 78/4806.
71. From the Commander of Aleppo and Adana to the Palace, 22/May 21, 1313/1897, *Haleb ve Adana Kumandan Vekaletine Mahsus [Defter]*, *BBA-Yıldız Esas Evrakı*, 36/2170–18/147/XVI.
72. To the Governor of Adana, May 20, 29, 1313/1897, Gumulcine Mutasarrifivla Adana, *Diyar-ibekir Vilayetleri Muhaberat Kaydına Mahsus Defterdir*, no. 48, *BBA-Yildiz Esas Evraki*, 36/139–54/139/ XXVI.
73. From Mehmed Kamil Bey to the Commander of Aleppo and Adana, *Haleb ve Adana . . .* , *BBA-Yildiz Esas Evraki* 36/2170–18/147/XVI.
74. From Beirut to the Palace, 51/July1, 1313/1897, *Beyrut Vilayetiyle Muhaberata Mahsus Defter*, no. 27, *BBA-Yıldız Esas Evrakı*, 36/2470– 6/147/XVI.
75. From the Palace to the Commander of Aleppo and Adana, 25/July 15, 1313/1897; 27/July 17, 1313; 28/July 26, 1313; 30/July 27, 1313; 33/July 28, 1313; 34/July 28, 1313; 35/August 9, 1313; 37/August 27, 1313; 86/January 19, 1313/January 31, 1898; and from this commander to the Palace, 29/July 27, 1313/1897, 36/August 11, 1313, 84/30 December 1313/January 11, 1897, *Haleb ve Adana Kumandan . . .* , *BBA-Yıldız Esas Evrakı*, 36/2470–18/147/XVI.
76. From the Palace to thé Governor of Aleppo and Adana, 25/July 15, 1313/1897, and 36/August 11, 1313/1897, ibid.
77. *BBA-Y/Mutenevvi (Günlük) Maruzat*, 18 Za 1319/no. 85–8766, *BBA-Yildiz Perakende*, 5 L 1316/no. 1023–8093, *BBA-BEO/Harbiye Giden*, 259–6/67, 213, (April 1318/April 15, 1902)/137166.
78. From Philip Currie to Foreign Office, Therapia, August 2, 1897/no. 518, PRO/FO 78/4805.
79. *BBA-BEO/VGG(2), Suriye Gelen:*345, telegraphs numbered 58 and 65/117521–118661.
80. "Konstantinopel: 14 Dezember 1897," *Pester Lloyd*, December 16, 1897.
81. From Marshall von Bieberstein to Schillingsfürst, Pera, December 3 1898 (pr. December 27, 1898 P.M.), no. 253/A. 14945, A 9184 and

A 9730, *Auswärtiges Amt:* 645/2, *Türkische Militärs,* 159–no. 3, (Bd. 2–3).
82. "Haleb'den," *Osmanlı,* no. 4, December 15 1898, p. 6.
83. He was Haydarpaşazâde Arif Bey; see his letter to Ishak Sükûti, Marseilles, August 17, 1899, *Arkivi Qëndror,* 19/106–3/144/969, and his card to Ishak Sükûti, Tunis, March 18, 1899, *Arkivi Qëndror,* 19/106–1/262/384.
84. "Le Comité Musulman de la Jeune-Turquie," *Correspondance Oriental* (Gibraltar), November 20, 1901, "El Harem del Sultan Abdul Hamid II' " *El Centinela Del Estrecho De Gibraltar,* no. 3 (November 24, 1901):2.
85. *Paris Büyükelcilici Arsivi,* D.278.
86. M.A., "Osmanli Ittihad," *Meşveret,* no. 5 (February 1, 1897):1.
87. "Kustahlik," *Şura-yi Ümmet,* no. 75 (May 30, 1905):1; Tunali Hilmi, *Peste'de Resit Efendi Ile* (Geneva), 1317/1901, p.96.
88. "Havadis: Istanbul'dan Yazıyorlar Ki," *Mizan,* no. 183 (July 1, 1896):2551.
89. From Ishak Sükûti to Dr. Nazim, n.d., Papers of *Bahaddin Sakir Bey.*
90. Şakir Bey, cypher from Mosul to the Sublime Porte, *BBA-BEO/VGG(2), Umum Defteri,* no. 880, 57/28 August 28, 1324/1908/255022.
91. *Arkivi Qëndror,* 19/60//445–30–1.

THREE

Ottomanism and Arabism in Syria Before 1914: A Reassessment

Rashid Khalidi

Different Views of Arab Nationalism. The study of early Arab nationalism has gone through a number of phases. The first was that encompassing the writings of participants in the early stages of the movement and their contemporaries. These included such men as As'ad Daghir, Muhammad 'Izzat Darwaza, Amin Sa'id, Sati-'al-Husri, and George Antonius. Each of them had witnessed and in some cases taken part—or had personally known the participants—in the events of the pre-1920 period. This phase has given us works that are often primary sources or contain primary source material.[1] They have also yielded many interpretations that remain relevant, as well as others that have become outdated or disputed.

A second phase included the first scholarly attempts to revise, build upon, or contradict the theses of these first chroniclers of the history of Arab nationalism. Notable among this second group are works mostly written in the 1950s and 1960s by such historians as C. Ernest Dawn, Albert Hourani, Abdel Latif Tibawi, Elie Kedourie, Zeine N. Zeine, Sylvia Haim, Suleiman Mousa (Sulayman Musa), and others.[2] They have introduced numerous corrections in the picture drawn by the writers of the first phase, although there have also been important differences between the assessments of some of these scholars.

Finally, while these established scholars have since developed their ideas further, a number of mainly younger historians have attempted to explore new areas or to go back over ground already worked on by earlier writers. Thus, such authors as the late Marwan Buheiry, William Cleveland, Philip Khoury, William Ochsenwald, Samir Seikaly, and others have focused on prominent leaders in the early era of Arab nationalism as well as on key regions or periods.[3]

Several of the main critiques in the 1950s and 1960s of the traditional view of early Arab nationalism presented by George Antonius in *The Arab Awakening* have been fully accepted. It is thus now generally agreed that Antonius and other early writers overemphasized the connections between the literary *nahda* linked to the earliest stirrings of protonationalist feeling in the late nineteenth century and the effervescence of the period from 1908 to 1914. Further, it is now accepted that the presence of Arabist trends in the late nineteenth-century literary movement dominated by Syrian Christians had a limited impact on the majority Muslim population, among whom there were developments of equal or greater importance at the same time. Similarly, the extent of the spread of Arabist feeling before World War I is now generally agreed to have been less great than was depicted by some members of the first generation of historians. Finally, the term "Arabism," implying protonationalism rather than full-fledged nationalism with the concomitant desire for separation of the Arabs from the Ottoman Empire, is now accepted as more appropriate to describe the prewar movement.

Perhaps the key revisions in the traditional view were the contributions from C. Ernest Dawn. In "The Rise of Arabism in Syria," Dawn dealt with Damascus and the areas that were later incorporated into the Syrian Republic.[4] He focused on Syrian members of the Arab movement whom he was able to identify, and who he found constituted the leadership of the movement and a "significant percentage" of its known active partisans, arguing that they were representative of the prewar Arab movement.[5] Defining the primary political conflict in the Arab provinces of the Ottoman Empire from 1908 to 1918 as one between Ottomanists and Arabists, Dawn argued that "most Arabs remained Ottomanists until 1918," and that the conflict between the two trends was one "between rival members of the Arab elite" (although he noted that middle-class elements were slightly more important among Arabists than among opponents).⁶

Dawn's arguments, and his strictures on the traditional view of Arab nationalism, have been generally accepted by recent writers. Thus, in his reappraisal of Antonius (in "The *Arab Awakening* Forty Years After"), Albert Hourani quotes Dawn approvingly while at the same time offering a number of refinements of his own. William Cleveland also relies on Dawn's assessment, stating that "the majority of the Arab elite sought survival within the framework of a strengthened Ottoman state, not in separation from it."⁷ And Philip Khoury, too, depends heavily on Dawn, concluding one discussion of the period from 1860 to 1920 by calling Arabism "a humble minority position in Damascus and elsewhere, unable to erode the loyalty of the dominant faction of the local political elite in Syria to Ottomanism."⁸

A Proposed Revision of the Revisionist Thesis. It is unfair to Dawn's sophisticated arguments to summarize thus the work of many years, embodied in several seminal articles and brought together in *From Ottomanism to Arabism,* or to cite so briefly the views of later historians who have accepted and built on his revisions of previous views of early Arab nationalism. However, such a review is necessary to understand some of the reservations that can be raised regarding the interpretations of various revisionist historians.

A significant problem with the work of many historians who have downplayed the extent of Arabist feeling before 1914 is that they seem to be arguing in the face of several important categories of primary evidence. These are: (1) the diplomatic and consular archives of the major powers as they relate to Syria; (2) the large body of contemporary material contained in the press during this period, which has only begun to be used by historians; and (3) recollections of those involved in the prewar Arab movement. Moreover, in very few cases do they rely on a fourth category of source material—the Ottoman archives.⁹

It is of course possible that our view of this period is influenced by the post-1918 success of Arab nationalism as an ideology in the *mashriq*. This criticism has been leveled in particular at Arab nationalist writers such as Amin Saʿid, Asʿad Daghir, and Antonius, whose recollections of the pre-1914 period may well have been colored by later events and by political preferences. Against the weaknesses in the analysis of these traditional writers, however, must be set the evidence of the other two categories of sources. Scores of consular and diplomatic dispatches in the British and French archives document a rising Arabist trend in Syria after 1910, frequently with specific references to events, individuals, and groups, reaching the point by 1912 or 1913 where it is described as a majority tendency.[10] For all their flaws as sources, whether due to their authors' ignorance of local languages and conditions, or their own biases, these dispatches paint a consistent and convincing picture, particularly when checked against other types of sources.

Similarly, the most prominent, forceful, and apparently popular Arabic-language papers of this period, whether those published in Beirut, Damascus, or Cairo, were Arabist in tone. These papers apparently constituted a majority of the Syrian press, whether in Syria or Egypt, and must have had a major effect at least on the urban population, and in particular the educated elite. While by itself the press can be misleading as a source (since in the last analysis it reflects the views of its publishers and journalists rather than its readers), it does provide a contemporary mirror of what people were reading, if not thinking.[11]

What is the explanation of this apparent discrepancy with the conclusions of the revisionist historians, who include most modern writers on the subject? To explain this discrepancy several points have to be made. The first has to do with a subject that has not been sufficiently factored into the discussion of early Arab nationalism by either the first revisionists of the 1950s and 1960s or their more recent followers. This is the pre-1914 development of Turkish nationalism as a political force, its impact on the rise of Arabism, and the way it affected local political conflicts in Syria. Although we have learned more in recent years of what Arabs in this era thought of Turkish nationalism, as Albert Hourani wrote a few years ago, "What the Turks, and in particular the Turks of the Committee of Union and Progress, thought about the Arabs is still largely an unanswered question."[12] The ongoing work of young Turkish scholars such as Hasan Kayali, who has analyzed Arab-Turkish relations in the parliaments of 1908–1914,[13] and M. Şükrü Hanioğlu, who is now publishing the secret papers for the secretaries of the CUP going back to 1889,[14] shows this to be an important subject and may provide surprising answers to Hourani's question.

Hanioğlu's work in particular reveals the CUP to have been a more intensely Turkish nationalist grouping, and one that was in existence earlier, than most historians have assumed. It also shows it to have had a secret, purely Turkish, inner leadership group and inner membership unknown to those citizens who joined after 1908. If substantiated by further research, these discoveries have major implications for our understanding of the policies of the CUP, and of how they were perceived by many Arabs. This is especially true of its so-called Turkification measures, which at the time may have looked more sinister than they really were—and which in some cases amounted to no more than the replacement of officials of the Hamidian era (often Arabs) with politically reliable CUP members, generally Turks. (On this point see C. Ernest Dawn's paper, in this volume.) These findings help us to understand the attitude of some politically aware Arabs to the CUP and to its increasing monopoly of power over the empire in the ten years from 1908 onward.

Such revelations throw a fresh light on much contemporary Arab material, making its accusations against the CUP more understandable, and making it somewhat more credible as a source. Hanioğlu's research, for example, bears out the description by an anonymous 1916 author (in fact, Asʿad Daghir) in *Thawrat al-ʿarab* (The revolt of the Arabs) of the CUP's internal organization and its exclusion of Arabs from the Central Committee and from its discussions of major issues of national policy. Similarly, they substantiate incidents reported in consular dispatches, such as that in Beirut in April 1911 when the "official committee" of the local CUP branch, headed by a Beiruti (Dr. ʿAsir), came into conflict with the branch's "secret committee," headed by a Turk (Ahmad Bey Fehmi), over instructions from the CUP's Central Committee in Salonika to censure two Arab deputies who had become "the champions of Arab grievances against the present Government."[15]

A second point relates to how we assess the importance of different centers and regions in the rise of Arabism. Most historians who deal with the period agree in assigning primacy to Damascus, which seems logical on the face of it. Dawn's claim of the representativity of the individuals he studies seems convincing, although he notes that "more biographical information is available for the inhabitants of Syria than of other Arab lands,"[16] and it is clear that his methodology (based on biographical dictionaries and similar sources) has partially influenced his choice of Syria. Later events may have had an effect, too: our focus on Damascus may be aptly a function of its having become the capital of Arab nationalism—"*qalb al-ʿuruba al-nabid*" ("the beating heart of Arabism"), to use the self-satisfied description adopted by a succession of modern Syrian regimes.

There are, however, a number of problems with this focus on Damascus and the areas that became the modern state of Syria. The first is that even if we concede the primacy of Damascus as a center of Arabism, we must weigh its importance vis-à-vis that of other centers, such as Beirut, Cairo, and Istanbul. It is also necessary to assess the relative significance of the cities of the Syrian interior from Damascus to Aleppo against that of cities along the Syrian littoral and in Palestine.

Although Khoury subscribes to the idea of the primacy of Damascus, he concedes in a footnote that "Beirut was also very active in promoting the 'Arab Movement' and in some respects rivalled Damascus in terms of its contribution to activating the idea of 'Arabism.' "[17] He adds in another: "But Beirut's contribution was more to the birth of the idea than to the physical growth of the national movement."[18] In fact, Beirut seems to have taken the political lead in late 1912 after the outbreak of the Balkan wars, when a movement from reform that started there swept the Arab provinces of the empire, leading ultimately to the First Arab Congress in Paris. At that congress, Beirutis such as ʿAbd al-Ghani al-ʿUraysi and Salim ʿAli Salam were prominent, alongside leaders from Damascus and Palestine.

It is significant that the newspaper that was arguably the most influential voice of the Arab movement, *al-Mufid*, was published in Beirut (its closest rival in this respect was *al-Muqtabas* in Damascus). *Al-Mufid* was the organ of what was probably the most important prewar Arab nationalist secret society, *al-Jamʿiyya al-ʿarabiyya al-fatat*.[19] It was widely read not only in Beirut and the *wilaya* of which it was the capital, but in neighboring *wilayas*. In addition, its articles were reprinted in other Arabist papers as far afield as Cairo, Istanbul, Haifa, and Damascus.[20] A reading of *al-Mufid* in its heyday, from 1911 to 1913, reveals the reasons for its popularity: it combined a lively style with impassioned rhetoric, and a respect for Islamic tradition and for the historic role of the Ottoman Empire with a modern insistence on reforms, equality, and national self-expression. Other Beirut Arabist papers included *al-Ittihad al-'uthmani, al-Haqiqa,* and *al-Iqbal.* It seems that most Beirut papers were Arabist and that this city had more Arabist newspapers than any other in *bilad al-sham.*[21]

Beirut had a particular importance in terms of the social, economic, and educational changes taking place throughout Syria in the late nineteenth and early twentieth centuries. These changes were probably most far-reaching in the port cities of the littoral. Foreign cultural and economic influences had penetrated most of this region, which was open to the sea and therefore also open to the powerful forces generated by trade, and which had a population more mixed in sectarian terms than elsewhere in Syria. Here, also, radical currents of thought were more widespread and less likely to be stifled by the status quo than in the more conservative cities of the interior. There was a particularly striking expansion of state, missionary, and private education along the coast. In Beirut *wilaya*, which included most of the littoral from north of Jaffa to north of Latakia the number of state schools alone rose from 153 in 1886 to 359 in 1914, a rate of growth faster than that of the population.[22]

While the great cities of the interior, notably Damascus and Aleppo, still retained their preeminence in a variety of ways, it is clear that both economic and demographic growth were faster along the coast. In the fifty years after 1865, Beirut's population doubled, to nearly 175,000. It took Damascus about a century to double its population of 1800, and that of Aleppo grew even more slowly.[23] Damascus had 250,000 inhabitants, and Aleppo 200,000, according to French statistics based on Ottoman figures and published in 1915 (these figures may be inexact; eighteenth-century estimates and French mandatory statistics show Aleppo's population as larger than that of Damascus). By 1914, Beirut, whose population was under 10,000 in 1800, had become the third-largest city in *bilad al-sham*, with a great gap between it and the next largest, Jerusalem, which had 84,000. According to Hourani, "The important fact of the growth of

Beirut in the nineteenth century was not simply the replacement of one major trading port by another ... but the growth of a new kind of city, a new kind of urban society with a new kind of relationship with the rural hinterland."[24]

Similar changes were also taking place in Palestine, whose population shared in the economic and demographic growth and the expansion of education going on in the coastal regions of *bilad al-sham*. In Palestine, there was the additional impetus of Zionist immigration and colonization. Thus Jerusalem's population, like that of Jaffa (which, with 55,000 people, was the second-largest port of the littoral after Beirut), included a large proportion of Jewish immigrants. These newcomers were mainly located in these two cities, where they made up as much as half of the total population according to some sources, and more than that according to others.[25]

Palestine was doubly important, as far as the issue of Arabism is concerned, because it was experiencing the same economic expansion that affected other coastal regions, with the attendant social transformations: in the words of Marwan Buheiry, a "new 'class' of Arab entrepreneurs" had emerged in the wake of the growth of Palestine's agricultural exports.[26] There was also a rapid spread of missionary, private, and state-sponsored education, and a multiplication in the number of newspapers, especially after 1908 (notably *Filastin* in Jaffa and *al-Karmil*, in Haifa): from 1908 to 1914, a total of thirty-four newspapers and magazines were established in Palestine, more than twenty of them achieving success and continuing to appear for several years.[27] Palestine was thus an area of economic, cultural, and political significance in its own right. It had all the more importance since it was one of the empire's sensitive border regions, and one where for various reasons the interests of major foreign powers had long been deeply engaged.

Palestine was simultaneously the scene of a confrontation with Zionism that became a key issue between Ottomanists and Arabists throughout the Empire in the five years before World War I. A survey of nine major organs of the Arabic press in Syria and Egypt revealed 441 articles on Zionism between 1911 and 1913, an indication of the extraordinary attention paid to Zionism.[28] Arabists in particular focused on this issue as evidence of the failure of the CUP to respond to local needs, while supporters of the CUP generally tried to avoid discussion of it.

(Dawn comes to similar conclusions in his essay, in this volume.) It is thus necessary to consider Palestine, like Beirut and other areas of the littoral, as part of a whole, of which Damascus and the interior regions of Syria were another (albeit more important) part. With a population of about a quarter million in its cities and towns, Palestine was an important political arena in the Arabist-Ottomanist conflict; at the same time, the spread of Zionism gave it a special salience.

Also underemphasized in much of the revisionist argument are the roles of the two great cities of the pre-1914 Levant, each of which played an essential part in the rise of Arabism. These were Istanbul and Cairo, the twin poles of a Western Islamic world that still retained a fragile sense of unity until it was shattered in the upheaval of World War I. Arabism did indeed arise in Syria, and Damascus was the leading city of *bilad al-sham*, but for many centuries this had been a region economically, intellectually, and often politically subordinate to one of those two poles, and sometimes to both.

It could be argued in long historical perspective that Arabism represented the first halting step toward a separate vocation for Syria, independent of Cairo and Istanbul as well as other centers—and that indeed seems to be its result today under the latest, Ba'thist, variety of Arabism, which has made Syria an important regional actor and an autonomous power center over the past few decades. However, there can be no doubt of the extent to which *bilad al-sham*, including Damascus, was still beholden to both of these great cities before 1914.

In view of this, it is not surprising that a preoccupation with Damascus leads us to miss a key element in the politics of the pre-1914 period: *majlis al-mab'uthan* (Chamber of Deputies), the lower chamber of the Ottoman parliament, for which elections were held in 1908, 1912, and 1914, and on which little historical work has been done, at least as far as the Arab deputies are concerned. While the local affairs of all parts of *bilad al-sham* (including those of the Damascus landed/bureaucratic elite on which most historians focus) could be all-consuming in their importance, these local struggles were quite often resolved in terms of national politics, for which the ultimate arena was in Istanbul.

The role of the first group of Syrian parliamentary deputies elected after the reinstatement of the constitution—most of whom, between the 1908 and 1912 elections, came to oppose the CUP and to identify with the bloc of Arab deputies linked to the opposition—is underemphasized by revisionist historians of Arabism. (See Dawn's discussion of this topic, in this volume.) Although further research is needed, it appears that of twenty-one Arab deputies from the *wilayas* of *bilad al-sham*, at least thirteen (Rushdi Sham'a, Shafiq Mu'ayyad, Shukri al-'Asali, 'Abd al-Hamid al-Zahrawi [Abdülhamid el-Zehravi], Khalid Barazi, Sa'd al-Din Khalil, and Tawfiq al-Majali of Damascus; Nafi' al-Jabiri of Aleppo; Rida al-Sulh, Kamil al-As'ad and Ahmad Khammash of Beirut; and Hafiz Sa'id and Sa'id al-Husayni of Jerusalem) had become identified with the opposition. All except al-As'ad and Barazi, both of whom abruptly went over to the CUP in the middle of the 1912 campaign, lost their seats in 1912. Only three of the twenty-one ('Abd al-Rahman Yusuf of Damascus, As'ad Shuqayr of Beirut, and Ruhi al-Khalidi of Jerusalem) were known partisans of the CUP. These three were the only Syrian Arab deputies elected in 1908 who were reelected in 1912, together with the two "defectors" from the opposition, al-As'ad and Barazi, in the rigged "big stick" election of 1912.[29]

The fact that, by the time they ran for reelection in 1912, most of the Syrian deputies elected in 1908 and in later by-elections were in opposition to the CUP and identified with the Arabist trend says something that the revisionists do not prepare us for. These officials presumably had the exquisite concern for their own self-interest that politicians have in all places and at all times. The implication is that they sensed that a majority of *electors* (who under the Ottoman two-tier system were largely representative of the elite) were also leaning toward Arabism. In practical terms, this meant opposition to the policies of the CUP, a call for decentralization and reform, and an emphasis on the Arabs, their language, culture, and history. If we join most historians in ignoring the Ottoman parliament, the three prewar election campaigns for it, and the experience of the Arab parliamentary bloc in Istanbul confronting the governing CUP from 1908 to 1912, then we are likely to miss this point. It should be noted that it is clearly emphasized in all three categories of sources already mentioned: diplomatic, press, and memoir materials.

Istanbul was further important in terms of its extensive trade with *bilad al-sham*. According to the research of Marwan Buheiry, for a three-year period early in this century, Jaffa, the second port of the littoral, had considerably more trade with other parts of the empire, notably with Istanbul, than with its largest foreign trading partner, Great Britain. Furthermore, it engaged in more trade with the rest of the empire than with the next two foreign trading partners, Germany and France, combined. Trade with Egypt was not quite as great as with Istanbul, but was only slightly less than with Germany and France combined in this period. This bespeaks a powerful current of trade with both Egypt and the rest of the empire that reinforced other links: this "new class" was engaged in "creating closer and closer ties ... in the Ottoman Empire and Egypt."[30] It also shows that the old Eastern Mediterranean economic system encompassing Syria, Egypt, and the central regions of the empire had not been entirely eroded by the powerful centrifugal economic pressures exerted by Europe.

Moreover, in pre-1914 Istanbul, at any one time there were normally several thousand Arab government officials, military officers, students, businessmen, journalists, and visitors. Most were drawn from the elite of the Arab provinces, however we define that group, and they were arguably as influential a group of Arabs as any in the Middle East, albeit lacking the direct contact with the rest of their own society and its local politics, which their compatriots at home retained. An Arabic-language paper, *al-Hadara* (Civilization), published in Istanbul by Shaykh ʿAbd al-Hamid al-Zahrawi, was influential in all Arabic-speaking regions, with its articles reprinted in the Cairo, Beirut, and Damascus press. (This newspaper, which still awaits in-depth research, is utilized in Ahmed Tarabein's essay on al-Zahrawi, in this volume.) We know, furthermore, that several Arabist societies were established in Istanbul, among them *al-Muntada al-adabi*, *al-Qahtaniyya*, and *al-ʿAhd*. These are only some indications of the importance of this metropolis in the rise of Arabism.

Cairo played a role of similar significance. It was home to a large community of Syrians (as were other Egyptian cities), some of whom had emigrated after the British occupation, but many of whom were already there in the early eighteenth century.[31] We have already noted the extent of Egypt's trade with Jaffa; it was probably even greater with Beirut. Between Cairo and the cities of *bilad al-sham* there was a web of trade and intellectual relations that went back centuries. Study at al-Azhar was the preferred course of scholarly advancement for Syrian ʿulamaʾ in the late nineteenth century, as before and since. And visiting scholars from Egypt had a great impact in Syria; thus Muhammad ʿAbduh's two years of teaching in Beirut, from 1886 to 1888, had a major effect on all who studied with him. Among those ʿAbduh taught were Shakib Arslan and Shaykh Ahmad ʿAbbas al-Azhari, founder of Beirut's influential Ottoman Islamic College, which became the training ground for a whole generation of pre-War Beiruti Arabists.[32]

More immediately relevant, several influential Arabist political groupings, such as *Hizb al-lamarkaziyya al-idariyya al-ʿuthmani* (the Ottoman Administrative Decentralization Party), were founded in Cairo. Journalists prominent in the press of Syria and Istanbul wrote in the Cairo press and often spent long periods in that city, as did many Arabist politicians during periods of repression by the CUP. Egypt was the home of a number of highly influential publications founded by Syrians— for example, *al-Manar, al-Muqattam, al-Ahram, al-Muqtataf,* and *al-Hilal,* all of which contributed significantly to the development of Arabic-language journalism and of Arabism.

It is hardly necessary to stress further the place of Cairo, which Khoury calls "a great intellectual center and haven or refuge for Syrian emigre intellectuals and political activists."[33] The growing bonds between Syria and Egypt were recognized and often deprecated by both the CUP in Istanbul and the British in Cairo. Thus in 1913, at the same time the British were discreetly encouraging the spread of Arabist feeling among Syrians in Egypt, Lord Kitchener wrote: "The direct influence of Syria on Egypt has already to be reckoned with, and any increase in this influence ... would in my opinion act as a disturbing factor in the Government of this country."[34] The Ottoman authorities were clearly worried about influences traveling in the opposite direction.

There remain two other issues that must be examined if the revisionist thesis is itself to be revised. The first centers on the definition of the terms "Ottomanists" and "Arabists," a more difficult problem than it may initially seem. Before 1914, Arabism involved stressing Arab elements of identity, generally at the expense of others (although Islamic, Ottoman, and regional loyalties also could be, and generally were, simultaneously stressed). But for most of its adherents, Arabism was not yet Arab nationalism, nor did it entail a demand for separation from the empire. In practical political terms, being an Arabist during the Ottoman constitutional period from 1908 to 1914 meant being in opposition to the policies of the CUP (notably "Turkification" and extreme Turkish nationalism), rigid centralization, and manipulation of the political system and utilization of administrative means to stifle electoral and press freedoms. It also meant supporting the policy of the opposition *Hürriyet ve Itilaf*, or Entente Liberale party—specifically, respect for the empire's nationalities, protection of democratic freedoms, and some measure of local autonomy and administrative decentralization. It is essential to stress that both Ottomanists and Arabists saw themselves as sincere Ottoman patriots, sometimes exclusively so.

For most of its adherents before 1914, Arabism did not mean Arab separatism, nor did it conflict with loyalty to the Ottoman Empire or to its religious legitimizing principle. Indeed, the Arabists argued that the Turkish nationalist and secular policies of the CUP threatened both, and their own advocacy of reform and decentralization was motivated by their devotion to the preservation of the empire in the face of foreign ambition. Thus, in 1913, at the height of the Balkan wars, al-ʿUraysi wrote in an editorial in *al-Mufid* that it was only possible to "shut the door of intervention in the face of any other country, whether Britain or France ... by satisfying the people .... Patriotism and love of country require that the leaders of the Ottoman Empire hurry to implement general reforms as a barrier to the ambition of the powers."[35]

The terminology being used by revisionist historians—by all of us—may obscure reality in this case. "Arabism" is perhaps unconsciously taken to mean fully developed Arab nationalism, and thus to exclude support for the Ottoman Empire. The implication is that only advocates of rigid centralization under the CUP can accurately be described as "Ottomanists." Until World War I this is not true in either case. Thus in *al-Mufid*, the most outspoken Arabist paper, we frequently find Arabist appeals with a strong nationalist overtone made in terms of the interest of the Ottoman nation or *umma*: Arabs and Turks are "brothers in patriotism [*wataniyya*]," and "the entire Ottoman *umma* is willing to sacrifice itself for any piece of its soil," al-ʿUraysi wrote of the Libyan war in 1911.[36] Similarly, the second major Arabist paper published in Beirut, *al-Ittihad al-ʿuthmani* (whose editor, Shaykh Ahmad Hasan Tabbara, was hanged, together with al-ʿUraysi, for Arab nationalistic activities during World War I), constantly emphasized the necessity of the Ottoman bond to protect Syria and Islam from external encroachment: the paper's very title means "Ottoman Union."

There were ideological differences between Ottomanists and Arabists in the Arab provinces of the Ottoman Empire, but these involved the concrete political issues of the day, such as the best means of resistance to imperialism or the proper balance of centralization versus decentralization, rather than whether the Arabs should remain part of the empire. This was simply not an issue for most Arabists before 1914. Indeed, both Ottomanists and Arabists saw preservation of the region from external encroachment under the Ottoman umbrella to be a primary goal: they differed bitterly on how to achieve this, and it was here that the endemic interfactional conflicts characteristic of the politics of the notables intersected with the macropolitical struggle in the empire as a whole. This conflict took place in terms of the existing Ottoman parties. As long as there was a credible opposition to the CUP with the potential for coming to power, Arabists were allied with it. After the CUP smashed the opposition in 1913–1914, the Arabists were cut loose, and this situation as much as the action of the CUP and the outbreak of war drove many of them to overt Arab nationalism.

This brings us to the second issue, which takes us to the heart of a revision of the revisionist thesis—and this is a definition of the elite in *bilad al-sham* before World War I. Certainly during this period many members of the old notable class of landlord/bureaucrats still retained their wealth, power, and privileged access to the spoils of office. But the following propositions can be suggested as part of a tentative broadening of our understanding of the Syrian elite before 1914:

1. There were major regional differences in the Syrian elite. By 1914 the coastal regions and much of Palestine showed a highly modified form of the classical "politics of the notables," described by Albert Hourani,[37] due to the socioeconomic changes we have already touched on. New groups of merchants and

speculative landlords were already on the scene and exercising growing influence, supported in many cases by their connections with Cairo and Istanbul, or by their modern educations in the hundreds of new schools, or by the new wealth that was more prevalent in many coastal regions. The old notables still existed and retained much of their influence, but were forced to share more and more of it with upstarts from other classes in these areas.

2. Throughout Syria there were new social formations, in some cases classes in embryo, in others new professional or occupational strata, coming into existence at this time and measurably changing the politics of the period. The Tanzimat and Abdülhamid's reforms had created vast numbers of military officers, government clerks, journalists, and teachers in modern schools. All were groups that had barely existed in Syrian society fifty years before, and that were now filled not just with sons of members of the old elite, but also with lower class newcomers. The social nature of the makeup of the top ranks of the CUP, which drew heavily from these new groups,[38] shows the extent to which access to politics was being broadened in the early twentieth century in a Turkish context; it is not unreasonable to assume similar, if delayed and less complete, transformations in the most developed and best integrated of the empire's Arab provinces, those in *bilad al-sham*.

3. From 1908 until 1914, *bilad al-sham*, for the first time, was the scene of press freedom, hotly contested election campaigns, active political parties and secret societies, and public speaking before meetings, rallies, and private groups—in short, the beginning of the era of modern mass politics. As a result, the traditionally exclusive notable role of intermediary with the state was being challenged, especially by the Arabists, who probably included larger numbers of dissident and younger members of the notable class, as well as many more members of the new and growing middle classes, than did their Ottomanist opponents. It is consequently not surprising to find most Damascene notables supporting Ottomanism, since in practical terms this meant that as local clients of the powerful, authoritarian, and centralizing CUP, they could still play the role of intermediaries, speaking for the people, to the mutual benefit of both their class and the CUP. The Arabists, aligned with the

more liberal, decentralizing, and reform-oriented opposition, did not offer this opportunity except during the period of the Libyan-Balkan wars, when the CUP seemed to be losing its grip. For the rest of the years from 1908 until 1918, the CUP was to all intents and purposes the government (*al-sulta* or *al-hukm*), and it was natural for older and more traditional members of this class to gravitate to it.

4. Of course, young men of the notable class could, and did, also obtain a modern education that provided the necessary training in the new skills of journalism, military science, public speaking, and so forth. And there can be no doubt that they were prominent in the leading ranks of the Arabists. But in spite of their many advantages, they had to compete with members of other classes who had acquired these same skills. We thus find men of relatively humble background, such as Rashid Rida, Muhammad Kurd ʿAli, ʿAbd al-'Ghani al-ʿUraysi, Shaykh Ahmad Hasan Tabbara, and Najib Nassar, editing influential newspapers, leading secret societies, or being in the ranks of the "martyrs" hanged in 1916. This marked the beginning of a broadening of the elite and the inclusion in its ranks of numerous members of nonnotable families in prominent roles.[39] Politics henceforth saw a mix of sons of the great families and others from the middle classes writing, speaking, and leading first the Arabist movement, and later the Arab nationalist movement and the various national movements it developed into in the post-World War I states into which the *mashriq* was partitioned.

The notables retained an advantage for many decades, and indeed through the mandate period, as has been conclusively shown by Philip Khoury.[40] However, it was not long before patterns established by the CUP on the national level in Ottoman politics asserted themselves in Syria and other parts of the Arab world. Street demonstrations, use of the media, and military coups became instruments of drastic political change. The first steps in that direction were taken before World War I—a period that, far from seeing only a stale repetition of the classical eighteenth- and nineteenth-century pattern of politics, witnessed the first stirrings of modern politics in the Arab *mashriq*.

Notes

1. The following can be mentioned (see the Bibliography for complete publishing details): As'ad Daghir, *Thawrat al-ʿarab* [The Revolt of the Arabs] (originally published anonymously as being by "a member of the Arab societies"); Muhammad 'Izzat Darwaza, *Nash'at al-haraka al-ʿarabiyya al-haditha* [The birth of the modern Arab movement]; Amin Saʿid, *al-Thawra al-ʿarabiyya al-kubra* [The great Arab revolt]; Satiʿ al-Husri, *al-Bilad al-ʿarabiyya wal-dawla al-ʿuthmaniyya* [The Arab countries and the Ottoman state]; and George Antonius, *The Arab Awakening*.
2. These include C. Ernest Dawn, *From Ottomanism to Arabism;* Albert Hourani, *Arabic Thought in the Liberal Age, 1798–1939;* A. L. Tibawi, *A Modern History of Syria, including Lebanon and Palestine;* Elie Kedourie, *The Chatham House Version and Other Middle Eastern Studies;* Zeine N. Zeine, *The Emergence of Arab Nationalism;* Sylvia Haim, ed., *Arab Nationalism: An Anthology;* Sulayman Mousa (Suleiman Mousa), *Al-Haraka al-ʿarabiyya: sirat al-marhala al-ula lil-nahda al-ʿarabiyya al-haditha 1908–1924* [The Arab movement: The story of the first period of the modern Arab awakening, 1908–1924]. See the Bibliography for complete publishing details.

    See also ʿAbd al-Karim Rafiq, *Al-'Arab wal-ʿuthmaniyyun, 1516–1916* [The Arabs and the Ottomans, 1516–1916]; and Tawfiq ʿAli Birru, *al-ʿArab wal-turk fil-ʿahd al-dusturi al-ʿuthmani, 1908–1914* [The Arabs and Turks during the Ottoman constitutional era, 1908–1914].
3. See, for example, Marwan R. Buhiery, ed., *Intellectual Life in the Arab East, 1890–1939;* William L. Cleveland, *Islam Against the West* and *The Making of an Arab Nationalist;* Philip Khoury, *Urban Notables and Arab Nationalism;* William Ochsenwald, *Religion, Society and the State in Arabia;* and Samir M. Seikaly, "Damascene Intellectual Life in the Opening Years of the 20th Century." See the Bibliography for complete publishing details.
4. Originally published in *Middle East Journal* 26 (1962): 145–68, it is reprinted in Dawn, *From Ottomanism to Arabism,* pp. 148–79, together with a number of other important studies.
5. Dawn, *From Ottomanism to Arabism,* p. 153.
6. Ibid., p. 147 (quotation from the article "From Ottomanism to Arabism: The Origin of an Ideology"), and p. 173.
7. Cleveland, *Islam Against the West,* p. 24.
8. Khoury, *Urban Notables,* p. 74.
9. The third category includes the works cited in note 1 above. The first category is utilized in Rashid Khalidi, *British Policy Towards*

Syria and Palestine, and Khoury, Urban Notables. The second is used in many articles in Buheiry, ed., Intellectual Life in the Arab East (including Seikaly, "Damascene Intellectual Life," pp. 125–53, and Khalidi, "ʿAbd al-Ghani al-ʿUraysi and al-Mufid: The Press and Arab Nationalism before 1914," pp. 38–61); as well as in Khalidi, "The Role of the Press in the Early Arab Reaction to Zionism," pp. 105–24; Khalidi, "Social Factors in the Rise of the Arab Movement in Syria," pp. 53–70; Khalidi, "The 1912 Election Campaign in the Cities of bilad al-sham," pp. 461–74; and Khalidi, "Palestinian Peasant Reactions to Zionism before World War I," pp. 207–33.

10. Khalidi, British Policy, ch. 5; see also Khalidi "The 1912 Election Campaign."
11. For more on the role of the press and its value as a source, see Khalidi, "ʿAbd al-Ghani al-ʿUraysi," and Khalidi, "The 1912 Election Campaign," p. 465. A French consular official who wrote a survey of the Syrian press in 1913 opined that a majority of papers were Arabist and anti-CUP (Ministère des affaires étrangères, Turquie, Nouvelle Serie 121, Guy to Pichon, April 30, 1913).
12. Albert Hourani, in the foreword to Khalidi, British Policy, p. ii.
13. Hasan Kayali, "Arabs and Young Turks: Turkish-Arab Relations in the Second Constitutional Period of the Ottoman Empire (1908–1918)" (Ph.D. diss., Harvard University, May 1988).
14. To date, only the first volume of papers has been published (with a second expected shortly): M. Şükrü Hanioğlu, Bir Siyasal Örgüt: Olarak Osmanli Ittihad ve Terakki Cemiyeti ve Jön Türklük, 1889–1902.
15. Daghir, Thawrat al-ʿarab, pp. 52–54. See also Birru, al-ʿarab wal-turk, p. 379. These sources also focus on the removal of Arab government officials and military officers and their replacement by Turks. For details on the Beirut incident see Khalidi, British Policy, pp. 228–29 (citing FO 195/2370/60, Cumberbatch to Lowther, April 13, 1911).
16. Dawn, From Ottomanism to Arabism, p. 152.
17. Khoury, Urban Notables, p. 125 n. 57.
18. Ibid., p. 101 n. 1.
19. Musa, Al-Haraka al-ʿarabiyya, p. 103.
20. Khalidi, "ʿAsd al-Ghani al-ʿUraisi," pp. 43–6.
21. To assess the significance of this tentative conclusion, it would be necessary to determine circulation figures for the papers of the period, which are not easily ascertainable. On this subject see Khalidi, "The Role of the Press," pp. 110, 121 n. 17.
22. The 1886 figures are taken from tables in ʿAbd al-ʿAziz ʿAwad, Al-Idara al-ʿuthmaniyya fi wilayat suriyya [The Ottoman administration in the province of Syria], pp. 363–67; the 1915 figures are

from Rafiq al-Tamimi and Muhammad Bahjat, *Wilayat Bayrut* [Beirut *vilayet*], 2:152–53.

23. The Beirut population figures are from the table in Leila Tarazi Fawwaz, *Merchants and Migrants in Nineteenth-Century Beirut*, p. 31. The Damascus and Aleppo figures for the end of the eighteenth century (90,000 and 120,000, respectively) are from Antoine Abdel Nour, *Introduction à l'histoire urbaine de la syrie ottomane (XVIe-XVIIIe siècle)*, pp. 73–74, 66–70. See also André Raymond, *The Great Arab Cities of the 16th and 18th Centuries: An Introduction*, pp. 5–7.

24. Hourani is cited in the editors' introduction in Polk and Chambers, eds., *Beginnings of Modernization in the Middle East*, p. 22. The 1915 population figures, "based on Ottoman figures," are from a table in Wajih Kawtharani, *Bilad al-sham*, p. 26, from a document entitled "Note sur la valeur economique de la syrie integrale," prepared by the Marseilles Chamber of Commerce for the French Foreign Ministry in 1915. Beirut's population is listed in this source as 140,000, but it is still the third-largest city in *bilad al-sham*. For French mandatory statistics on Syria see Philip Khoury, *Syria and the French Mandate*, p. 11.

25. For Jerusalem see Yehoshua Ben-Arieh, *Jerusalem in the 19th Century: The Old City* (New York: 1984), p. 358, which summarized 1910 figures indicating 45,000 Jews to 25,000 non-Jews. Many of the former were apparently citizens of states at war with the empire during World War I, and as such were forced to leave Palestine, since by 1916, Ben-Arieh notes, the number of Jews was reduced to 26,571. For the definitive work on Palestinian demography see Justin McCarthy, *The Population of Palestine: Population Statistics of the Late Ottoman Period and the Mandate*.

26. Marwan Buheiry, "Exportations agricoles de la Palestine meridionale 1885–1914," pp. 49–70; and Alexander Schölch, "European Economic Penetration and the Economic Development of Palestine, 1856–82," pp. 10–87.

27. Yusuf Khuri, comp., *al-Sihafa al-ʿarabiyya fi filastin, 1876–1948*, pp. 7–26.

28. Khalidi, "The Role of the Press," p. 107. See also Neville Mandel, *The Arabs and Zionism before World War I*.

29. Dawn's essay in this volume disputes these conclusions, but they are generally borne out by Feroz Ahmad and Dankwart A. Rustow, "Ikinci Mesrutiyet Döneminde Meclisler: 1908–1918," in *Güney-Dogu Avrupa Arastirmalari Dergisi*, pp. 245–84, which includes a list of all deputies with party affiliations. This yields twelve Arabs from *bilad al-sham* affiliated to the opposition, and only three to the CUP for the 1908–1912 Parliament. For a table listing the Syrian deputies elected to all three parliaments, see Khalidi, *Brit-*

ish Policy, pp. 258–59. See also Khalidi "The 1912 Election Campaign," p. 470, for more on the 1912 election results. Little research has been done on the Ottoman parliamentary debates recorded in *Tekvim-i vekai'*, although Kayali's work, cited in note 13 above, utilizes them.
30. Buheiry, "Exportations agricoles."
31. Thomas Philipp, *The Syrians in Egypt (1725–1975)*.
32. Cleveland, *Islam Against the West*, pp. 8–10. This school seems to deserve considerable further study. Another school that played an important role in the early rise of Arabism was Maktab ʿAnbar in Damascus: see Khoury, *Urban Notables*, p. 71 and n. 64, p. 125; and ʿAbdallah Khalid, "Maktab ʿAnbar: suwar min safhat al-butula fi dimashq al-ʿuruba" [Maktab ʿAnbar: Scenes from the pages of heroism in Arab Damascus], pp. 110–18. For more on the place of Arabism in the intellectual life of Damascus in this period, see Joseph Escovitz, "He Was the Muhammad ʿAbduh of Syria: A Study of Tahir al-Jazaʾiri and His Influence," pp. 293–310; and David Commins, "Religious Reformers and Arabists in Damascus, 1885–1914," pp. 405–25. See also Commins' book, *Islamic Reform: Politics and Social Change in Late Ottoman Syria* (New York, 1990).
33. Khoury, *Urban Notables*, p. 101.
34. FO 371/1813/18858/22533, Lord Kitchener to Edward Grey, May 11, 1913, cited in Khalidi, *British Policy*, pp. 307–8.
35. *Al-Mufid*, January 7, 1913, cited in Khalidi, "ʿAbd al-Ghani al-ʿUraysi," p. 58.
36. *Al-Mufid*, October 1, 1911, cited in Khalidi, "ʿAbd al-Ghani al-ʿUraysi," p. 57.
37. The phrase is from Hourani's article, "Ottoman Reform and the Politics of the Notables," pp. 41–68.
38. A sense of how access to leadership positions in the Ottoman Empire was expanded by the 1908 revolution and the CUP domination of politics that followed can be obtained from a perusal of the brief entries for CUP leaders in the biographical appendix to Feroz Ahmad, *The Young Turks*, pp. 166–81. The cases of Haci Adil, Ahmed Agayev, Yusuf Akçura, Hüseyin Cahit, Mehmed Cavit, Ahmed Cemal, Enver Pasa, and Mehmed Talât, among others, show the important new role junior military officers, journalists, low-ranking government officials, teachers, and individuals of relatively humble origins played in politics. The contrast with previous periods of Ottoman history is striking.
39. For more on the social origins of the groups of *salafi* and Arabist figures in Damscus whom he studies, see Commins, "Religious Reformers," pp. 408–10.
40. Khoury, *Syria and the French Mandate*.

PART TWO
Syria and Iraq

FOUR

Shukri al-ʿAsali: A Case Study of a Political Activist

Samir Seikaly

The inductive method, ideally at the core of all historical writing, requires that generalization be based upon, and issued from, an aggregate of particular facts that have been conclusively established and systematically verified. In the case of the historical literature pertaining to the dawn of Arab nationalism, this procedure has at times been ignored: many existing histories have been constructed upon a narrow foundation of facts that have been drawn, in the first place, from non-Arabic sources or that depended upon the testimony of only a few men.[1] Even today, professional monographs devoted exclusively to a systematic examination of the conditions that engendered Arab nationalism and to the roles played by various men and ideas in its ideological formation are scarce. Recently, the link between socioeconomic transformation and the rise of Arab nationalism has received some attention.[2] By contrast, the study of overt nationalist manifestations, as expressed in the creation of Arab cultural clubs or the establishment of party organizations, is practically at a standstill. Thus, *al-Muntada al-adabi* is invoked by name rather than studied.[3] In turn, the Ottoman Administrative Decentralization party *(Hizb al-lamarkaziyya al-idariyya al-ʿuthmani)*, which constituted, according to George Antonius, the most authoritative spokesman of Arab aspirations and represented the first essay in the science of organized effort on the part of the Arab movement, remains the subject of determined neglect.[4]

Biographical accounts emphasizing the guiding role played by individuals in promoting Arab demands and in articulating the Arab movement's nascent ideology fare only marginally better. In fact, apart from a few recent studies that represent new departures,[5] historians have repeatedly examined, to the point of redundancy, the thought and political achievements of people whose importance has long been recognized (al-Kawakibi, Azoury, and Rashid Rida readily come to mind here). Others, arguably more important as political activists and as exponents of a new nationalism, have been consistently overlooked. To prove the point it is sufficient to note that to date there are few academic inquiries concerned with the political and intellectual lead given to Arab nationalism by prominent Syrians, such as ʿAbd al-Hamid al-Zahrawi (Abdülhamid el-Zehravi; see Ahmed Tarabein's essay, in this volume), Haqqi al-ʿAzm, or Shukri al-ʿAsali—to name just a few.

To attribute this manifest gap in the historical record to Orientalism is ingenious but not quite adequate. There are, in fact, other more convincing explanations that range from methodological bias to the persisting failure of practicing historians to utilize the local press as the single most important source for any systematic study of early Arab nationalism. As a result, political activists who owned or edited newspapers and for whom the press was simultaneously a means of self-expression and an instrument for the acquisition of influence remain unknown or are known only in outline, as the cases of al-Zahrawi and al-ʿAsali testify. Insofar as it extends to the former, this judgment may be defensible; as it relates to al-ʿAsali, it seems to be somewhat less valid. This is owing to the fact that he figures prominently in Mandel's *The Arabs and Zionism before World War I* as well as in the work of Rashid Khalidi.[6] It is, of course, true that both have done much to enhance our knowledge of the man and his political preoccupations. But that knowledge, which is mainly derived from non-Arabic sources, is incomplete; it is confined in large measure to his role as a relentless foe of Zionism. The purpose of this paper is, therefore, corrective in nature; it aims, by a closer examination of the record, to re-create the thought of the man and to shed new light on some unknown aspects of his career as a political activist and as a principal defender of Arab rights. Perhaps, as a result, we will understand the man, and the complex circumstances in which he operated, a little better.

The salient features of al-ʿAsali's life are fairly well known. He was born in 1878 into a moderately prosperous Damascene family that had attained some recognition but did not as yet belong to the socioeconomic or political elite of the city.[7] After an indifferent primary education, he transferred to the only state secondary school in Damascus (*Maktab ʿAnbar*). There he was taught a variety of subjects, but his knowledge of Turkish developed rapidly. At the same time, he appears to have drifted into the circle that had grown around Shaykh Tahir al-Jazaʾiri. This association influenced the life of al-ʿAsali decisively; in that circle he was awakened to his identity as an Arab, to the cultural patrimony of his ancestors, and to the need for bringing about reform in his society and in the empire at large. In that circle, too, he became a member of an organized group of Syrian youth who were to emerge at a later date as the most determined defenders of Arab rights in the Ottoman Empire.[8]

Toward the end of the century, probably in 1896, he went to Istanbul where, as a student in *Mekteb-i Mülkiye*, he followed a course of advanced technical training designed to prepare him for a career in the civil service. Upon the completion of his formal education, he served a period of apprenticeship in a number of minor posts and eventually entered full government service which, except for a brief spell, he never left. From the start, he was a member of the state administrative system serving in several of the empire's local governments before his appointment, probably in 1909, as subgovernor (*qaʾimaqam*) of the district of Nazareth in the southern part of the *wilaya* of Beirut.

It is clear from this brief survey that in an economic and social sense, al-ʿAsali was, to employ Ruth Roded's terminology, an "upstart" who deliberately opted to acquire a modern secular education as a preliminary for government employment that would, in turn, operate to enhance his socioeconomic and political status in the Syrian society of the day.[9]

It is likely that al-ʿAsali would have risen gradually in the bureaucracy during an ordinary career, gaining, by virtue of his official position, access to new sources of wealth and establishing himself firmly as a rising member of Damascus' new urban elite. But the normal course of events took an unexpected turn; in July 1908, the Young Turk revolt altered the condition of the empire and introduced a significant detour in the life of al-ʿAsali. From the views he expressed in the pages of newspapers that mushroomed at the time, we know that he was an outspoken supporter of the revolt. It was, he said, "sacred," aiming at the creation of a new state (*dawla jadida*) based upon freedom and equality before the law.[10] The revolt, besides, was an act of liberation, important in itself because it had substituted constitutional government for tyranny in the Ottoman Empire. But it was significant in another sense as well: it represented a continuation of the Oriental struggle for freedom that had opened with the rise of Japan to ascendancy and with the outbreak of the 1905 revolution in Russia.[11] The enthusiasm that al-ʿAsali evinced was not, if we are to believe Mustafa al-Shihabi, fake. It was, rather, the normal reaction at the achievement of a goal for which he had worked secretly as a youth in school.[12] But even if Shihabi's account is discounted, the fact remains that al-ʿAsali, for some time at least, held the optimistic view that the revolt had inaugurated a new age of liberty and progress.

From the beginning, al-ʿAsali believed that the building of the new order could not be undertaken by old hands. As a result, he pressed for a government purge. Only by such radical means, he affirmed, would the administration be freed of its Hamidian legacy of corrupt and reactionary officials. Their removal would allow for the employment of young people who were dynamic, incorruptible, and dedicated to the principles of the constitution.[13]

In all probability, it was his conviction that a new order required new men that led al-ʿAsali to present himself as a candidate to the restored Ottoman parliament. There are indications that he ran as a candidate in the first round of elections late in 1908. But he seems to have been rebuffed by the secondary electors, who voted overwhelmingly for ʿAbd al-Rahman Yusuf.[14] Three years later, in a by-election, he did much better. Although he did not receive the unqualified support of the city of Damascus, the votes coming in from the secondary electors belonging to that city's districts swung the result in his direction. To some of al-ʿAsali's friends, this was a remarkable victory. It demonstrated, in the first place, the determination of the secondary electors not to succumb to external pressure exercised by the rich and the traditionally powerful. In their view, it also marked the entry of the middle class (*al-tabaqa al-wusta*) into the political arena.[15] But it is possible to account for this victory in other terms: al-ʿAsali, we now know, was president of the Nazareth branch of the Committee of Union and Progress (CUP).[16] It is possible that this affiliation decided the election in his favor.

Whatever the case may be, there is little doubt that al-ʿAsali's election to Parliament represented the zenith of his career. For a brief moment he occupied the political centerstage; in the process he became involved in a controversy that reverberated throughout the empire. His career as a representative will be examined separately; it is necessary now to turn to other aspects of his life and activities.

After 1908 the encounter between the historian and the intellectual (or the political activist who was at the same time a thinker) invariably occurs in the pages of the press. This is a statement that applies to Shukri al-ʿAsali and to many of his compatriots.[17] For most of them, the new press of Beirut, and the older one of Cairo, served as an outlet. But as a Damascene, it was almost inevitable that al-ʿAsali should write in *al-Muqtabas*: that periodical, and the newspaper that carried the same name, constituted the two most important prewar publications in that city. There was, however, another, ultimately more crucial consideration. The two publications were owned and edited by Muhammad Kurd ʿAli, a close friend and associate with whom he shared a common social and educational background as well as similar attitudes to politics in general and to developments in Syria in particular. But it is essential, at the outset, to remember that by comparison to his friend, al-ʿAsali was not a systematic thinker nor did any subject long occupy his critical attention. For apart from being a high civil servant acquainted with the operation of local government and its limitations, al-ʿAsali was first of all a political activist who contemplated the condition of his society and expressed his views about it occasionally and in a most selective manner.

Like other contemporary Syrian thinkers, al-ʿAsali's understanding of Syrian society was predetermined, perhaps even distorted, by the supposition that it was in a state of general decline. On the broader, socioeconomic plane, Syrian society was marked by a profound schism between rich and poor. The former, as landowners, acquired and multiplied their wealth by abusing their status as tax-farmers (*multazimi al-aʿashar*). Having procured their *iltizams* by auction, they methodically overtaxed the peasants, in the process enriching themselves and causing peasant poverty. But for al-ʿAsali, the peasants were trapped in a kind of vise between the *multazim*, who overtaxed them, and the usurer, who normally charged them exorbitant rates of interest on loans that they were compelled to take out in order to purchase provisions, seed, and livestock.[18]

There are in the articles of al-ʿAsali many indications that, in a sentimental sense, he was on the side of the peasants: deprived and ignorant, they nevertheless were (he maintained) contented, kind, and concerned about their children.[19] By contrast, the rich were heartless, indifferent to the suffering of the poor, and glad to exploit them. Indeed, were they not in need of the poor to work for them and serve them, they would suck their blood dry.[20] Perhaps al-ʿAsali's righteous indignation may have been aroused by his feeling that there was not much that could be done to rectify the situation. Radical change was impossible (*al-tafra muhal*).[21] To ameliorate the plight of the poor, those who were primarily peasants, al-ʿAsali recommended the replacement of the *iltizam al-aʿshar* system by a direct and regular land tax based upon the actual productivity of the land as superior, inferior, or intermediate. Whether this purely administrative measure can be regarded as a realistic solution for the problem of peasant poverty is debatable. But al-ʿAsali believed that perpetuation of the current system would poison human relations in his native land. In what must have been one of the earliest novellas written by any Syrian, a sort of debased exercise in social realism, al-ʿAsali tried to dramatize the chasm that divided rich and poor, pasha and commoner, in the Syria of his day. Entitled *Fajaʾiʿ al-baʾisin* (best translated into French as *Les Misérables*), it tells the story of the hopeless love between Saʿid, son of an ordinary policeman, and Jamila, herself a pasha's daughter. Because of the deep class division that separates them, they are unable to marry until the pasha is about to die and Saʿid has divorced the wife he had taken in the meantime. Cheated by their class affiliation once, they are also cheated by fate when Saʿid is killed by his ex-wife's brother.[22] *Fajaʾiʿ al-*

ba'isin is forgettable; indeed, it seems to have had little impact at the time. But its importance for our purpose lies in the fact that it discloses some of the preoccupations of al-ʿAsali as a thinker and his concern over some of Syria's social ills, such as divorce, female illiteracy, and the exaction of blood vengeance. Above all, it demonstrates his concern about class antagonisms in Syria and the need to reduce them.

For Shukri al-ʿAsali, as for many of his associates, widespread ignorance was the hallmark of Syrian deterioration. Early in 1909, just a few months after the outbreak of the Young Turk revolt, he described the state of Syrian culture and learning as pitiable. Adopting an attitude that was becoming increasingly popular at the time, he attributed Syrian illiteracy to the benighted policies of Sultan Abdülhamid. Education, for this sultan, he claimed, was essentially harmful (*madarra*); it represented a hazard against which the state and the people had to guard. In an attempt to attenuate its dangers, Abdülhamid intentionally reduced government expenditure for education to a minimum. Money raised by supplementary taxes for the improvement of educational facilities was instead diverted into the hands of his favorites, who dissipated it foolishly in pursuit of fame and reputation. In the time of Abdülhamid, the censor was the custodian of culture and, in the school, the teacher was replaced by the spy.[23]

But al-ʿAsali was careful to point out that the Syrians themselves were not entirely blameless in this regard; apathetic and lacking all sense of initiative, they relied upon the government to meet, as it could not, all their needs.[24] Moreover, they callously neglected the few learning centers already in existence: schools maintained by *waqf* were allowed to revert to stables and into coal dumps.[25] The state of Syrian ignorance, for al-ʿAsali, was most evident among the female segment of the population. In al-ʿAsali's view, the male attitude toward women was, to begin with, wrong. The average Syrian male regarded women as inferior, playthings (sing., *ulʿuba*) fit for his service or entertainment. Over the question of female education, Syrian opinion was split; for most men, the education of women was harmful while ignorance served as a cloak for virtue (*ʿafaf*). But an enlightened minority regarded education as a prerogative that men and women both ought to enjoy. Shukri al-ʿAsali himself maintained that in their quality as human beings, men and women were equal, similar in their feelings and possessing similar abilities. In fact, owing to their social predisposition, men and women needed and complemented each other; their mutual well-being was conducive to the welfare of society as a whole. And for women to become successful marriage partners and useful members of society, it was necessary that they should have access to education. As he conceived of it, this education was not exclusively vocational in character; it was rather a rounded education that released all their potential, that developed their minds and raised their ethical standards, and that adapted them for their role as guardians of society and as productive members in it. In other words, it was an education that would prepare them simultaneously for motherhood and employment. For al-ʿAsali believed that female unemployment turned women into parasites, at home as well as in society. By contrast, an honorable profession (sanʿa sharifa) would liberate women from apathy and financial dependence, would enhance their role as partners in marriage, and would allow them to participate in the economic cycle of production.[26] At a stage when female emancipation was not a reality anywhere in the region, al-ʿAsali's views were audacious and well ahead of their time.

The resolution of the problem of male and female illiteracy depended upon the creation of more and better primary and secondary schools. By 1911, as al-ʿAsali noted with relief, the establishment of new schools in Damascus was well in progress. But this development was not the result of any government program; it was, rather, the outcome of self-help as expressed in the creation of local benevolent societies actively involved in the promotion of education in the capital and the remainder of the province.[27] Although he himself was educated with a view to eventual government employment, al-ʿAsali nevertheless insisted that educational programs be designed to provide the groundwork for an independent career in commerce or industry or in any of the new professions—such as law, medicine, or engineering—that were proliferating at the time.[28]

Like other Arab thinkers of the time, al-ʿAsali subscribed to the view that Europe was ahead of the rest of the world educationally, and because of this he advised Syrian students demanding an advanced education to go to Europe. In 1910 he openly congratulated his political adversary, ʿAbd al-Rahman

Yusuf, for his decision to send two students on a mission to Europe. At the same time, he called upon other Arab parliamentary representatives, the municipality of Damascus, as well as its wealthy citizens, to follow the example set by their compatriots.[29]

It is possible, however, to maintain that al-ʿAsali's message lacked conviction or, at least, that it was sent out hesitantly. As he saw it, Europe was the center of world learning, but the process of European education entailed serious implications. In the first place, as an alternative dynamic civilization, Europe, by the fact of its superiority, could undermine the students' cultural heritage, leading them to drift between a culture that was not their own and their own culture, which they might come to scorn. To avoid such an eventuality, only students of sound mind and morality, those who would not relinquish their culture nor desert their ethical norms, should be permitted to embark upon this perilous journey.[30]

The purpose of al-ʿAsali's admonition was to control, even limit, Syrian access to Europe. But there was little, apart from protestation and dire warning, that he could do about the spread in Syria of European cultural manifestations and patterns of behavior.

To begin with, he was upset by the view that the acquisition of a European language placed its recipients at the pinnacle of human knowledge. Given the fact that foreign schools in Syria were both popular and successful, he felt that gaining a foreign language was inevitable and even desirable. But, for him, this ought to represent only part of the educational process, not its entirety. Put a little differently, this meant that pupils ought at the same time to develop and prize the mother tongue and remain in contact with, and build upon, their Arab-Islamic culture.[31] Perhaps there is in all this an element of autobiography. Shukri al-ʿAsali does not seem to have learned a European language well. Additionally, his Arabic, when be began his public career, was not very profound. It was, as Kurd ʿAli noted, only as a result of personal and painstaking study that al-ʿAsali became fluent in Arabic and knowledgeable about his Arab and Islamic culture.[32] Certainly, if one can judge by his almost exclusive reference to it, Arabic-Islamic culture, its history, literature, and law, represented the starting point of, and the point of reference for, most of his thought.

In addition to the issue of language, al-ʿAsali was much disturbed by the popular belief that what was European was necessarily better. He also criticized the corollary—namely, the view that Europeans, as individuals, were superior, capable of achieving feats that no local man could even begin to consider. For al-ʿAsali, this fallacious contention constituted Syria's malignant disease (*ʿillatuna al-mash'uma*).[33]

In the end, however, it was the influence of Europe upon traditional morality that most perturbed al-ʿAsali. Reflecting an opinion that was common among Arab intellectuals at the time, he accused his Syrian compatriots of subverting the essence of European civilization and adopting instead its external features only. Thus freedom, which he regarded as at the heart of European culture, became license as it traveled from West to East. As it was practiced in Syria, freedom, in its degraded form, entailed the renunciation of received values and traditional norms. Rather than freedom of expression, association, and education, there was in Syria freedom to consume alcoholic drinks, freedom to gamble, and freedom for both sexes to consort openly. In short, freedom in Syria represented an affront to virtue and an insult to common decency. It was the freedom of depravity (*hurriyyat al-radha'il*).[34]

It was a mark of al-ʿAsali's sophistication that he did not as a result renounce Europe altogether, nor freedom as an ideal. What he desired was to regain freedom in its original purity and allow it to elevate life morally, intellectually, and politically, instead of demeaning it.

As Shukri al-ʿAsali prepared to leave for Istanbul to occupy his seat in Parliament, he was leaving a Syria that had been touched by the Young Turk revolt but not transformed by it. In the government of the province, corrupt officials were still in place; in the law courts, justice was being administered by untrained judges who paid little respect to the law; and in the administrative council of the city, power was still routinely abused.[35] Nevertheless, al-ʿAsali was not entirely disillusioned; he was, however, somewhat chastened. His simple optimism had given way to realism; he now acknowledged, and probably accepted, that change could only come slowly and over an extended period of time.[36] Yet he was also aware that, in Syria, internal divisions were beginning to manifest themselves.

When he went to Parliament in 1911 as Damascus' elected deputy, al-ʿAsali was preceded by his reputation as one of the earliest, most informed, and most determined opponents of the Zionist program as it was unfolding in Palestine. In the chamber itself, where he joined in the attack against former CUP allies, he was to emerge, probably unintentionally, as the main defender of Arab rights in Parliament. His preoccupation with the political and socioeconomic implications of Zionism, his apprehension lest Palestine forfeit its Arab identity, is known and well documented. As such, it will be accorded attention only tangentially. Instead, an attempt will be made to trace his path to opposition and, more importantly, to what brought him to the forefront of a controversy that, in 1908, he did not fully anticipate.

From the viewpoint of an ardent supporter of the Young Turk revolt, al-ʿAsali regarded the first demands for an Arab caliphate (*al-khilafa al-ʿarabiyya*) and Arab independence (*istiqlal al-ʿArab*), which surfaced early in 1909, as being an outcome of definite political intrigue. Fabricated by reactionaries who had been overturned in 1908, the call was designed to manipulate the Arabs into profound disagreement with the CUP and, in the process, to discredit them and demonstrate their inability to maintain internal peace and harmony among the empire's many races. Judging by his reaction to that call, it appears that al-ʿAsali recognized its inherent emotional potential, but he was nevertheless convinced that as a demand it was absurd and as a program it was impractical. For any people to form a government or to gain autonomy, the three prerequisites of place (*al-makan*), time (*al-zaman*), and mental disposition (*istiʿdad al-nufus*) had to converge. According to this analysis, the Arabs, al-ʿAsali maintained, occupied a definite landmass. But owing to the absence of permanent links of communication, each region—Yemen, Iraq, al-Hijaz (Hejaz), Syria, and Tripolitania—existed in a kind of isolation; that is, each region exhibited a unique way of life, special forms of social structure, and distinct patterns of trade and commercial relations. Time, likewise, was not conducive to self-rule; indeed, every Arab region was on the point of being overwhelmed by external enemies. The will to independence, expressed in a kind of mental disposition, was nowhere in evidence: the Arabs who had yet to make an impression in the Ottoman parliament were incapable of re-creating an Arab caliphate or achieving any form of independence.

But for al-ʿAsali, Arab independence was unacceptable even as an ideal. Indeed, even to begin to consider it as a possibility was a form of madness (*junun*) and an act of treason, threatening both the Arabs and Islam. Writing in the spring of 1909, in a real and metaphoric sense al-ʿAsali could assert that the Arabs must continue to be what they had been for four centuries, an integral part of the Ottoman Empire. This view was supported by his conviction that a new dawn of unity and equality had set in and that, under the CUP, the Turks and Arabs were jointly involved in the process of reconstructing the empire. However, whether in the government or outside of it, there was, he declared, no life for the Arabs except by union with the Turks. Secession or autonomy entailed for the Arabs certain death (*mawt muhaqqaq*).[37]

One year later, al-ʿAsali found that his confident projection of a new era of Arab-Turkish harmony and cooperation had not in fact materialized. Rather than participating together in the task of rebuilding the Empire, the Ottomans—that is, the Turks and the Arabs—were involved in a kind of cold warfare in which each exalted his own culture and heritage, and both simultaneously demeaned the other. This act of gratuitous fragmentation, which threatened to undermine the foundations of the empire from within at the same time as it was being menaced by foreign aggression, had to be overcome; the inflammatory press must be restrained and the Ottomans must redirect their energies toward the more immediate task of resuscitating their empire. In the same breath, and somewhat paradoxically, al-ʿAsali expressed his belief that his plan for reconciliation did not imply opposition to the presentation of equitable Arab demands, nor did it entail a repudiation of the effort to preserve and reinvigorate the Arabic language that was beloved by every Arab (*maʿshuqat kul ʿArabi*).[38]

In less than two years, al-ʿAsali had traveled a long way. At first dismissing Arab demands as either pure fabrication or sheer insanity, he was now implying that the Arabs had cause for legitimate complaint and were entitled, in fact duty bound, to safeguard their language. This change in tone (though not yet in course) was, in all probability, a reflection of the grave public dissatisfaction with the CUP's program of provincial reorganization and administrative centralization. The first part of the program, which involved large-scale dismissals of pro-Hamidian government functionaries, was consistent with one of al-ʿAsali's early demands. But since those removed in Syria were in large measure Arabs who had been replaced by politically reliable Turks, the feeling developed that as a race and a separate nationality, the Arabs were being subjected to deliberate discrimination. It appears that al-ʿAsali himself was gradually coming around to this viewpoint. The second part of the program, really a necessary outgrowth of the first, was even more objectionable on the popular plane; it was not confined, in its effect, to the administrative machine but extended to influence the daily life of the vast majority of Syrians. By administrative decree the local Arabs were expected to become Turks in the conduct of their lives. (See C. Ernest Dawn's essay, in this volume, on this subject.) In order to acquire an education, they were obliged to perfect their knowledge of the Turkish language; in order to execute commercial transactions they were compelled to use Turkish; and in order to bring litigation they were forced to follow court proceedings in Turkish and to be sentenced by magistrates who were, in the majority, ignorant of Arabic and unacquainted with local customs and practices. The drive of the CUP to modernize the Ottoman Empire and thus extricate it from virtual moribundity was seen by many in Damascus as an attempt to humiliate the Arabs and subvert their language. Judging by his public statements, al-ʿAsali was far from sharing this opinion. It is certain that this shift was, at least in part, occasioned by his failure, as an Arab official, to convince the Turkish *wali* of Beirut and the central government in Istanbul to block the transfer of the land of ʿAfula from its Arab tenants to Zionist colonists.[39]

There is nothing in the record to show that al-ʿAsali had severed his links with the CUP prior to his departure to Istanbul. But the record does show that his mind was in a state of political ferment, torn between conviction that had begun to waver and certainties that had not fully crystallized.

Upon his arrival in Istanbul, probably sometime in February 1911, it is said that al-ʿAsali reinvigorated the Arab parliamentary bloc. It is also likely that he was himself energized, and his political thought given definite orientation, as a result of establishing intimate contacts with a number of Arab deputies, among whom the most important were Shafiq Mu'ayyad al-ʿAzm, ʿAbd al-Hamid al-Zahrawi, and Rida al-Sulh. It is certain that the three, in addition to al-ʿAsali, were the main architects of the short-lived Arab party (al-Hizb al-ʿArabi), an informal organization grouping nearly all the Arab representatives in defense of Arab rights in the Ottoman Empire.

From the moment of creation, toward the end of March 1911, the party outlined its demands plainly. It wanted, it said, to secure full equality for the Arabs, to make Arabic the language of instruction in primary and secondary state schools, to protect the interests of dismissed Arab government employees, and to work for the appointment of government officers knowledgeable in the language of the region in which they were stationed.

Early in April 1911, the party held a meeting that was attended by ʿAbd al-Rahman Yusuf, one of the deputies for Damascus, but not a constituent member of the new organization. In the debate that occurred, Yusuf (a registered member of the CUP) argued that the creation of an Arab party was unnecessary and maintained that the Turks were the rightful rulers of the empire and that their rule, under the CUP, was essentially enlightened and benevolent in nature. This was a standpoint with which al-ʿAsali could not agree. He began his rebuttal by pointing out that in the new constitutional era rule was not restricted to the Turks but was instead the prerogative of the *umma* acting collectively. And just as rule was not the hereditary right of any group, so, too, no racial element within the empire was entitled to monopolize the services of the state and become its sole beneficiary.[40]

As it turned out, the life of the party proved ephemeral. Its importance, however, ought not to be underestimated. It was the first time that the Arab deputies had acted together as a bloc outside Parliament independently of earlier political affiliations. It was important as well because it evoked wide support in the Arab divisions of the Ottoman Empire, principally in the *wilaya* of Beirut and the city of Damascus. An item in *al-Ittihad al-ʿuthmani* reveals that support for the party and its positions emanated from many of the *ʿulama'* of Damascus, its *aʿyan* as well as its traders.[41] The party, in other words, was not a voice crying in the wilderness; rather, it echoed the profound disquiet felt in many Arab circles at the policies of the CUP. Finally, and from the perspective of this study, it was significant because it served as a forum for al-ʿAsali and constituted an arena for the views he was to express soon after in Parliament.

It is not possible, at this stage, to determine whether al-ʿAsali's speech in Parliament was a product of his own initiative or resulted from a preconcerted strategy on the part of the Arab delegates. It is likely, however, that he had divulged the contents to some of them in expectation of support. In the debates that followed he was strongly supported by Rida al-Sulh.

The speech that al-ʿAsali delivered on Wednesday, April 5, 1911, provoked a storm that lasted for some time. But the speech was essentially a mild one in which he attempted to show, by reference to official statistics, that the Arabs were being excluded from the senior posts in central ministries. He ended his address (which was interrupted several times) by making a plea, in his capacity as representative of the *umma*, for the termination of all forms of discrimination against his people.[42]

In Damascus and in Beirut, as well as among the Syrians of Cairo, al-ʿAsali's speech was hailed as a milestone. But it was perhaps ʿAbd al-Rahman Shahbandar who best captured the spirit of the moment. According to him, al-ʿAsali, by his act, had wiped out the traditional image of Arab deputies as meek men who had no voice and no convictions, and who invariably toed the government line. Moreover, by his courage and composure, al-ʿAsali had demonstrated that the Arabs had men of dignity capable of defending their cause anywhere. Notwithstanding this rhetorical flourish, Shahbandar realized that al-ʿAsali's speech was unlikely to radically alter the conditions of the Arabs in the empire. But its real importance for him lay in the fact that it was delivered in the highest forum of the land in such a way that Arab grievances could no longer be overlooked or bypassed.[43]

The reaction of the Turkish press in Istanbul was spearheaded by *Tanin* and *al-Dia*, which accused al-ʿAsali of perfidy and downright hypocrisy.[44] The virulence of the press campaign was such that he had to restate his position unambiguously. He reiterated the rights of the Arabs to occupy senior administrative posts, but he denied categorically that his speech in Parliament implied disloyalty to the Ottoman Empire. He was, he said, an opponent of those who discriminated against the Arabs, but his loyalty, and Arab loyalty, to the empire and sultanate was irrevocable; the bond that linked Turks and Arabs together was permanent for all time (*ribat abadi*).[45]

In May 1911, just before he delivered his farewell speech on the subject of Zionism, al-ʿAsali once again responded to charges made by *Tanin* against him and against the Syrians by extension. But this time he took the offensive. He began (as indeed he closed) by reasserting his loyalty, and the loyalty of all Syrians, to Ottomanism. But then he introduced a significant change. The Syrians, he insisted, would not submit to just any government; their allegiance and obedience belonged to the Ottoman sultan who was also the caliph of all Muslims. It is clear that here al-ʿAsali was bypassing the CUP and suggesting that in the Ottoman order of things they were, or could become, superfluous. Whatever the case, al-ʿAsali proceeded to imply that the CUP, by its misguided centralizing policies, was itself responsible for Syrian exasperation and estrangement.[46]

Shukri al-ʿAsali returned to Syria in June to a warm public reception. But as far as his relations with the CUP were concerned, the die was cast. Upon his return to his native city, he publicly withdrew his membership from the local CUP branch.[47] In the months leading to the year's end, this symbolic act of defiance was to evolve in the direction of outright hostility. Instead of simply alluding to his disagreements with the CUP, he now openly displayed his antagonism. Thus he used a goodwill visit of the CUP's Salonika branch to Syria as an opportunity to castigate the government and its CUP leadership, accusing it of deliberately working to humiliate the Arabs and to obstruct the progress that Syria had achieved independently.[48] In August and December of 1911, he went further and accused the CUP of undermining the foundations of the empire by its reckless bid for autocracy and by its arrogant indifference to the interests and fate of non-Turkish races and nationalities.[49] Its misguided autocracy, as far as he was concerned, was illustrated by its resort to brute force in order to deal with an unstable situation in Hawran and Karak.[50] Its indifference was demonstrated by its inability to stem the Italian invasion of Tripoli in spite of the unanimous support it had received from the Arabs, who had transcended their differences with the CUP and had rededicated themselves to Ottomanism and expressed their desire to die in defense of a sister Arab province in order that it might remain an integral part of the Ottoman Empire.[51]

But it must have been his personal attack on Hakki Paşa, the CUP collaborator who resigned as Prime Minister in September 1911, that made coexistence with that party temporarily impossible. In October 1911, as he was preparing to set sail for the capital to regain his seat in the Parliament that would soon be dissolved, he bitterly criticized the CUP for engineering the appointment of the incompetent Hakki and insisted that he, together with his main CUP supporters, be brought to trial for negligence in the performance of their duty to preserve the territorial integrity of the empire.[52]

The years 1912–1913 were ripe in consequence for Shukri al-ʿAsali. For part of the period he attempted to redefine his political commitments and establish new allies. After the dissolution of Parliament early in 1912, which in effect left him out in the cold, al-ʿAsali gravitated toward the Entente Liberale. This may have been politically convenient or he may have genuinely believed that it represented a viable alternative to the discredited CUP. Its program, which was a variation on the earlier one of the Union Liberale, leaned in the direction of greater provincial and national autonomy and thus seemed to promise whatever the CUP denied.[53] In the run-up to the elections due in April, Shukri al-ʿAsali campaigned actively on behalf of the opposition candidates. The campaigns that took the shape of rallies in the major towns of Syria were a popular success, but they did not influence the elections. The result, in fact, was almost predetermined: the CUP, with a firm hold on the provincial administration and with a network of subsidiary branches, was able to win a conclusive victory.[54]

As a renegade, Shukri al-ʿAsali represented a problem with which the CUP had to contend. In its measures, it oscillated between the wish to eliminate and the desire to conciliate. Thus, in March 1912, he survived a botched attempt on his life, and soon after was forced to flee to Cairo. When he returned to Damascus in the summer of 1912 he was probably expecting his new party's accession to power to last. However, early in 1913 the Entente Liberale was forced out of office by a military coup of the CUP.

The year 1913 opened somewhat inauspiciously for al-ʿAsali. Still a man attached to his political principles, he turned down, in March, the offer of Hazim Bey, *wali* of Beirut, to become *mustarrif* of Latakia. He was, he said, after reform in the empire and not a post bestowed upon him by a government opposed to reforms.⁵⁵

In June of that year the Arab partisans of reforms, or at least some of them, held the First Arab Congress, in Paris. Shukri al-ʿAsali was not at all involved. Why this should have been the case is difficult to determine, especially as he had anticipated the convening of the congress as early as January 1913, when he called for a pan-Arab meeting to be held either in Damascus or Beirut to consider the question of reform in the Arab provinces of the Ottoman Empire and the fate of the *khilafa*.⁵⁶ He may have lacked the funds to travel,⁵⁷ but this does not explain why he did not send a telegram of support, as his compatriot Muhammad Kurd ʿAli had done.⁵⁸ It is difficult as well to determine his general attitude to the congress owing to the closure of *al-Muqtabas* at the time. It could be, of course, that he was reconsidering his attitude to reform and to the CUP, now back in full control.

When *al-Muqtabas* was suspended in September 1913, al-ʿAsali reissued it under a slightly different name, *al-Qabas*, and, in fact, became its editor.⁵⁹ In that capacity he published several articles that were generally mild in character but, at the same time, revealed his continuing preoccupation with reform in Syria and with defining the nature of the relationship between it and the central government in Istanbul. Thus, he called for the appointment of provincial government officers who served the people rather than abused their privileges and who were both reasonable and conscientious.⁶⁰ It was in this context that he recommended the appointment of foreign experts to help direct the administrative machine and supervise its proper and efficient functioning.⁶¹

In October 1913, al-ʿAsali wrote what would prove to be one of his last articles; it simultaneously revealed his commitment to change in Syria and his willingness to compromise. He reaffirmed the view that the resolution of the empire's political ills lay in the construction of a decentralized order and declared that, as an Arab, he was prepared to cooperate with any government that would respond to legitimate Arab demands.⁶² In February 1914, *al-Muqtabas* reported that al-ʿAsali had accepted the post of civil inspector in the *wilaya* of Syria. ʿAbd al-Karim al-Khalil, president of *al-Muntada al-adabi*, explained al-ʿAsali's action and that of a few others: it was, he said, in recognition of the CUP's stated intentions to implement reform in Syria as well as a kind of guarantee that the process of reform once underway would not be unilaterally abandoned.[63] But notwithstanding al-Khalil's explanation, which has an apologetic ring to it, it is impossible to ignore economic factors as a partial cause for this turnabout. As has already been noted, al-ʿAsali's livelihood depended almost entirely upon his employment in government. Once outside it, he tried to locate an alternative source of income. His post as editor of *al-Qabas* was precarious, lasting as long as the suspension of *al-Muqtabas* lasted. His attempt to establish himself as a lawyer in the city of Damascus was not successful either.[64] It is probably that al-ʿAsali's return to government service was facilitated by the expectation of immediate economic relief and the receipt of a regular salary.

The fact that al-ʿAsali was hanged two years later by Cemal Pasa has led many historians to conclude that al-ʿAsali's opposition was complete, and that he was actively working to undermine the empire and to replace it with a new Arab order—and it was for this, presumably, that he was executed. This study has, on the contrary, revealed that at no time did al-ʿAsali actively encourage, or even seriously consider, the possibility of Arab independence. From the beginning of his career up to the time of his appointment, al-ʿAsali was committed to the continuation of the empire as a political entity in which all races would be equal and in which Arabs and Turks, bound by the links of a re-created Ottomanism, would jointly cooperate in its government. It is, of course, true that there were protonationalist resonances in what he said and did, but essentially these were in the form of a defense mechanism: the more the CUP pressed for Turkification the more was he compelled to emphasize the uniqueness of his culture and his existence as an Arab. But until 1914, this represented an affirmation of an identity and not a program of revolutionary transformation. If the CUP mistakenly interpreted opposition to itself as prelude to the dismantlement of the Ottoman Empire, it does not mean that the historian should make the same mistake.

In this study, the Ottomanist/Arabist model has been deliberately avoided, not only because al-ʿAsali does not fit into it easily but because a modified model relating to the "politics of the notables" is, in his case, far more compelling. In its classical form, this model postulates the existence of a class of local notables who, as intermediaries between the ruler and the ruled, exercised real political power. In the case of al-ʿAsali, member of a new urban elite, the path to political power was blocked by the exclusionist policies of the CUP. His intention, most certainly, was to deprive the CUP of its political hegemony, not for the purpose of destroying the historic Ottoman Empire, but in order for him, as a representative of an emerging urban notability, to participate in the process of government.

Notes

1. In *The Arab Awakening*, George Antonius based his account of the early manifestations of Arab nationalism on the recollections of one man, Faris Nimr.
2. The reference here is to Philip Khoury, *Urban Notables and Arab Nationalism*.
3. Apart from Tawfiq ʿAli Birru's *"al-Muntada al-adabi"* [The literary club], I know of no other work devoted exclusively to the study of that organization.
4. This requires some modification. Miss Salma Saʿd, a graduate student at the Lebanese University, has written, under my supervision, an exploratory thesis (1983) on the subject under discussion.
5. See Rashid Khalidi, "ʿAbd al-Ghani al-Uraysi and *al-Mufid*," and Samir Seikaly, "Damascene Intellectual Life."
6. Khalidi, *British Policy Towards Syria and Palestine*, and "Arab Nationalism in Syria." The second purports to study al-ʿAsali in some detail (see pp. 281ff). See also Khalidi's "The Role of the Press," pp. 105–23 (esp. pp. 116–20) for more on al-ʿAsali.
7. The claim that al-ʿAsali came from "a prominent landowning family of the Maydan" is not, perhaps, entirely justifiable. His family is not mentioned in ʿAbd al-Razzaz al Bitar's *Hilyat al-bashar fi tarikh al-thalith ashar* [The embellishment of mankind in the thirteenth century], 3 vols. (Damascus, 1961–1963). This suggests that the family did not have historic roots in the city. In any event, when Muhammad Kurd ʿAli presented a profile of the man following his (al-ʿAsali's) election he referred to him as the son of an *agha*, not specifically as a scion of a prominent landowning family. See "Mabʿuth Dimashq," *al-Muqtabas*, January 26, 1911. Additional information can be found in Muhammad al-Husni, *Kitab*

muntakhabat al-tawarikh li-dimashq [Book of selections from the histories of Damascus], as well as in Adham al-Jundi, *Shuhada' al-harb al-ʿalamiyya al-kubra* [Martyrs of the first world war].

8. Regarding his association with al-Jaza'iri's circle, see Mustafa al-Shihabi, *al-Qawmiyya al-ʿarabiyya* [Arab nationalism], and David Commins, "Religious Reformers and Arabists," pp. 405–25.
9. For the "upstart" concept, see Ruth Roded, "Ottoman Service," pp. 63–94. The substance of the same argument is contained in Ruth Roded, "Social Patterns."
10. This usage occurred in "al-Shuyukh wal-shubban," *al-Muqtabas*, September 4, 1908.
11. For the details of this analysis, see his "Nazra fil-Sharq," *al-Muqtabas*, July 25, 1910.
12. Al-Shihabi, *al-Qawmiyya al-ʿarabiyya*, p. 51.
13. For his campaign against the appointees of Abdülhamid see the article cited in note 10 above; "al-Jawasis wal-suʿat," *al-Muqtabas*, January 28, 1909; and "Mata nasir ʿala al-tariq," *al-Muqtabas*, June 7, 1909.
14. *al-Umma*, December 20, 1909. This was a sister paper of *al-Muqtabas* that appeared during the latter's many suspensions. Its editor was Ahmad Kurd ʿAli, Muhammad's brother.
15. For the details of al-ʿAsali's election and its significance, see "Dars ʿan al-intikhab," *al-Muqtabas*, January 29, 1911.
16. This disclosure occurred in "Ila al-iʿtidal," *al-Muqtabas*, June 29, 1911. In two successive issues the same daily reproduced a speech delivered by al-ʿAsali to the Union and Progress club in Nazareth (*al-Muqtabas*, July 9 and 10, 1910).
17. In fact, al-ʿAsali criticized the overwhelming reliance upon the press as an outlet for intellectual activity. See "al-ʿArab wal-ta'lif," *al-Muqtabas*, September 7, 1910.
18. For a more detailed treatment of the burdens of the peasants in Syria, consult al-ʿAsali's important study, "al-Jibaya fil-Islam," in the periodical *al-Muqtabas* 2, no. 4 (1907); and 4, nos. 2 and 3 (1909).
19. His views about peasant morality are contained in "al-Fuqara' wal-aghniya," *al-Muqtabas* 1, no. 5 (1906–1907).
20. His critical attitude toward the rich can be found in the article cited in note 19 above; and in "al-Zur wa al-buhtan," *al-Muqtabas*, July 9, 1910.
21. This is taken from "Hikam munawwaʿa," *al-Muqtabas*, August 18, 1910.
22. *Faja'iʿ al-ba'isin* was serialized in the periodical *al-Muqtabas* 2, nos. 1, 2, 5, and 6 (1907).

23. The study cited in note 18 above contains several references to Abdülhamid's educational policies. See also the article cited in note 20 above.
24. For Syrian reliance upon the government see "al-Aʿmal khayr min al-intiqad," *al-Muqtabas*, April 27, 1910.
25. The neglect that had overcome *waqf*-supported schools is discussed in *al-Muqtabas*, February 23, 1909.
26. Al-ʿAsali's attitude toward education for women, and women in general, is contained in "al-Fudlayat al-dimashqiyyat," *al-Muqtabas*, March 16, 1909, and in "al-Mar'a wal-hirfa," *al-Muqtabas*, April 14, 1909.
27. See "al-Nahda al-fikriyya," *al-Muqtabas*, July 25, 1911.
28. His call for the sponsorship of crafts and industries as well as the education related to them is found in "al-Raja," *al-Muqtabas*, July 29, 1911.
29. This encouragement appeared in the article cited in note 17 above.
30. On the moral characteristics of Syrian delegates to Europe see "Hikam munawwaʿa," *al-Muqtabas* 7, no. 6 (1912).
31. See ibid.
32. This is related in the article cited in note 7 above that Kurd ʿAli devoted to his friend on the eve of his election.
33. "A sahih ma yaqulun?," *al-Muqtabas*, May 6, 1910.
34. The abuse of freedom and its supposed consequences is presented graphically in "Nata'ij al-ihmal," *al-Muqtabas* 7, no. 6 (1912).
35. For the failure to root out government corruption, see "al-Rashwa haqiqa," *al-Muqtabas*, February 22, 1910. The poor condition of judges is described in "al-Qudat wal-nuwwab," *al-Muqtabas* 4, no. 10 (1909). The abuse of power in administrative councils is found in "al-Mufti wal-mafdi," *al-Muqtabas*, March 30, 1909.
36. Refer to al-ʿAsali's article in note 27 above.
37. All this appears in "Hayat al-ʿarab bi al-ittihad maʿa al-atrak," *al-Muqtabas*, May 1, 1909.
38. See al-ʿAsali's article, "al-ʿUthmaniyyun yumazziq baʿduhum baʿda," *al-Muqtabas*, June 5, 1910.
39. Al-ʿAsali's personal account of this transaction can be found in *al-Mufid*, February 11 and 19, 1911. The clearest expression of his view occurs in an article that he wrote entitled "Qalʿat al-fula," *al-Ittihad al-ʿuthmani*, February 18, 1911. (The fortress of al-Fula, which al-ʿAsali claimed dated back to the time of Saladin, was on the land of the village of ʿAfula.)
40. The following articles contain much information about the creation of the Arab party: "al-Hizb al-ʿarabi," *al-Mufid*, March 22, 1911; and "al-Hizb al-ʿarabi," *al-Muqtabas*, April 2, 1911. For the

actual exchange between Yusuf and al-ʿAsali, see Haqqi al-ʿAzm's account in *al-Mufid*, April 5, 1911.
41. A document containing the names of Damascenes supporting the party can be found in *al-Ittihad al-ʿuthmani*, April 26, 1911.
42. There are many, though not dissimilar, renditions of the speech in the Arab press of the day. See, for example, *al-Muqtabas*, April 7, 1911; *al-Muqattam*, April 7, 1911, and *al-Mufid*, April 10, 1911.
43. For Shahbandar's article entitled "Tahni'a," see *al-Muqtabas*, April 7, 1911.
44. There are translations of Turkish articles in "Rudud suhuf al-asitana," *al-Muqattam*, April 8, 1911.
45. The reaction of al-ʿAsali to the Turkish press campaign can be found in "Rad Shukri al-ʿAsali," *al-Muqattam*, April 11, 1911.
46. These views appeared in an article entitled "Shukri al-ʿAsali yudafiʿ ʿan al-ʿarab," *al-Mufid*, May 17, 1911. This article also includes a graphic description of the vexatious measures to which the Syrians were submitted.
47. *Al-Muqtabas*, June 29, 1911.
48. For this goodwill visit and al-ʿAsali's reaction to it, see *al-Muqtabas*, June 5, 1911, and *al-Muqattam*, July 6, 1911.
49. Probably his bitterest attacks against the CUP appeared in "Hala ghariba," *al-Muqtabas*, August 27, 1911, and "Jamʿiyyat al-ittihad wa al-taraqqi," *al-Muqtabas*, December 20, 1911.
50. His comments regarding the troubles of Hawran and Karak occurred in "Ahwal Suriya," *al-Muqtabas*, September 9, 1911.
51. For an example of Arab reaction to the Italian invasion of Tripoli and their resolve to resist it, see "Ila al-mustasrikh al-tarabulsi," *al-Mufid*, October 15, 1911.
52. *Al-Ittihad al-ʿuthmani*, October 9, 1911.
53. The political program of the Union Liberale was commented upon by al-ʿAsali in *al-Muqtabas*, June 24, 1911.
54. For a contemporary but somewhat prejudiced account of the 1912 election, see Haqqi al-Azm, *Haqa'iq ʿan al-intikhabat fil-ʿiraq wa surriya wa filastin* [Verities regarding the elections in Iraq, Syria, and Palestine] (Cairo, 1912). More modern accounts are available in Tawfiq ʿAli Birru, *al-ʿArab wal-turk* [The Arabs and the Turks], and Khalidi "The 1912 Election Campaign," pp. 461–74.
55. The details of this offer can be found in *al-Mufid*, March 12 and 20, 1913.
56. *Al-Ittihad al-ʿuthmani*, January 20, 1913.
57. See his statement about this matter in M.A.E., *Turquie*, N.S.120. Consul General in Damascus to Pichon.
58. A list of Syrian personalities who sent telegrams of support can be

found in M. al-Khatib, *al-Mu'tamar al-ʿarabi al-awwal* [The first Arab congress] (Cairo, 1913), pp. 152–53.
59. For this development see *al-Qabas*, September 3, 1913.
60. See his article entitled "Kayfa tudar al-bilad," *al-Qabas*, October 2, 1913.
61. The reference to foreign experts can be found in *al-Qabas*, October 5, 1913.
62. See his "ʿAzm al-hukuma ʿala al-islah," *al-Qabas*, October 19, 1913.
63. For al-ʿAsali's appointment and al-Khalil's justification, see *al-Muqtabas*, February 11, 1914.
64. There are references to Shukri al-ʿAsali's attempt to establish himself as a lawyer in Damascus in *al-Qabas*, October 25, 1913.

FIVE

'Abd al-Hamid al-Zahrawi: The Career and Thought of an Arab Nationalist

Ahmed Tarabein

'Abd al-Hamid al-Zahrawi (Abdülhamid el-Zehravi), one of the most active proponents of the Arab movement, was born, probably in 1871,[1] in Homs, in the central part of Syria. His father claimed descent from Muhammud Shakir, son of Ibrahim al-Zahrawi, who claimed descent from al-Imam al-Husayn, son of 'Ali b. Abi Talib, cousin of the Prophet and the fourth caliph, and his mother Fatima al-Zahra, from whose name the al-Zahrawi family took its own, and from whom it inherited the position of *naqib al-ashraf*.

When al-Zahrawi was seven years old he entered the traditional *kuttab* supervised by Shaykh Mustafa al-Turk, where he studied Arabic and Turkish linguistics. He then moved to a government *rushdiyya* (*rüşdiye*, elementary) school; when he graduated, he began to deepen his general knowledge of jurisprudence, Quranic (Koranic) interpretation, theology, Hadith, and other rational sciences under prominent teachers of the period in Homs, such as Shaykh 'Abd al-Sattar Al-Atasi and Shaykh 'Abd al-Qadir al-Afghani. He also studied sociology and read the works of al-Qadi al-Fadil (1135–1200), Ibn Khaldun (1332–1406), Ibn Taymiyya (1263–1328), and Ibn Qayyim al-Jawziyya (1292–1350), and was influenced by them all.

In his twenties he traveled to Istanbul to broaden his knowledge and experience. There he began to realized how his compatriots suffered from the autocratic rule of Sultan Abdülhamid II. He then moved to Cairo, where he was welcomed as a respected guest in the house of Tawfiq al-Bakri, *naqib al-ashraf*, with whom he shared common descent from the Prophet. Al-Zahrawi attended the literary circle held at al-Bakri's house. When he returned to Homs he had three facts in mind: the tyranny of the Hamidian regime, the predominance of ignorance among the majority of the people, and the alienation of many traditional scholars from the spirit of Islam. He decided to fight on these three fronts, and began to issue a newspaper called *al-Munir*, which he printed and distributed secretly in Syria to support the cause of the Young Turks against the Hamidian regime. The paper, however, was short-lived and was suppressed by the Ottoman authorities.

Al-Zahrawi then returned to commercial activities in Istanbul, but met with no success; instead he spent most of his time reading Arab manuscripts in public libraries in the capital. Shortly before the turn of the century, al-Zahrawi became editor of the Arabic section of the Turkish newspaper *Malumat*, in which he wrote many literary, social, and reformist essays before the authorities had him exiled to Damascus. Despite this, in 1901 he managed to write "The Imamate and Its Conditions," in which he hinted implicitly that the Ottoman sultans had usurped the caliphate and had violated the legal conditions for the Imamate. He also published a study entitled "Jurisprudence and Mysticism," which aroused fanatical scholars against him. Nazim Pasha, the governor of Damascus, organized a debate in his palace between al-Zahrawi and his opponents, from which al-Zahrawi emerged the victor, thanks to his logical arguments and religious evidence. However, the pasha sent him under escort to Istanbul so that the central government might decide his case. Many Arab intellectuals were in sympathy with his ideas, especially Muhammad ʿAbduh, who declared that al-Zahrawi "merely states what is compatible with the roots of religion." It seems most likely, according to Rashid Rida, editor of *al-Manar*, that the reason for his several months' arrest in Istanbul was his article on the caliphate published in the Cairo newspaper, *al-Muqattam*.[2]

No sooner did al-Zahrawi escape to Egypt in 1906 than he took a very active public role, publishing articles in the Cairo newspapers, which he found receptive to his ideas. He wrote first for *al-Muʾayyad*, edited by Shaykh ʿAli Yusuf; then for *al-Jarida*, edited by Ahmad Lutfi al-Sayyid. In Egypt in 1908 he published his book *Khadija, the Mother of Believers*, in which he described the Prophet's life as an example for the Arabs to follow. He also wrote a book on jurisprudence at the request of Rashid Rida and others. His articles in *al-Manar* were collected in a book entitled *The System of Love and Hate*, in which he explained the factors lying behind love among people, and concluded that these factors contributed to national unity.

Already an accomplished journalist and deeply involved in politics, and possessing a good grasp of the Turkish language, he seemed to have benefited considerably from his stay in Cairo and Istanbul. But politics attracted him once more when his compatriots called him back to his hometown of Homs, after the restoration of the Ottoman constitution in 1908. There he was elected a deputy in the *majlis al-mabʿuthan* (Chamber of Deputies), the lower chamber of the Ottoman parliament.

After the Young Turk revolution of 1908 and the substitution of the rule of the Committee of Union and Progress (CUP) for that of Sultan Abdülhamid, it soon became clear that the CUP was much less sympathetic to Arab aspirations than the sultan had been. In the years immediately following the restoration of the Ottoman constitution, the Arab movement that had started as a cultural nationalist phenomenon began to develop into an extensive network of associations, parties, secret societies, and clubs working for reforms and decentralization throughout the Arab provinces of the empire, and calling for Arabic to be a recognized official language.

As a member of Parliament for nearly four years, al-Zahrawi witnessed how the CUP became increasingly influenced by Turkish nationalism, gradually throwing the principle of equality overboard and using its power to promote Turkish interests to the detriment of those of other Ottoman elements. The CUP failed to see the incompatibility of Turkish nationalism with Ottomanism, which aimed at uniting the different elements of the Empire on the basis of equality. While the CUP adopted a centralized form of government and proceeded to tighten its grip on the central bureaucracy, the diverse non-Turkish elements within the Empire increasingly called for a decentralized form of government, to ensure them a larger measure of autonomy. When Parliament assembled in December 1908, al-Zahrawi realized that although the Arabs were one of the largest elements in the Empire, perhaps as numerous as the Turks and perhaps outnumbering them, they were represented in the Chamber of Deputies by 60 members, while the Turks were represented by 150 members.³ The CUP also usurped Arab rights in the Senate *(Majlis al-Aʿyan)*, in the Cabinet, in the governorship of provinces, and in other high ranking posts. Although the Arabs constituted a very large proportion of the population of the Empire, they were reserved only one portfolio, the Ministry of Awqaf, whereas other elements were reserved one or two portfolios.

Al-Zahrawi was among the founders of the Liberal Moderate Party while the members were largely Arabs, which can be understood as a reaction to the attempts of the CUP to use their power to dominate the Arabs and undermine the unity of their fellow Ottomans. The CUP later dissolved the Entente Liberale Party, formed somewhat afterward by some liberal Turks and other elements including al-Zahrawi, who was elected together with Shukri al-ʿAsali, the deputy for Damascus, to its Central Committee. Al-Zahrawi declared that this party's objects were twofold: combating tyranny and reconciling other elements in the Empire.

Al-Zahrawi's talents emerged plainly in his numerous addresses delivered in the Chamber, defending Arab rights, warning against foreign colonial intrigues threatening the Ottoman Empire, and deploring the neglect and ignorance which led to the loss of Tripoli. With tears in his eyes, he gave a speech in the Chamber saying that the Italian occupation of Tripoli meant the fall of a great Arab region into the grip of foreign colonialism. To a deputy who had tried to console him by saying that Tripoli would be restored shortly, he answered: "I am not weeping for the loss of Tripoli; I am weeping for the loss of Rumelia, Iraq, the Hijaz, and Syria." When the CUP attempted to dissociate itself from responsibility for the loss of Libya (alleging in the Chamber on October 19, 1911, that the empire had not the fleet to confront the enemy), al-Zahrawi and Shafiq al-Mu-'ayyad of Damascus insisted that the Unionists alone were responsible for that invasion. But the Ottoman opposition parties, with whom the Arab nationalists and most Arab deputies were in alliance, realized that the empire was facing a catastrophe. They tried to reach an agreement with the CUP to consolidate a united front capable of dealing with the critical situation resulting from the war in Libya. The only condition the opposition put forth was removal of the speaker of the Chamber, Ahmad Riza, for reasons of incompetence. The CUP refused categorically and insisted on reelecting him for a new term. While Riza barely obtained the necessary votes for his post, al-Zahrawi acquired 86 votes for the position of deputy speaker. He declined, however, lest his acceptance be interpreted as a gesture of cooperation with the CUP, and another Arab deputy was elected in his stead. Then the opposition parties proceeded to join together in the opposition Entente Liberale party.

The CUP's attempts to strengthen the unity of the empire in a Draconian fashion were doomed to failure. The clumsy steps they took in pursuance of their centralization policy intensified the bitterness it engendered. By monopolizing political power, the CUP only succeeded in alarming the other elements, particularly the Arabs, into a belief that Ottomanism, which they were asked loyally to accept, was a sham, and that if it meant anything, it could mean that they would have to abandon their national identity and allow themselves to be Turkified for the sake of unity.

The opposition Entente Liberale party benefited from the diminishing popularity of the CUP and consolidated its political philosophy, based on decentralization. The CUP was angered when it saw many Unionists deserting the party to join the opposition, thus increasing the competition's strength in the Chamber. It also drew its conclusions from the failure of its candidate in the December 1911 by-election held in Istanbul. Thus, before the opposition could win more ground, the CUP hastened to modify Article 35 of the constitution to make the dissolution of the Chamber easier. Al-Zahrawi warned against the modification of Article 35, arguing that the government could dissolve the Chamber when difficulties arose, but his warnings went unheeded.

No sooner did the CUP dissolve the Chamber than al-Zahrawi started his trip home to Syria to campaign with his associates: Shukri al-ʿAsali (see Samir Seikaly's essay, in this volume), Khalid al-Barazi, Kamil al-Asʿad, and the famous Turkish deputy Lutfi Fikri. They were given a warm welcome in Beirut and Damascus.

The elections for the new Chamber were held under restrictive measures and had been so geared as to ensure a great majority for the CUP nominees. These rigged elections, in which

Zahrawi was defeated, made him pessimistic; he became convinced that the CUP had established a tyranny no less despotic than that of Abdülhamid's. But al-Zahrawi regained his hopes in July 1912, when the army in the Balkans overthrew the government, and a new cabinet was formed by Ahmad Mukhtar Pasha to reestablish entente among all the Ottoman elements. The Cabinet, which kept strong links with the Entente Liberale party, received an enthusiastic welcome from the press, after restoring freedom of speech and announcing a general amnesty for all political crimes. Al-Zahrawi called the collapse of the Unionist Cabinet "the fall of the second persecution" and recalled that this happened in July, the same month in which Abdülhamid had fallen four years before.[4] A month later the new Parliament was dissolved and new elections were called for September 1912. Al-Zahrawi urged his compatriots to use their right to choose those who were known for their integrity and patriotism among the Entente Liberale nominees.[5] He bitterly criticized the indifference shown by some and warned of its catastrophic effects on the whole nation.

The new Cabinet asked the general provincial councils in the Arab provinces to draw up a scheme for the necessary reforms, and for home rule on the basis of decentralization. Arab Reform Committees were formed in Beirut, Damascus, Aleppo, Jerusalem, Baghdad, and Basra. But the sudden defeat of the Ottoman armies soon after the first Balkan war led to a military coup that returned the CUP to power in January 1913.

In power again, the CUP decided to proceed with a new policy of repression and tough measures toward the Ottoman provinces in general and the Arabs in particular. After the first Balkan war, the Arab provinces became more important in relation to the remaining provinces, especially following the loss of eight of the most important provinces in the Balkan Peninsula. Some Ottoman politicians had even suggested in 1912 that the Arab provinces should form a single kingdom with its own parliament and local government; this kingdom was to be part of a Turkish-Arab empire, along the lines of the Austro-Hungarian Empire. But before these ideas could crystallize, the CUP had returned to power, and in April 1913 the reform movements in Beirut and elsewhere were repressed.

At the same time, Arab circles realized that foreign powers were moving to assert their claims in the Ottoman Empire, and the victory of the Balkan states had revived the "Eastern Question" once again. Widespread rumors about the colonial ambitions of France, Britain, Germany, and Russia brought dismay that turned to despair. Watchful Arabs among the Syrians and Lebanese in Egypt were moved to defend the Arab countries against European intervention, and toward the end of December 1912 founded the Ottoman Administrative Decentralization party in Cairo. The aim of this party was to impress upon the ruling class in Turkey the need for decentralizing the administration of the empire and to mobilize Arab opinion in support of decentralization. The founders of the party argued that the Ottomans, who were incapable of protecting Rumelia, which was adjacent to Istanbul, would inevitably be unable to protect the more distant Arab provinces.[6] Although al-Zahrawi attended the foundation of the party in Cairo, he abstained from entering its administrative committee, since he was domiciled in Istanbul, not Cairo.[7]

All Arab hopes collapsed after the repression of the Arab Reform Committees in 1913. There was general dismay and anger in Beirut and Damascus, and the agitation evoked demonstrations of solidarity all over Syria. While some Arab groups resorted to underground channels, fed by secret organizations, others envisaged the holding of an Arab Congress outside the Ottoman territories, in some neutral and free atmosphere. The First Arab Congress was therefore held in Paris in June 1913.

The Decentralization party was represented at the Congress by al-Zahrawi and Iskandar ʿAmmun. Al-Zahrawi declared to the editor of the Paris newspaper *Le Temps* that the Arabs held the Congress after recent Ottoman defeats in Europe in order to head off their possible negative results for the Arabs, who constituted numerically the most important element in the empire. He added: "This Arab race has its characteristics in the unity of language, customs, interests, and tendencies that have emphasized Arab rights still ignored to this hour. For that reason, we, as Ottomans, demanded to have an effective share in the administration of the affairs of the empire, and to expose, as Arabs, special demands with reference to our nationalism and status."[8] The Congress, he said, would first examine the subject of protecting national life in general, and introduce reform on the basis of decentralization; second, it would express the Arab demands in particular, and examine the problems of those moving to and from the homeland. Al-Zahrawi stressed that the Congress had no religious character, and that its work was focused on social and political affairs, so the membership was made up of both Muslims and Christians, and the idea of convoking the Congress had been born following recent events in Beirut.

When al-Zahrawi was asked whether the Congress would cause dismay to the Ottoman government although the latter expressed a willingness to accept the Arabic language officially, he replied that "the government would have the right to be dismayed had the Arabs demanded secession, for example. As for us, we want the contrary. Our demands would improve both the status of the empire and the Arab race."[9] The Arab right, he said, "is not to expose the demands, but to put them into effect." He criticized the negative attitude of some Turks toward the Arabic language and their refusal to consider it an official language. Although they narrowed the authority of the central government, they did not expand the authority of the nation, "and this would lead to the breakdown of Ottoman unity, which we do not want."[10]

Asked if the Congress aimed at supporting Ottoman unity for the sake of religious ties, al-Zahrawi answered: "We are not attached to political unity for the sake of a religious link; we are, rather, willing to establish a strong Ottoman entity in which the Arabs would prosper without obstacles in their way, and in the hope that we shall have a share in the national government. The Ottoman state could realize our wishes if it committed itself to the reform requirements that we consistently insist on. But if it refrains, I declare to you as I declared in Cairo, that our plan to deal with it would change completely."[11]

The First Arab Congress held its opening meeting on June 18, and al-Zahrawi was elected president. The Congress lasted for six days, during which four formal sessions were held. At the first session al-Zahrawi delivered his inaugural speech (discussed below). Throughout the proceedings, many references were prudently veiled, hinting, as they did, at French ambitions and the possibility of foreign intervention as dangers resolutely to be warded off. Also, there was no mention whatsoever of secession; on the contrary, all speakers stressed the general desire to maintain the integrity of the Ottoman Empire, provided the Arabs were recognized as partners.

The CUP, however, took a hostile attitude and accused the promoters of the Congress of being agents of foreign governments. Having failed to block the Congress, CUP officials sent the party's secretary to Paris to negotiate with the heads of the Congress. Agreement was reached with al-Zahrawi and his colleagues as a basis for further negotiations in Istanbul. To prove their desire for reform, even if it came gradually, the Arabs accepted something less than the Decentralization party program. The agreement did meet Arab demands for the use of Arabic as an official language in the Arab provinces, and for its use as a medium of instruction in the primary and secondary schools. Also, administrative reform in the Arab provinces would follow principles of decentralization, and there would be effective participation by the Arabs in the central government by the reserving of certain posts for them.

Al-Zahrawi remained in Paris to await the implementation of the agreement; 'Abd al-Karim al-Khalil, the delegate of the Arab youth in Istanbul and president of the Arab Literary Club, returned home with the CUP delegate to press implementation of all that had been agreed to. Al-Zahrawi received a telegram from al-Khalil asking him to come soon to Istanbul; the Decentralization party permitted al-Zahrawi to stop off at Istanbul on his way back to Cairo.[12] He arrived in Istanbul at the end of October 1913, where Arab notables and more than seventy Arab officers, together with many Arab students, gave him a warm welcome.[13]

Al-Zahrawi began his contacts with the CUP about putting the reforms into effect; they told him that they had already started the reforms by establishing two *sultaniyya* (secondary) schools in Damascus and Beirut that were teaching in Arabic.[14] While he was satisfied with the Imperial Decree on the use of Arabic in the local courts, he patiently awaited the enforcement of other demands, swaying between "despair and hope," according to his close associate, Rashid Rida.[15]

After a long period of patient waiting, al-Zahrawi decided to leave Istanbul. He held a press conference in which he referred to the division in the government between the moderates and the extremists. However, in time the moderates blamed the extremists for the delay in the implementation of reforms, and asked the government to take immediate steps. On January 4, 1914, another Imperial Decree nominated al-Zahrawi and six other Arabs to be members of the Senate (*majlis al-aʿyan*). Among the six, three were independents and three were Unionists. Shukri al-ʿAsali and ʿAbd al-Wahhab al-Inklizi were appointed to the Ministry of Justice as inspectors in Syria, while the others were nominated to various high-ranking posts.[16]

Although al-Zahrawi did not consult the Decentralization Party about his nomination, the party confirmed him in that post because it trusted him and believed that he had been sincere in serving the Arab nation, and that he was the best among the Arabs who could brief the party on CUP policy. The party saw fit not to sever relations with the CUP, even though it was not sure whether the Paris agreement would really be ratified. But al-Zahrawi's acceptance of the nomination was regarded in some Arab circles as a betrayal. Al-Khalil, who himself was criticized, defended al-Zahrawi's motives, arguing that he could do inside the Senate what he could not outside, and that was to continue to convince the government to fulfill Arab demands that could only be carried out gradually for fear of agitation on the part of other.s Al-Zahrawi, he said, accepted his post only when he was faced with the escalating ambitions of the colonial powers in the Arab countries and their intention to exploit the differences between Arabs and Turks to fulfill their objectives.[17]

In despair al-Zahrawi sent a secret letter to Rashid Rida, in which he explained his motives for accepting the appointment, revealing the critical conditions on the Arab political scene and pointing to the lack of qualified men for political action in Istanbul. He began by summing up the intention of Europe to interfere in Ottoman affairs. Then he referred to the Unionists who stood alone; no other party could defy them, except the rich organized associations and societies of the Greeks and Armenians. The Arabs, he said, had nothing like that, except the Decentralization party and the Reform Committee of Beirut. The Unionists had the upper hand; they had a strong will and the intention to regenerate the empire as conditions permitted. He added, "They have confessed their past mistakes and intend not to return to them again." Al-Zahrawi admitted that he believed them on many grounds, but he doubted "their ability to carry out their intention; however, I see that not leaving them alone is better than leaving them; it is to be hoped that their ability would be enhanced." Al-Zahrawi proceeded to describe the Arabs in Istanbul whom he represented: indifferent merchants, educated youths not qualified for politics, pragmatic employees, and officers without experience. As for the Syrians and Iraqis, "They do not understand and they do not want to understand; they do not help and they do not intend to help." He expressed hope in the Arabs of Yemen, ʿAsir, Najd (Nejd), and Hadramaut. Then he stated that his presence in Istanbul was a necessity, and that he suffered from the lack of dependable men, hoping that by his presence "the number of our men would increase; men of true reform who combine theory and practice."[18]

In the end, al-Zahrawi probably accepted membership of the Senate because it did not imply a post in the government; it was, rather, a control on the government, not a service. It was like membership as a deputy, concerned with the enactment of laws and supervising their proper application. Furthermore, al-Zahrawi believed, rightly or wrongly, that the government had proceeded in the implementation of reforms, and it was not logical or fair to abstain from a post or employment until the reforms had been entirely fulfilled.

However, al-Zahrawi sought to adopt a conciliatory attitude toward the ruling CUP in good faith after the Unionists confessed their past mistakes (which had caused the revulsion of the Arabs) and expressed their willingness to make up for them in an effort to regenerate the strength of the empire. Al-Zahrawi was inclined to believe them since he viewed his nomination by the CUP, after his bitter opposition to them, as evidence of their sincerity. He henceforth became convinced that the reformists should help the Unionists; if they refrained, hypocrites and pragmatists would replace them.[19] Fearing foreign intervention, al-Zahrawi and al-Khalil, supported by leading Arab officers such as Colonel Salim al-Jaza'iri, wished to show goodwill to the Ottoman government, realizing the critical position of the Arabs and the government's inclination to fulfill some of their demands. Al-Zahrawi even wrote to Rafiq al-ʿAzm, president of the Decentralization party, and Rashid Rida, one of its prominent members, asking them to come to Istanbul to occupy the high-ranking posts promised them. Both men, however, thought it was a trap to get rid of them. Those Arabs who deplored al-Zahrawi's conciliatory steps considered that what the government had announced to meet the Arab demands fell far short of the Paris agreement. The concessions, they maintained, were limited and illusory, and the whole process was a well-planned spectacle mounted by the CUP to disseminate dissension among the Arab reformists.

The steps taken by the CUP included many points compatible with the Arab demands, though they did fall short of the Paris agreement. But al-Zahrawi's and al-Khalil's call for patience and trust in the CUP overestimated the goodwill of the governing party, while al-Khalil's interpretations were not devoid of illusions. On the other hand, the critical Arab group was wrong in its negative attitude, which weakened the reformist front, caused discord, and gave the CUP a pretext to stop the reformist steps. Some Arab nationalists, not necessarily from either group, suggested that had harmony and entente dominated both Arab groups, the CUP might have taken other steps, and Turkish-Arab relations probably would not have deteriorated to the breaking point during World War I.[20]

Yet the CUP bore a great share of the responsibility for the deadlock; they had reached a definite agreement with the Arab nationalists in Paris. They were obliged to commit themselves to it honestly without modification or trickery, and their evasive conduct after this agreement was concluded provoked suspicion and skepticism among the Arabs in general. Until the beginning of World War I, the reform procedure went very slowly because of the differences arising among leading Ottoman politicians over decentralization. While some of them suggested a dual Turkish-Arab state, others remained hostile to reforms, feeling the necessity of ruling the Arabs by force. There was also a third group made up of Arab intellectuals whom the CUP had attracted; these people, although not in sympathy with Turkish policy toward the Arabs, believed that the dangers of breaking up the union of Arabs and Turks were too great, and that it would be best to work for a change in CUP policy. Added to this group was the majority of Muslim Arabs, who were influenced not by political trends but by religious allegiance to the Ottoman caliphate.

Following his letter to Rashid Rida, al-Zahrawi did not remain long at his post; he soon left Istanbul for Cairo, where he joined his associates in the Decentralization Party. Together they were soon convinced that the CUP was no longer willing to meet the Arab claims beyond what little they had done. Al-Zahrawi stayed in Egypt until 1914, when he returned to Istanbul, where he lived until his arrest during the war.

On the eve of World War I, three Unionist politicians dominated the CUP and the government: Talât Bey (later Paşa), minister of the interior and adherent of Ottomanism; Enver Bey, minister of war and an advocate of Islamism with a slight inclination to Turkish nationalism; and Cemal Bey (later Paşa), navy minister and a sympathizer with Turkish nationalism. When World War I broke out, throwing the Ottoman Empire onto the side of the Central Powers, the Arabs, for fear of internal dispute, suspended all their claims and demands and declared their support for all the decisions of the government. However, the CUP did not merely postpone the promised reforms: it also proceeded to prosecute all the nationalists, particularly those who had concluded the reform agreement. When the Egyptian campaign failed, Cemal Pasa began his Arab policy with a terrorist wave that swept up eminent figures known for their national allegiance and patriotic spirit. Among them was ʿAbd al-Hamid al-Zahrawi, who was executed because "he was a member of the Decentralization Party, and went so far as to ask the permission of the party by telegram before accepting his nomination to the *majlis al-aʿyan*, as if the authority which granted him that post were not the government, but the Decentralization Party."[21]

After it became clear, by the end of 1913, that a compromise between the Arabs and CUP was impossible, al-Zahrawi and his associates slowly edged toward the idea of independence.[22] This idea, added to his outspoken stand in the Chamber in defense of Arab rights and his editorials in the Istanbul newspaper, *al-Hadara* (Civilization), constituted the basis of his trial and execution in Damascus in 1916.

Al-Zahrawi's Arab Nationalist Thought. Not only was al-Zahrawi a Muslim scholar, he was also a political militant, social reformer, jurist, orator, and a man of letters. He was a true Muslim, enjoying the privileged position of membership of the *ash-*

raf, and wearing the traditional dress of shaykh with a turban on the head; he was also proud of his Arab origins and had a deeply rooted loyalty to the Arab nation. He inherited the tradition of attachment to the Arabic language and Arab history, and he had a sense of pride in what the Arabs had done for Islam, which reinforced his sense of responsibility toward his nation. He had great sympathy with national and patriotic ideals; he preached fraternity among Muslims and Christians, with an Arab coloring, asserting the identity of the Arab nation. While al-Zahrawi maintained that the caliphate was essentially connected with the fact that the Arabs had been the pioneering elements of Islam, he claimed that consequently the caliph could only be an Arab. This meant that the Ottoman sultan, who had assumed his claim to the caliphate in the mid-nineteenth century, had no legal justification for it. We already know how al-Zahrawi was detained in his early days for his essay on the caliphate. That was in the time of autocratic Hamidian rule, of which al-Zahrawi was a strong opponent, denouncing the sultan as usurper of the title of caliph. After the downfall of Abdülhamid II, al-Zahrawi made no further references to the caliphate; instead, he laid greater emphasis on the despotic rule of the CUP, which he regarded as a separate form of corruption, decay, and weakness. Like his fellow Arab nationalists of the day, he seemed to have been inclined to form the Arab provinces along the lines of decentralization and to emphasize their national unity within the framework of the Ottoman Empire.

Today we can see more clearly that al-Zahrawi's struggle and thought in the late Hamidian period, and more particularly in the later constitutional period (1911–1914), was focused directly or indirectly on national matters in general. A study of his editorials in *al-Hadara* (the name of which reflected his objectives and ambitions) reveals the trend of his ideas. The current exposition of al-Zahrawi's national and patriotic views is based on the only two available volumes of his paper, dated 1911 and 1912 (that for the first year, 1910, has not yet been found). The eighty-three editorials written by al-Zahrawi were in numbers 53 through 140, covering the period between April 13, 1911, and December 18, 1912.[23] These editorials were either signed by him or published under such sobriquets as "An Ottoman" or "A Free Ottoman"; regardless of what epithet appeared, he definitely wrote all of them, since all reflect his familiar style and a consistent line of argument.

The paper was founded, according to al-Zahrawi, its owner and chief editor, "to be a platform for rational men with concern for our political education."[24] Before the Libyan war of 1911, al-Zahrawi's positive expectation of a new era with the CUP in power had not yet been shaken by that party's bitter and unjustified press attacks on the Arabs; he had not abandoned his view of reforming the empire to stand firm in the face of foreign powers, supporting equality among Ottoman elements based on Ottoman patriotism.

Al-Zahrawi rejected the idea of a highly centralized government, and he resented the predominance of the Turks, who claimed to be seeking to preserve the unity of the empire. He regarded reform along the lines of decentralization as an inevitable step, not only to promote the Arab entity and develop it, but also to consolidate a real union among Ottoman elements, thus thwarting foreign ambitions. "When Arabs and Turks are united," he wrote, "the Eastern Question will disappear; for the strength of the state lies in the recognition of Arab rights, the Arab entity and the Arabic language." That is why he repeatedly called on the CUP to give the Arabs their due share in the Chamber of Deputies and the Senate in the Cabinet, in governorships of *vilayets*, and other high-ranking posts.[25]

Arab nationalism was one of the most outstanding preoccupations of al-Zahrawi; he stressed the major importance of the Arabic language and Arab history as ties binding together those Arabs who differed in inherited religious beliefs. An editorial he wrote in mid-1911, entitled "Who Are the Arabs," begins by mentioning the Arab civilizations in Yemen, Iraq, Syria, and the North African coast. The Quran (Koran), he said, preserved the language of the Arabs and united them until today; "those [Arabs] who speak Arabic and write in Arabic are 50 to 60 million people; their homes and countries are in close proximity to each other, and not water separates them but the Suez Canal." The Arabs today, he continued, "are the speakers of this language, whose life and progress have been known since the dawn of history. They are the inhabitants of these beautiful homelands that occupy a central position in the land adjacent to the Atlantic Ocean, the Indian Ocean, and the Mediterranean Sea. They are the owners of those intelligent minds, which they inherited more than seven thousand years ago, from ancestors known as builders of civilizations, reviving construction and developing knowledge."[26]

This very clear definition of the Arabs and, consequently, of Arab nationalism, which al-Zahrawi never mentioned directly, is comparable to the then-current concepts of European nationalism in general, and its German school in particular, which advocated language and history as being the most important factors in nationalism.

Al-Zahrawi, too, considered Arab history a basic incentive to revive national consciousness; there was a deep sense of anger and resentment in a number of editorials against any encroachment on Arab history and heritage. He urged the Arabs to know their history and cultural achievements better; for some extreme Turkish nationalists, notably the pan-Turanians, sought to expand the concept of "Turks and Mongols as one nation." Whether this was right or wrong, al-Zahrawi was alarmed by its immediate effect, which he claimed tended to lead toward national arrogance on the part of the Turks. Thus, when a proponent of Turkish nationalism, Yusuf Akçura, alleged in a speech given in Istanbul that Turks and Tatars had a common origin, and that most of the civilizations in medieval Asia and Russia had been established by the Turks, al-Zahrawi scornfully deplored this underestimation of the Arab heritage and the ingratitude shown by the speaker. He turned to his fellow Arabs and warned them that if they continued to neglect preserving their ancestors' heritage, other nations might claim it for themselves.

Earlier, al-Zahrawi had called on all Arabs to revive their past glories, although the CUP tolerated such steps by all other elements and denied them to Arabs. He urged his fellow Arabs to cooperate and adopt that moral strength with which their ancestors loved other people as they loved themselves. Glory, he said, can only be realized through cooperation, and cooperation can only be achieved through ties, and ties can only be established through the love of one's self: "Those who have no ties have no glory; and those who have no glory have no policy to protect them."[27]

He also called upon the Ottoman Arabs—Syrians, Iraqi Hijazis (Hejazis), Yemenis, Egyptians, and North Africans; Muslims and non-Muslims; conservatives, Socialists, or liberals—

to reach an agreement to fulfill the Arab identity. Al-Zahrawi urged the Arabs not to conform to the image of them projected by their enemies, who claimed that it was impossible for the Arabs to come closer to one another. He warned those who had been betting on Arab discord to remember that the present situation could change, and that accord among Arabs was possible. He concluded that the Arabs had to agree on the need for:

1. Awakening after a long sleep
2. Favoring mutual sympathy over discord
3. Keenness on supporting the Arabic language and resisting every idea aimed at undermining it or replacing it gradually in their countries
4. Respecting their entities as a whole
5. Playing a leading role in the scientific field and in all welfare activities[28]

After the Italian invasion of Libya, al-Zahrawi's attitude toward the ruling CUP, like that of many Arab nationalists, became highly critical of their repressive and despotic measures. He condemned the government's destructive expeditions to put down internal revolts, particularly in the Arab provinces of Yemen, ʿAsir, Hawran, and Karak. In an emotional editorial entitled "Woe Betide the Country and the People," al-Zahrawi thoughtfully exposed the political situation in the wake of the outbreak of the Balkan wars in 1912. He repeated his attacks on the CUP, for weakening the empire whenever it crushed revolts in remote areas, and he appealed frankly to the Arabs to trust themselves and to oppose the CUP, recalling Arab sufferings under Abdülhamid and his successors, the chauvinistic Unionists:

O my people we've had enough of sleep, we've had enough nonchalance towards the future. We've had enough of underestimating ourselves; we've had enough dependence on those whose realities have come to the surface; we've had enough of negligence of the lessons of time; we've had enough of pride in the elaborate sermons of the remote ones which would hide the facts. May God be with you my Arab brethren; you constitute an important part of this Kingdom, you should examine your position therein yesterday, today and the future. Only yesterday there was no foreign element in Egypt and Tunisia, which are major Arab countries, but today there are foreign elements therein. Only yesterday Tripoli was peaceful and secure, but today it is suffering under foreign occupation. Only yesterday the coasts of Najd were peaceful and today they are sad. Tell me O my people: is Syria free of fears?[29]

Al-Zahrawi thought that his being an Arab nationalist was not incompatible with being committed to Ottomanism. In a number of his editorials he took pains to emphasize this outspoken conviction; he went on to stress the bonds of Islamic fraternity and Ottoman patriotism that had linked Arabs and Turks, warning that their neglect would end the union between them. But he reacted strongly to the consistent endeavors of Turkification pressed by the CUP, stressing that true union is that in which the Arab remains Arab, and the Greeks Greek, and Albanians remain what they are; no one misunderstands the other when he wants to serve his language and proceeds to enhance the ideas of his people so as to enable them to get to know one another and consolidate their efforts to promote their social conditions. Al-Zahrawi also deplored union "if it leads to ignoring the origin of its elements, their language, their relatives and their peoples. Not only is such a union impossible, but imposing it on people is far from being practical; none but a fool would trust anybody who forgets his people and his nationalism; he who forgets his people has forgotten his homeland before."[30]

According to al-Zahrawi, the conditions for real union could be fulfilled when Ottoman elements intensify their love and friendship for one another. When the union is keen on the welfare of its homelands and the mutual respect of its other elements, and when it is aware that they are all participating in political rights, "then we would witness the disappearance of the term 'the ruling element' not only from the minds of the people, but also from the political dictionary." Al-Zahrawi maintained that "the extremely difficult union is that by which the Turk, for example, renounces his nationalism, the Arab his Arabism, for the sake of union"; he was trying to emphasize that Arab rights and identity should be safeguarded; the Arabs in no way renounce their Arabism for the benefit of another dominant group. Union is possible, he concluded, only when every element preserves its own national bonds, sharing equally in the common welfare of the union.[31]

While al-Zahrawi called on all the Ottoman elements to preserve the Ottoman link and strengthen it, so that everyone would respect his brethren as justice dictated, he urged his people not to despise those who stick to their nationalism or religion, since the dominant CUP was vulnerable to charges of being anti-Muslim because of its policies of suppressing the Arabic language and its indifference to Islam. The effects of Turkification did not escape al-Zahrawi; he realized how this policy encroached on the rights of Arabs; it united them in opposition, thus leading them to form the first open and secret organized groups. "If the Turks maintain that the Tatars and themselves are but one entity, then they should not be upset when we say that the Arabs in the East and West are but one entity."[32]

Al-Zahrawi seems to have exploited every event of the day for the promotion of national objectives. In this respect he proved to be farsighted and well informed of political realities, locally, nationally, and internationally, and thus could be counted among the most notable political figures of the time. Though he was a true Muslim, the national or patriotic feeling of his editorials took a secular form. This was clear from the articles he wrote on fraternity among the different faiths in the Ottoman Empire, stressing the unity of Muslims and non-Muslims. He seemed to have viewed seriously what some Turkish and Egyptian newspapers termed "European fanaticism" and the ascribing of a religious motive to the Italian invasion of Libya. But Al-Zahrawi rejected the kind of rhetoric used by those elements who seemed to discern farfetched religious motives for the Italian invasion of Tripoli, and pointed out that non-Muslim Arabs were not spared the hardships inflicted on the homeland. Al-Zahrawi maintained that "adherence to such rhetoric would throw suspicion on our patriotic fraternity. It is necessary that all the communities from different faiths in the Ottoman homeland should remember that they have partners therein; there are the Muslims who are attached to the caliphate, but the Ottoman homeland is a political homeland for all Ottomans, Muslims and non-Muslims."[33]

It is clear that al-Zahrawi seized the opportunity to stress the theme with which he was preoccupied—that is, how to enhance the cordial relations between his Muslim and non-Muslim compatriots to block the way against foreign designs. He also wanted his people to realize that group solidarity is one of the basic pillars on which nations stood, that indiscriminate fanaticism was tantamount to suicide since it led to foreign occupations, whereas group solidarity, which aimed at redressing what is right, was a call to strengthen the bonds among people. But this, he advocated, "requires sincere rational men who know how to control it, so as to make the non-Ottoman Muslim a brother, acting for his religious homeland, and who know how the Ottoman Muslims and non-Muslims can become two cooperating brothers in their political homeland." Al-Zahrawi also drew attention to the fact that the "disease" lay in ourselves, not in Europe alone, and that the Ottomans were drowned in debts and invasions from Europe: "we are dependent on Europe even for the flour with which we make our bread, and the thread with which we sew our clothes." He ascribed all that to the evil resulting from the appointment of unqualified men to high-ranking posts.[34]

It is evident from al-Zahrawi's overriding preoccupation with Arab nationalism and the Ottoman reform movement, together with consciousness of the danger of foreign control and partition hanging over the empire in general and the Arab provinces in particular, that he was extremely apprehensive of European political designs. He noticed that Europe frequently took the protection of Christians in Ottoman territories as a pretext to fulfill its colonial objectives. He referred to "the Crusades" that had arrived in the Islamic East as a form of aggression hiding behind the veil of religion. He criticized the Europeans' unwillingness to recognize that Islamic rule had been more benevolent to the Christians living among the Muslims than had Christian rule to Muslims, and that Muslims were more disposed to protect their Christian compatriots than intruding foreigners. Al-Zahrawi then drew the following conclusions:

1. Not to arouse the hostility of the peoples of Europe
2. That people should spare no efforts to strengthen themselves
3. That people should remember the good and evil of Europe, and be on the alert; they should also be on the alert to foster a climate of friendliness and sympathy, acting prudently and not disturbing the world with talk, most of which is nonsense.

The only means to foil European intrigues, in al-Zahrawi's view, was to "strengthen ourselves and censure the government for its unnecessary wars, which are self-defeating, and for appointing hypocrites who praise every dominant force in Istanbul, even if it causes destruction and weakness."[35]

Before concluding this exposition of al-Zahrawi's Arab nationalist thought, it may be appropriate to sum up his inaugural speech at the First Arab Congress in Paris, in which he underlined the topics that he had previously dealt with in his articles, particularly those connected with political education.[36]

Al-Zahrawi criticized the monopoly on political activities by politicians, and he deplored the people's aversion to politics (which was tantamount to denouncing their political rights) and their acceptance of absolute rule. While the West had bypassed this stage, many in the East were still ignorant of the right of the people to question and criticize their government and bring it to task.

He criticized some Europeans who begrudged the Arabs their freedoms and political rights. His concept of political activity was twofold—to help the government to improve the conditions of the country, and to oppose the government when it adopted measures detrimental to the country. This can only be achieved when the people are always on the alert. Al-Zahrawi concluded that after the Arabs had seen the sad conditions in the empire resulting from the politics of the Turks, they realized they should play an active role side by side with the Turks. Al-Zahrawi also stressed that the Arabs had come to Europe for enlightenment and the acquisition of knowledge as well as to tell Europe that it does not need those attending the Congress to expand its territories, and neither did they accept to shoulder this task. The Arabs declared that they were seeking to reform their countries on the basis of decentralization, and would like to have their national entity within the framework of the Ottoman Empire because this was in their own interests as well as in the interest of the state as a whole.

Finally, it is appropriate to touch on an article by al-Zahrawi published in *Mir'at al-gharb* (Mirror of the West)[37] four months before his appointment to the Senate. This article (entitled "Where Is the Nation of the Syrian?") has an implicit though very strong nationalistic tone akin to that of the European philosophers of nationalism in the nineteenth century. Thus he says:

Where and how can I seek my nation, or you might say, isn't my nation the selfsame communities living in beautiful Syria? Yes, this is your nation, but the nation you mean are those communities in whose consciousness the spirit of nationalism is ever reverberating; without such a spirit the whole nation would be dispersed and fragmented. The aim of our struggle today is to revive the spirit which is instrumental in the formation of nations. Once we acquire this spirit we become a nation in no time. As long as this spirit is remotely distant, our whole existence would be that of ghosts with no place under the sun, and no position in the eyes of the political world.

The article embodies al-Zahrawi's innermost Arab nationalist feelings. He seems to tell his readers that unless the nationalism of the Arabs throughout the Arab homeland binds them together in conscious awareness that they belong to one nation (albeit extending over long stretches of territories and constituting a multiplicity of communities), they can never establish their true identity and will remain mere ghosts, unable to establish their place in the world.

Notes

1. According to Rashid Rida, editor of *al-Manar*, al-Zahrawi was over fifty years old at the time of his nomination to membership of the Senate in 1913. If we believe Rida, who was his close associate, and consider that al-Zahrawi was fifty years old in 1913, and fifty-three when he was hanged in 1916, then his birth date should be 1863 not 1871, the date given by most writers. See *al-Manar* 19 (1913): 172.
2. *Al-Manar* 19 (1913): 169.
3. George Antonius, in *The Arab Awakening*, p. 104, says Arabs outnumbered Turks three to two. For more details, see al-Zahwari's editorials in *al-Hadara*, nos. 64 and 65 (June 29, 1911, and July 6, 1911, respectively). These ratios are open to some question.
4. "After Four Years," *al-Hadara*, no. 123 (July 25, 1912).
5. "Have Mercy on Your Country," *al-Hadara*, no 123 (August 15, 1912).
6. *Al-Manar* 19 (1913): 77.
7. *Al-Manar* 17 (1911): 238.
8. M. al-Khatib, *al-Mu'tamar al-'arabi al-awwal* [The first Arab congress], pp. 17–18.
9. Ibid., p. 19.
10. Ibid., p. 20.
11. Ibid.
12. *Al-Manar*, 19 (1913): 235.
13. *Al-Mufid*, no. 1406 (October 20, 1913).
14. *Al-Manar*, 19 (1913): 235.

15. Ibid.
16. Muhammad 'Izzat Darwaza, *Nash'at al-haraka al-'arabiyya al-haditha* [The birth of the modern Arab movement], p. 449.
17. As'ad Daghir, *Mudhakkirati 'ala hamish al-qadiyya al-'arabiyya* [My memoirs on the margins of the Arab cause], p. 68.
18. See the complete text in *al-Manar* 19 (1913): 175–81.
19. *Al-Manar*, 19 (1913): 180–81.
20. Among those holding this view is Darwaza, *Nash'at al-haraka*, pp. 451–52.
21. Quoted in Sati' al-Husri, *Nushu' al-fikra al-qawmiyya* [The birth of the nationalist idea], p. 215.
22. According to Amir Shakib Arslan (Emir Şekib Arslan), al-Zahrawi and Rashid Rida, whom he had met in Cairo, advocated Arab cooperation with England to get rid of Turkey, while Arslan expressed his adherence to the Ottomans. See Shakib Arslan, *al-Sayyid Rashid Rida aw ikha' arba'in sana* [Al-Sayyid Rashid Rida, or the friendship of forty years], pp. 152–55.
23. Al-Zahrawi's editorials were collected in a book, *al-Irth al-fikri lil-muslih al-ijtima'i 'Abd al-Hamid al-Zahrawi* [The intellectual legacy of the social reformer 'Abd al-Hamid al-Zahrawi], published in Damascus in 1963.
24. "Our Political Education," *al-Hadara*, no. 53 (April 13, 1911).
25. See his editorials based on statistical data on this theme: "The Ministers," *al-Hadara*, no. 61 (August 1, 1911), and "The Governors," *al-Hadara*, no. 71 (August 17, 1911). See also "Our Political Education-6," *al-Hadara*, no. 58 (May 18, 1911).
26. "Who Are the Arabs?" *al-Hadara*, no. 60 (June 1, 1911).
27. "Our Political Education-5," *al-Hadara*, no. 57 (May 11, 1911).
28. "Our Political Education-8," *al-Hadara*, no. 62 (June 15, 1911).
29. *al-Madaniyya*, no. 91 (January 5, 1912). It is to be noted that after this editorial was published, the authorities closed *al-Madaniyya* (earlier the censor had closed *al-Hadara*; it had reappeared as *al-Madaniyya*, which, after it was closed, reappeared as *al-Idara*).
30. "Our Political Education-3," *al-Hadara*, no. 55 (April 27, 1911).
31. Ibid.
32. "Our Political Education-4," *al-Hadara*, no. 56 (May 4, 1911).
33. "Today and After-3," *al-Hadara*, no. 82 (November 3, 1911).
34. "Today and After-4," *al-Hadara*, no. 83 (November 10, 1911).
35. "Today and After-6" and "Awakening After Sleep," *al-Hadara*, no. 85 (November 23, 1911); see also "Our Internal Wars," *al-Hadara*, no. 118 (July 11, 1912).
36. For the complete text of al-Zahrawi's speech see al-Khatib, *al-Mu'tamar al-'arabi al-awwal*, pp. 28–39.
37. Republished in *al-Mufid*, no. 1370 (September 8, 1913).

SIX

Iraq Before World War I: A Case of Anti-European Arab Ottomanism

Mahmoud Haddad

The first idea that springs to mind when addressing the topic of Arab nationalism, or more precisely proto-Arab nationalism, during the period of the Young Turks (1908–1914), is the idea of Arab versus Turk, or the Arab provinces versus the Ottoman central government. While this is a proper approach, it is incomplete, because we may speak of two general patterns within "Arab nationalism" at that stage. One reflected a reaction to Turkish domination, the other reflected a reaction to European or Western economic, political, and cultural penetration. Although the first pattern was not marginal and should not be taken lightly, it was, relatively speaking, minor. It was overshadowed and dwarfed by the anti-European pattern that was more important, more broadly based, and more socially and politically significant, at least in the case of Iraq.

The central government, and especially that of the Committee of Union and Progress (CUP), was increasingly perceived as representing the dual peril of both Turkish nationalism and increased European penetration. For the Arabs of Iraq, the CUP was the origin of Turkification and increased centralization policies on the one hand, and the authority that was either upholding or giving in to foreign interests on the other.

The anti-European pattern developed in opposition to two particular schemes that kept reappearing independently or concurrently in Iraq during the rule of the Young Turks (1908–

1914). The first scheme was the attempt of foreign capital to monopolize the rights of navigation on the Tigris and Euphrates rivers, while the second was related to other attempts by foreign capital to penetrate agriculture. It appeared in two distinct phases—an initial phase at the end of 1909, and a later more broadly based phase during the last half of 1913. Although the first phase can be described as having only partially a national or protonational character, a close look at it may be helpful toward acquiring a good understanding of the subsequent phase.

The 1909 phase started when the Ottoman cabinet approved a project to amalgamate the Ottoman steamer line, the *Nahriyya*, with the British Messrs. Lynch Brothers Company. For all practical purposes, the project meant the absorption of the former by the latter. Messrs. Lynch was to enjoy a virtual monopoly for navigating the Tigris and the Euphrates for seventy-five years, subject to termination by the Ottoman government after thirty-seven years.[1]

The course of events during December 1909 concerning the "Lynch Affair" reads like a diary of turbulent local uprising. According to an extremely informative memorandum by the British consul-general at Baghdad around December 14,[2] a number of merchants, Christians and Jews as well as Muslims, protested by telegram to Istanbul against the supposed intention of *majlis al-mabʿuthan* (Chamber of Deputies, the lower chamber of the Ottoman parliament) to sanction a concession for navigation in favor of Messrs. Lynch, and to sell them the *Nahriyya* steamer line. The merchants also sent a long memorandum to the president of the Chamber in which they recited their fears about three main sources—namely, British trade advantage, British political designs, and Arab tribal misconduct. The detailed arguments were put as follows:

1. Freight and fares between Bagdad and Bussorah [Basra] would probably be increased, as *there would no longer be any competition.*

2. The working of the steamers might be manipulated so as to give an advantage to British over that of other trade.

3. In case of tribal disturbances upon the river, the firm would probably demand compensation for the interruption of their business,

which they could not do so long as there were also Turkish steamers on the river.

4. An opportunity would be created, in case of tribal disturbances, *for political interference by the British government.*

5. The Turkish government would no longer have any steamers at its disposal for the transport of troops, in case of tribal disturbances.

6. The transfer of the steamers would have a bad political effect upon the rebellious tribes, *and the steamers might even be used by the British in such a way as to assist and encourage those tribes. India was an excellent example of how political designs might be pushed under the guise of trade.*

7. The same price could be obtained from themselves (the merchants) as from Messrs. Lynch and they would agree to conditions more favorable to the Turkish government. [emphasis added]

On December 15, the Baghdad branch of the CUP met and passed a resolution:

to the effect that the grant of a navigation concession to foreigners would be very injurious to the interests of Turkey. The Committee appointed a deputation consisting of Abdul-Jabbar Khaiyatzadah (a Christian lawyer), Manahim Salih (a Jewish lawyer), Yahuda Zaluf (a Jewish merchant), Wafik Bey (a Turk, *mudir* of the local customhouse), and Yusuf Shantub (a Jewish merchant), to interview the *Vali* and protest against the concession in the name of the mercantile community and other inhabitants of Baghdad.

On December 19, a telegram sent from Istanbul carried the news that the Chamber of Deputies, "notwithstanding the united opposition of the deputies for Baghdad, Bussorah, Musal [Mosul], and Dair-az-Zor [Dayr-al-Zur], had decided by a majority of votes to approve the concession."

On December 20, a telegram was sent from Baghdad

to the prime minister and the other members of the Turkish cabinet, to the presidents of the Senate and Chamber of Deputies, to the deputies for Bagdad, Bussorah, Musal, Dair-az-Zor, Hedjaz [Hejaz], and Yemen, to Nazim Pasha (the *vali*-elect of Bagdad), and to the editors of a number of newspapers at Constantinople. It stated that the life of Irak depended on the rivers Tigris and Euphrates, and that to give a concession for their navigation to foreigners would be to destroy the country.

In the absence of a favorable answer, the local deputies would be recalled from Constantinople and other measures taken. The actual sender of these telegrams was probably Abdul Kadir Pasha ("Khadhairi"), a merchant.

On this day a mass meeting was held on the plain north of Bagdad City. It was, I believe, organized by Abdul Kadir Pasha and Mahmud ("Shabandar") another merchant. The meeting lasted an hour, and the number of people taking part was estimated at 5,000 to 10,000.... The organizers, with the assumed consent of the meeting, then nominated a committee of about fifty members (Mohammedans, Jews, and Christians) to watch the interests of the inhabitants of Bagdad in the matter of the concession. The committee thus appointed included the Khadhairi and the Shabandar themselves, a number of government officials and ex-officials, a number of merchants (mostly Jewish and Christian), the editors of one Christian and five Mohammedan newspapers, and one Mohammedan schoolmaster.

On December 21, the *vali* of Baghdad replied to an earlier telegram from the minister of the interior in Istanbul, stating in a somewhat sympathetic manner "the following remarks of the 'Turkish merchants of Bagdad' ":

1. The concession should not involve any kind of monopoly.
2. If the steamers must be sold, the Turkish merchants themselves would buy them on any reasonable conditions.
3. A company, if formed, should consist of Turkish subjects only, and should be bound to comply with all reasonable requirements of the government. Messrs. Lynch should retain their present two steamers.
4. The arrangements explained in the minister's telegram to the *vali* would be most harmful, and they were not acquiesced in by the people.
5. The people would accept any proposals by the Government which did not involve the intrusion of foreigners.[3]

On the same day, twenty-seven "private individuals" sent a letter from Basra "protesting against a concession to foreigners" (ibid.). The Mosul branch of the CUP sent a "strong protest" directly to Istanbul against the concession.

From the above it is clear that the impetus for this movement against foreign monopoly capital came from the merchants of Baghdad. However, the most vocal representatives of this class were the two Sunni merchants (*chalabis*) ʿAbd al-Qadir al-Khudayri and Mahmud Shabandar, who together with "their chief associates were still practically inhabiting the telegraph office" on December 22. We must add here the name of a third *chalabi* which does not appear in the British consul-general's memorandum but is mentioned in an Arabic historical work; he is the Shiʿi Jaʿfar Abu al-Timman;[4] and while he played a minor role in this instance, he was to become "a key leader and inspirer of the 1920 uprising"[5] against the British and "stood, until his death in 1945, as the symbol of irreconcilable opposition to British influence."[6]

That al-Khudayri in particular was centerstage during the 1909 episode is significant not only because he referred to himself at one point as the "representative of the people,"[7] but also because he was the first director of the CUP branch in Baghdad and the head of its club.[8] It is possible to shed some light on what was really at stake for him if we draw attention to the fact that he seems to have been the richest of the three owners of "freelance" river steamers in service on the Tigris.[9]

It should be noted, moreover, that, relatively speaking, both Abu al-Timman and al-Khudayri were lesser local capitalists. The richest merchants in Iraq were the merchant-intermediaries who were agents of British firms. To this last class belonged Mahmud al-Shabandar, who was the agent of the British firm Allan Brothers of Aberdeen.[10] What incited Mahmud al-Shabandar can easily be deduced. He was, like all members of this class of merchants of different religious persuasions (which even included independent British merchants),[11] fearful of the reimposition of an earlier practical monopoly by the Lynch Company, which had started around the middle of the nineteenth century and ended in 1904.[12] During that period regular freight from Basra to Baghdad was 40s. per ton, but often rose to as much as 80s. per ton.[13] In 1904, Sultan Abdülhamid bought the old Ottoman steamship service, brought it under the administration of his private estate (the *Saniyya* administration), and gave it the new name of the *Hamidiyya* steamship company. Under the new management, the service was overhauled and the freight charges were substantially reduced. At the beginning of 1910, they stood at 25s. per ton for upriver freight and 5s.6d. per ton for downriver freight. This last figure is especially important because local merchants usually transported grain grown for export by steamships from Baghdad to Basra. Before the days of the Hamidiyya, the merchants had to pay whatever the

British charged, usually more than sevenfold the 1909–1910 rate.[14]

Thus, we can reaffirm with Hanna Batatu that: "The whole episode illustrates in an unequivocal manner how a class, threatened in its vital interests, quickly coheres, regardless of the diversity of its elements or of the differences in its religious beliefs."[15]

Yet the participants in this episode were not confined to members of the merchant class. On the more popular level, the British consul-general at Baghdad observed, on December 22, that:

It was now the talk of the Bagdad cafes that three members of the Turkish Cabinet had accepted a bribe of £T50,000 from Messrs. Lynch (!). At Kadhimain, a Shi'ah town 3 miles from Bagdad, there was a great stir on this date. Inflammatory harangues were delivered urging the people not to let the sacred land of Ali and Husain be "sold" to unbelievers, and matters reached such a pass that the shopkeepers in the bazaar closed their shops. Here a number of the demonstrators were probably not even Turkish subjects, but Persians.[16]

On December 26, the authorities reinforced the police guards near the British residency and the premises of Messrs. Lynch at Baghdad for fear of demonstrations against them.[17] Furthermore:

The merchants generally, including Oriental Christians and Jews, were at first inclined to throw in their lot with the agitation; but, as the language of the agitators grew more and more extreme, they separated themselves from it. By the end of December the agitators had the field left to themselves and the permanent following, almost entirely Mohammedans which they had succeeded in attaching to themselves. I am under the impression that this following is not now, to any great extent, of a commercial character.[18]

A few days before the resignation of Hilmi Paşa's government in Istanbul—over this and other issues—events in both Basra and Baghdad had become serious enough for the Porte to consider proclaiming martial law.[19]

Interestingly enough, popular feeling was turning against Sir William Willcocks' irrigation schemes. Willcocks, a distinguished British irrigation expert, had been commissioned by the Ottoman government to improve irrigation facilities in the

Iraqi provinces. According to the British consul-general at Baghdad there was

> a tendency for popular feeling to turn against Sir William Willcocks' schemes, which by many are regarded as a British rather than a Turkish concern. That this should have been so was not unnatural, for the dangerously foreign character of Sir William's enterprise had been insisted on by the agitators during the agitation.[20]

The correspondent of *The Times* of London was to report similar observations later:

> For a time British residents were not without anxiety that they might be made the object of a popular demonstration. At a mass meeting attended by about 5,000 people the speakers used very plain language, alleging that the British Government was supporting the amalgamation in pursuance of its policy of penetration into and absorption of Turkish Arabia. All forms of British enterprise in the country, including the irrigation projects in charge of Sir William Willcocks, who is a servant of the Turkish government, were enlarged upon as evidence of sinister intentions.[21]

We do not know for certain what specific "sinister intentions" the demonstrators were attributing to British enterprise at that point. We can only draw attention to the fact that Sir William Willcocks himself mentions in his memoirs his preference for settling Indians in Iraq. For him: "The Euphrates-Tigris delta will be reclaimed and settled by millions of natives of India, who will make it again the Garden of the East."[22]

Although the British government did not seriously consider such a project until 1914–1915, some British officials entertained the possibility of utilizing Iraq as an "outlet for the surplus population of India"[23] as early as 1906. We also know that certain elite groups in Iraq were not unaware of these ideas. When an informer in the pay of the British was visiting what appears to have been a prominent religious family in Baghdad in January 1910, a most revealing exchange took place. In the course of the conversation, the informer denied any political motives behind Willcocks' works, but was rebuffed by one of the religious dignitaries in the following manner:

> We know better. It is the same old story. The drama of Egypt shall be re-enacted in Iraq. First comes the irrigation scheme, which entails the

service of 25,000 coolies and agriculturists from India. Then, all of a sudden, it is discovered that it will be no good to make the soil productive unless there are means of exporting the superabundant produce to profitable markets. To achieve this purpose railways must be established. This means more Indians, say, 10,000 to 15,000 as railway employees, &c. Then there is the question of money, for the Turkish Government is insolvent. Sir William Willcocks obtains permission to raise a loan in England. Either the British Government or the British people find the money. The loan is raised; irrigation and railway schemes are completed. New schemes crop up and the loan is never repaid. A foolish Arab tribe makes a raid upon the Indian colony. Military intervention becomes imperative; India is near; and occupation follows and Mesopotamia becomes Egypt.[24]

Although we do not have a clear indication about the stance of the landowners, it is fair to assume that their interests would have been adversely affected by a new Lynch monopoly. The freight rate that the Lynch Company was charging the merchants on transporting grain before 1904 was "equal to 50 percent of its costs in the markets of Baghdad and thus the money which should have been coming back to enrich the agriculturists and the country generally was going to the pockets of the Lynch Company."[25]

Yet the position of the landed interests was an uneasy one. While they did not seem to back a Lynch monopoly, they looked favorably toward Willcocks' irrigation schemes, from which their agricultural estates could benefit. Their complex attitude was expressed by the *naqib al-ashraf* of Baghdad on December 27, 1909. According to the British consul-general in the city, the *naqib*

who is pecuniarily interested in irrigation of the country and who in a quiet way seems well-disposed towards things British, took up the line that irrigation and navigation are incompatible,[26] and that there can therefore be no collusion between Sir W. Willcocks and Messrs. Lynch. He had also been endeavoring to impress upon excited patriots the view that the abolition of Messrs. Lynch's perpetual concession will be advantageous purchased at the expense even of a thirty-seven years' monopoly. (This argument seems to involve an unwarranted assumption.)[27]

The Shi'i *mujtahids* were clearly against a Lynch monopoly concession. The manifestation of religious zeal at Kazimayn in particular attests to this conclusion. The British consul-general referred to a certain Shaykh Ibrahim ("Khurasani" of Kazimayn) as a "a ringleader in the disturbance which took place there on the 22nd [of December]."[28]

There was one important social element that did not express its position. It did not need to do so, since the merchants made no secret of their hostility to it. This element was the tribes. Not only did the merchants fear an interruption of river transport in the event Ottoman troops should lose access to steamers, they also suspected an alliance of sorts between the British and the tribes. Indeed, on December 25, ʿAbd al-Qadir al-Khudayri and Mahmud Shabandar "wired to the Prime Minister and others in somewhat violent language, accusing Messrs. Lynch of having in the past supplied the Arab tribes with modern rifles."[29]

In Basra, Sayyid Talib al-Naqib represented both the landed and the merchant classes.[30] Being the deputy of the city in the Ottoman parliament, he declared his position on the Lynch Concession inside the Chamber of Deputies in Istanbul. On December 14, 1909, he spoke in strong terms against the concession, stating "this will be the beginning of great Catastrophes."[31] Fearing British expansion in Iraq, Sayyid Talib was joined by a parliamentary bloc composed of forty out of a total of about sixty Arab delegates who opposed the concession.[32] The most prominent spokesmen of this bloc were Shafiq Muʾayyad al-ʿAzm (deputy of Damascus), Ahmad Pasha al-Zuhayr (deputy of Basra), Shawkat Pasha (deputy of Diwaniyya), and Khudr Lutfi (deputy of Dayr al-Zur).[33] The last explained to the Chamber, on December 13, that "We Arabs [Arab deputies] have no bad intentions toward the government. Our aim is the preservation of the safety of the fatherland (*watan*). We denounce, however, all attempts to endanger that safety by granting such economic concession to foreign companies."[34]

At this juncture it is imperative to say more about the wider political context within which this episode took place. In Istanbul there was a struggle for effective political power between the CUP and the military, headed by Mahmud Shawkat (Sevket) Paşa, who had suppressed the counterrevolution of April 1909.[35] A weak government headed by Hüseyin Hilmi Paşa was trying to keep its balance between these political groups. In the area of foreign affairs, the military opted for an Ottoman-German alliance, while the civilian CUP preferred a rapprochement with Great Britain. Furthermore, the CUP members in the Chamber did not form a monolithic body; in fact, they lacked unity.[36] Thus, while it is true that the main body of the CUP, focusing on the necessity of improving relations with London, reluctantly acquiesced with the government's amalgamation scheme, some of its members were initially opposed to it. Two cases in point are available. The first is the case of Sasson Hasqail, a Jewish financier, ex-director of the *Hamidiyya* steamship company,[37] CUP member, and deputy of Baghdad who "journeyed from Basrah up the Tigris arousing the local traders and notables to the danger that the scheme could bring."[38] The second case is that of Isma'il Haqqi Baban, a prominent CUP deputy of Baghdad. He opposed the amalgamation "on the grounds that Britain was already powerful in Iraq, and control of the river system would make her even more powerful. As a good Unionist, he wanted the Porte to strengthen its hold in Iraq, rather than make it weaker."[39]

That both Sasson and Baban were CUP members raises suspicions about whether the opposition in the Chamber was drawn up along sharp CUP/non-CUP lines. Similarly, on the Iraqi scene itself, the local CUP branches, whether in response to local pressure or out of established policy, protested to Istanbul against the *Nahriyya*-Lynch amalgamation. Moreover, a key role in the whole episode was played by 'Abd al Qadir al-Khudayri, who was a merchant as well as a high-ranking local CUP member.[40]

Thus, the dominant character of the 1909 episode was neither anti-Turk nor anti-CUP. It was protonationalistic and anti-European on the popular plane and antimonopoly capital on the mercantile plane.

The second phase of the manifestation of the anti-European pattern before World War I in Iraq occurred in 1913. In this case it was directly linked with the movement of proto-Arab nationalism.

The Ottoman government was in very tight financial situation after two wars, one with Italy over Tripoli in 1911–1912, the other in the Balkans in 1912–1913. It seems that the Ottoman government's leaders thought they could acquire badly needed funds by selling concessions for exploiting the lands formerly owned by Sultan Abdülhamid (the *Saniyya* or Crown lands), but transferred in 1909 to the Finance Ministry[41] and brought under direct state control and renamed the *mudawwara* lands, the *çiftliks* (referred to generally as *miri*, or state lands). On February 10, 1913, *The Times* correspondent reported from Istanbul that "a [European] Jewish group . . . [has] offered an immediate advance for the concession of certain Crown Lands in Syria and Palestine which, presumably, it proposed to colonize."[42] Less than two weeks later the same newspaper reported (again from Istanbul) that "the Council of Ministers are discussing a new law of Real Property which will permit the sale or transfer of land to corporations, not only, as heretofore, to persons. The promulgation of the law will presumably be followed at no distant date by the establishment of mortgage banks and kindred institutions in Turkey."[43] By July 1913, Arab newspapers were carrying the news that the Ministry of Finance had auctioned the *mudawwara* lands in the provinces of Baghdad, Mosul, Syria, Beirut, Maʿmurat al-ʿAziz, Sivas, and Aleppo.[44] One paper's estimate of the area of the lands involved was put at 28 million dunums.[45] *Al-Mufid* of Beirut said that this was "a matter of grave danger . . . all Ottomans, especially those who live in the provinces that have large areas of state land, should look into this matter wisely, not overlooking its consequences."[46]

There is some room to suspect that if the proposed 1913 auction had been carried out along the lines of an earlier aborted one, it would have been in fact confined to the *mudawwara* lands of the provinces of Baghdad, Aleppo, Beirut, and Syria.[47]

Whether that was the case or not is a matter open for further research. Nevertheless, the whole issue was of particular importance in the above-mentioned Arab provinces. It was looked at against the background of Jewish immigration to Palestine, on the one hand, and the fear of Western economic and political penetration on the other. According to a British source, the Arab press, for example, held that "the acquisition of such vast tracts of land by foreign Capitalists would be the first step towards foreign occupation, and in the case of Palestine the further argument of the 'Jewish Peril' is adduced."[48]

Moreover, the Arabs could have perceived, rightly or wrongly, an element of Turkish anti-Arab mischief in the whole affair. One can imagine what impression was left on them when Arabic newspapers reported, for example, the unconfirmed yet startling news that Husayn Jahid (Cahid), the CUP deputy and editor of the influential *Tanin* of Istanbul, told one editor of an Arabic newspaper published in Beirut that if the Arabs persisted in opposing the central government, the Turks would sell the Arab countries to foreigners and invest the proceeds in Anatolia.[49]

The news of the proposed project for auctioning the *mudawwara* lands traveled fast. On July 19, 1913, a British correspondent writing from Basra (where the populace was not sure whether the province was exempted from the auction)[50] reported that:

Considerable excitement has been caused in the town by a report that the Senia property (i.e., the lands formerly owned by the ex-sultan) is about to be sold to a foreigner—according to one version, a London Jew. The leading Arabs have held a meeting of protest, and declared that this will not be tolerated. The affair seems to have brought the long-existent dissatisfaction to a head, and last night the Arabs, headed by Seyd Talib, telegraphed to Constantinople demanding that no part of the revenues of the *Vilayet* should be forwarded to the capital, and that only three Turkish officials—the *Vali*, the Commandant, and a judge—should be left here.

The Government telegraphed instructions to the *Vali* to declare martial law, obtaining assistance from Baghdad if necessary. The *Vali*, however, is afraid to act. Today business is at a standstill in the town, Seyd Talib having ordered that all shops should be shut and prohibited gharries and bellums (the local gondola) from plying for hire.... The Arabs all along the Euphrates are in a state of ferment. They declare that they know now that there is no longer any government with power to act.[51]

In another letter, this one dated July 26, the same correspondent added:

The Vali has resigned, and it is stated that he will leave immediately. One report has it that he has been dismissed, but it is impossible to find out the truth of this yet. It is observed that Seyd Talib absented himself from the official reception given by the Vali last Wednesday—the National Holiday; and the next day the Vali resigned. Until the arrival of the new Governor, the Commandant, Izzet Bey, will act. He is reported to be on very intimate terms with Seyd Talib. The latter had intended going to India for his health's sake, but he has now postponed his visit.[52]

The July 19 letter is particularly important not only because it mentions the sale of the *mudawwara* lands to foreigners as the source of trouble, but also because it gives an idea of the magnitude and dimension of the episode by pointing to the fact that "the Arabs all along the Euphrates"[53] were involved in it. In this context, "Arabs" should be read as "Arab tribes." We get an even more excited picture when we travel upstream on the Tigris. In Baghdad, the center of the province, where the *mudawwara* lands were said "to cover more than half"[54] (or, according to another source, 30 percent) of its cultivated lands[55] the situation was quite serious. A meeting attended by "Iraqi notables including merchants, landowners, ʿulamaʾ, journalists, lawyers, and some Arab [tribal] Amirs took place in the National Scientific Club."[56]

The meeting took two decisions. First, it elected as president none other than ʿAbd al-Qadir Pasha al-Khudayri, who does not seem to have retained his past affiliation with the CUP. Second, it decided to arrange for a large demonstration to protest the sale of these lands.

When the organizers petitioned the *wali* for permission to proceed with their plans, the latter, acting under extreme pressure, granted permission, but cabled the Ministry of Interior at the same time describing in "strong words" the dangers the central government would face because of its land sale project. The government, sensing that the situation was about to get out of hand, backed down. Talât Bey, the minister of the interior, after consultations at the Porte, cabled back to Baghdad explaining that "the Government had auctioned the *mudawwara* lands in order to finalise a financial transaction of which it was very needy. However, since the Government was able to have access to some funds in a different manner, there was no longer any need to sell the State lands.... On the contrary, [Talât Bey went on in his volte-face cable] the Government has formed a special committee to study a legislation that would permit settling the tribes and distributing the[se] lands among them."[57]

Concurrently with these developments, another issue was brought into the open again. At the beginning of 1913, after the Hürriyet ve Ittilaf opposition party held office between July 1912 and January 1913, the CUP, once again in power in Istanbul, started a fresh effort to improve British-Ottoman relations. In this context, Hakki Paşa, minister plenipotentiary and extraordinary of the Ottoman government arrived in London in February 1913. His instructions were "to leave no stone unturned to settle outstanding differences with Great Britain."[58] After months of negotiations between Hakki Paşa and Sir Edward Grey, the British secretary of state for foreign affairs, an Anglo-Ottoman agreement was reached in May 1913. Britain was to support an increase of 4 percent of the custom duties of the Ottoman Empire. In return, Istanbul recognized the special position of Great Britain in the Persian Gulf, pledged a policy of noninterference in the affairs of Kuwait, agreed to make Basra (not Kuwait) the terminus of the Baghdad Railway, and permitted the election of two British citizens to the board of directors of the Baghdad Railway company.[59] Furthermore, navigation by steamers and barges on the Tigris, the Euphrates, and the Shatt al-ʿArab was to form a monopoly granted to an international company of which the shares were to be divided equally between Great Britain and the Ottoman government. The international company, "the Ottoman River Navigation Company," was to be headed by Lord Inchcape (chairman of the Peninsula and Oriental and the British Steam Navigation companies), who would also represent British interests.[60]

Equally important, the agreement provided for establishing a joint Ottoman-British commission to supervise and police navigation along the Shatt al-ʿArab waterway. The commission was to enjoy the treaty rights normally exercised by foreign powers under the Capitulations and to have the right to levy dues and to exercise the rights that the government would normally possess at the Port of Basra when that should have been built. Furthermore, the commission "was to deal directly with the central government and not through local authorities of the area."[61] In short, the agreement seems to have satisfied Britain's long-standing position that it possessed "certain rights and privileges"[62] with regard to navigation on the Tigris, the Euphrates, and the Shatt al-ʿArab. Regardless of whether they were "rights" or "privileges," *The Times* of London described them as being essential for "giving British trade an independent right of access to the markets of Mesopotamia."[63]

A British-Ottoman draft convention was signed on July 29, 1913.[64] In reaction to it[65] and to the *mudawwara* lands auction scheme, the Basra Reform Committee formed in February of the same year[66] and led by Sayyid Talib al-Naqib, changed its priorities. In February it advocated virtually complete autonomy, claiming, according to the British consul in the city "the right of employing local revenue for local purposes, the balance only, if any, being remitted for Constantinople after these requirements have been satisfied."[67] In April it somewhat toned down its demands but rejected the new law of March 26 on provincial administration that was designed to establish a quasi-autonomous administration in the Ottoman provinces. The Committee perceived the new law as another attempt at centralization through the vali rather than through the capital in Istanbul. It took issue principally with the clauses that gave the *wali* wide powers over the local general council, which was controlled by the notables.[68]

By contrast, the detailed program of the committee, published in August, showed a distinctly different orientation. Although the notables insisted on their demands for local control, they projected a subtle attempt to construct a delicate compromise between matters local and matters imperial. Articles 4 and 16 make this point clear.[69] Article 4 states:

Matters relating to this [central] authority and its branches, e.g., foreign and military affairs, customs, posts, telegraphs, laws, regulations, dues, and taxes appertain to the central government, but local matters relating to the internal concerns of the vilayet, its administration, progress, and development appertain to the General Council of the vilayet.

Similarly, Article 16 states:

Revenue is of two kinds. Customs receipts, posts, telegraphs, and military exemption tax appertain to the central Government entirely. The rest belongs to the vilayet and is to be spent in it.

More significant still is the fact that Sayyid Talib warned British Consul Crow on April 28 that the Basra notables "would not hesitate to resort to methods of violence in order to attain their ends."[70] But he assured him that "as far as the Arab notables themselves were concerned, *British interests would be respected*" (emphasis added).[71]

By contrast again, the August program of the committee declared, in a somewhat horrified and assertive tone: "No concessions to be given to foreigners in Irak. Foreigners to be repelled, the country to be protected from their intrigues, and foreign influence to be checked in every way."[72]

A British correspondent reported in October that native opinion in both Baghdad and Basra was "not unnaturally . . . exercised over the subject" of Hakki Paşa's negotiations.[73] In Basra:

> the energetic Sayyid Talib called together a meeting of the leading Arabs, and a protest against the Turkish boats being allowed to fall into foreign hands was drawn up and handed to the Vali for transmission to Constantinople. It is even said that the protestants offered to form a native company to take the boats over on the same terms as the English company, whichever it may be, to which they are being offered. This agitation, it may be advisable to point out, is not due to any ill feeling against either B[ritish] I[ndia] or Messrs. Lynch, both of which firms are, in fact, quite popular; but it is a part of the policy of keeping *"Arabia for the Arabs,"* which Sayyid Talib and his adherents wish to see followed [emphasis added].[74]

When accused of being intent on merely gaining provincial autonomy for the *wilaya* (*vilayet*) of Basra, Sayyid Talib himself came out into the open to explain his position. In a long proclamation,[75] he denied any motives for such schemes describing the *wilaya* as "exclusively Ottoman" (*'uthmaniyya mahda*). He accused those who circulate such rumors of trying to sow discord within the ranks of "the oppressed Arab nation," to distract it from seeking reform and remaining thus under despotic rule, deprived of its just rights, "threatened by the dangers of this Western torrent that has come with the insistent intention of acquiring it [the Arab nation] whether it likes it or not." As for the CUP leaders, Sayyid Talib described them as atheists who deprived the Islamic caliphate of its power and who were auctioning the Islamic countries in European capitals in a way similar to the slave trade. For him, the CUP sold Tripoli, "this Arab country which is purely Muslim," to Italy and were intent on selling "Palestine to the Jews of foreign nationalities."

There is a great deal of rhetoric in all of this, but Sayyid Talib was more specific when he spoke about Iraq:

> They [the CUP] sent Haqqi Pasha, their clever merchant, to London to sell the Iraqi assets. He did in fact start to do so gradually. . . . Thus they granted her [Great Britain] the right of inspection at Basra and the Persian Gulf and granted her an important concession that can destroy the whole of Iraq, namely forming companies to navigate both

the Tigris and the Euphrates in addition to the railway concession from Baghdad to Basra to Kuwait.[76] Furthermore, they put up the Mudawwara [or] Crown lands to auction in Istanbul, granting only thirty days for the period of auction, making it impossible for the tribes to buy their own lands, thus these lands would be sold to foreigners.[77]

Sayyid Talib's proclamation does not prove that he was not working for autonomy, yet he and the Basra Reform Committee found themselves between the hammer and the anvil. They realized that autonomy meant distancing themselves not only from Istanbul but from Britain and British India in the first place. Both the anti-European and anticentralization patterns are well reflected in the committee's program.

Sayyid Talib might have had an ulterior motive in feeling ill at ease at the prospect of the formation of the Ottoman-British Commission, which was invested with wide powers to execute the rules concerning the navigation and policing of the Shatt al-ʿArab waterway. The commission had the independent power to inflict penalties on violators of those rules.[78] There is no escaping the fact that Sayyid Talib was engaged in acts of "freeboating" and "undertakings of piratical emprise at the bar or in the river."[79] Though a landed *sayyid*, he was not very wealthy by Iraqi standards of his time. According to one source, part of the funding for his political activities was "obtained by levies . . . on wealthy Arabs in southern Iraq."[80]

There is more to be said about Sayyid Talib's political activities. Generally speaking, he was a maverick who tried to cultivate good relations with different and opposing power bases, apparently with the intent of establishing himself as the arbiter among them all.[81] In regard to the two most influential powers in his region—the Turks and the British—he seems to have been playing each against the other. He was, of course, opposed to Ottoman centralization policies and tried to keep effective local authority in the *wilaya* of Basra in his own hands. But, as we have observed earlier, Sayyid Talib's greatest worry was not Turkish domination but increasing British economic and political penetration. This fact may explain why the Turkish authorities tried to win him back at the end of 1913 and why he was also ready to meet the Turks halfway.[82] By early 1914 he reached an agreement with Istanbul ending his differences with the central government and pledging to preserve "Ottoman unity."[83]

One can only wonder if the abortion of the *mudawwara* lands sale and/or the postponement and later nonratification of the British-Ottoman draft convention had anything to do with this rapprochement.[84]

Sayyid Talib may have acquiesced with the conversion of the nonratified convention into a tripartite Anglo-German-Ottoman draft convention a year later in July 1914.[85] Yet this does not seem to have endeared him to the British nor did it endear the latter to the majority of the population of Basra. In August 1914, the British acting-consul at Basra remarked that "all Moslems in the town were anti-British."[86] A month earlier some British officials had described Sayyid Talib as "a worthless and corrupt intriguer" and of being of "untrustworthy" character.[87] Indeed, during the same month, the Ottoman minister of the interior told Sir Louis Mallet, the British ambassador to Istanbul "in confidence that he was recalling the Vali of Basra, who is quite discredited, and means to appoint Sayyid Talib in his place."[88] A week later, the ambassador, under instructions from London, visited the minister and apparently convinced him to abandon the appointment.[89]

On the social plane it is evident from the foregoing that there existed a coalition of many Iraqi classes and groups that were opposed to colonization and foreign capital penetration. The meeting held in Baghdad in protest against the proposed sale of *mudawwara* lands included landowners, merchants, *'ulama'*, tribal amirs (emirs), journalists, and lawyers.

That the tribal element was not excluded in the second phase is of particular importance because of the hostility the merchants exhibited in the first phase. It is possible that some of the tribal amirs sensed that the sale of the *mudawwara* lands would be the first step in a process that would ultimately displace their tribes. In this regard, it is relevant to quote a British editor who wrote, in 1916, that "a change of rule would be beneficial to all the inhabitants of Mesopotamia with the possible exception of the bedouins. We sympathize with them, but of course they could not be allowed to occupy indefinitely such splendid lands they neither use nor allow others to use."[90]

At any rate, the program of the Basra Reform Committee of 1913 was attentive to the interests of the landowners and the merchants as well as to those of the tribes.[91] Article 11 of the program suggested selling or distributing the state lands among these groups: "Lands to which the title has lapsed and *miri* lands in the vilayet are to be handed over to the [local] General Council, which may sell what is required or build, and may distribute vacant lands among the tribes."[92]

The most striking feature of the 1913 episode, in comparison with its prelude in 1909, was the association the Arabs of Iraq began to draw between British or European designs on the one hand and CUP policies on the other. Iraqi Arabs, at that point, perceived the CUP to be in league with foreigners. Resisting the latter of necessity implied resisting the former. Unlike 1909, no CUP voices made common cause with indigenous Iraqi sentiments. Sasson Hasqail, for example, who was agitating, for whatever motives,[93] against a British monopoly in river navigation in 1909, had a reverse role in 1913. He accompanied Hakki Paşa to London where he assisted in arriving at the British-Ottoman draft convention of June 29.[94]

Nevertheless, this anti-European aspect of the Iraqi version of "Arab nationalism" was not incompatible with Ottomanism. Instead, it pushed the two concepts closer together. The Arabs sought in this instance to ally themselves with the Ottoman Caliph, the symbol of Islamic authority, against the CUP which was perceived as representative of Turkish nationalism. The first and third articles of the Basra Reform Committee's program state: "Our dear fatherland (*watan*) shall be an exclusively Ottoman territory under the Banner of the Crescent"; and: "The Ottoman state (al-dawla al-ʿaliyya) is a Muslim state under the sovereignty of the supreme Caliph of the Muslims and not an Empire as held by those devoid of virtue."[95]

Remarking on these articles, Sir Charles Marling, the British chargé d'affaires in Istanbul, acutely observed, "It may be noticed that the underlying tendency in the Basra Programme is one of aversion from the rule of the Committee of Union and Progress, rather than that of separation from the Ottoman 'Turkish' Government."[96]

In fact, "Ottomanism" was an integral part of the basic ideology of the mainstream "Arab nationalists" before World War I in Iraq. Thus, it is possible to speak of "Arab-Ottoman nationalism" as a concept that attempted to reconcile Arab resistance to Europe's designs and CUP policies with the Arabs' need to retain a workable relationship with Istanbul. After all, and ironically, the Arabs needed the Turks to counterbalance European encroachment on their lands. Clinging to the traditional framework of the Ottoman caliphate was the loose formula that served both goals. Decentralization and autonomy—not separation and independence—were thought to be the way out.

In his seminal work on modern Iraq, Hanna Batatu was not concerned with a comprehensive study of "Arab nationalism" during the period of the Young Turks. Concentrating on the role of the landed *sadah* in the movement and on class conflict as one of its aspects, he notes, "Arab 'nationalism' in its incipient form proved to be the palladium of their class—the last dyke of the old order, so to say."[97] He goes on to add:

> it is not only concern for their Arab cultural identity or for the old Islamic beliefs that drove the *sadah* and other Arab landed magnates to seek autonomy. They sought it also for the same reason that the privileged Turkish pashas sought the downfall of the Young Turks, that is, to prolong the life of the old social institutions from which they benefitted. It is more in this light than as a manifestation of authentic nationalism that the *sadah*'s demand for autonomy must be viewed.[98]

This may well have been the case. But for our purpose here it is necessary to speak of other aspects and other social elements that were instrumental in pushing the movement to the surface.

The rise of "Arab nationalism," or of "Arab-Ottoman nationalism" took place in a complex and paradoxical historical framework. It was a response to policies of increased Turkish centralization and schemes of European colonization. If the response to the first process was not an expression of "authentic nationalism," the response to the second was.

Originating from different termini, the prospects of centralization and colonization simultaneously hit all components of Iraqi society, high and low, whether they were part of the traditional social structure or the still embryonic modern one. The common defense of class, territory, nation, and religion was activated. The conjuncture allowed likewise for the simultaneous deployment of diverse terminologies in the ensuing ideological engagement. The terms "fatherland" (*watan*), "reform" (implying autonomy), "Basra," "Iraq," "Arab nation," "Ottoman caliphate," and "Islam" were all concurrently used in the face of the dual challenge. If Sayyid Talib's cry "Arabia for the

Arabs"[99] was raised in Basra against the Europeans, the cry "Iraq for the Iraqis" was raised in Baghdad in the face of the Young Turks.[100]

For the long socioeconomic view, the conclusion of the present study is in basic agreement with Batatu's main thesis. He finds the sources of post-World War I's "insurrectionary trend" (which was manifested above all in the 1920 armed uprising against British occupation) in the structural consequence of integrating the country into the world market economy.[101] This process, which started in the nineteenth century, dislocated and undermined the traditional social fabric:

> old local economies, based on the handicraft of boat-building industries and the traditional means of transport (camels and sailing ships) declined or broke asunder; a tribal tillage, essentially self-sufficient and subordinate to pastoralism, gave way to a settled, market-related, tribal agriculture.

From this it is deduced that

> the moving spirits of the agitation against dominance by the English that culminated in the 1920 armed uprising sprang from *chalabis* bound up with the old modes of transport; or from "aristocrat" officials connected with the former Ottoman administration; or from the *mujtahids* and *'ulama'*, the chief exponents of the hereditary social conceptions; or from landed tribal shaikhs or tribal *sadah*, who resented the unaccustomed rigor in English revenue collection or had been badly affected by the English management of the Euphrates waters.

The point at which we arrive, then, is that pre-1914 "Arab nationalism" in Iraq was, essentially, a reaction to a high pitch in this same general process described above by Batatu. Looked at from this angle, it is easy to perceive the common features between the anti-European episode of 1913 and the armed uprising of 1920. The former was the forerunner of the latter.

Two further points must be made regarding the merchants' vigorous defense of their interests in river transportation. The first is that this class was trying neither to dominate Iraq's international trade, which had by then become a virtual British monopoly,[102] nor to dominate the country's internal trade (or even the river transport), since the merchants did not call for the abolition of the foreign companies' right to navigate these rivers. The real bone of contention was the local merchants' share in the internal Tigris and Euphrates trade or the competition from which they were benefiting, both of which were threatened by foreign monopoly capital.

The other point that bears special emphasis has to do with a statement by Batatu about the Iraqi social groups that agitated against British dominance in the 1920 armed uprising. One of these groups, according to him, were "the *chalabis* bound up with the old modes of transport."[103] This is certainly true. The key role that Ja'far Abu al-Timman played in 1920 attests to this conclusion. His family had "heavy investments in camels and sailing ships" and could have "naturally suffered from the country's shift to new forms of transportation."[104] But we can add now that the *chabalis* who employed modern modes of river transport had a prominent role in opposing British dominance before World War I. The British Lynch Company, the Ottoman *Nahriyya* Company, and al-Khudayri's freelance steamers were all employing the same mode of transport. 'Abd al-Qadir al-Khudayri's business was not threatened by a superior mode of technology in 1909 and 1913, but by one that was basically monopolistic and foreign in nature.

What accounts, then, for Abu al-Timman's relatively minor role, in comparison to al-Khudayri's, in anti-British agitation before the war and his key role in the 1920 uprising? In the same spirit, what accounts for al-Khudayri's active participation against the British amalgamation schemes before the war and his passivity after the war?

A partial clue may be located in the fact that British attempts to monopolize river transport on the Tigris and the Euphrates before the war applied only to steamers. It exempted sailing ships and boats. Evidently, al-Khudayri was to be the party hard hit by the prospect of a monopoly. It seems that it was the fear of losing his steamers that drove him to join hands with Ja'far Abu al-Timman in 1910 to form the "Iraqi sailing ships company."[105] There is nothing to indicate that the venture did actually come to fruition. On the contrary, circumstantial evidence suggests that al-Khudayri was engaged in some business dealings with the British during and directly after the war.[106] Later on, in 1924, the al-Khudayri steamers were absorbed by British interests.[107] On the other hand, Abu al-Timman's old modes of transport could have felt the brunt of competition with the new modes after the war.

It is worthwhile, finally, to repeat that my research has focused on the anti-Western pattern within early "Arab nationalism" in Iraq. There is enough evidence to suggest that the pattern of anti-Turkish dominance was not dormant in the social, political, or intellectual realms.[108] Yet in referring to the former as the major pattern, this study is merely underlining the central sociopolitical fact in the Arab Ottoman East during the late nineteenth and the early twentieth centuries. This fact, which is often overlooked when addressing the issue of early Arab nationalism, emphasizes that if the Turk, as the administrator of the Ottoman Empire, was above the Arab, the European, by virtue of his economic clout and political/military might, was above both Arab and Turk.

Notes

I would like to express my gratitude to Hanna Batatu for his criticisms on an earlier draft. I am also grateful to Richard Bulliet, J. C. Hurewitz, Rashid Khalidi, Reeva Simon, and Muhammad Muslih for their astute suggestions and to Najla Fahd for her assistance with the research for this paper.

1. Tawfiq ʿAli Birru, *al-ʿArab wal-turk fil-ʿahd al-dusturi al-ʿuthmani, 1908–1914* [The Arabs and the Turks during the Ottoman constitutional era, 1908–1914], p. 129.
2. Memorandum by Consul-General Lorimer respecting "Affaire Lynch in Irak (December and January 1910)." Enclosure 2 in a letter dated January 31, 1910, from Consul-General Lorimer, Baghdad, to Sir G. Lowther, Istanbul. Foreign Office Archives, Public Record Office, London, FO 424/222, pp. 101–6 (hereafter, "Memorandum").
3. Ibid., pp. 101–4.
4. ʿAbd al-Razzaq al-Darraji, *Jaʿfar Abu al-Timman wa dawruhu fi al-haraka al-wataniyya fil-ʿIraq* [Jaʿfar Abu al-Timman and his role in the national movement in Iraq], p. 38.
5. Hanna Batatu, *The Old Social Classes and the Revolutionary Movement of Iraq*, p. 293.
6. Ibid., p. 294.
7. "Memorandum," p. 105.
8. Faysal Muhammad al-Arhayyam, *Tatuwwur al-ʿIraq taht hukm al-*

itihadiyyin [The development of Iraq under the rule of the Unionists], p. 241.
9. Stephen Hemsley Longrigg, *Iraq, 1900 to 1950: A Political, Social, and Economic History* (London: 1953), p. 61.
10. Batatu, *Old Social Classes*, pp. 242–43. Ibrahim, the son of Mahmud al-Shabandar, is the only Muslim name that appears on the earliest available list of the "First Class" merchants of the Baghdad Chamber of Commerce for 1938–1939. All the other twenty-four members were either foreigners or non-Muslims (see table 9–4, "'First Class' Members of the Baghdad Chamber of Commerce...," in ibid., p. 246). It should be noted, however, that a letter dated August 25, 1911, indicates that a member of the Khudayri family, ʿAbd al-Jabbar, resident of Basra, was the agent of Messrs. Andrew Weir & Co., of London. FO 602/53.
11. See letter of February 7, 1910, from Mr. Cree, a partner of the British firm Blockey, Cree and Co., to the editor of *Truth* (FO 424/222, pp. 158–62).
12. Ibid., pp. 160–61. See also "The Story of the Euphrates Company," p. 150; and Batatu, *Old Social Classes*, p. 239.
13. Mr. Cree's letter, pp. 160–61 (see note 11 above).
14. Ibid.
15. Batatu, *Old Social Classes*, p. 282.
16. "Memorandum," p. 104.
17. Ibid., p. 105.
18. Ibid.
19. Technically, the Ottoman government of Hilmi Paşa won a vote of confidence over the Lynch affair in the Chamber. However, awakened to the fact that it could neither grant the concession for fear of British expansion in Iraq, nor reject the British for reasons of foreign policy, the government resigned on December 28, 1909. See Feroz Ahmad, *The Young Turks*, pp. 65–67.
20. "Memorandum," p. 105.
21. "Baghdad Trade and Politics," *The Times*, June 11, 1910, pp. 7–8.
22. Sir William Willcocks, *Sixty Years in the East* (London: 1935), p. 72. Willcocks ignored a similar proposal in 1905. See also Stuart Cohen, *British Policy in Mesopotamia, 1903–1914*, p. 141.
23. Cohen, *British Policy*.
24. "Memorandum," p. 107.
25. Mr. Cree's letter (note 11 above).
26. Willcocks had indicated in 1909 that the irrigation works would consume so much water that the Euphrates and the Tigris would become unnavigable. See Cohen, *British Policy in Mesopotamia*, p. 177.
27. "Memorandum," p. 105.

28. Ibid., p. 104.
29. Ibid., p. 105.
30. The first administrative council of the "Liberty and Accord party" that Sayyid Talib formed in Basra in 1911 in opposition to the CUP was composed (aside from Sayyid Talib himself) of three landowners, two merchants, one lawyer, and one newspaper editor. See Ghassan R. Atiyyah, *Iraq: 1908–1921*, p. 58; and Sulayman Faydi, *Fi ghamrat al-nidal* [In the deluge of struggle] (Baghdad: 1952), p. 96.
31. Birru, *al-ʿArab wal-turk*, p. 183.
32. Ahmad, *The Young Turks*, p. 67.
33. For details on the parliamentary discussions regarding the affair, see Birru, *al-ʿArab wal-turk*, pp. 180–87; and Tag Mohammad Harran, "Turkish-Syrian Relations in the Ottoman Constitutional Period, 1908–1914" (Ph.D. Thesis, University of London, 1969), pp. 149–50.
34. Cited in Harran, "Turkish-Syrian Relations," p. 149.
35. Ahmad, *The Young Turks*, p. 56.
36. Ibid., pp. 54–55.
37. See "Government Steamers on Tigris, 1904," in Charles Issawi, *The Fertile Crescent, 1800–1914*, pp. 249–50.
38. Batatu, *Old Social Classes*, p. 275. As for Hasqail's motives, however, Sir G. Lowther, the British ambassador in Istanbul, reported that he was "supported financially by Germany" in order to fight British influence in Iraq. See telegram of June 20, 1909, form Sir Lowther, Istanbul, to Sir Edward Grey, London. FO 424/219, p. 190.
39. Ahmad, *The Young Turks*, p. 56, n. 6.
40. Batatu, *Old Social Classes*, p. 314.
41. Walid Khadduri, "Social Background of Modern Iraqi Politics" (Ph.D. Thesis, Johns Hopkins University, 1970), p. 249.
42. "Turkish Efforts to Raise a Loan," *The Times*, February 10, 1913, p. 7.
43. "The Committee and the Army," *The Times*, February 22, 1913, p. 5.
44. "Al-Aradi al-ʿamiriyya," *al-Mufid*, July 7, 1913, p. 2.
45. A *dunum* equals 0.618 acres.
46. "Al-Aradi al-ʿamiriyya," *al-Mufid*, July 7, 1913.
47. "A Turkish Chartered Company," *The Near East and the Anglo-Egyptian Mail* (hereafter *The Near East*), October 1910, p. 123.
48. "Notes from Beirut," *The Near East*, August 22, 1913, p. 448.
49. An Egyptian newspaper published an accounts of Cahid's conversation with Taha al-Mudawar, the editor of the pro-CUP *al-Raʾi al-ʿAmm* of Beirut. When *al-Haqiqa* of Beirut republished an account of this conversation, the authorities closed it down for an indefinite

period of time (see *al-Muqattam*, July 20, 1913, p. 2). Interestingly enough, Cahid had written earlier, on March 16, 1911, in *Tanin* itself, an article describing Istanbul's dilemma in dealing with foreign capitalists. He considered the question from two standpoints—the situation of the government vis-à-vis the foreign capitalists, and the sentiment of public opinion toward the government. Cahid urged the government not to be too exacting in its attitude toward the foreign capitalists since that might drive them to withdraw from the country. Furthermore, his description of the situation concerning this matter was quite telling: "In all negotiations undertaken with a group of financiers, while on the one side the Government is afraid of being duped, public opinion on the other is afraid that the men in power are in league with the capitalists" (cited in "Foreign Capital in Turkey," *The Near East*, March 1911, p. 220).

50. That was according to a telegram sent from *al-Dustur*, a newspaper published at Basra, to the Beiruti newspaper, *al-Mufid* (see *al-Mufid*, July 7, 1913, p. 3). According to the telegram, the *mudawwara* lands were to be sold within a month in Istanbul.
51. "The Unrest at Basreh," *The Near East*, August 29, 1913, p. 476. Since the same company proposed buying the *mudawwara* lands in Palestine as well, it was described by some Arabic newspapers as a "Zionist Company" (see "Anba' al-ʿIraq," *al-Muqtabas*, August 14, 1913, p. 1). For an account of the protest against selling the *mudawwara* lands in Palestine, see Mandel, *The Arabs and Zionism*, pp. 167–68.
52. "The Unrest at Basreh," *The Near East*, August 29, 1913.
53. See note 50 above.
54. "A Turkish Chartered Company," *The Near East*, October 1910.
55. Khadduri, "Social Background," p. 218.
56. "ʾAnba ʾal-bilad al-ʿarabiyya," *al-Muqtabas*, August 14, 1913, p. 1.
57. Ibid.
58. Edward Mead Earle, *Turkey, the Great Powers and the Baghdad Railway: A Study in Imperialism* (New York: 1924), p. 255.
59. Ibid., pp. 255–56.
60. Ibid.
61. Maybelle Kennedy Chapman, *Great Britain and the Baghdad Railway*, (Northampton: 1948), p. 158.
62. "British Interests in the Gulf," *The Times*, May 17, 1913, p. 8.
63. Ibid.
64. G. P. Gooch and Harold Temperley, eds., *British Documents on the Origins of the War, 1898–1914* (London: His Majesty's Stationery Office, 1939), 10:2.183–94.
65. This convention was never ratified. See J. C. Hurewitz, ed., *The*

Middle East and North Africa, 1:567. It should be noted, however, that Edward Earle *(Turkey and the Great Powers)* mistakenly mentions that it was.

66. One source mentions that "On February 20, 1913, at a meeting in Sayyid Talib's house a petition was signed by the notables of Basra, condemning the deteriorating social and economic conditions in the *wilaya* and requesting the establishment of a General Council of the *wilaya*. For the notables of Basra the General Council of the *wilaya* would enable them to control the expenditures of the local revenue" (cited in Atiyyah, *Iraq: 1908–1921*, p. 66). See also Birru, *al-ʿArab wal-turk*, p. 490.
67. Telegram of February 24, 1913, from Consul Crow, Basra, to Sir G. Lowther, Istanbul. Enclosure 1 in No. 171 FO 424/237, p. 119.
68. Telegram of April 29, 1913, from Consul Crow, Basra, to Sir G. Lowther, Istanbul. Enclosure in No. 237 FO 424/238, pp. 260–61.
69. "Programme of the Basra Reform Committee." Enclosure 2 in No. 13. Letter dated August 28, 1913, from Consul Crow, Basra, to Chargé d'Affaires Marling, Istanbul, FO 424/240, pp. 13–14 (hereafter "Programme").
70. However, Sayyid Talib frankly admitted that "a condition of things might arise which could be beyond their [the notables] control, and he anticipated general danger from excess on the part of the lower classes of the population if they got out of hand in the course of these events." It is this last part of Sayyid Talib's remarks that stimulated the British consul to suggest dispatching British ships-of-war to Basra "in order to protect British lives and property if threatened" (ibid.). See also Phillip Willard Ireland, *Iraq: A Study in Political Development* (New York: 1939), pp. 233–34.
71. "Programme," FO 424/238.
72. Ibid.
73. "Tigris Navigation Question," *The Near East*, November 28, 1913, p. 101.
74. Ibid. Interestingly enough, Lord Inchcape strongly suspected that Mr. Lynch was mobilizing Turkish opinion against the concession. See telegram of October 31, 1913, from Sir Edward Grey, London, to Sir Louis Mallet, Istanbul. FO 424/240, p. 61.
75. This proclamation was first published in *al-Dustur*, a newspaper in Basra and picked up by the Damascene *al-Muqtabas* (see "al-Nahda al-ʿarabiyya," *al-Muqtabas*, September 14, 1913, p. 1). Strangely enough, there is no trace of this proclamation in the British Archives nor is there a discussion of the local reaction to the Anglo-Ottoman convention or the project of the *Saniyya* lands sale. On the contrary, British Consul Crow at Basra was content to comment on the second article of the program of the Basra Reform

Committee as follows: "I hardly think this clause expresses the unanimous opinion of the country on the subject. My own experience is that, apart from a small chauvinistic element chiefly formed by Turks and officials, popular sentiment is generally not averse to the development of Irak under foreign auspices. The Arabs are Anglophile, and are certainly much drawn toward India; they are, however, less fond of the Germans." Enclosure 1 in No. 13, letter dated August 29, 1913, from Consul Crow, Basra, to Mr. Marling, Istanbul. FO 424/240, p. 12.

76. Sayyid Talib was not very precise in regard to the railway concession point.
77. "Al-nahda al-ʿarabiyya," *al-Muqtabas*, September 14, 1913.
78. See Articles 6(c), 7, and 8 of the "Anglo-Turkish Agreement" in Gooch and Temperley, *British Documents*, pp. 183–87.
79. Batatu, *Old Social Classes*, p. 164.
80. Ireland, *Iraq*, p. 232.
81. A good biographical work on Sayyid Talib is lacking. For a glimpse into his political vicissitudes see: Phillip Graves, *The Life of Sir Percy Cox* (London: n.d.), pp. 171–72; Elie Kedourie, *England and the Middle East*, pp. 204–5; Makki Shabikah, *al-ʿArab wal-siyasa al-baritaniyya fil-harb al-ʿalamiyya al-ʿula* [The Arabs and British policy during the first world war], pp. 33–34, 46–55 (1970 ed.), pp. 41–46 (1975 ed.).
82. Atiyyah, *Iraq: 1908–1921*, p. 67. In 1911, Sayyid Talib refused a British offer to protect and patronize his then anti-CUP political activities (see Faydi, *Fi ghamrat al-nidal*, pp. 97–98).
83. According to Atiyyah, this agreement was reached in January 1914; al-Arhayyam, however, gives April as its date (see Atiyyah, *Iraq: 1908–1921*, p. 67; al-Arhayyam *Tatuwwur al-ʿIraq*, p. 226).

Although the Ottoman government had a policy of trying to come to terms with Great Britain in order to counterbalance Russian pressure on the empire, it was not at all content with the British posture in Iraq, particularly at Basra. On December 26, 1910, Ismaʿil Haqqi Baban, the CUP deputy of Baghdad, wrote in *Tanin:* "At whatever part of Basra you look, a thousand different things connected with England will immediately strike your attention and you will feel how deep the claws of English influence have sunk into our country's flesh. The very *hammals*—street porters—adapt to their own dialect the naval and other technical terms which have been Arabicized from the English and decline and conjugate them" (cited in Batatu, *Old Social Classes*, p. 243).

On December 28, 1910, the weekly *al-Rashad* published an article the contents of which, according to the British consul at the town, the *wali* was aware beforehand. The article stated that: "The

British Government interferes with Turkish commercial matters by financing companies formed in Turkey, with a view to carry out their own designs in the Companies' name as they have done in India. British ambition has increased and their Government has tried without success to get concessions in Arabia. Having obtained a concession from the Persian Government for working oil in Abadan, the British Government makes this a pretext for laying down rails etc. and lending arms, ammunition, cannon and soldiers and for establishing British subjects there—and afterwards they will bring their men of war ..." (letter of January 18, 1911, from British Consul Crow, Basra, to Chargé d'Affaires, Istanbul; FO 602-52, pp. 12-14).

In 1911, a member of the Baghdad branch of the CUP said in a speech: "Listen, dear compatriots—For a number of years England had been endeavoring to increase her political influence in the Persian Gulf. This influence is being felt in Basra.... We must be ready to resist any political aggression on our territories.... We must awaken our Government to take immediate steps to protect Basra" (cited in Ireland, *Iraq*, p. 44 n. 1).

84. See note 64 above; and Birru, *al-ʿArab wal-turk*, p. 572. Since the Lynch Company was the symbol of British influence in the country, it was subject to frequent attacks in the local press. On March 14, 1913, *al-Misbah* of Baghdad warned its readers that "Great Britain intended to do in Turkish Iraq what she had done in India," that the Lynch Company, supported by England, was one of the "harbingers of a vast colony there," and it advised readers "to arm [themselves] to fight the pioneers of the colonizing army" (cited in Ireland, *Iraq*, p. 44 n. 1). On March 13, 1914, the same newspaper attacked British commercial influence in the country, expressing the suspicion that it was a prelude to political control. The paper described the Lynch navigation company as the company that "holds the rein of trade in their iron hands and the native merchants are nothing but subordinates and brokers without influence" (cited in Atiyyah, *Iraq: 1908-1912*, p. 64). On December 11, 1913, *al-Rashad* "urged the fortification of Fao, Iraq's main port, against possible British encroachment" (cited in Atiyyah, *Iraq: 1908-1921*).

85. See Gooch and Temperley, *British Documents*, pp. 397-402; and Earle, *Turkey and the Great Powers*, pp. 255-56.

86. Cited in Cohen, *British Policy in Mesopotamia*, p. 306.

87. The first remark was made in July 1914 by Crowe, the assistant under-secretary in the British Foreign Office; the second in October of that year by Louis Mallet, the British ambassador to Istanbul (cited in ibid., p. 307).

88. Telegrams of July 2, 1914, from Mallet to Grey. FO 424/253, p. 4.
89. Telegrams of July 6 and 9, 1914, from Mallet to Grey, ibid., pp. 10, 13. Although the political activities of Sayyid Talib after the proclamation of World War I fall outside the scope of the present study, it is interesting to note that he contacted the British in order to reach an agreement with them. Yet when these negotiations ended in failure in early December 1914, a number of British officials—including Lord Herbert Kitchener, the consul-general in Cairo, Sir Edward Grey, secretary of state for foreign affairs, Sir Arthur Nicolson, permanent under-secretary of state, and Sir Eyre Crowe, head of the Eastern (and Western) department—approved the following amazing remark made by Sir George Clerk, senior clerk at the Eastern department of the Foreign Office: "He [Sayyid Talib] will now be against us, and, unless we are lucky enough to kill him fairly soon, can do much harm." Cited in Joseph Heller, *British Policy Towards the Ottoman Empire, 1908–1914* (London: Frank Cass, 1983), p. 211 n. 78. For a different perspective see Eliezer Tauber, "Sayyid Talib and the Young Turks in Basra," *Middle East Studies* (January 1989): 3–22.
90. Cited in Khadduri, "Social Background," p. 250.
91. In the late nineteenth and early twentieth centuries, the failure of Ottoman attempts at land reform in Iraq left the door open for some merchants to acquire agricultural land (see ibid., p. 220).
92. "Programme."
93. See note 45 above.
94. Gooch and Temperley, *British Policy in Mesopotamia*, pp. 276–79.
95. This is the correct translation of the two articles as they appear in the original Arabic program. Enclosure in dispatch No. 51 dated August 28, 1913, from British Consul Crow, Basra, to Chargé d'Affaires Marling, Istanbul. FO 195/2451/423. See also Zeine, *Emergence of Arab Nationalism*, p. 109 n. 4; and Birru, *al-ʿArab wal-turk*, pp. 501–2.
96. Cited in Zeine, *Emergence of Arab Nationalism*, p. 109.
97. Batatu, *Old Social Classes*, p. 171.
98. Ibid., pp. 171–72.
99. See "The Unrest in Basreh," *The Near East*, August 29, 1913, p. 476.
100. The American Vice Consul in Baghdad reported the following incident during the proceedings of *al-majlis al-ʿumumi* (local General Council) of the *vilayet* on October 14, 1913: "A member of a rather influential Baghdad Mohammedan family, a certain Fuad Effendi, made in one of his speeches the bold remark that the Irak (the Arabic term for Mesopotamia) belonged and had to belong to

the People of Irak (on the principle of *L'Egypte aux Egyptians*). The *vali*, who was presiding at that meeting of the *majlis*, asked Fuad Effendi at once to repeat what he had said. On this Fuad Effendi replied that he was ready to repeat and to maintain what he had said and so he did. The *vali* ordered then the Secretary of the Majlis [sic] to write down exactly and carefully all that he had heard at this moment. After that the discussion proceeded, Fuad Effendi *not* having retracted by no means his former statements." Dispatch dated November 12, 1913, from Carl F. Richarz, Vice Consul, Baghdad, to American Ambassador, Istanbul. Records of the United States Department of State, Relating to the Internal Affairs of Turkey 1910–1929, 867.00/592. I am indebted to Hasan Kayali for first drawing my attention to this dispatch.

101. Batatu, *Old Social Classes*, p. 1113.
102. Khadduri, "Social Background," p. 251. Between 1906 and 1913, Britain's economic position in Iraq was partially challenged by another power, Germany (see Batatu, *Old Social Classes*, p. 243 n. 115; and Cohen, *British Policy in Mesopotamia*, pp. 53–58). It should be noted also that "whereas the major share of Iraqi trade prior to 1870 was with Middle Eastern countries, especially with Iran, this picture changed completely shortly before World War I: 48 percent of the exports and 82 percent of the imports were directed towards India" (Khadduri, "Social Background," p. 252). In comparison, 7 percent of Iraq's exports and 9 percent of its imports were directed toward Germany (see table 25 in ibid., p. 253).
103. Batatu, *Old Social Classes*, p. 1114.
104. Ibid., p. 294.
105. Al-Arhayyam, *Tatuwwur al-ʿIraq*, p. 200.
106. Batatu, *Old Social Classes*, pp. 314–15.
107. "The Story of the Euphrates Company," p. 152. Yet in 1958 a company was operating in Iraq under the name of Abd al-Munʿim al-Khudayri River Steamship Company (see table 9–13, "Iraq: Capitalists Worth A Million or More Dinars in 1958," in Batatu, *Old Social Classes*, between pp. 275 and 282).
108. For the intellectual angle, see Abdul Wahhab Abbas al-Qaysi, "The Impact of Modernization on Iraqi Society During the Ottoman Era," ch. 2.

SEVEN

The Education of an Iraqi Ottoman Army Officer

Reeva S. Simon

It was not until 1634 that most of what is Iraq today came under Ottoman rule as a consequence of a series of wars between the Ottomans and the Safavi rulers of Persia. Because of the general instability in the area due to the intermittent warfare, natural catastrophes, and the lack of a strong central government in Istanbul whose writ extended to the limits of the empire, Iraq remained a backwater region neglected by the Ottomans until the mid-nineteenth century. This period, beginning with the rule of Sultan Mahmud II, was known as the Tanzimat, when administrative and military reorganization and reform were undertaken by the Porte. Directed from the capital, these policies had a direct impact upon Iraq, which until this time had been ruled almost independently of Istanbul. In 1831, an Ottoman governor replaced Mamluk rule in Baghdad by force, and by the last quarter of the nineteenth century, when Ottoman control was firmly established, Iraq entered the mainstream of the Ottoman empire.[1]

Two events that occurred at this time had a lasting effect on Iraq. First, in 1848, in the context of centralization and the reorganization for the empire, the Ottoman government created a 6th Army Corps to be stationed in Iraq. Baghdad became an integral part of the empire and Iraqis began to participate more fully in the bureaucratic life of the Ottoman state. The educational reforms that followed provided the means for an Iraqi

Arab to join the Ottoman army or civil service, to be educated in Istanbul, and return to work in Iraq. Access to civil service jobs for Iraqis and their families provided prestige, a regular income, and prospects for advancement.[2]

The second event was the appointment of Midhat Pasha as governor of the *vilayet* of Baghdad in 1869. Of his reforms, the establishment of secular schools in Iraq was the key to bringing Iraqis into the orbit of cosmopolitan Istanbul. Iraqis were now directly exposed to the currents of the new political thinking that began to filter through the secular educational process. Until the era of Midhat Pasha, education for most Iraqis was largely traditional except for a few Christian and Jewish schools established earlier, which had introduced secular subjects into their curricula. Centered around the mosque, the Islamic schools were based upon the study of the Qur'an (Koran) reading, some arithmetic, and penmanship. The child entered school anywhere from the age of three to seven. He attended a local religious school that prepared him for a future clerical career through advanced study in Cairo at al-Azhar or at Shi'i *madrasas* (schools) in al-Najaf.

At one point it was thought that the graduates of these religious schools could proceed directly to secular careers in administration or the military, and students headed for military careers were sent directly to Istanbul,[3] but it was realized quickly that the religious curriculum provided inadequate preparation for the secular education that the central government began to institute in its program of reform. The Education Law of 1868 (Maarif-i Umumiye Nizamnamesi) was issued in recognition of the need for secular preparatory schools in the empire. The Ottomans set up a network of primary and secondary schools in the provincial capitals.[4]

As one of his goals, Midhat Pasha began to establish secular schools in Baghdad in order to provide a pool of local military and bureaucratic talent for service to the empire. In 1868 and 1870 he set up military and civilian *rüşdiye* schools.[5] It was not until the practical means for career advancement were provided by the central government, however, that Iraqis began to study first in Baghdad and later in Istanbul in great numbers. The need for a stable supply of officers stationed in the Arab provinces prompted the Porte in 1871 to invite Iraqis to choose the military as a career:

Due to the fact that Baghdad, our city, is the headquarters of the Imperial 6th Army of the Iraqi districts, the establishment of a military high school there is very necessary. Students who complete their studies in this school will be sent to the Imperial Military College in Istanbul to continue their education, so that they might graduate as officers. The school opens a clear future to its graduates up to the rank of Field Marshall [*mushir*] and it is indispensable for the progress of our countrymen (*abna' al-watan*).[6]

The military *idadi* school was established in Baghdad in 1879[7] and a civilian *idadi* two years later. The government paid the student's expenses in Baghdad, including room and board, and sent the graduates of the military school in Baghdad to Istanbul, reimbursing their travel fees and supporting them through the Military Academy (Mekteb-i Harbiye). The first group of thirteen Iraqis to complete the course graduated in 1881.[8] Graduates of the Military College in Istanbul were commissioned as lieutenants and most of them were later stationed in Iraq.[9]

Other occupations were open to Iraqis of means. Some, such as Tawfiq al-Suwaydi, went through Iraqi schools and on to the Baghdad Law College (1908) or the Teachers Training College, then remaining in Iraq for their advanced studies. Some attended university abroad or the American University of Beirut, while others attended the Law and Civil Service Academies (Mekteb-i Mülkiye) established in Istanbul. Shi'ites had their own network of schools and rarely sent their children to the government schools for fear of Sunni indoctrination.

For lower-class and poor Sunni families, military education became a popular means for social mobility. Talib Mushtaq, who later taught in Iraq, recounts that poor families made their sons attend the military schools in Baghdad so that they could complete their studies in Istanbul. "Istanbul was the Mecca [Ka'aba] of ambitious Iraqis," he wrote:

For whoever wanted an important position filled his bag with expensive presents and hurried to Istanbul, and whoever wanted advancement and promotion filled his pockets with tens of gold liras and went to Istanbul; and those wealthy families who wanted to give their sons a higher education sent them [there] the majority of these attended the College of Law and the Mulkiye Shahana, the College of Political and Administrative Sciences as it is now called. As for poor families, they made their sons attend the military school in Baghdad so that it might lead to their completing their higher studies in the Military College in Istanbul and graduate as officers in the Ottoman army.[10]

They traveled to school despite the hardships incurred even in reaching Baghdad from other parts of Iraq. Ibrahim al-Rawi had to study in Baghdad because Ramadi, his hometown, had only two religious elementary schools and a state primary school.[11] For ʿAli Jawdat, the trip from Mosul to Baghdad was an eight-day river ride on a raft of inflated skins.[12]

The trip from Baghdad to Istanbul was even more arduous. Once in the capital, poor students studied at night. ʿAli Jawdat was fortunate. He lived with relatives. Despite the problem, however, the first group of Iraqis to graduate from the lower school in Baghdad and to go on to the Military College in Istanbul arrived in the capital in 1872. ʿAli Jawdat tells us that seventy students entered the Military College with him in 1903.[13] From 1872 through 1912, between 500 and 1,200 Iraqis had gone through the military educational process.[14]

By that time, military education throughout the Ottoman empire had undergone a major transformation. The Ottomans had established a War College in 1846; a two-year course of study here included mathematics and foreign languages.[15] A French military mission to Istanbul advised the Ottomans and French became the second language in the Ottoman military schools. But the French defeat in 1870 and the refusal of France to renew the military mission in 1877, coupled with the Ottoman defeat in the Russo-Turkish War of 1877–1878, led to a reassessment of the situation. In 1880, Abdülhamid II commissioned a study of Ottoman and foreign military capabilities and institutions, which resulted in recommendations of reform along the German modes.[16]

The Creation of a Cohesive Officer Corps. Germany was an attractive model because it had achieved unity and a centralized regime in a short time. Of no less importance to the Ottomans, Germany also emerged after the Congress of Berlin in 1878 as the true friend of the empire, and a power not outwardly concerned with the "minorities question" (as was Britain), or one suspected of "landgrabbing."[17] Kaiser Wilhelm II's visit to Istanbul in 1898 reaffirmed Ottoman confidence at a time when no other European sovereign would have even met Abdülhamid II, the "Red ('bloody') Sultan."[18]

Thus, in 1880, negotiations between the Ottomans and Germany began for the dispatch of German military advisers. It was not until the end of 1881, however, that Bismarck consented to send a military mission, telling the Ottomans he needed time to select the most qualified officers, while in truth he was occupied by diplomatic concerns related to Austro-Hungary. Finally in May 1882, the first German military contingent arrived in Istanbul.[19]

Its most famous member, Colmar Freiherr von der Goltz, commanded the German mission from 1885 to 1895 and was most responsible for the reorganization of the Ottoman army and its military education system.[20] Von der Goltz returned to Turkey from time to time for short visits and commanded the 6th Army Corps at Baghdad during World War I, where he died in 1916. German advisers took command of selected Ottoman military units until the end of the war.

The creation of a new officer corps and the reform of military education in the interest of greater military effectiveness were given priority both by Abdülhamid II and by von der Goltz, but for different reasons. Fully aware of the fate of Sultans Selim III and Mahmud II, who had attempted military reform,[21] Abdülhamid II decided to create his own younger, educated officer corps, specifically loyal to him, which would be able to cope with the problems of decentralization and nationalist uprising within the empire. Wary of forming another potential threat to its regime, however, he instituted a spy system and morals lectures in the military academy to reinforce the gratitude of cadets for their sultan's munificence. Practical training was rare and the rifles remained in their crates.[22]

Von der Goltz, on the other hand, saw an officer corps as an elite, homogeneous, unified group, albeit in this case drawn from the various ethnic and social groupings that made up the empire, but which would exist as a distinct social class and would be the heart and souls of the army. In Germany, as in Abdülhamid's Ottoman empire, the officer corps was meant to serve the authority of the ruler against demands for democratization and to act as a "School for the Nation" that is, in the German sense, a means to educate the people to be loyal subjects of the state. In prewar Germany, the imperial army, led by the officer corps, was the unifying factor in the state.[23]

In the Ottoman empire, however, the unity of the officer corps would not necessarily become a political force directly loyal to the sultan, despite the classes and lectures in pan-Islam mandating it so. Rather, the unity of its membership would emerge through the sharing of common experiences and professionalism. Having common interests and duties, the entire corps would thus render itself responsible to each individual member. In reality, the creation of the new Ottoman officer corps as a distinct entity superseding political loyalties would outlast the empire itself, disintegrating as a whole but regrouping its members in the new states (especially Iraq) created after the war.

The key to the creation of the new Ottoman army officer corps was education. Because the few graduates of the Military College and the entering students were ill-prepared, and many of the officers in the Ottoman army who rose through the ranks were illiterate, reaching their positions through patronage,[24] von der Goltz began increasing the number of military preparatory schools throughout the empire on three levels. He modified the *rüşdiye* schools on the model of the German cadet school, which educated the child from approximately eight to ten years of age.[25] Military education, like all government-sponsored education, was centralized, all direction emanating from Istanbul. Although located in military centers and staffed by military officers, these secular schools came under the direct control of the general staff. In 1893 the army opened twenty-one *rüsdiye* schools and by 1911 there were thirty-two throughout the empire, exposing the students to science as well as the traditional Ottoman curriculum.

The *idadiye* schools came under the jurisdiction of the local *ordu* (military division) commanders and were located in the major provincial capitals: Istanbul, Adrianople (Edirne), Manastir, Bursa, Erzurum, Damascus, and Baghdad. If there was no school in his area, a promising student was sent directly to Istanbul to attend a military school there. The course of study lasted three years.

Von der Goltz also took control of the Mekteb-i Harbiye. His goal was quality not quantity, and so from 1884 to 1896 the officer corps grew from some 10,000 officers to just over 18,000. More significantly, the percentage of Military College graduates in the entire officer corps increased from 10 percent to 25 percent. Harbiye graduates were also sent abroad to study, beginning with ten officers sent to train with German military units in 1883.[26]

Education and the Politicization of the Officer Corps. The General Staff in Istanbul assigned the teachers and mandated the curriculum for the military schools throughout the empire. Most of the teachers in the military *rüşdiye* and *idadi* schools were Turkish military officers.[27] In 1870 all twenty-five teachers in the Baghdad *rüşdiye* were Turks, and as late as 1908 most of the teachers were Turks and military officers.[28] As more Arab students from the provinces graduated from the Harbiye, however, they were stationed close to home and many taught in the local *rüşdiye* and *idadi* schools.[29] Both Nuri al-Sa'id and Ja'far al-'Askari, for example, taught in Iraqi schools before World War I.[30] When Arabic was included in the curriculum. it was frequently taught by Iraqi Arab graduates of local *madrassas*, who also taught religion and penmanship.[31]

The curriculum of the military and the civilian *rüşdiye* schools were similar except for the emphasis on gymnastics in the military schools.[32] Instruction was in Turkish rather than in French, as had previously been the case, and for those who did not know Turkish, an extra year was required to catch up. Entering students also needed some knowledge of arithmetic and reading. The course of study was four years long and included Islamic history, Ottoman geography, elementary engineering, arithmetic, natural science, Arabic, Turkish, French, hygiene, and gymnastics.[33]

The course of study in the *idadi* schools was three years and included trigonometry, algebra, engineering, hygiene, astronomy, geography, religion, calligraphy, drawing, gymnastics, Turkish, Arabic, Persian, French, and English. Those students who did not have an *idadi* school in the vicinity had access to education in Istanbul. There was a special class for them before they went on to the regular *idadi* school.[34]

Once in the Military College, students could specialize. For the first three years they enrolled either in a course for infantry or cavalry, with the majority choosing the infantry. Selected students continued for another three years in the General Staff course while the rest remained for a fourth year, graduating as lieutenants. The General Staff graduates received commissions as captains.

The General Staff curriculum was divided into scientific and military specialization. Before the arrival of von der Goltz, the only purely military course was one on fixed fortifications and the scientific section taught courses in mechanics, construction, and railways. Von der Goltz was able to add courses in German and Russian in addition to French, history of war, weapons, military organization, strategic geography, tactics, and military literature. He was also able to manage to have students take visits to active military units, despite the rigid control instituted by Abdülhamid II.[35]

In the early days, most of the teachers in the Harbiye were Germans who taught through interpreters.[36] By World War I, however, Harbiye graduates, some of whom went on to advanced training in Germany, taught in the Military College in Istanbul and later in the Iraqi Military College.

The curriculum was determined directly from Istanbul, even to the amount of hours spent per subject, down to scheduling, textbooks, and study plans for each grade. In addition to military reform, the goal of the government schools was to encourage loyalty to the Ottoman state and to the sultan who was also the caliph of Islam. When nonscientific subjects such as history were taught, therefore, Ottoman history was emphasized. There was little foreign history. Fahmi Bey, a retired colonel of the Ottoman General Staff who was born in Tripoli and went through the Ottoman military school system, says that "it was wise to avoid this sort of thing. Isma'il Pasha, the spy from the palace was always around to check on what was being taught."[37]

Thus, when the Ottoman government began to implement the Turkification process, textbooks reflected the shift from Ottomanism to Turkism in historical study. Influenced by the Romantic "pan" nationalists of Germany, Central Europe, and Russia, whose nationalism or the earlier liberal thinkers, Turkish historiography became the means for discussion of Turkish nationalism in a society that prohibited the discussion of politics. After 1877, Turkish history began to focus on the early Turkish and pre-Islamic Turkish antecedents of the Ottomans, relegating Arab and Persian contributions to Ottoman culture to limited roles. Where earlier texts published for the *rüsdiye* did not mention the Turkish ancestry of the Ottomans, now practically all of the texts related that the ancestors of the Ottomans were from "Turkish tribes of Central Asia" who fathered the Ottomans, the Tatars, and the Mongols.[38]

With the new Turkish national consciousness, links became philological and ethnic rather than religious. Turkish replaced French as the language of instruction in the school and Arabic and Persian words were purged from the language in attempts to purify Ottoman Turkish and enrich it with additions from Chagatay and other Central Asian Turkish languages. Authors used studies by European Orientalists on racial kinship between Aryans and Turks, and newspapers underlined the virtues of the Turks through frequent comparisons with Europeans, both as a mechanism for self-defense and for self-glorification. While pointing out Turkish military qualities, for example, they were also eager to demonstrate that the Turk was not the "bloodthirsty creature" he was depicted to be.[39]

Some of these ideas were later incorporated in the nationalist philosophy of Ziya Gökalp, the theoretician of Turkish nationalism. Gökalp rejected the idea of racial purity, but he was attracted by the similar problems that faced Germany in the nineteenth century and Turkey in the twentieth, namely, ethnic unity and industrialization/modernization. And like a number of Ottoman writers in the nineteenth century, he was attracted by the Romantic nationalism that caused him to look to Turkish rather than to Islamic roots. Both he and his military protégé, Mustafa Kemal Ataturk, looked to the concept of an elite that would educate the nation in the new Turkish nationalism, a variation of von der Goltz's "School for the Nation." Although Ataturk later criticized Germany and German military advice during the war, under his direction Turkey underwent a massive cultural transformation using the concepts of a "Leader" and an elite pulling the nation into the twentieth century.[40] Similarly, the ideological underpinnings of what was later to become pan-Arabism was provided by Sati' al-Husri, who used Germany as his ideological paradigm,[41] just as the Iraqi officers did for their political and military model in the new Iraq.

The Young Turks, whose regime followed the 1908 coup in Anatolia, accelerated the education program while implementing their policy of Turkification of the non-Turkish population via the schools. When they mandated Turkish as the language of instruction, taught Sunni doctrine in religion classes, and emphasized Turkish history and culture to the exclusion of Arab, there was a decline in enrollment in government schools in Iraq.[42]

Iraqis studying at the Istanbul Harbiye before 1908 were comfortable in the Ottoman milieu. As Iraqi Sunnis under Ottoman suzerainty for more than three hundred years, they had become acclimatized, accepting the spiritual and temporal leadership of the Ottoman sultan and looking to Iraqis such as Mahmud Shawkat (Shevket) (who had attained a high position in the Ottoman establishment) as an ideal example of upward mobility. They appreciated the opportunity to study in cosmopolitan Istanbul, the center of intellectual ferment, despite the omnipresent imperial espionage system.

As military men, they were impressed with the technical and military education they received, by the General Staff system that instilled order and respect for efficiency, and with the elevation of the methods of war to the level of science, once again creating the possibility of Muslim military ascendance. Reading von der Goltz's *The Nation in Arms*, they were impressed by his thoughts on the role of the army and education in society. But just as their Turkish colleagues secretly read the works of Namik Kemal, they, too, read writings of the Ottoman liberals and they joined Arab-Ottoman societies that advocated equality for all members of the Ottoman empire. 'Ali Jawdat, who became the Iraqi prime minister in 1934, tells us that he read the books by 'Abd al-Haqq Hamid, who wrote in Turkish but who told the exciting tales of Arab heroes and of the Arab conquests of Spain. These stories awakened Jawdat's Arab consciousness and he began to question Ottoman discrimination against the Arabs in the Ottoman empire, finding new respect and admiration for the Arabic language and Arab culture.[43]

The Turkification policy of the Young Turks and their imposition of the Turkish language and culture on the Arabs was a turning point in Arab-Ottoman relations, which sparked the development of an antidote—Arab nationalism. (See C. Ernest Dawn's essay on the subject, in this volume.)

In Iraq, the poets Ma'ruf al-Rusafi (1875–1945) and Jamil al-Zahawi (1836–1936) criticized Hamidian injustices all the while remaining loyal Ottoman subjects. When the Young Turk revolt occurred, they saw the new regime as one of reform. Branches of the Committee of Union and Progress (CUP) were founded first in Basra by an Iraqi colonel in the Ottoman army, Rashid al-Khuja, and later in Baghdad and Mosul. They sponsored meetings, lectures, and a daily Arabic-Turkish newspaper, *Baghdad*.[44]

When the Turanists, who advocated the union of Turkish-speaking peoples, became influential within the CUP, however, the Iraqi literati and the army officers began to reconsider their allegiance. Some, like Mahmud Shawkat, served the regime, while others tried to accommodate Arab-Turkish interests. They resigned from the CUP to form more liberal societies that advocated reform. One, the Reform Committee, founded by a Basra notable, Sayyid Talib al-Naqib, went even further, demanding that the government-appointed administrator in Iraq be an Iraqi native, that Arabic be the official language in all government departments and courts, and that all arts and sciences be taught in Arabic in the schools. (See Mahmud Haddad's essay, in this volume, for more details). The Reform Committee's newspaper, *Bayna al-Nahrayn* (Mesopotamia), attacked the CUP for its Turanic policy and its unfriendly attitude toward the Arabs.

The career army men tended to join the short-lived secret societies that came and went with government pressure. The most important of these, al-ʿAhd, was formed just before World War I and became the vehicle for the political Arab nationalism that burgeoned under Faysal (Faisal) in Syria and finally in Iraq. It was said that some 315 out of the total of 490 Arab officers stationed in Istanbul joined al-ʿAhd. Most of these officers were Iraqis who subsequently returned with Faysal to rule Iraq after World War I, later instituting the ideology of pan-Arabism as the focus for loyalty in the new Iraqi state.[45]

The Impact of Ottoman Military Education on the Iraqi Officers.
The legacy of this Ottoman military education transcended purely military matters. It led to a system of networking and politicization that would play a large role in Iraqi and Arab politics during the interwar years.

Iraqis who passed through the military system maintained a bond even though they may have fought on different sides during World War I. For example, Yasin al-Hashimi (who served with the Ottoman forces and was wounded in the fighting in Palestine) was rescued by Nuri al-Saʿid (who was fighting with the British), not only because Yasin was an Iraqi but because both men were comrades in arms from the Military College.⁴⁶ Later, in Iraq, they were political adversaries during most of their careers, working together only when politics required their cooperation.⁴⁷

Indeed, in interwar Iraq, these allegiances were pronounced because the Sunni officers who returned to Iraq and worked under Faysal filled most of the civilian and military posts in the bureaucracy and government. By the end of the 1920s, they became the political elite in Iraq, remaining in power throughout the interwar period. Nine of the fourteen prime ministers from 1921 to 1932, for example, were former Ottoman military officers, as were thirty-two out of fifty-six major cabinet members.⁴⁸ By 1936, among the Iraqi officers holding posts of commander and above in the new Iraqi army, fifty out of sixty-one were ex-Ottoman officers who had received their education in Istanbul.⁴⁹

There is also a direct link between the politicized officers who controlled the Iraqi government after 1936 and the Ottoman military system. Two teachers in the Iraqi Military Academy, in particular, propagated the active role of the army in politics. The first, Tawfiq Husayn, a product of the Ottoman military system, remained in the Turkish army until his return to Iraq in the early 1930s. Appointed lecturer in military history by Taha al-Hashimi, who knew him from Istanbul, Tawfiq Husayn lectured extensively on nationalism. He influenced the post-1930 generation of Iraqi officers by advocating that Iraq be like Turkey, and that the military intervene in politics. His hero was Mustafa Kemal Ataturk and, as Mahmud al-Durrah describes, his lectures inspired more than one officer to envision himself in the role of the Turkish leader. By 1934, Tawfiq Husayn had more than seventy officers in his circle, including the leader of the subsequent pan-Arab coup in Iraq, Salah al-Din al-Sabbagh.⁵⁰

The second teacher was Taha al-Hashimi, a graduate of the Baghdad military *rüşdiye* and *idadi* schools, who attended the Istanbul Harbiye and Staff College. He was also a founding member of al-ʿAhd. Although Taha served in the Ottoman army, where he reached the rank of lieutenant colonel, he was better known as a teacher because of his predilection for military studies, history, and geography. Most of his career in Iraq was as commander in chief of the Iraqi army, where he was eventually promoted to general. Taha also taught in the Military Academy and wrote textbooks. He entered politics after the death of his brother, Yasin al-Hashimi, but was considered a weak replacement. From 1939 to 1941 he was the intermediary between the four pan-Arab colonels, Nuri al-Sa'id, and the Mufti of Jerusalem, al-Hajj Amin al-Husayni, believing that the army's role was to fill the political void and to institute the pan-Arab ideology that had been propagated in the Iraqi schools and the army throughout the 1920s and 1930s.[51]

There is evidence that attendance at distinctive secondary schools was a most influential experience for many who later achieved political power in the Middle East.[52] To be sure, other facts such as a social background, family, and religion played a large role in forming a person's later political world view. Nonetheless, the shared schooling and experiences, and the friendships many of these officers made during this period of early adulthood, lasted and, for many of them, determined the circle of persons with whom they stayed in contact throughout the remainder of their lives. Both 'Ali Jawdat and Ibrahim al-Rawi report that outside of the Ottoman army experience and service with Faysal, neither had much contact with the outside world before returning to Iraq.

Notes

1. Phebe A. Marr, *The Modern History of Iraq*, pp. 19–21.
2. Walid Khadduri, "Social Background of Modern Iraqi Politics," pp. 38–42.
3. Matta Akrawi, *Curriculum Construction in the Public Primary School of Iraq* pp. 126–31.
4. The other motive for the reorganization of Ottoman education was clearly to use education as the means to wield the diverse ethinic and religious groups of the empire into a "Western-oriented and corporated Ottoman state" (Andraes M. Kazamis, *Education and the Quest for Modernity in Turkey*, pp. 63–64). See also Kemal H. Karpat, "Reinterpreting Ottoman History: A Note on the Condition of Education in 1874," *International Journal of Turkish Studies* 2 (1981–82): 93–100, wherein he notes changes in the usage of the terms *rüşdiye* and *idadiye*.

    Generally, the *rüşdiye* was equivalent to an intermediate school (American junior high school) and the *idadi* was a secondary school (senior high school). However, grade levels and school frequently merged and designations for schools changed. Sometimes a *rüşdiye* could include all of the grades above the *mullah* school through junior high school (primary school). In some places *ibtida'i* school was added, shortening the student's stay at the *mullah* school. The ages of student's in each division varied, depending upon the kinds of schools in the area and the students' educational backgrounds. See also Akrawi, *Curriculum Construction*, pp. 126–31.

5. 'Abd al-Razzaq al-Hilali, *Tarikh al-ta'lim fi al-'Iraq fi al-'ahd al-'uthmani, 1638–1917* [The history of education in Iraq during the Ottoman Era, 1638–1917], pp. 155, 162. The school of military sciences took the few students from the provinces as well as the Turkish students. The first group of Iraqis graduated in 1869. They were immediately stationed with the 6th Army Corps (ibid.).

6. Abdul Wahhab Abbas al-Qaysi, "The Impact of Modernization on Iraqi Society During the Ottoman Era," pp. 85–86.

7. Attendance in 1898 was 269 students; in 1900 it was 256. An average of thirty to forty students per year went on to Istanbul. By 1900 a second *idadiye* school had been opened in Sulaymaniyyah (al-Hilali, *Tarikh al-ta' im*, pp. 164, 220).

8. Ibid, p. 164.

9. By imperial decree, officers from Arabic-speaking areas were sent back to their own areas; other officers drew lots for assignment (Interview with Fahmi Bey, in M. A. Griffiths, "The Reorganization of the Ottoman Army under Abdülhamid II, 1880–1897" p. 177.

10. Talib Mushtaq, *Awraq ayyami, 1900–1956* [The papers of my days] p. 36. The translation from David Pool, "From Elite to Class, the Transformation of Iraqi Leadership 1921–1939," *International Journal of Middle East Studies* 12 (1980): 331–51. The wealthier families sent their sons to the nonmilitary colleges such as law and medicine. Of the Iraqis, these were less than 8 percent of the number who received military degrees (Ayad al-Qazzaz, "The Changing Patterns of the Iraqi Army" [Paper delivered at the Middle East Studies Association of North America Conference, 1969], p. 5).

11. Ibrahim al-Rawi, *Min al-thawra al-'arabiyya al-kubra ila al-'iraq al-hadith: dhikriyat* [From the great arab revolt to modern iraq: Memoirs], p. 3.

12. 'Ali Jawdat, *Dhikriyat 'Ali Jawdat, 1900–1958* [Memoirs of 'Ali Jawdat, 1900–1958], p. 16.

13. Ibid.

14. Al-Qaysi maintains that the number is as high as 1,200. Walid Khadduri contends that the number of Iraqi officers trained in Istanbul prior to World War I could not have exceeded 500. This

figure, however, does not include the number of reserve officers hastily trained on the eve of World War I. Khaduri concludes that no more that an average of fifteen students were sent to Istanbul annually from Baghdad (al-Qaysi, "The Impact of Modernization," pp. 85–87; and Khadduri, "Social Background," p. 40).

15. J. C. Hurewitz, *Middle East Politics: The Military Dimension* (New York: 1969), pp. 36–38.
16. Griffiths, "Reorganization of the Ottoman Army," pp. 44–45.
17. Arminius Vambéry, "Personal Recollections of Abdülhamid and his Court," *Nineteenth Century* 66 (1909): 81.
18. Ernest E. Ramsaur, *The Young Turks*, p. 140.
19. Griffiths, "Reorganization of the Ottoman Army," pp. 41–51.
20. Von der Goltz succeeded Kahler Pasha, who died in 1885 (ibid., p. 66).
21. Kemal H. Karpat, "Transformation of the Ottoman State," pp. 243–81.
22. "Annual Report for 1907," in G. P. Gooch and Harold Temperly, eds. *British Documents on the Origins of the War 1898–1914*, 5: pp. 29–31.
23. Griffiths, "Reorganization of the Ottoman Army," pp. 57–61. On the officer corps in Imperial Germany, see Colmar von der Goltz, *The Nation in Arms, a Treatise on Modern Military Systems and the Conduct of War*, trans. by Philip A. Ashworth (London, 1906); and Martin Kitchen, *The German Officer Corps, 1808–1914* (New York: 1968).
24. In 1884 the total number of active officers was 9,810, while estimates of the total officer corps including reserve officers ranged up to 30,000 (Griffiths, "Reorganization of the Ottoman Army," pp. 98–99).
25. In Baghdad, the *rüşdiye* was four years (al-Hilali, *Tarikh al-ta ʿlim*, p. 162).
26. Griffiths, "Reorganization of the Ottoman Army," p. 53.
27. al-Hilali, *Tarikh al-ta ʿlim*, pp. 162–63.
28. Khadduri, "Social Background," p. 37.
29. Ibid., p. 59.
30. al-Hilali, *Tarikh al-ta ʿlim*, p. 162. They may have taught in the special six-month course set up before World War I to get graduates into military units quickly (p. 234).
31. According to al-Hilali, Arabic was not included in the 1870 curriculum; it was included in the 1889 curriculum (ibid., p. 164).
32. al-Qaysi, "The Impact of Modernization," p. 59.
33. al-Hilali, *Tarikh al-ta ʿlim*, p. 234.
34. Ibid., p. 164; and ʿAli Jawdat, *Dhikriyat*, p. 17.
35. al-Hilali, *Tarikh al-ta ʿlim*, p. 164.

36. Interview with Fahmi Bey, in Griffiths, "Reorganization of the Ottoman Army," p. 175.
37. Ibid.
38. David Kushner, *The Rise of Turkish Nationalism*, p. 29.
39. Ibid., pp. 32–33, 37–38.
40. Uriel Heyd, *Foundations of Turkish Nationalism*, pp. 164–70; and Taha Parla, "The Social and Political Thought of Ziya Gökalp."
41. Bassam Tibi, *Arab Nationalism*.
42. Akrawi, *Curriculum Construction*, p. 131.
43. ʿAli Jawdat, *Dhikriyat*, pp. 20–21.
44. al-Qaysi, "The Impact of Modernization," pp. 92–94.
45. For material on the Arab nationalist societies see Muhammad ʿIzzat I. Darwaza, *Hawla al-haraka al-ʿarabiyya al-haditha* [Regarding the modern Arab movement]; and al-Rawi, *Min al-thawra*, pp. 25–60.
46. Phebe A. Marr, "Yasin al-Hashimi" pp. 71–72.
47. Reeva S. Simon, *Iraq Between the Two World Wars*, pp. 57–65.
48. Al-Qazzaz, "Changing Patterns" pp. 3–5; see also his "Power Elite in Iraq, 1920–1958," *The Muslim World* 61 (1971): 279.
49. Mohammad Tarbush, "The Role of the Military in Politics: A Case Study of Iraq to 1941" (Ph.D. diss. Oxford University, 1977), pp. 101–3.
50. Mahmud al-Durrah, *al-Harb al-ʿiraqiyya al-baritaniyya 1941* [The Iraqi-British War, 1941] (Beirut: 1969), pp. 47–52. The perpetrators of the first military coup in the modern Middle East were not the bureaucrats and the literati, but units of the cohesive body of the officer corps with its esprit de corps and the Western techniques acquired at military school (see Ahmad, *The Young Turks*, p. 48, 177; Dankwart A. Rustow, "The Military: Turkey," in R. E. Ward and D. A. Rustow, eds., *Political Modernization in Japan and Turkey* ([Princeton: 1968], p. 360; and *The Young Turks: Prelude to 1908*, p. 118).
51. Simon, *Iraq Between the Two World Wars*.
52. See, for example, P. J. Vatikiotis, *The Egyptian Army* (Bloomington, Ind.: 1961); M. Van Dusen, "Political Integration and Regionalism in Syria," *Middle East Journal* 26 (1972): 123–36; and Frederick W. Frey, *The Turkish Political Elite*.

EIGHT

The Rise of Local Nationalism in the Arab East

Muhammad Muslih

Scholarly studies on the origins and ideas of Arab nationalism abound.[1] Few works, however, explore the rise of local nationalism (*wataniyya*) and the internal Arab conditions that made it strike root in the Arab East after World War I. This study will attempt to fill the gap. It is an analysis of the Arab factors that contributed to the weakening of the framework of Arab nationalism in Syria, and consequently helped usher into existence the forces of territorial nationalism. Of course, the imperial powers England and France played an important part in this process, but their story has been told and retold by many parties and from different perspectives.[2]

This essay concentrates on the politics of influential Syrians and Palestinians who dominated the Young Arab Society (al-Jam'iyyat al-'arabiyya al-fatat). Four factors account for this approach: first, al-Fatat played a central role in the dissemination of the idea of Arab nationalism in geographic Syria before the Ottoman capitulation; second, many al-Fatat members played particularly active roles in Syrian politics after the war; third, the society formed the backbone of Faysal (Faisal) ibn al-Husayn's Arab state in Syria (1918–1920); and fourth, the interaction among the Syrian and Palestinian bosses of al-Fatat was bound to affect the future of Arab nationalism.

Al-Fatat: Its Origins and Factions. The origins of al-Fatat can be traced to 1911, when a group of young Syrian, Palestinian, and Lebanese Muslim Arabs[3] who were pursuing their higher studies in Paris decided to found an organization devoted to the aim of "raising the level of the Arab *umma* [nation] to the level of modern nations," (a reference to Western nations.)[4] Prior to World War I, al-Fatat was more concerned with equal rights and obligations for Arabs and Turks within the framework of a unified Ottoman state[5] than with Arab independence from Ottoman rule as Antonius and some other writers maintain.[6] With the CUP's (Committee of Union and Progress) suppression of Syrian political organizations including the Damascus branch of Hizb al-lamarkaziyya al-idariyya al-ʿuthmani (the Ottoman Administrative Decentralization party) and the Beirut Reform Committee al-Fatat started rechanneling its energies into clandestine work on behalf of rebellion against Turkish rule. The offices of the society were moved to Beirut late in 1913 and a branch was set up in Damascus around the same time.[7]

The complex developments pertaining to the Syrian provinces during the war years, including Jamal Pasha's execution of Arab nationalists on charges of treasonable activities, created a drastically new environment for al-Fatat: now the society amended its political program and sought, in general terms, full independence and unity for the Arab provinces.[8] Although the activities of al-Fatat and of politicized Syrians were ruthlessly suppressed by the Turks during the war, the society added to its roster some prominent members, including Faysal ibn al-Husayn and a number of Syrian and Iraqi civilians and military officers.[9] The ideology that these men espoused was not clearly defined until the eve of World War II. Secular as they were, they were not inclined to accept a state based solely on religious solidarity. They stressed language, culture, and history rather than Divine Law as the binding substance of the envisioned Arab nation.[10] In the words of one authority, they "believed implicitly in the existence of an Arab nation: in schools, in barracks, in the Ottoman Parliament, in exile in Cairo, and in the Sharifian forces they had come to know each other and acquired the ease of discourse which possession of a common language and a common education gives."[11] To state it differently, their concept of nationalism took an Arab rather than a specific Syrian, Lebanese, Palestinian, or Iraqi form.

Three factors account for this. One was the self-view of the creators and advocates of the idea of Arab nationalism: their conception of themselves was for the most part shaped by the glories of the period of the Prophet Muhammad, of the Orthodox caliphs Abu Bakr, ʿUmar, ʿUthman, and ʿAli, and their successors the Sufyani and Marwani Umayyads and Abbasids, all of whom were seen increasingly in terms of their Arab identity. Thus they were conscious of themselves as members of a distinct community that had played a determining role in the civilization of Islam, a community that had not only occupied a position of paramountcy in the Islamic empire but had also constituted the backbone of the Islamic *umma*.

Another factor was the Arabic language. Islam made full use of the particular structure of the language and the admirable composition of the Qur'an (Koran) was considered "miraculous." No popular expression reflects the importance of Arabic in the psychology of the Arab better than the old Arab adage *"jamal al-insan fi fasahat al-lisan"* ("The beauty of man lies in the eloquence of his tongue").[12] That Arabic was the main vehicle of Islamic civilization in Islam's intellectual golden age made the language even more glorious.

The third factor was the common way of looking at the Arab provinces of the Ottoman Empire. In the minds of the Arabs at least those inhabiting the areas east of Egypt the Arab provinces constituted one single unit within the larger Ottoman framework. What reinforced this view was the unity the Ottomans had imposed on the Arab provinces and their peoples in terms of buildings, schools, mosques, social manners, and style of government and politics.

The world resulting from the Ottoman defeat in 1918 put to the test the new idea of Arab nationalism. The prime movers behind this world were the two imperial powers, England and France, whose direct interests in the Arab East were pervasive. Insofar as France was concerned, she was adamant about securing her strategic interests in Syria and Lebanon, and these were: maintaining of her position as a Mediterranean power in northwest Africa; the protection of her access to the Far East and to the oil of Iraq by means of the Kirkuk-Tripoli pipeline; the protection of the Catholic communities, the work of the missions; and, the position of French culture; and the enhancement of her domiant position in North Africa by contracting so important a center of Arab opinion in the Levant. By contrast, Britain had no similar interests of first-rate importance. Her primary concern was to ensure that Syria and Lebanon remained in friendly hands, and that the policy adopted by the controlling government, indigenous or foreign, be in general conformity with that of Britain.[13]

In the Levant, on the other hand, Britain's eyes were upon Palestine and Iraq, where tremendous resources had been engaged. A commitment to the Zionist cause, enshrined in the Balfour Declaration of November 2, 1917, was meant to achieve two goals—strategic considerations and the restriction of Jewish immigration from Eastern Europe into Britain and the United States. Central to Britain's strategic evaluations was her desire to establish a buffer region, populated by settlers from overseas, between Sinai and the Levant for safeguarding the Suez Canal and the communications to India.[14] It fell to Biblical sentimentality, and the Western sense of guilt toward the Jews, to make British realpolitik an article of faith as far as the embrace of Zionism was concerned.

British interests in Iraq were also of first-rate importance, and sprang mainly from the desire to protect the route to British India by blocking German penetration from the north and Russian encroachments from the east. Iraq therefore figured very high as a key point of the Britain's strategic system in the eastern Mediterranean, and Iraq's oil fields occupied a central position in His Majesty's Government's imperial calculus.[15] Those, in brief, were the interests that shaped the course of the policies of the two imperial powers in the Arab East after the Ottoman defeat. On the eve of the capitulation in October 1918, General Sir Edmund Allenby, commander of the Egyptian Expeditionary Force, divided geographical Syria into three administrative areas called Occupied Enemy Territory (OET): North (Lebanon and the Syrian coast), South (Palestine), and East (Transjordan and the Syrian interior). Although the boundaries of these administrations departed from the Sykes-Picot Agreement of October 1916, they represented the postwar power configuration between England and France. France coveted, and in the end secured, Syria and Lebanon, while England assumed control over Palestine and Iraq. The arrangement between the two powers, reached after intense negotiations, was enshrined in the instrument of the mandate that was concluded at San Remo on April 25, 1920.[16]

How did dominant members of the first generation of Arab nationalists respond to these challenges? How strong was their consciousness of solidarity and their commitment to the pan-Arab ideal? By looking at the political agendas of two major groups within al-Fatat during Faysal's short reign in Damascus, answers to these queries can be provided.

The Syrian Agenda. Syrian personalities, many of whom occupied key positions in Faysal's Syrian state, were perhaps the leading actors in the politics of Arab nationalism after the war. Being on their home turf, they had an obvious political edge over the Palestinians and Iraqis. Their capital, Damascus, was a magnet that attracted Arab nationalists from all over the Levant by virtue of being the birthplace of Arab nationalism and the political seat of Faysal, the first Arab "sovereign" after roughly four centuries of Turkish suzerainty. Furthermore, Syria was politically and socially familiar to the Arab nationalists of Lebanon, Palestine, and Iraq, and geographically close to the primary focus of their attention. Baghdad, Beirut, and Jerusalem could be looked to for support, but they were not places from which to launch the Arab nationalist struggle. Little wonder, therefore, that Damascus served after the war as the major coordinating center of the infant Arab nationalist movement. Its cultural and political credentials were compelling attractions for transnational elites who rode the tide of Arab nationalism.

For all its appeal, Syria projected an image of contradiction and factionalism. Syrian political elites were divided in their political ideas and preferences. Perhaps the most visible and serious tension was between Arab nationalism's highest ideal, the creation of a single independent political unit comprising all who shared the Arabic language and heritage, and the tendency toward giving precedence to local ambitions and concerns. A further element was added to the tension by the wounded prestige of older members of urban upper-class Syrian families who, during the brief period of Faysal's Arab kingdom in the Syrian interior, were pushed to the sidelines of the political process. Their effective challengers were young individuals who were close to the Amir: his Hijazi (Hejazi) troops, Iraqi and Syrian military officers who deserted to his northern Arab army during the war, and a number of Arab nationalist Syrian and Palestinian intellectuals and officials who were well schooled in the intricacies of Ottoman plotting and counterplotting.[17]

Thus the grounds already existed for a conflict among the Syrian political actors. Within al-Fatat, the conflict manifested itself in the clash between the old political guard and the young upstarts who filled the higher and lower echelons of the Syrian government. The two groups differed widely in their self-views; and there were local interests and jealousies that were stimulated but not altogether created by the divisive policies of England and France.

Most representative of the old guard was the al-Rikabi and al-Bakri faction. ʻAli Rida Pasha al-Rikabi was born to a notable landowning Damascene family. He served as a general in the Ottoman army, and during the war he established his connections with Amir Faysal. Toward the end of the war he joined al-Fatat and in December 1918 he was elected to its central committee. Late in October of the same year, General Allenby appointed him military governor of OET-East, and later Faysal appointed him military governor of Syria. On March 8, 1920, the amir entrusted him with forming the first Syrian Cabinet.

ʻAli Rida al-Rikabi was one of the most influential military figures in Syria. In certain quarters, he developed the reputation of being too lenient toward the French and contemptuous of the Arab nationalist members of al-Fatat, particularly the Palestinians and Iraqis.[18] The most outstanding talent that al-Rikabi exhibited was the military expertise he had acquired from Ottoman military schools.

Associated with al-Rikabi was Nasib Bey al-Bakri. A graduate of the al-Sultaniyya school in Beirut, al-Bakri also came from a wealthy landowning Damascene family. He had been an early acquaintance of the Sharifian family, and it was at the al-Bakri house in Damascus in the spring of 1915 that Faysal for the first time met the leading members of al-Fatat.[19] After the war, al-Bakri served as private consultant to Faysal until the French conquest in July 1920.[20] Nasib al-Bakri's French connection caused him many difficulties with the Arab nationalists whose ideas he had little appreciation and for whose rise to power he had difficulty accepting.[21]

'Ali Rida al-Rikabi and Nasib al-Bakri, together with several like-minded Syrians, showed their disdain for the desires and wishes of the young Arab nationalists in act and word. Their concerns were specifically Syrian, aimed at the creation of an independent Syrian state with a parliamentary monarchy;[22] and this for a number of reasons.

First, capricious French designs in Syria made nationalism the chief political instrument with which members of the traditional Syrian elite hoped to broaden their constituency and reestablish their position of local dominance. The fact that Syria was threatened with a French invasion overshadowed in their minds the principles of pan-Arab unity and independence.

Second, the idea of Arab nationalism did not look particularly attractive to older members of Syrian upper-class families who had been tied to the Ottoman system of government, and who therefore had had a vested interest in the continuation of the empire. From their perspective, therefore, the accommodation of Syrian nationalism after the war was more comfortable than the accommodation of Arab nationalism. This was not only because an Arab nationalist victory threatened their monopolistic control of political power, but also because these men felt more at home with local concerns than with the vague and broader aims of Arab nationalism.

Third, the advent of a Sharifian amir to Damascus was disturbing to the old Syrian elites because Sharif Husayn and his family had dynastic interests that, they felt, could only be achieved at the expense of the Syrian notability and masses. Arab nationalism was the ideological instrument with which the Sharifians tried to achieve their ambitions. Moreover, the Sharifians were viewed as strangers to Syria, with no real stake in the land, and no local interests to promote and defend. True, some members of the Syrian notability had their Sharifian connections, but these were more for political convenience than for reasons of ideology.[23]

The presence of Palestinians and Iraqis who became, in the space of five years, the masters of the local political scene was a source of serious complaint by the old Syrian elite. Neither in their ideology nor in their social origins were the young upstarts appealing to this indigenous Syrian class. The Baghdadis were not men of wealth and position in their country, and the Palestinians were either of a middle-class background or unestablished members of high-status families. Furthermore, Palestinians and Iraqis were putting their Syrian government positions in the service of political ideals that were not at the top of the notables' agenda. "In forming his government," laments the local chronicler Muhammad Kurd ʿAli, "al-Rikabi relied on foreigners more than he relied on nationals."[24] The "wise" notables of Damascus disliked, according to him, the young Iraqis and Palestinians who had acquired standing with Faysal and had the power to do or undo things in Syrian national politics.[25] This is the description provided by Ihsan al-Jabiri, then Faysal's chamberlain, of the anger of the notables: "It is true," he wrote, "that some of the notables of Damascus, who were used to occupying high positions under the former Turkish government, became alarmed at the invasion of intellectuals from all classes who wanted to make the administration democratic. These notables preferred to ask for protection from the French liaison officer rather than lose their privileged position. They ended by forming a party of retrograde and reactionary malcontents who remained ineffective until the invasion of the French army."[26] The party to which al-Jabiri refers was the al-Hizb al-watani al-suri (the Syrian National party), which al-Rikabi, al-Bakri, and a number of Syrian notables had set up in January 1920 to protect Syrian rights against the non-Syrian "strangers."[27] In the party's parlance, the Palestinian and Iraqi "strangers" were no more than "confused, hot-headed youths who belonged to a world of shadows and abstractions."[28]

If the older notables tell part of the Syrians' story, the younger Arab nationalists tell a different and more complex one. The Arab nationalists from Syria had to fight not only against France and the encroachments of the West, but also against the traditional elites of Damascus. This group of nationalists was a counter to the more strictly Syrian nationalist perspective of the older notables. There is a revolutionary theme to their lives (revolutionary in the Syrian context of this period): it is the story of young men, many of affluent background, who could have chosen to swim with the current but instead chose to oppose, to rebel, and to lose out.

Among the Syrian Arab nationalists, three figures stood out: Muhib al-Din al-Khatib, ʿAbd al-Rahman Shahbandar, and ʿAdil Arslan. The world of these men, though by no means a comprehensive chronicle of Arab nationalism, tells a lot about the politics of the new movement. Theirs was the short era of the search for pan-Syrian unity, of the fight for independence, of the crusade for pan-Arabism, and of the collapse of Faysal's rule in Syria.

All three men were linked by more than a common devotion to Arab nationalism. In education and upbringing they were very similar: Muhib al-Din al-Khatib studied in Damascus, Beirut, and Istanbul where he focused on law and literature;[29] ʿAbd al-Rahman Shahbandar specialized in medicine at the Syrian Protestant College (later the American University of Beirut);[30] and ʿAdil Arslan graduated with a degree in literature from Paris.[31] None of them had, therefore, acquired an education laden with the values of high Ottoman-Arab culture, nor were they members of the Ottoman imperial bureaucracy. Moreover, they all hailed from wealthy landowning families. They also had a strong fondness for Arab language and culture. Finally, due to personal ambition and ideological preference, they remained close to Amir Faysal, notwithstanding the dislike and distrust some of them later exhibited toward Sharif Husayn and his son ʿAbdallah (Abdullah) on account of the latter's connections with the British.[32]

The party through which the Syrian Arab nationalists tried to promote their views was the secularist, pan-Arab *Hizb al-istiqal al-ʿarabi* [the Arab Independence party]. Founded by al-Fatat in February 1919, its major principle was to achieve Arab unity and complete Arab independence. To mute the opposition of the Syrian National party, and to impart an image of extensive political participation, al-Fatat maintained a policy of open registration. Such a course of action had the additional advantage of screening potential members: unknown individuals were admitted to Hizb al-istiqal but not to the mother organization.[33]

A fairly steady stream of Syrian and Palestinian political activists (among them Asʿad Daghir, Shukri al-Quwwatli, and Muhammad ʿIzzat Darwaza) joined the party, which counted, according to one source, 75,000 members.[34] Although the number seems to be inflated, one thing is clear: the party's rank and file was predominantly Syrian.[35] The Arab Independence party was headquartered in Damascus with branches in various Syrian towns. It received political and financial support from Amir Faysal, but it relied for its survival on the inner circle of al-

Fatat. Its political vision was, therefore, a replica of al-Fatat's and, indeed, their memberships on the leadership level overlapped.

However, despite a common outlook rooted in a consciousness of Arab history, deep cracks appeared in the Syrian Arab nationalists' edifice. ʿAbd al-Rahman Shahbandar irked his colleagues by his pro-British stance. Anglophile that he was, he could hardly escape the accusation of being a British agent, even though it was not untypical of members of his generation to seek British cooperation in the hollow hope of attaining Syrian independence.[36] On the other hand, ʿAdil Arslan was inclined to rule out any cooperation with the British, and partly due to his heavier involvement in Arab culture he had a stronger penchant for the ultimate goal of Arab unity.[37] Moreover, Shahbandar favored the Faysal-Clemenceau agreement of January 1920,[38] whereas the Damascenes al-Shaykh Kamil al-Qassab and Ahmad Maryud rejected it out of hand.[39]

Their rivalry and ideological differences notwithstanding, the Syrian Arab nationalists and their contenders among the old political guard shared a common denominator-namely, the political independence of Syria. The Syrian Arab nationalists as a dissident force opposing Ottoman rule were one thing; the nationalists outside the Ottoman fold facing the prospect of a French invasion were quite another. While these young men were "committed" to the cause of Palestine and Iraq, they were more directly concerned with Syrian affairs. The division of geographical Syria, and the personal and political disputes of the Syrian elites, fractured the nascent Arab nationalist movement. As far as the Syrians were concerned, their local interests came before everything else. In this way, the ideals of pan-Arabism were scaled down, not in theory but in practice.

The Palestinian Agenda. From the center of the political arena in Damascus, the Palestinians observed firsthand the harsh realities of inter-Arab politics. Their perceptions clashed with those of the traditional Syrian elite. And for all the appeal of pan-Arabism, the romance of the Syrian Arab nationalists was with the Syrian question. For the Palestinians, concentrating all efforts on stopping the Zionist incursion took precedence over everything else.

Two trends competed with one another in the world of the

Palestinians-the push of pan-Syrian unity (the reality of geographical Syria) and the pull of local Palestinian concerns. The first suggested a shared destiny with Syria and provided the raw ideological material with which its supporters worked. The second theme was the product of the designs of the British and Zionists. The first was the universe of the young pan-Arabists; the second was the realm of the old Palestinian elite.

The yearning for pan-Syrian unity on the part of the Palestinian Arab nationalists had ideological and realpolitik underpinnings. The ideological can be located in the Palestinian involvement in the early stages of Arab nationalism. Politicized individuals such as ʿAwni ʿAbd al-Hadi, Muhammad ʿIzzat Darwaza, Rushdi al-Imam al-Husayni, and Muʿin al-Madi belonged to the founding generation of Arab nationalism.[40] For them, conscious of their history as Arabs, the issue of CUP centralization and Turkification became a civilizational and cultural question. At the heart of the crisis lay the explosive problem of cultural dualism between an Arab self and an Ottoman wrapping. Disaffected as they were, certain Palestinians who were not integrated in the Ottoman state apparatus joined a narrowly based group of Syrians and Iraqis, and together they formulated the idiom of Arab nationalism, always lured by the Western concepts of patriotism, constitutionalism, liberal parliamentary forms, and personal freedoms.

On the other hand, the realpolitik origins of the Palestinian quest for pan-Syrian unity can be found in the fear engendered by the encroachment of the British-Zionist alliance. The articulate Palestinian opposition to Zionism gave an insider's view of an indigenous society whose very existence was threatened by a colonial settler movement of European provenance.[41] What in 1882 began as Jewish immigration rapidly turned into a determined process of colonization that later, under direct British protection, was allowed to expand and establish firm foundations for hegemony in Palestine without regard to the wishes of the indigenous Arab majority.

To resist Zionism, the Palestinians looked to the larger Ottoman framework for salvation, and despite its soft spots the framework did the job. But with the disintegration of the Ottoman Empire after the war, the Palestinians sought to put together another answer to their struggle against Zionism, which some did by focusing on Palestine, while others worked for

Syrian-Palestinian unity. The young Palestinians who went to Syria did not go just for the attractions of Damascus. Above all, they went to realize a pan-Arab dream and, equally important, to forge a protective shield that would ward off the British-Zionist incursion.

This is where the ideology and the power politics of the Palestinian pan-Arabists intersected. While in Damascus, the Palestinians were perhaps the most resolute group in their pursuit of pan-Syrian unity. In Palestine proper, the pan-Arabists were equally vigorous in their attempts to create a mass-based propagation of the idea of unity. Without unity, they maintained, Palestine would be amputated-cut off from the Arab world-and would stand vulnerable and exposed. In their propaganda at home and abroad, they extolled the virtues of pan-Arabism and threw into the political debate hard geopolitical realities. They preached that Palestinians could not go at it alone against the British and Zionists.[42] Their perspective in Damascus was a mirror image of political views they tried to disseminate in Palestine through al-Nadi al-ʿarabi (The Arab Club), a nationalist organization that emerged in January 1918 under the leadership of younger members of the al-Nashashibi family.[43]

With few exceptions, the men who constituted the Palestinian camp in Damascus were activists of a younger generation of upper-class families. Among the most important of them were three Nablusites: ʿAwni ʿAbd al-Hadi, who was born in 1882 to a Sunni Arab family noted for its wealth and social status; Rafiq al-Tamimi, who was born in 1889 to a Sunni Arab landowning family; and Muhammad ʿIzzat Darwaza, who was born in 1888 to a middle-class Sunni Arab family. Their political closeness to each other is explained not just by where they came from, but more significantly by the role they had played in founding al-Fatat and the doctrine of Arab nationalism that they all shared. Two of them in particular, ʿAbd al-Hadi and Darwaza, were highly articulate individuals-they thought aloud; they argued out the pressing issues of the time; and they dealt as best they could with questions of Palestinian and collective Arab purpose.

ʿIzzat Darwaza, a self-taught intellectual and political activist, captured and expressed the secularist content of early Arab nationalism. His case was atypical because, unlike the overwhelming majority of the young group of early Arab nationalists to which he belonged, he had had no formal training in Ottoman professional schools, or in the Syrian Protestant College in Beirut, or in Europe. The politics that Darwaza knew were the politics of the cell and the underground organization in late Ottoman times. This helps explain the manner of his presentation-simple, direct, and to the point.

'Izzat Darwaza's ideas helped spread the word in Palestine on behalf of secular pan-Arabism against religious nationalists, and against theose who believed in separate Palestinian, or Syrian, or Lebanese destinies. Moved as he was by the civilization of the Arabs, he evoked a distant Arab past. For obvious reasons, Islam was central to that past. But in the case of Darwaza, Islam was important not as the binding substance of the nation, but as a culture and civilization. In other words, culture, language, and history rather than religious solidarity were posited as the glue that was to hold the Arab nation together.[44]

Darwaza had pronounced anti-British tendencies. He was reluctant to align with the traditional Palestinian elite. His use of Damascus as a major center for his propaganda campaign against the British and Zionists, his firm conviction in Syrian-Palestinian unity, and his resort to political activism placed him on the British and French lists of suspected nationalists. In the early stage of his career, Darwaza kept his activities under wraps, but later he was harassed, chased, and incarcerated by the British authorities in Palestine.

While 'Izzat Darwaza's contribution to the Arab nationalist movement lay in the practical and intellectual domains, that of 'Awni 'Abd al-Hadi was mainly confined to practical politics. Judging by his biography, there was a profound intellectual compatibility between 'Abd al-Hadi and Darwaza despite differences in social background, education, and political strategy toward the British. 'Abd al-Hadi was much closer to Faysal than Darwaza; he filled the position of director of the Hijazi office in Paris and served as private secretary to the amir. As such, he was more understanding of Faysal's relations with the British, and more receptive to the idea of cooperating with them to secure Arab independence.[45]

At home in Palestine, there were other Palestinians who had a different perspective. They constituted the group of early Palestinian nationalists, or "Palestine First." The group included some of the most prominent senior statesmen of Palestinian society, including the Jerusalemites Musa Kazim Pasha al-Husayni (b. 1853) and ʿArif Pasha al-Dajani (b. 1856). On the whole, these bearers of proud names belonged to the local ruling elite of urban notables; they had a tradition of social leadership and, as officers or civil servants, had played a part in the Ottoman system of local and provincial government. Their age and background colored their political outlook. For the most part, they tended to stress local Palestinian independence; most of them favored cooperation with the British, were suspicious of the Hashemites, and were generally unimpressed with pan-Arabism.

Local patriotism and political interests were at the heart of the ideological preferences of these older elites. Seeing Palestine put under a separate military administration and alarmed at Britain and her pro-Zionist policy, they chose to focus on Palestine first and other Arab matters second. From their perspective, therefore, Palestinian nationalism was the appropriate response because the British and Zionists were a direct danger to Palestine in particular.

Moveover, the short-run goal of monopolizing local political power on the part of the traditional Palestinian elite enhanced their emphasis on local political independence for Palestine. Familiar as they were with the local political game, they foresaw the challenge that the elite of such Syrian cities as Damascus and Aleppo would pose to their positions of local control. The network of propertied urban families in Syria was much larger and, on the whole, wealthier than the network of Palestinian urban families. Compared with Palestinian cities, Damascus and Aleppo had much larger populations and greater commercial importance. Equally significant was the fact that Damascus had a decisive ideological edge by virtue of being the birthplace of Arab nationalism. Therefore, were Palestine to merge with a greater Syria, it was likely that the Syrian notables would overwhelm their Palestinian counterparts, a scenario the older Palestinians were keen to avoid.[46]

And they did. By 1920 the conflicts and differences in the order of priorities were sufficiently pronounced to create permanent lines of division in the Arab nationalist movement. The pull of Palestinian nationalism ultimately prevailed. The inhospitable universe of the traditional Syrian elite exposed the vulnerability of the doctrine of pan-Arabism. Painful as they were, the assaults by members of this elite on the Arab "foreigners" provided a recipe for the reorientation of the politics of the Palestinian pan-Arabists. If an important segment of the Syrian body politic was too preoccupied with domestic concerns and priorities, then why not a Palestinian focus on Palestine before anything else? Did not the Syrian Arab nationalists themselves put the Syrian question at the top of their action agenda, in the process relegating the Palestine cause to a secondary position? Zionism and the imposition of the Mandate system provided the spark and added to the fuel that had already been there. Early in 1920 a perceptive Zionist agent offered an astute summation of the consequences of the clash of political priorities in the Syrian arena. He described the fracturing of the Arab nationalist movement and predicted the emergence of what he called the "Arab Nationalist Movement of Palestine."[47]

Indeed, by the end of 1920 nationalism in Palestine had acquired a rather narrow focus. Palestinian independence became nationalism's highest aim. The Palestinian pan-Arabists came to concentrate all their efforts on achieving this goal before all else. They had already learned their lesson in Damascus. Even for Faysal, their idol, the stakes were different. In his political calculus Syria came first, Palestine was second. Britain was too important to his dynastic ambitions, and Faysal was of the view that the Zionists would help him in checking French designs in Syria, a perspective that made him conclude a conditional, yet controversial, agreement with Chaim Weizmann, the Zionist leader, in January 1919.[48]

Thus, in keeping with the tenor of inter-Arab politics after the war, the Palestinian pan-Arabists made peace with Palestine's new "national" situation and accommodated the particularism of the Palestine cause within the "universalism" of their Arab nationalist doctrine. Their organizations in Damascus, most notably *al-Nadi al-ʿarabi* and *Jamʿiyyat fatat filastin* (The Palestinian Youth Society), were set up in the name of Palestinian nationalism. Despite the pan-Syrian fervor of the two organizations, Palestinian rights and the distancing of Faysal from the Zionists came to the fore of their issues and demands.[49] Ethnoculturally, the Palestinian pan-Arabists did not break with Arab nationalism, but organizationally and politically they accepted the paramountcy of *raison de la nation*.

This was the story of early Arab nationalism in its birthplace

Syria. The narrative is far from complete, but it reveals some salient features of inter-Arab processes as well as the political priorities of those engaged in them. Arab nationalism, the only viable ideology destined to fill the ideological void caused by the death of Ottomanism, proved to be tender and precarious. The colonial policies of England and France contributed to this development, but so did the internal Arab factors outlined in this essay. And even though a group of intellectuals and politically conscious Arabs continued the pursuit of pan-Arabism, it had to compete with local nationalisms in the political life of the Arab East.

Notes

1. C. Ernest Dawn, *From Ottomanism to Arabism;* Albert Hourani, *Arabic Thought in the Liberal Age;* Rashid I. Khalidi, *British Policy Towards Syria and Palestine;* and Philip S. Khoury, *Urban Notables and Arab Nationalism.* See the Bibliography for complete details.
2. See, for instance, George Antonius, *The Arab Awakening;* A. L. Tibawi, *A Modern History of Syria;* and Jukka Nevakivi, *Britain, France, and the Arab Middle East, 1914–1920* (London: 1969).
3. Among those were: Jamil Mardam (Damascus); ʿAwani ʿAbd al-Hadi (Jinin); Rafiq al-Tamimi (Nablus); Muhammad al-Mahmasani (Beirut); Tawfiq al-Natur (Beirut); ʿAbd al-Ghani al-ʿUraysi (Beirut); and Rustum Haydar (Baalbak).
4. Muhammad ʿIzzat Darwaza, *Nashat al-haraka al-ʿarabiyya al-haditha* [The birth of the modern Arab movement], pp. 481–82.
5. Ibid., pp. 480ff. See also Amin Saʿid, *al-Thawra al-ʿarabiyya al-kubra* [The great Arab revolt], 1:9–10; Khayriyya Qasimiyya, *al-Hukuma al-ʿarabiyya fi dimashq bayna 1918–1920* [The Arab government in Damascus between 1918 and 1920], pp. 19–20; and Zeine N. Zeine, *The Emergence of Arab Nationalism*, p. 84. Darwaza draws on his own experience in al-Fatat, while Qasimiyya draws on the records of the society and Zeine on information provided to him by Tawfiq al-Natur.
6. Antonius, *The Arab Awakening*, p. 111; and Khoury, *Urban Notables*, p. 65.
7. Darwaza, *Nash'at al-haraka*, p. 503.
8. See Antonius, *The Arab Awakening*, pp. 202–3; Dawn, *From Ottomanism to Arabism*, pp. 155–56; and Saʿid, *al-Thawra al-ʿarabiyya al-kubra*, 1:9–10.
9. For a partial list of names see Darwaza, *Nash'at al-haraka*, p. 502.

10. Albert Hourani, *The Emergence of the Modern Middle East*, pp. 179–93; and Khoury, *Urban Notables*, pp. 98–99.
11. Hourani, *Arabic Thought*, p. 293.
12. Philip K. Hitti, *The Arabs: A Short History* (Chicago: 1985), p. 26. For details on the significance of Arabic, see Anwar G. Chejne, *The Arabic Language*.
13. Albert Hourani, *Syria and Lebanon: A Political Essay* (Beirut: 1968), pp. 155–58.
14. See, for instance, Herbert Sidebotham, *England and Palestine: Essays Toward the Restoration of the Jewish State* (London) cht. 10; Oskar K. Rabinowicz, *Winston Churchill on Jewish Problems* (New York and London 1960), pp. 46–80; and Walid Khalidi, ed., *From Haven to Conquest* (Beirut: 1971), introduction, pp. xxi-xxxiii.
15. See Peter Sluglett, *Britain in Iraq 1914–1932* (Oxford: 1976).
16. For details, see J. C. Hurewitz, *The Struggle for Palestine*, pp. 17–18; Nevakivi, *Britain, France, and the Arab Middle East*, pp. 241–60; and A. L. Tibawi, *Anglo-Arab Relations and the Question of Palestine, 1914–1921* (London: Luzac, 1978), p. 399.
17. For details, see Khoury, *Urban Notables*, pp. 78–81.
18. Muhammad ʿIzzat Darwaza, "Tisʿuna ʿaman fil-Hayat" [Sixty years of life], 2:94 (xeroxed manuscript in my possession). Biographical data on the personalities discussed in this essay draws on information provided in Muhammad Muslih, *The Origins of Palestinian Nationalism*, pp. 135–43.
19. Antonius, *The Arab Awakening*, p. 152.
20. Ahmad Qudama, *Maʿalim wa aʿlam fi bilad al-ʿarab* [Places and eminent personalities in the Arab lands], 1:142.
21. Darwaza, "Tisʿuna ʿaman," 2:141; and Ahmad Qadri, *Mudhakkirati ʿan al-thawra al-ʿarabiyya al-kubra* [My memoirs of the great Arab revolt], pp. 172–73.
22. Saʿid, *al-Thawra al-ʿarabiyya al-kubra*, vol. 2:42.
23. For details on the political outlook of the Syrian notables, see Muslih, *Origins of Palestinian Nationalism*, pp. 131–56; Khoury, *Urban Notables*, pp. 78–88; and Khoury, *Syria and the French Mandate*, pp. 3–27.
24. Muhammad Kurd ʿAli, *al-Mudhakkirat* [Memoirs] 1:232.
25. Ibid., 6:170.
26. As cited in Elie Kedourie, *England and the Middle East*, pp. 160–61.
27. Darwaza, "Tisʿuna ʿaman," 2:140.
28. Khalid al-ʿAzm, *Mudhakkirat Khalid al-ʿAzm* [Memoirs of Khalid al-ʿAzm], 1:94–95.
29. Qudama, *Maʿalim wa-aʿlam*, 1:380; Anwar al-Jundi, *Muffakiruna wa udabaʾ min khilal atharihim* [Thinkers and men of literature through their works] (Beirut: n.d.), p. 201.

30. Philip S. Khoury, "Factionalism Among Syrian Nationalists During the French Mandate," pp. 445, 465.
31. Darwaza, "Tisʿuna ʿaman," 2:113–14; Khoury, "Factionalism Among Syrian Nationalists," p. 449; and Qudama, Maʿalim wa-aʿlam, 1:23.
32. Khoury, Syria and the French Mandate, pp. 229–30.
33. Darwaza, "Tisʿuna ʿaman," 2:113–38; and Qasimiyya, al-Hukuma al-ʿarabiyya fi dimashq, p. 69.
34. Asʿad Daghir, Mudhakkirati ʿala hamish al-qadiyya al-ʿarabiyya [My memoirs on the margins of the Arab cause] p. 107.
35. Khoury, Urban Notables, p. 84.
36. Khoury, "Factionalism Among Syrian and Arab Nationalists," pp. 445, 462.
37. Ibid., p. 462.
38. This provisional agreement (reached with the encouragement of the British) provided for the right of Syria to independence and unity, on condition that it would be dependent on, advised by, and represented abroad by France.
39. Darwaza, "Tisʿuna ʿaman," 2:163; Yusuf al-Hakim, Suriya wa al-ʿahd al-faysali [Syria and the Faysal era], pp. 128–130.
40. For details, see Muhammad Muslih, "Arab Politics and the Rise of Palestinian Nationalism," Journal of Palestinian Studies (Summer 1987): 77–95.
41. For the Palestinian reaction to Zionism, see Neville J. Mandel, The Arabs and Zionism; Before World War I (Berkeley: 1976); Khayriyya Qasimiyya, al-Nash at al-sahyuni fil-sharq al-ʿarabi wa sadahu 1908–1918 [Zionist activity in the Arab East and its echo, 1908–1918] (Beirut: 1973); and Khalidi, "The Role of the Press" pp. 105–123.
42. Central Zionist Archives (C.Z.A.), September 1919, Record Group L4, File no. 765; April 11, 1920, Record Group L4, File no. 743; June 1, 1920, Record Group Z4, File no. 1454; and Darwaza, "Tisʿuna ʿaman," 2:141ff.
43. For details of these organizations see Muslih, Origins of Palestinian Nationalism, ch. 7; Yehoshua Porath, The Emergence of the Palestinian-Arab National Movement, pp. 74–79; Bayan Nuwayhid al-Hut, al-Qiyadat wa al-muʿassasat al-siyasiyya fi filastin 1917–1948 [Political leadership and institutions in Palestine, 1917–1948], pp. 86–89.
44. Darwaza, "Tisʿuna ʿaman," 1:22–50, and Hawla al-haraka al-ʿarabiyya al-haditha [Regarding the modern Arab movement], 1:5–10.
45. ʿAwni ʿAbd al-Hadi, Awraq khassa, pp. 30–33.
46. Muslih, "Arab Politics," pp. 85–86.
47. Zionist intelligence report (C.Z.A.), January 31, 1920, Record Group L3, File no. 278.

48. For the full text of this agreement see Antonius, *The Arab Awakening*, pp. 437–39.
49. For details on these organizations, see Darwaza, "Tisʿuna ʿaman," 2:143–44; Porath, *The Palestinian-Arab National Movement*, pp. 74–79; Khoury, *Urban Notables*, pp. 126–27; and C.Z.A., Record Group L3, File no. 278, and Record Group Z4, File no. 1366.

PART THREE
The Hijaz

NINE

Ironic Origins: Arab Nationalism in the Hijaz, 1882–1914

William Ochsenwald

The most significant expression of early Arab nationalism was the Arab Revolt against the Ottoman empire. Sharif Husayn of Mecca announced the revolt on June 10, 1916. This revolt became the key starting point not only for the independence of the short-lived kingdom founded by Husayn but also for the history of independent Iraq and Syria. The Hashemite kingdom of Jordan continues today as the direct heir of Husayn's action. The Arab Revolt of 1916 that began in the Hijaz (Hejaz) also involved promises of support made by the British to Husayn before June 1916. In these promises, according to the interpretation placed upon them by Arab nationalists, the British made commitments to Husayn that included, among other things, Arab control over Palestine. For all of these reasons, the Arab Revolt of 1916 was vitally important for Arab nationalism. It marked the end point of the beginning phase of Arab nationalist intellectual thought and development, and it was the only concrete result of the secret societies that had planned Arab independence since before World War I began. The revolt also signaled the second phase of Arab nationalism—a phase that involved independent or semi-independent Arab governments struggling to secure full control over their own destinies while at the same time spreading nationalist consciousness to the masses of Arab society.

Yet the Arab Revolt was in many ways an ironic beginning

for secular Arab nationalism and independence. The revolt was formed by and took place in a province of the Ottoman empire that was not at all nationalistic, and the first leader of the revolt, Sharif Husayn, was a very late recruit to the cause of Arab nationalism. The political, economic, military, and intellectual prerequisites for the emergence of nationalism among the elite were singularly lacking in the Hijaz during the period leading up to the outbreak of World War I in 1914. Moreover, in the first declaration outlining the reasons for the revolt, Husayn said that the chief causes were religious rather than nationalistic. Thus, if one considers the initial impetus and place of origin, the Arab Revolt and its leaders developed a more nationalistic overtone only after 1916.

The Hijaz, 1882–1908. Religion was the dominant force in the intellectual and political life of western Arabia in the nineteenth century.[1] Secularizing reforms had had little impact on the area, and the new ideas of nationalism that had begun to be discussed in Beirut, Damascus, and Cairo by the latter part of the century found few, if any, adherents in the Hijaz.[2]

Mecca and Medina in one sense had been peripheral to the Ottoman empire since their inclusion in the state during the sixteenth century. They were far removed from Istanbul and were poor. The Hijaz paid very little in taxes other than import duties and provided no troops to the imperial armed forces. Instead, the Ottomans sent men, money, and food to the area because of the religious importance it held for Muslims throughout the world and because of the prestige provided the Ottoman sultans by the use of the title "servant of the Harams" of Mecca and Medina.

The Ottoman Hijaz had little agriculture and few natural resources. Income for both the nomadic tribal majority and the settled minority of the population was largely derived from pilgrims who came to visit the Haram in Mecca and the Prophet Muhammad's tomb in Medina.

Governmental power in the Hijaz reflected this close relationship between religion and the economy, for it was shared between the agent of the Ottoman state, the *vali*, and the amir or prince of Mecca, a descendant of Muhammad, who was selected by the Ottomans but whose family held this position because of its religious prestige. The local balance of power between amir and *vali* fluctuated according to several factors, including Istanbul's interventions, the personal abilities of the participants, and popular feeling. The amirs of Mecca operated within the Ottoman system and were, to a degree, Ottomanized in language and style of life. Many of the amirs in the nineteenth century had lived part of their lives in the imperial capital. When a new amir took office, he sought chiefly local autonomy, presents and subsidies from Istanbul, and guarantees from external attack. In return, the amir assisted the Ottomans in maintaining order, so as to protect the pilgrims, and he acknowledged the overlordship of the sultan.[3]

While it is extremely difficult to characterize with any certainty the political feelings of the majority of Hijazis, who lived in towns, it would appear that most of them were reasonably happy with the Ottoman-amirate government. Popular goals that were generally achieved included minimal government, the continuation of gifts of grain and money from the Ottoman empire (including Egypt), security against marauders and robbers, and the carrying out of the holy law. There were few expressions of opposition to Ottoman rule by the townspeople. In the 1850s, riots and a massacre took place over the issuance of an imperial antislave trade edict, the deposition of an amir, and a commercial-religious rivalry between foreign Christian merchants in Jidda and Muslim Arab officials and merchants. But after 1859 the Hijaz towns were largely tranquil. On the other hand, nomads were often unhappy with the Ottomans, especially when the imperial forces shortchanged the protection money paid to the tribes as tribute for safe pilgrimage, or when the central government on rare occasions attempted to impose its rule directly in the countryside. This unhappiness usually found only an isolated and limited expression, and was easily assuaged by the amirate or imperial government.

Both townspeople and tribesmen wanted the Hijaz to remain semiautonomous. In 1880–1882 the aged and irascible amir, ʿAbd al-Muttalib ibn Ghalib, faced severe problems that led to his recall; chief among these was the new and active *vali*, Osman Nuri, a personal favorite of Sultan Abdülhamid II, who sought to increase the power of the central government and decrease the local autonomy of the amirate.[4]

ʿAbd al-Muttalib's successor, Amir ʿAwn al-Rafiq ibn Muhammad (r. 1882–1905), faced two challenges from Istanbul that were designed to decrease Hijazi autonomy. The first was the renewed attempt by the *Vali* Osman Nuri at direct rule; the second was Sultan Abdülhamid's pan-Islamic policy that found a concrete expression in the Hijaz Railroad. Resistance by the amir to centralization was not based on nationalism, nor did it lead, at that time, to the development of political and intellectual alternatives to Ottoman rule. Rather, ʿAwn al-Rafiq, in the 1880s and again in the 1900s, appealed to Hijazis to oppose centralization on the basis of preserving old local privileges and the special religious and political role of the Hijaz within the Ottoman state. Osman Nuri was dismissed as *vali* as a result of the amir's actions, and ʿAwn al-Rafiq established his own political dominance in the Hijaz.

The 1886–1905 period saw a stable rule wherein the amir gained money through pilgrimage and appointments, and then used bribes to the central authorities to stop centralizing measures. ʿAwn al-Rafiq could also call upon some of the bedouin tribes to cut the trade and pilgrimage routes, so as to apply pressure upon pilgrims, pilgrimage officials, and merchants. Despite the mishandling of the cholera epidemic of the 1890s, and the frequent insecurity of the routes leading to the coast from the chief inland cities, ʿAwn al-Rafiq overcame all opposition and retained imperial favor up to his death in 1905, when his nephew ʿAli ibn ʿAbdallah (r. 1905–1908) succeeded him and continued his basic policies.

The amirs did nothing to foster Arab nationalism, while the Ottomans, in desultory fashion, attempted to spread Ottoman patriotism through education and literature. Even though the cultural revival of Arabic learning was in full sway in Syria, Lebanon, and Egypt, there were no signs of a similar renaissance in the Hijaz. The professional groups so influential in the spread of nationalistic ideas elsewhere—secularly minded teachers, newspaper writers, army officers—were few in number and often were not ethnically Arabs.[5]

Cultural life revolved around religion. Systems of thought and modes of expression were permeated by Islam. Most of the educated elite, and they were few, had attended private schools, where religious subjects predominated, or had studied with tutors; secular fields such as geography, politics, recent history, and economics, which were all possibly conducive to a development of nationalistic ideas, were not taught. Most of the population did not receive any formal education at all. The educational system was fragmented along linguistic lines; many of the private schools were established by the large expatriate non-Arab communities, particularly the Indian Muslims, Only a few of the private tutors and teachers in the Harams were native Hijazis.[6]

Government schools enrolled far fewer students than did the private schools, and most of the students in the Ottoman schools were the sons of officials who spoke Turkish as their first language. Most Arabs resisted sending their sons to government schools because the education received there was viewed as preparatory to government and military services, an unpopular career choice.[7] So the new secular subjects taught in Mecca, Medina, and Jidda in the government schools were generally taught in Turkish and to very few Arab students. In contrast, many more government schools were built in Syria and Arab attendance was much higher. Schools there served as vehicles for recruiting the elite into the Ottoman government, and concepts such as nationalism were often encountered, especially in the higher training schools in Istanbul.

Authors in the Hijaz were often cosmopolitan and widely traveled, but they usually wrote on religious topics and often in verse in the form of commentaries, not in original works. Many writers had originally come to the Hijaz for religious reasons; very few, if any, were Arab nationalists. Books and newspapers from abroad, such as Jamal al-Din al-Afghani al-Asadabadi and Muhammad ʿAbdu's *al-ʿUrwa al-wuthqa* and the *salafi* writings of ʿAbdu and Rashid Rida, were read in western Arabia but only in small numbers. Also, press censorship in the Ottoman empire was strict, and the Ottoman censors were strongly antinationalistic.[8]

The only printing press in the Hijaz up to 1908 was owned by the Ottoman government. There were no newspapers published before 1908, but more than thirty books in Arabic were issued. Most of these dealt with religious subjects, and no translations from books originally published in European languages appeared in the Hijaz from the local press.

Just as there were apparently no nationally oriented teachers, writers, and newspapermen, there was also an absence of Arab nationalism in the army stationed in the Hijaz. By 1908 most of the government-sanctioned armed forces in the area consisted of regular (*nizami*) Ottoman soldiers. Since conscription did not exist in the Hijaz, and apparently no Hijazis volunteered for service, there were no Hijazis in the Ottoman army. However, the amirs of Mecca recruited their own armed forces from among tribesmen, sharifs, Meccans, and freed slaves. This small, diverse, and somewhat irregularly trained group was a source of power for the amirs, but it did not provide a training ground for nationalists, such as existed for some of the Arabs from Iraq and Syria who served in the Ottoman armed forces.

Politics in the Hijaz, 1908–1914. While the Hijaz was a singularly infertile area for the emergence of nationalism, it did become somewhat more receptive after changes in the empire's central government, which were brought about by the restoration of the constitution in 1908, the overthrow of Sultan Abdülhamid II in 1909, and the ultimate accession to power of the Committee of Union and Progress (CUP) during much of the period 1909–1914. In the Hijaz, the amir, the *vali*, and the governor of Medina were removed in 1908. The new amir, Sharif Husayn ibn ʿAli (r. as amir 1908–1916), almost immediately began a long struggle against the local CUP representatives. Husayn strongly opposed the centralizing and secularizing policies of the CUP while it feared his independence and sought to limit or abolish the autonomy of the Hijaz.

Upon his arrival in Jidda, Sharif Husayn rebuffed the local CUP leadership, which was composed of ethnic Turks, and began an ultimately successful campaign to persuade Istanbul to remove *valis* he deemed to be interfering. Between 1908 and 1916 there were six *valis*, none of whom had the personal authority to best the amir.[9]

Despite this conflict with the CUP and the *valis*, Husayn publicly remained loyal to the Ottoman empire. There were strong interests that bound him to the state. These included his long residence in Istanbul, where he had forged personal links to a number of high officials; the financial aid given him and the province by the Ottomans; Husayn's ambition to extend his influence into nearby areas (an ambition that could best be realized with the help of Ottoman troops); the amir's statement in 1911 that foreign powers posed a danger to the independence of Islam and the Ottomans could protect the holy places from the threat of their encroachments; and Ottoman assistance in providing security for the land pilgrimage that was crucial to the welfare of Mecca.[10] Husayn's political ideology was a pragmatic and flexible one. He had lived long in Istanbul and identified himself as an imperial official. He was, therefore, an Ottoman, but this was true only as long as the empire encouraged the application of the *shariʿa* and allowed for Hijazi autonomy. Husayn was not yet a nationalist of any sort—neither Ottoman nor Arab.

Even though he generally supported the Ottoman empire at this time, Husayn opposed centralization and especially the Hijaz Railroad. Before he was appointed amir, the tribes of the northern Hijaz had attacked the railroad as it approached the city of Medina in 1908. They managed to stop its extension to its original goal of Mecca, but the ease of transporting troops to Medina from Syria still enabled the Ottoman government to directly administer the city. Medina was made a separate administrative unit directly under the Ottoman ministry of the interior, and Husayn's delegate in the city was deprived of much of his power.[11]

Husayn and other Meccans feared that if the railroad was extended to Mecca the Ottoman government would also extend its direct political authority there, as it had done in Medina. In 1913–1914 the *vali*, Vehib Bey, and the CUP in Istanbul revived the plan of finishing the railroad to Mecca and Jidda. They also wished to bring the Hijaz under the Law of the *Vilayets* of March 1913, a step that would have curbed the power of Amir Husayn and the autonomy of the Hijaz. In 1913, Husayn also objected strongly to the imposition of conscription in the Hijaz *vilayet*. The *vali* had contingency plans for removing the amir if he continued to oppose centralization. In response to these events, the nomads rose in rebellion, commerce came to a halt, there were riots in Mecca, and the grand vizier of the empire agreed to the amir's request that the extension of the railroad, conscription, and the local implementation of the Law of the *Vilayets* be abandoned.[12]

Although in public the central government officially abandoned its centralizing policies for the Hijaz, in private, Talât Paşa (Talât Bey), the CUP leader and minister of the interior, told a son of the amir that if Husayn continued to oppose the railroad he would be deposed. On the other hand, if he supported the railroad's construction to Mecca, Husayn would receive a number of benefits.¹³

While Husayn resisted CUP pressure after 1912, he and his sons began to assiduously cultivate ties with the Arab nationalists of Syria and with the British in Cairo. If the autonomy of Mecca was to come under direct assault, as seemed likely, Husayn hoped to turn to one or the other group for help. He received a good deal of encouragement from the Arab nationalists and, initially at least, polite discouragement from the British. The outbreak of World War I in Europe and Ottoman neutrality in regard to it seemed likely to alter such calculations made before the war. Husayn wrote the sultan asking the empire to stay out of the conflict.¹⁴ When it entered the war on the side of Germany, a new, threatening, and radically different military-political situation was created for the Ottoman state and for the province of the Hijaz. Under the threat of foreign attack or, at the least, an embargo of the food and pilgrims upon which the Hijazis depended for their lives and livelihoods, independence from the Ottoman empire seemed a more desirable course of action than had earlier been the case. Also, the wartime leadership of the empire was now even more insistent on rigid centralized rule over the provinces than before the war began. These dual pressures might well have led to the loss of power for Husayn and his family; with independence, however, freedom for the Hijaz and restoration of the pilgrimage were certain, and the territory beyond the holy places might be brought under the sway of an independent Arab state, led by the Hashemites. A separate nation-state, independent of the Ottoman empire, became enormously appealing under these circumstances.

Culture and Ideology, 1908–1914. The transformation of the political situation of the Hijaz between 1908 and 1914 was matched by similar changes in its literary climate. New writers, especially in newspaper essays, called for general reforms and changes in society and welcomed Western influence in Arabic literature. Political culture, however, changed little at this time, in part because public critics of the Ottoman empire, such as Ibrahim ibn Hasan al-Uskubi (1847–1913), got into serious trouble with the imperial government as a result of expressing their views.

Nationalism did not spread to significant numbers of the population, while those who wanted independence for the Hijaz were, for the most part, impractical foreigners who envisaged Mecca as the seat of an independent caliphate rather than the capital of an Arab nationalist state.

Hijazi journalism really began after the revolution of 1908 in Istanbul. The first newspaper to appear was the official *al-Hijaz* in 1908; this was an organ of the *vilayet* administration. *Al-Hijaz* followed the policy line of the central government by calling for the unity of Arabs and Turks inside a reformed and reinvigorated Ottoman empire. The short-lived Meccan *Shams al-Haqiqa* in 1909 used as its motto "love of country [*al-watan*] is part of faith"; it was owned and managed by ethnic Turks who were sympathetic to the CUP. Sharif Husayn secured its closing.[15]

Al-Islah al-Hijazi of Jidda was a more influential journal. It was owned by a Syrian, Raghib Mustafa Tawakkul, and edited by a Lebanese, Adib Daud Hariri, and was dedicated to "service to the *umma*." Sharif Husayn supported the paper financially. Although it only lasted a few months, its articles, drawn in part from the Egyptian press, were controversial. It advocated purging the country of despots and the development of progress in the Ottoman empire. The other three newspapers published in the Hijaz province were too ephemeral or unimportant to merit discussion. Ultimately, the amir secured control over the press of the Hijaz by allowing the papers to die a natural death because of a lack of readership, by gaining approval from Istanbul for their suppression, and by influencing the *vilayet* administration in regard to the official newspaper. Despite this situation, there were in the schools and in private life individuals who were familiarizing themselves with the new thoughts coming from Syria and Egypt; in the 1930s and 1940s they would create a new intellectual and literary climate in western Arabia.[16]

In education there were some reforms designed to improve the quality and quantity of students, but apparently little was done to substantially change education between 1908 and 1914, in part because the time period was so short. Official government schools increased in number in the towns. In the curricula by 1909 there was an emphasis on courses that might very well have inculcated both an awareness of the existence of national states elsewhere and Ottoman, though not Arab, loyalty. Courses included European and Ottoman geography, foreign languages such as French, and Ottoman history. The Meccan CUP even established a school of its own in 1910 with about fifty students for the purpose of promoting Ottomanism. In the government schools, including the new normal institute in Medina, students did study Arabic, and the languages of instruction were Turkish and Arabic. Still, popular opinion continued to identify these schools with serving in the Ottoman armed forces and in the government bureaucracy, and, as a result, their enrollments remained lower than those of the private schools.[17]

The premier schools in the province were those of the *haramayn* (mosques of Mecca and Medina). The government reform decree of December 1913 was intended to regulate and regularize the organization of teaching in the Meccan Haram, where the language of instruction was Arabic. Lessons were to include logic, history, and mathematics, but religion naturally continued to dominate.[18]

New private schools outside the harams began to open after 1908, and some new curricula were introduced as well. In Mecca in 1908 the Khayriyya religious school opened; by 1910 it had enrolled around three hundred students. The al-Falah school of Mecca began in 1912, and its curriculum included, significantly, the geography of the Arabian peninsula, intended especially for Hijazi students. Many of al-Falah's students were the children of non-Arabic-speaking foreign residents. The al-Sawlatiyya school reformed its curriculum along Indian lines in 1913.[19]

While these changes were transpiring in the Hijaz, some non-Hijazi Muslims living outside the Arabian peninsula began to think of an independent Hijaz. Even before 1908, rumors of plots in or about Mecca began to surface. In 1879, ʿAbd al-Qadir al-Jazaʾiri was said to be interested in establishing an Arab kingdom that would include Mecca and Medina. In 1883, Jamal al-Din al-Afghani al-Asadabadi erroneously suggested that Great Britain wanted to establish an Arabian caliphate based at Mecca. Some of these speculations were ultimately derived from British sources: G. C. M. Birdwood, Wilfrid Scawen Blunt, and one of the British consuls in Jidda, James Zohrab.[20]

An elective Arab caliphate drawn from among the sharifs of Mecca was envisaged by ʿAbd al-Rahman al-Kawakibi in 1900. In his fictional account of a congress held in Mecca to promote this goal, al-Kawakibi discussed Mecca as the capital of a new state and the center of an effort to revitalize and reform Islam. In 1905, Najib ʿAzuri speculated about a separate Hijazi state with an Arab caliph as its sovereign. Mirza ʿAli Aqa Shirazi, a Persian writer who was a resident of Mecca in 1908–1909, published one issue of a newspaper there, in which he called for an assembly of Muslims to meet in Mecca to address religious reform.[21]

These rumors and speculations found very little resonance in the Hijaz. Most Hijazis, in all probability, did not even know of them. And when in nearby areas circumstances created uprisings against Ottoman authority or political upheavals that might have been presumed to have a nationalistic tinge, there was almost no support or sympathy displayed in the Hijaz. This was the case for the ʿUrabi events in Egypt in 1882, the Mahdiyya in the Sudan throughout the 1880s and 1890s, and the revolts in Yemen and ʿAsir in 1902–1905.[22]

The reasons for the near absence of Arab nationalism in the Hijaz were numerous. Most important among them was the strength of religious identity and interests among the people and elites of the Hijaz.

It was precisely religion that made the province important to the Ottomans, the British, and, in general, the outside world. The enthusiastic reception given by the Ottomans to the Prophet Muhammad's banner that was sent from Medina to Damascus and Jerusalem in December 1914 was an indication of this, as was the constant pressure from the imperial government upon the amir for his joining in the declaration of holy war (jihad) against the enemies of the empire during World War I. Great Britain sought an alliance with Husayn primarily for the same reason—to gain his religious prestige—as well as for the strategic location of the Hijaz and the amir's potential leadership of a general Arab insurrection in the other Arab provinces of the Ottoman empire. Within the Hijaz religion dominated most aspects of public life, and the power and prestige of the amirs rested upon a religious foundation.[23]

Secular nationalism was weak in the Hijaz because the sort of people who were nationalists elsewhere were largely missing from this region. There were few, if any, Arab nationalists among the resident teachers and journalists, while external nationalistic writings had very little appeal in Mecca, Medina, and Jidda. Because there was no conscription and Hijazis did not wish to volunteer, there were probably no Hijazis in the Ottoman regular armed forces.

Feuding factions among the ruling elite, and younger members of the ruling elite who sought to displace their elders, were recruits to nationalism elsewhere.[24] In the Hijaz, the younger members of the amir's family were becoming nationalists in the 1910s, but there seem to have been few other Hijazis who felt as they did. One reason for this was the extraordinary ethnic and social diversity of the Muslim communities in the chief towns. Muslims from all parts of the world came to the Hijaz on pilgrimage, to study in the harams, and to conduct business. Many stayed, and large resident communities of Javanese, Indians, Malays, Algerians, Egyptians, and so on, came into existence. Insofar as there was a common identity among these peoples, it was based on religion, not on Arab ethnicity.

Arab nationalism also spread among merchants, landowners, and bureaucrats in other places as a result of European encroachments or as a means by which an indigenous Christian minority might bridge the gap between themselves and fellow Arabs who were Muslims. In the Hijaz after 1858 there was little direct European encroachment, and because known Christians were not permitted to visit the holy cities of Mecca and Medina, there was no Christian European group in these towns. Similarly, nearly the entire population of the province was Muslim, so there was no large Ottoman Christian minority to become nationalist.

Nationalism itself was a relatively new set of ideas and values in the Middle East in the late nineteenth and early twentieth centuries. Its terms, meaning, and implications were amorphous and were poorly understood even by those who sought decentralization or independence. In the Hijaz, localistic patriotism identified with a specific, usually small, territory, and group identity based on Sunni Islam certainly existed. The perception of a large number of people that "they belong to a community that is entitled to and capable of maintaining independent statehood and who grant that community... primary terminal loyalty"[25] was clearly missing, unless it might take the form of loyalty to the universal Islamic *umma*.

Despite the weakness of nationalism in the Hijaz, the Arab

Revolt that began there in 1916 did succeed. The townspeople of Mecca and Jidda supported Sharif Husayn, and he received substantial backing from many of the nomads. The leaders of the towns and the tribes were strongly in favor of keeping the privileges of the Hijaz, including its exemption from conscription and many forms of taxes. They opposed the centralizing and secularizing policies of the CUP, as seen in the drive to extend the Hijaz Railroad to Mecca and Jidda, just as their predecessors had opposed similar attempts at changes during the Tanzimat and Hamidian periods. Sharif Husayn and his sons demonstrated considerable skill in leading the Hijazis toward independence; their personal abilities, prestige, rank, and courage were major ingredients in bringing about the success of the revolt. Also, the disasters that befell the Ottoman empire in the Balkans and North Africa before 1914, and the naval power of the British in the Red Sea during World War I, indicated that the Hijaz could no longer be protected by the Ottoman state, and that the leadership of that state was quite prepared to sacrifice the fragile economy of the Hijaz in its illusory pursuit of victory in the war. By 1916 the Hijazis faced an inescapable choice between economic destruction and possible foreign occupation, or independence and relative economic well-being under the leadership of the amir.[26] As a result, most Hijazis, despite the uncertainty about the outcome of the war, cooperated with Sharif Husayn when he announced the Arab Revolt. And Arab national independence began in the nonnationalistic Hijaz.

Notes

1. For a more detailed discussion of the Ottoman Hijaz (Hejaz) in the nineteenth century, see William Ochsenwald, *Religion, Society and the State in Arabia*.
2. Randall Baker, *King Husain and the Kingdom of the Hijaz*, p. 33.
3. Ochsenwald, *Religion*, pp. 3–7.
4. Ibid., pp. 178–83; Turkey, Istanbul, Bashbakanlik Arsivi, Yildiz 31.995.103.88, instructions to the *vali;* 31.995.103.88, instructions to the *vali* and amir; 12.112/3.112.6, instructions to Osman. For a valuable general survey of relations between Istanbul and Mecca, see Butrus Abu-Manneh, "Sultan Abdülhamid II and the Sharifs of Mecca (1880–1900)," pp. 1–21. A recent Turkish discussion empha-

sizes the suspicions the sultan had in regard to the Hijaz; see Omer Kürkchuoglu, *Osmanli Devleti'ne Karshi Arap Bagimsizlik Hareketi (1908–1918)* [Arab independence movements against the Ottoman state], especially pp. 68–70.

5. The crucial role of the press in Arab nationalism is stressed in most of the essays contained in Marwan R. Buheiry, ed., *Intellectual Life in the Arab East, 1809–1939*, ed. Marwan R. Buheiry .
6. For a discussion of education in the Hijaz see Muhammad ʿAbd al-Rahman al-Shamikh, *al-Taʿlim fi makka wa al-madina* [Education in Mecca and Medina] (Riyadh: n.p., 1973); Ochsenwald, *Religion*, pp. 74–84; and C. Snouck Hurgronje, *Mekka in the Latter Part of the 19th Century* (Leiden: 1970 reprint), pp. 162–69.
7. Al-Shamikh, *al-Taʿlim*, p. 33.
8. Muhammad ʿAbd al- Rahman al-Shamikh, *The Rise of Modern Prose in Saudi Arabia* (Riyadh: King Saud University and University Libraries, 1984), pp. 9–20; and Caesar Farah, "Censorship and Freedom of Expression in Ottoman Syria and Egypt," in pp. 151–94.
9. Sulayman (Suleiman) Musa, *al-Haraka al-ʿarabiyya* [The Arab movement], pp. 49–52.
10. C. Ernest Dawn, *From Ottomanism to Arabism*, pp. 14–15, 50; and Musa, *al-Haraka*, p. 56. When Husayn went to ʿAsir to lead the battle to regain that area for the empire, he spoke to the notables of Mecca of his sacrificing himself for "his country [*bilad*], and his nation [*watan*], and his sultan" (ibid., pp. 53–55). Country and nation refer to the Ottoman Empire.
11. William Ochsenwald, "Opposition to Political Centralization in South Jordan and the Hijaz, 1900–1914," pp. 303–4; and Dawn, *From Ottomanism to Arabism*, p. 9.
12. William Ochsenwald, *The Hijaz Railroad*, pp. 130–1; Musa, *al-Haraka*, pp. 75–78; Dawn, *From Ottomanism to Arabism*, p. 17; and Elie Kedourie, *England and the Middle East*, p. 50. T. E. Lawrence, *Secret Despatches from Arabia* (London: 1939), p. 27, claimed during World War I that the nomads of the Hijaz had been deadly enemies to the Turks for generations; this seems to be an exaggerated view, as is his discussion of the rise of nationalist sentiment in general (see p. 39).
13. Musa, *al-Haraka*, p. 79; Ochsenwald, *The Hijaz Railroad*, pp. 131–32.
14. Zeine N. Zeine, *Emergence of Arab Nationalism*, p. 105 n.2, on entry into the war. A discussion of the contacts of Husayn with the nationalists and the British falls outside the scope of this paper.
15. Muhammad ʿAbd al-Rahman al-Shamikh, *al-Sihafa fi al-Hijaz 1908–1941* [The press in the Hijaz, 1908–1941], pp. 27–31, 38, 42.
16. Al-Shamikh, *al-Sihafa*, pp. 45, 82; al-Shamikh, *Rise of Modern Prose*, p. 18; and ʿAbdallah al-Jabbar, *al-Tayyarat al-adabiyya al-haditha fi*

qalb al-jazirat al-ʿarabiyya [Modern literary currents in the heart of the Arabian peninsula], pp. 136–41. I wish to thank Professor Ahmed Tarabein for drawing my attention to al-Jabbar's work.
17. Al-Shamikh, al-Taʿlim, pp. 31–34, 75, 81–82.
18. Ibid., pp. 14–17.
19. Ibid., pp. 42–44, 50, 57.
20. Zeine, *Emergence of Arab Nationalism*, p. 56 n. 23 (and see p. 59 n. 30); and Martin Kramer, *Islam Assembled*, pp. 10–18.
21. Ochsenwald, *Religion*, p. 201; Kramer, *Islam Assembled*, pp. 40–41, 48–49; and Zeine, *Emergence of Arab Nationalism*, pp. 66–67.
22. Ochsenwald, *Religion*, pp. 202–4.
23. George Antonius, *The Arab Awakening*, pp. 140, 147–48; and C. Snouck Hurgronje, *The Revolt in Arabia* (New York: 1917), pp. 5, 7.
24. Philip S. Khoury, *Urban Notables*; and Rashid Khalidi, "Social Factors in the Rise of the Arab Movement in Syria," pp. 54, 57.
25. Richard Cottam, "Nationalism in the Middle East: A Behavioural Approach," in Said Amir Arjomand, ed., *From Nationalism to Revolutionary Islam*, p. 29. Also see Albert Hourani, *Emergence of the Modern Middle East*, p. 186; Hisham Sharabi, *Arab Intellectuals and the West*, pp. 105–9; William Haddad, "Nationalism in the Ottoman Empire," pp. 3–24, especially p. 19; and Michael Hudson, *Arab Politics: The Search for Legitimacy* (New Haven: 1977), pp. 34–35.
26. Hourani, *Emergence of the Modern Middle East*, p. 203; Hurgronje, *Revolt in Arabia*, pp. 36–38; Gerald de Gaury, *Rulers of Mecca* (London: 1951), p. 264; Zayn Nur al-Din Zayn, "Asbab al-thawra al-ʿarabiyya al-kubra," in *Dirasat fi al-thawra al-ʿarabiyya al-kubra* [Studies on the great Arab revolt] (Amman: n.d.), pp. 39, 55; and Khayriyyah Qasimiyyah, *al-Hukuma al-ʿarabiyya fi Dimashq bayna 1918–1920* [The Arab government in Damascus between 1918 and 1920], pp. 24–25.

TEN

The Hashemites, the Arab Revolt, and Arab Nationalism

Mary C. Wilson

Most historians of Arab nationalism now agree that the ideology was spawned in the cities of the Fertile Crescent among a class of provincial notables that had lost power because of changes in Istanbul between 1908 and 1914. Yet despite its place of origin, the first organized movement that arose in its name—the Arab revolt—emerged out of the Arabian peninsula led by Sharif Husayn of Mecca. Scholars such as George Antonius, C. Ernest Dawn, and Elie Kedourie have been intrigued by the strange parentage of the Arab revolt, but they have questioned neither the revolt's Arab nationalist identity nor its unique position in Arab history. (See Dawn's latest formulation, in this respect, in his essay in this volume.)

For historians of the Middle East, the Arab revolt is the symbolic touchstone of Arab nationalism. As such it was certainly used to good purpose by its Hashemite leaders, who later came to rule Transjordan and Iraq. Nonetheless, one is tempted to question the assumed simple and straightforward relationship of the Arab revolt to the development of Arab nationalism. For example, in the formation of nationalist parties in the newly created Arab states after the war, men who had not taken part in the revolt, or who had fought on the Ottoman side, were not necessarily at a disadvantage.[1] Only in Iraq did a coterie of "Sharifian officers" form a distinct and privileged group within the political hierarchy.[2] Others who took part in the revolt switched loyalties later, not away from Arab nationalism but from the Hashemites to the Saudis when the consequences of the Hashemite-British relationship began to unfold. As for the tribesmen who had been the rank and file of the revolt, they returned to the politics of tribal feuds and alliances that customarily governed their political lives, and had little concern for the ideology that had once thrust them onto the stage of world history.

The nationalism that became the reigning ideology in the Arab world after the demise of the Ottoman Empire owed its spread less perhaps to the Arab revolt than to the end of the Ottoman empire, the consequent demise of the reigning ideology of Ottomanism, and the imposition of European control in the Fertile Crescent. Indeed, in some ways it makes better sense to view the revolt as the death rattle of the traditional Ottoman order, the last gasp of a repetitive cycle of tension and struggle between Istanbul and a provincial elite, than as the birth pangs of a new state system in the Arab East. How else to explain the dilemma presented by the Hashemites, who at one and the same time were the acknowledged leaders of the struggle for "independence" from the Ottomans as well as the conduits of British power into the heart of Arab affairs?

The historical development of Arab nationalism is usually viewed as follows: (1) the idea of Arabism emerges in the cities of the Fertile Crescent, especially Damascus and Beirut, in reaction to post-1908 changes emanating from Istanbul; (2) World War I makes it possible for some Arabs, with the encouragement of their new British ally, to revolt against the empire; and (3) the empire is destroyed, and Arab nationalism becomes the dominant ideology in the region when Britain reneges on its promises to the Arabs and agrees to the imposition of British and French mandates in the Fertile Crescent.

In this sequence, steps one and two are usually stressed. It is step three, however, that made the primacy of Arab nationalism inevitable. Step two is less important in its creation of an active militant nationalism on the basis of Arabism than it is in its introduction of new actors and forces-namely, the Hashemites and their British allies. The British, with their primary concern being to protect Britain's imperial routes of communication, would ultimately be at odds with Arab nationalism. As for the Hashemites, they, like other political leaders, were searching for an ideology tailored to their ambitions. That they found such an ideology in Arab nationalism is without doubt. But, given their alliance with Britain, the ideology was not a perfect fit. At what point and in what circumstances did Hashemite ambitions and Arab nationalism come together? And once they did, was it irreversible? Here there is perhaps an unresolvable problem of definition—for at different times and in different places, what did it mean to be an Arab nationalist? In an imperfect world where the dictates of realpolitik were harsh and no one was pure, where was the line between self-interest and national interest, collaboration and judicious restraint? Was participation in the Arab revolt—even a leading position in it— enough to establish nationalist credentials?

In the absence of objective criteria, one may fall back on the public perceptions of the people concerned-the Arabs. Looking over the careers of two Hashemite brothers, one, Faysal (Faisal) is definitely accorded nationalist kudos; the other, ʿAbdallah (Abdullah) is not. Since both took a leading part in fomenting and leading the Arab revolt, a comparative look at their political lives may shed some light on the nationalist identity of the Arab revolt and its objective importance to the coalescence of an Arab nationalist movement.

One of the problems in studying the Hashemites and Arab nationalism before World War I is that sources are scarce. Jordanian historian Sulayman (Suleiman) Musa has done more than anyone to try to bring Hashemite correspondence within the reach of scholars. But his first volume of *al-Murasalat al-tarikhiyya* (Historical Correspondence) begins only in 1914.[3] Without diaries and letters to tell us what the Hashemites were thinking before the war made a break with the Ottoman Empire not only possible but imperative, one can so far only judge their aims and interests by what has been recorded of their actions.

Sharif Husayn, ʿAbdallah and Faysal's father and the figurehead of the revolt, was appointed Sharif of Mecca in November 1908 after the Young Turk revolution. The configuration of circumstances and influences that led to his appointment is not entirely clear. George Antonius wrote that Husayn owed his appointment to the Young Turks; ʿAbdallah's memoirs, published after Antonius' book, indicate that his father's appointment was generated within the Palace.[4] Historical evidence goes against a Husayn-Young Turk alliance and suggests that from the outset Husayn was at odds with Young Turk ideology and the policies that emanated from that ideology.[5]

Certainly Husayn's appointment crowned a lifetime of striving. Among the many he had tried to influence in his favor was the British ambassador in Istanbul. Some months before his appointment he had sent the ambassador a "very friendly message expressing his feelings of gratitude to England for her sympathy towards the Ottoman constitutional movement." Thus the ambassador was later able to approve of the new Sharif of Mecca as "an upright man who is unlikely to connive at or condone the extortions on pilgrims or other malpractices of his predecessor under the old regime."[6] That Husayn was trying to impress Britain is clear from his message, for he was not, in fact, favorably disposed toward constitutions. While British approbation could not by itself secure the appointment of a particular candidate, Britain's interest in Hijazi affairs was well known and British disapproval would have been a serious hindrance to any candidate.

When Husayn arrived in Mecca, the town was in turmoil over expected changes stemming from the events in Istanbul. He had, however, been given a written assurance by Grand Vizier Kamil Pasha that the customary rights of the Sharif of Mecca would not be affected by the introduction of a constitutional government in Istanbul (evidence that his appointment did not originate with the Young Turks). Hence he announced to his new constituents that "the constitution of the country of God is the law of God [shari'a] and the saying and doing [sunna] of His Prophet."[7] Nonetheless, in the years before World War I, Ottoman policies of centralization increasingly threatened to limit Husayn's exercise of power in the Hijaz (Hejaz). The symbol of encroaching Ottoman authority was the Hijaz Railroad, which had been been completed to Medina in 1908. Although the railroad had been a pet project of Sultan Abdülhamid's and was completed as far as it ever would be before his fall from power, its extension to Mecca was pursued by his successors. This project and other changes in provincial government threatened Husayn's autonomy and put him in a position similar to that of the Arab urban notables in the Fertile Crescent, whose loss of power after 1908 led to the coalescence of the ideology of Arabism.

'Abdallah thus took a leading part in familiar maneuvering to stave off Ottoman intrusion in the years from 1908 to 1914.

In the winter of 1908–1909, for example, he accompanied the pilgrimage caravan back to Damascus in order to refute the contention of the *amir al-hajj* (Commander of the pilgrimage), ʿAbd al-Rahman Pasha al-Yusuf, that the land route was not safe. Since a large part of the sharif's prestige rested on his ability to ensure a safe pilgrimage, such a charge was dangerous. It appeared, moreover, to have been politically motivated as ʿAbd al-Rahman Pasha was identified with the Committee of Union and Progress (CUP).[8] Occurring so soon after Husayn's arrival in the Hijaz, it also suggests that the CUP was not pleased with his appointment. In any event, the caravan returned safely to Damascus by land while the *amir al-hajj* sailed home alone.

This trip to Damascus was ʿAbdallah's first and only visit to the city, and his only visit to the Fertile Crescent before he became Amir of Transjordan. He spent seven days in Damascus with the aristocratic al-Bakri family whom he knew from Istanbul. Thirty years later he was to write in his memoirs that the al-Bakris and similar Damascene families were disaffected from the Ottoman government and on the verge "of splitting the bonds."[9] But this is a judgment shaped by hindsight. The disaffection of the Damascene elite at the time was focused not on the Ottoman system as a whole, but on the Young Turk revolution. And ʿAbdallah at the time, so recently returned to Mecca after fifteen years in Istanbul, would not have been a figure to whom such a startling confidence could safely be made. (When Faysal visited Damascus in 1915, he, too, stayed with the al-Bakri family. Antonius relates that even then "it was some time before they [members of al-Fatat] spoke their mind openly, for Faysal was a stranger to them and he was known to favor cooperation with the Turks").[10] That Husayn was at odds with the CUP was clear, but this did not by any means make him anti-Ottoman. During the winter of 1908–1909 the CUP was still a phase in Ottoman affairs that might yet be transcended. It was not until after the unsuccessful counterrevolution of April 1909 that the changes precipitated by the Young Turk revolution began to look durable.

ʿAbdallah's actions over the next five years were not notably affected by his experiences in Damascus, at least not as he recorded them in his memoirs. Rather, they were shaped wholly by tactics—that were well within the bounds of normal central-peripheral tensions of the Ottoman systems—to maintain and enhance his father's position as Sharif of Mecca.

ʿAbdallah was a key figure in maintaining the Istanbul-Mecca axis since he traveled regularly to Istanbul as a representative to the Ottoman parliament from Mecca. If he got the worst of both worlds in a climatic sense, he got the best of both in a political sense. It was he, rather than his older brother ʿAli or his younger brother Faysal, who represented his father in Istanbul. He cultivated good relations with the Ottoman elite, whom he knew from his residence in the capital from 1893 to 1908. In addition, he always stopped in Cairo on his way to and from Istanbul to stay with his friend the Khedive ʿAbbas Hilmi II, certainly a most important political friend for any ruler of the Hijaz. In the Hijaz, he (along with his brothers) was an important link in his father's tribal policies, which were described by a contemporary observer: "Sharif Husayn sent out one son in one direction and another son in another direction until the area had been brought under control."[11]

While ʿAbdallah was a known figure in Istanbul, there is no evidence that he played much part in parliamentary politics. In his memoirs he refers to his first two terms as ones of "examination and exploration."[12] There is no indication that his later term was one of increased participation. Neither brother's name appears on Ottoman lists of party affiliations,[13] and British records mention the brothers only to remark on their lack of activity.[14] In assessing the Hashemites' knowledge of and involvement with nascent Arabism, it is of particular importance that there is no record of their reaction to such issues as Zionist settlement in Palestine or the British Lynch concession on the Tigris and Euphrates. (For details, see the essays by Samir Seikaly and Mahmoud Haddad in this volume.) These issues were actively debated in Parliament by Arab deputies from the Fertile Crescent, and Arab interests were recognized as such by Istanbul to the extent that Zionist settlement in Palestine was forbidden, a ministerial crisis was precipitated in order to reverse the British Lynch concession, and Ottoman troops were sent to Libya against the Italians.

During the years 1908–1914, Sharif Husayn was considered to be an Ottoman loyalist by Arabs beginning to think in terms of Arab interests. As C. Ernest Dawn has pointed out, although Sharif Husayn had his own problems with Ottoman authority, it was in his interest to act as the agent of Ottoman authority in his relations with neighboring tribes. Thus, in 1910, after a successful foray into Najd (Nejd), the Hashemites secured from ʿAbd al-ʿAziz ibn ʿAbd al-Rahman al-Saʿud an agreement confirming his attachment to the Ottoman Empire and to the sharifs of Mecca.[15] And in 1911, Husayn intervened in ʿAsir as an agent of Ottoman power against the Idrisi rebels. ʿAbdallah had rushed home from Istanbul to take part in this campaign, ignoring the advice proffered by the Khedive that for the Sharif to undertake such an action on behalf of Istanbul would antagonize Arab opinion.[16]

Yet if to some Arabs it looked as though Husayn was an Ottoman loyalist, to some Ottomans it looked as though Husayn, under an Ottoman aegis, was acting mainly in his own interests. For example, the Ottoman commander at Ibha, Sulayman Pasha, argued against Husayn's involvement in the ʿAsir campaign. He warned the Porte that if the empire called on Husayn in its defense, Husayn would use his new importance to aggrandize his own position. Sulayman Pasha did not, however, see the threat that Husayn posed in terms of an ethnic Arab nationalism. Rather, he saw him as a personally ambitious man whose ambitions might eventually get in the way of a smooth-running empire.

The Hashemites' intervention in ʿAsir was only a superficial success. Husayn helped to relieve the siege of Ibha, but he did not add permanently to his own power by doing so. Sulayman Pasha described Husayn's progress through ʿAsir as "a ship in the water, its prow cutting waves in the front and the water returning to harmony behind it leaving nothing but a faint trace which soon passed away."[17]

Nonetheless, Husayn returned to the Hijaz in a combative and independent frame of mind, just as Sulayman Pasha had warned. The two years from 1912 to the outbreak of the war saw increased tension between Mecca and Istanbul. Husayn does not appear to have initiated the tension, however. Rather, Ottoman policies threatened him. For example, in 1910 the *muhafiz* of Medina had announced that the sharif's deputy in the city was no longer needed. The sharif would continue to be responsible for pilgrims throughout the Hijaz, but because the telegraph and railway had greatly increased the speed of communication between Medina and Istanbul, the *muhafaza* of Medina would be bound directly to the ministry of the interior in the capital for administrative purposes.[18] In short, technological innovations enabled Husayn's religious duties to be separated from his administrative ones and thus his activities were to be confined to the religious sphere. In 1910 and thereafter, tribal revolts in the vicinity of Medina were rumored to have been encouraged by Husayn in order to challenge the new Ottoman administrative arrangements. The threat to extend the Hijaz Railway to Mecca and to impose the new Law of the *Vilayets* (March 1913), which would regularize and rationalize provincial government and thus destroy the special status and privileges of the Hijaz, further demonstrated to Husayn the trend of Ottoman policy. He naturally reacted in ways designed to protect the traditional autonomy of the Hijaz and his own position.

It was within the framework of protecting the traditional place of the Hijaz in the Ottoman order that 'Abdallah had his famous conversation with Lord Kitchener in Cairo in February 1914. 'Abdallah was on his way to Istanbul for the delayed opening of Parliament. In the Red Sea he had seen the ship, bristling with Ottoman troops, bringing the new Ottoman *vali* to Mecca. This, he felt, indicated the onset of a stricter Ottoman policy. Disquieted, he asked Kitchener if Britain would support his father against any Ottoman attempt to dismiss him. Kitchener did not give him a positive answer but was not unfriendly. News of his meeting with Kitchener traveled rapidly, and when he arrived in Istanbul he found the Ottoman government conciliatory. The Law of the *Vilayets* had already been repudiated, and in return for allowing the Hijaz Railroad to be extended to Mecca, his father would be granted his position for his lifetime and to his descendants after him; also he would get L250,000 outright and one-third of the annual revenue from the railway; and, finally, he himself would take command of the security forces sent to protect the railway during its construction.[19]

With this message, 'Abdallah returned to Mecca. He saw Ronald Storrs in Cairo on the way home and reiterated his desire that Britain should guarantee the status quo in Arabia against "wanton Turkish aggression."[20] In other words, he hoped Britain would throw its diplomatic weight against Ottoman centralization in the Hijaz, and that in the balance the Hijaz would retain its traditional autonomy within the Ottoman Empire.

At the outbreak of World War I, 'Abdallah was in Istanbul again, armed with the time-honored delaying tactic that a committee should be formed to study the problem of the extension of the Hijaz Railroad. Thus, as war broke out, Mecca and Istanbul had reached a stale-mate. Istanbul insisted on the extension of the railway; Husayn continued to see the extension as a long-term threat to his position regardless of what Istanbul might offer as concessions in the short term.

The war added a new ingredient to Husayn's negotiations with the Porte. 'Abdallah's meetings with British representatives in Cairo before the war had already helped win some concessions from Istanbul. Now, Britain had suddenly begun to vie for his favor. To Britain's first feelers concerning an anti-Ottoman alliance, 'Abdallah replied for his father that "the people of the Hedjaz will accept and be well-satisfied with more close union with Great Britain ..., owing to the notorious neglect by Constantinople of religion and its rights... Great Britain will take first place in their eyes so long as she protects the right of our country ... and its independence."[21] What he meant by "independence" is open to dispute; however, it is clear that initially the frame of reference was kept carefully to the Hijaz. The next message from Britain was more ambitious; according to Antonius, "it spoke of 'the Arab nation' and of 'the emancipation of the Arabs.'"[22] Returning from Damascus six months later, Faysal carried with him a protocol, drawn up by members of the secret nationalist societies in Damascus, that defined, geographically, the Arab nation.[23] By the time Sharif Husayn began his famous correspondence with Sir Henry McMahon in July 1915, the language of Arab nationalism was in place.

The Husayn-McMahon correspondence shows clearly that in negotiating with Britain, the Sharif consciously adopted the language and terms of nationalism. In a sense, he chose an idiom that was especially comprehensible to European sensibilities. He began his first letter, "Whereas the entire Arab nation without exception is determined to assert its right to live, gain its freedom and administer its own affairs in name and in fact..."[24] In a similar manner, McMahon thought he was speaking to Husayn's particular sensibilities when he spoke in terms of the caliphate. Succeeding letters from Husayn have no similar grandiose phrases. They concentrate instead on the borders of the future Arab kingdom, borders that were named in conformity with the Damascus protocol.

If the discussion of borders indicates Husayn's awareness of his new Arab constituency, it also shows his clear understanding of the risks involved in revolt. An impressive justification was needed for a Muslim leader to seek an alliance with a Christian power in order to challenge the foremost Muslim state of the period. Personal ambition was not enough. In particular, it was not enough for the Sharif of Mecca, who depended on the support and approbation of Muslims the world over. Husayn knew that the Hijaz could not stand alone. It depended on subventions from the Ottoman Empire and from the Muslim world at large. If he were to destroy the framework of empire, he would have to replace it with another sort of framework, one that would relieve the Hijaz of its material indigence.

By all accounts it was 'Abdallah who most strongly urged alliance with Britain on his father. Lawrence described him as the "spur" of his father.[25] Behind his impatience lay his experience, since 1910, of shuttling between Istanbul and Mecca. At best his efforts had gained time while maintaining the status quo in the Hijaz. But the threat of increased Ottoman supervision hung as ever over his father's ambitions and the family's future prospects. His focus at this time appears to have been the Hijaz, where only the intervention of a new force could break the stalemate between Istanbul's policy and the Sharif's will. He may also have been thinking of the succession to the Sharifate where, if it was to be kept in his natal family, he appeared to be the favorite over his older brother 'Ali. Faysal, who was the intermediary with Arab nationalist organizations in Syria between 1914 and 1916, was more cautious about declaring a revolt, perhaps because he knew better the strength of the Ottoman presence in Syria and the weakness of the Arab movement in terms of both organization and appeal. But with the imposition of a British embargo on trade in the Red Sea, calculations concerning the immediate provisioning of the Hijaz proved decisive and the revolt was declared.

The language of nationalism suited Husayn's needs in some ways, but in Mecca itself and in other important forums, the language of Islam was an equally important tool. William Cleveland has shown that the Meccan newspaper *al-Qibla*, which was founded to propagate and justify the Arab revolt, did so mainly in terms of Islam: "The Ottoman Empire has been taken over by a reckless party which has launched an attack on Islam, an attack which is *fitna* [sedition] in every sense of the term. The leaders of the state do not care about religion or the *shari'a* ... and have begun to live under the signs of apostasy and unbelief."[26] *Al-Qibla* also objected to the political appropriation of Islam by the CUP, and accused it of replacing Islamic solidarity with Turkish nationalism.

Hence the ideology of Arabism was not espoused by the Hashemites until it became of particular use to them with particular audiences. It became useful insofar as they began to take political action in areas outside of the bounds of their traditional sphere in Arabia. It also became useful when they began a dialogue with a European power whose political frame of reference was ethnic nationalism. Until 1916, and perhaps even afterward, their struggle for power with a centralizing Ottoman regime was not directed at the destruction of that regime or at independence. Such a course was too perilous to pursue in a region that had always depended for its material well-being on healthy infusions from the outside. And in material ways, Istanbul had always been most generous to Mecca. But with the appearance of a new protector, Britain, the Hashemites suddenly had a choice: they could trade on their loyalty to the Ottoman Empire to restore the sort of regional autonomy within the empire that they had envisioned all along; or, with Britain temporarily willing to fill the material gap, they could break with the empire and construct a new framework of support—an Arab state made up of territories outside the customary Hashemite purview. The creation of this state would be legitimized by the ideology of Arab nationalism.

One must be somewhat wary of putting too rational and too functional an interpretation on the espousal of nationalism by the Hashemites, but as the revolt progressed one can continue to see the attraction of the Hashemites to Arabism in terms of particular interests. This becomes especially clear when considering the different roles of 'Abdallah and Faysal in the revolt and the resulting divergence of their relations with the Arab nationalist movement. For Faysal, whose military activities took him outside traditional Hashemite spheres of influence and into Syria, Arabism provided the necessary ideological justification both for his particular leadership and for his actions against the empire. Through T. E. Lawrence and other British officers, he was also in immediate contact with British representatives whose ears were particularly attuned to the ethnic nationalist idiom of revolt and whose records have largely defined the terms of the revolt for historians. His geographical location allowed him to supersede ʿAbdallah who, until the declaration of the revolt, had been the chief Hashemite interlocutor with Europe.

ʿAbdallah spent the revolt in Arabia, distant from the fronts that were of major concern to Europe and from the nationalist movement of the Fertile Crescent. His military activities consisted of reducing Ottoman outposts in areas where Hashemite authority was an accepted feature of the political landscape. Hence he had less need than Faysal to justify his actions in the language of Arabism. Where ʿAbdallah had been eager for the alliance with Britain, he was now patient as the long-drawn-out sieges, first of Ta'if and later of Medina, reached their slow culmination.

The British were displeased with ʿAbdallah's methods. They noted, with a whiff of disapproval, that he had decided to lose time rather than lives.[27] But as a local leader, his battle plan was understandable and justified. He went out of his way to be lenient with civilians in the towns, who were allowed to leave as food dwindled, for these civilians were his father's subjects. He also treated the surrendering Turkish garrisons with scrupulous honor and respect. At Medina, the second holy city of Islam after Mecca and where the Prophet lies buried, ʿAbdallah had an additional reason not to press an attack, since he did not want to be accused of desecrating a sacred place. He could not claim to be fighting against the godless Turks and at the same time destroy the Prophet's tomb. Indeed, Medina did not surrender until three months after the Armistice of Mudros, and then it did so owing to a mutiny within the garrison rather than to an increased use of force from ʿAbdallah's side.[28] Nevertheless, his lack of vigorous action in Arabia cost him his place in British esteem, where he was supplanted by Faysal.

There was a method to ʿAbdallah's madness, however. His ambitions at this time lay in Arabia, and Britain believed that he would inherit his father's position.[29] Hence he was anxious to expand his father's domain and he was said to be the instigator of Husayn's claims to be "King of the Arabs." Although the title has a distinct nationalist ring to it, ʿAbdallah seems to have seen such a title chiefly in an Arabian framework. When Britain refused to recognize this new title, he defended his father's right to it by citing the other Arab rulers and tribal chiefs in the peninsula, one by one: Ibn Saʿud was a shaykh and Husayn did not propose to interfere with his work or his land; the Idrisi of ʿAsir was not recognized by anyone to be anything; the Imam of Yemen could rule his land, but he would not deny that the Sharif of Mecca should be the ruler of Hijaz and king of the Arabs. As for the Arab tribes, none would oppose the Sharif's becoming king of the Arabs since the history of the sharifs of Mecca went back to the time of the Arab kingdom of the ʿAbbasids.[30]

ʿAbdallah also explicitly told Lawrence that he was interested in a kingdom of south Arabia, comprising ʿAsir and Yemen.[31] Hence, staying in Arabia was a rational choice for him rather than taking part in the riskier forays farther north. Still, his interests in Arabia set him against other Arabs, namely Ibn Saʿud. Against such local enemies, Arab nationalism was at this time a useless ideology. And so in this way, too, ʿAbdallah grew more distant from the ideology of Arab nationalism that, as the war reached its end, came to dominate the political elites in the north.

For the final year of the war, ʿAbdallah remained outside Medina. He needed no special justification to get his bedouin forces to attack the railway, which they had always opposed. Indeed, his greatest concern was not with Medina, but with events in central Arabia where Ibn Saʿud was waxing stronger. In the spring of 1918 the tribes centered around Khurma oasis, to the east of Ta'if, refused to pay taxes to the Sharif's tax collector. Instead they began paying taxes to Ibn Saʿud. Khalid ibn Luwa'y, the Sharifian agent installed there, went over to Ibn Saʿud as well, reportedly because ʿAbdallah had previously insulted him.[32] The refusal to pay taxes, which was the customary expression of tribal fealty, was tantamount to a declaration of war. From that time on, up to half of ʿAbdallah's troops were diverted to Khurma.

It was in the vicinity of Khurma, rather than against the

Turks at Medina, that ʿAbdallah's supporters were actively engaged in battle. In such clashes, tribal loyalties as well as (on Ibn Saʿud's side) the ideology of a reformed and purified Islam were at work. Throughout 1918 the skirmishing between Hashemite forces and those of Ibn Saʿud went on without a decisive victory for either side. Finally, in the spring of 1919 after the surrender of Medina, ʿAbdallah was free to move with his full strength toward Khurma. Nearby, at the village of Turaba, he was disastrously defeated by forces loyal to Ibn Saʿud. He described his losses to the British consul: "I have unfortunately escaped from amongst the very dear people who were killed in a most abominable manner. All my attendants and staff were killed before I left them while I myself was surrounded by the enemy but I managed to escape."[33] Such a decisive rout killed his dreams of a kingdom in Arabia as well.

Until 1919, ʿAbdallah and Faysal, though both leaders of the Arab revolt, moved in quite different spheres and spoke different political languages. Faysal, the chief liaison with both Britain and the nationalists of the Fertile Crescent, used the new language of Arab nationalism. ʿAbdallah, concerned with the protection and extension of his patrimony in Arabia, relied on the old language of religion and of tribal and familial loyalties. After his defeat at Turaba he returned to Mecca and busied himself as he had before the war, as his father's go-between with Britain. But the business in which he was involved had only to do with Hijazi affairs. So while Faysal was at the peace conference in Paris, ʿAbdallah was discussing quarantine arrangements with the British consul in Jidda.

Despite Faysal's mastery of the new language of Arab nationalism, he met initially with defeat as well. Not everyone in Damascus jumped on the bandwagon of the new movement and its youthful leaders. (See Muhammad Muslih's essay, in this volume, for more on this topic.) When France occupied Damascus, Faysal and his nationalist government were ousted. A year later, though, he was put on the throne of the British mandate of Iraq. On the one hand, if British officials felt a nagging sense of responsibility toward Faysal for his wartime activities, on the other they felt he had learned a valuable lesson in Syria that would make him an ideal ruler in Iraq. He had learned the limits of Arab nationalism and of Europe's superior strength.[34] He had come to understand that full independence was not possible and so was "willing to settle for something less." Here his upbringing in the Ottoman system helped to make him "more comfortable than [he] would otherwise have been in that 'something less.' "[35] In this regard, Faysal did not differ from other interwar Arab nationalist leaders. Indeed, he was the foremost among them, the acknowledged leader of the pan-Arab nationalist movement. Although he had been placed on the Iraqi throne by the British, he was able to win concessions from them, enough to maintain and add to his stature as a nationalist.

The structure of Iraqi society aided Faysal in this struggle. It was a complex society, difficult for him to master, but even more so for Britain. Hence, Britain needed him, and he could pose Britain's need against the interplay of social forces—urban masses, a growing middle class, tribes, peasants, Shi'ites, Sunnis, Kurds—to create elbow room for himself and greater independence for Iraq. Arab nationalism was the ideology that helped both to weld these disparate forces into one nation and to mobilize some of them into timely manifestations against British interference. He created a new ruling elite of sharifian officers but made a strategic alliance with established forces in society, which he had failed to do in Damascus. "In his efforts to refashion Iraq on national foundations, Faisal I proceeded with care and, keeping his eyes fastened not on what was purely desirable but on what could in practice be achieved, he avoided any step suggestive of adventurism. Of course, in this and in other relevant lines of policy, he was not actuated by sheer devotion to the interests of his people, for he was laying the base for the power of his own family, even as he was laying the base for a compact state."[36]

In Transjordan, 'Abdallah took a different tack. To the Arab nationalists who had supported Faysal in Damascus, Transjordan was a province of Faysal's kingdom of Syria. After the French occupied Damascus in July 1920, these men were anxious to stave off French expansion into the whole of Syria and to establish a base for the diplomatic and military reconquest of French-occupied areas. They were also aware of Anglo-French rivalries and hoped to use them to advantage. They found the Hashemites to be useful symbols that gave the Arab nationalist movement an appearance of unity while stressing the continuity of nationalist demands with the unfulfilled promises made by Britain to Sharif Husayn during the war. Therefore, Faysal's supporters, who had regrouped in ʿAmman after being forced out of Damascus, invited ʿAbdallah to stand in for Faysal at their head. Responsive to nationalist urgings that offered him a chance to make up for his losses in Arabia, ʿAbdallah marched northward. Like Faysal five years earlier, he did so to the tune of Arab nationalism.[37]

ʿAbdallah struck a deal with Britain in Transjordan, as Faysal had in Iraq. Unlike Faysal, however, he was unable to do so and at the same time maintain a nationalist identity. Transjordan did not provide the interplay of varied social forces that might have helped him, as it helped Faysal in Iraq, to create some distance between himself and his British overlords.[38] Though he used nationalist rhetoric, ʿAbdallah's actions were defined by his dependence on Britain. He stymied criticism of his stance by invoking memories of the Arab revolt,[39] but with the passing years the nationalist glow imparted by his participation grew very dim indeed.

The failure of the Hashemites to create a self-sufficient Arab kingdom along the lines envisioned in the Damascus protocol of 1915 led to their inability to live up to the ideals of Arab nationalism. Within their separate countries, their wartime alliance with Britain proved to be not temporary but ongoing, and therefore a grave embarrassment to their nationalist credentials. In Iraq, Faysal was more fortunate, for the country provided pockets of independent influence that allowed him to both deal with Britain and maintain his stature as a nationalist. In Transjordan, ʿAbdallah was less fortunate, for his dependence on Britain there was unmitigated. In the Hijaz, Husayn refused to continue his alliance with Britain after the war. Although he subsequently lost his throne, his refusal to sanction the Anglo-French division of the Fertile Crescent secured for him a place in the annals of Arab nationalism.

The Arab revolt first brought the Hashemites and Arab nationalism together. But what was decisive to their reputations as nationalists was the nature of their compromises with Britain after World War I. Hence the development of Arab nationalism rested less on the revolt itself than on the imposition of the mandates just afterward.

Notes

1. Philip S. Khoury, *Urban Notables*, pp. 75–92.
2. Hanna Batatu, *Old Social Classes*, pp. 319–61.
3. Sulayman (Suleiman) Musa, *al-Murasalat al-tarikhiyya* [Historical Correspondence] ('Amman, 1973), vol. 1, *1914–18*.
4. George Antonius, *The Arab Awakening*, p. 103. King 'Abdallah, *al-Mudhakkirat* in 'Umar Madani, ed., *al-Athar al-Kamila lil-Malik 'Abdallah*, pp. 46–48.
5. Mary C. Wilson, *King Abdullah, Britain and the Making of Jordan* (Cambridge, Eng., 1988), p. 15.
6. PRO F0371/561, Sir G. Lowther to FO, 24 November 1908.
7. King 'Abdallah, "al-Mudhakkirat," in 'Umar Madani, ed., *al-Athar al-kamila li al-malik Abdallah* [The complete works of King 'Abdallah] ('Amman, 1977), p. 60.
8. Khoury, *Urban Notables*, p. 87.
9. King 'Abdallah, "al-Mudhakkirat," p. 68.
10. Antonius, *The Arab Awakening*, p. 152.
11. Muhammad Labib al-Batanuni, *al-Rihla al-hijaziyya* [The Hijazi journey] (Cairo, 1911), p. 81.
12. King 'Abdallah, "al-Mudhakkirat," p. 89.
13. Tarik Z. Tunaya, *Turkiye'de Siyasi Partiler, 1859–1952* [Turkish political parties].
14. Monahan to Lowther, March 7, 1912, FO 371/1487.
15. C. Ernest Dawn, *From Ottomanism to Arabism*, p. 7.
16. King 'Abdallah, "al-Mudhakkirat," pp. 78–79.
17. "Fi mudhakkirat Sulayman Pasha," *al-'Arab* 6, no. 5 (January 1972): 358.
18. King 'Abdallah, "al-Mudhakkirat," pp. 102–3.
19. Ibid.
20. Note by Ronald Storrs, October 20, 1914, FO 141/460.
21. 'Abdallah to Storrs, October 20, 1914, FO 371/6273.
22. Antonius, *The Arab Awakening*, p. 133.
23. Ibid., pp. 157–58.
24. Ibid., p. 414.
25. "The Sherifs," by T. E. Lawrence, October 27, 1916, FO 882/5.
26. William L. Cleveland, "The Role of Islam as Political Ideology in the First World War," p. 89.
27. *Arab Bulletin*, no. 23 (September 26, 1916): 303.
28. Elie Kedourie, "The Surrender of Medain, January 1919," *Middle Eastern Studies* 13, no. 1 (January 1977): 134.
29. Wilson, *King Abdullah*, pp. 31–32.
30. Telephone message from 'Abdallah, November 1, 1916, PRO FO882/5.

31. Report by T. E. Lawrence, April 16, 1917, PRO FO686/6, part 2.
32. Khayr al-Din al-Zirikli, *al-A'lam* [Eminent personalities], 2:340–41.
33. 'Abdallah to C. E. Wilson, June 3, 1919, PRO FO686/17.
34. PRO FO371/5038, A. T. Wilson to FO, July 31, 1920.
35. Albert Hourani, *Emergence of the Modern Middle East*, p. 71.
36. Batatu, *Old Social Classes*, pp. 25–26.
37. PRO FO371/6371, "To Our Syrian Brethren," January 7, 1921.
38. Mary C. Wilson, "A Passage to Independence: King Abdullah and Transjordan, 1920–1950," pp. 187–205.
39. King Hussein, *Uneasy Lies the Head* (London: 1962), p. 17.

PART FOUR
Northeast Africa

ELEVEN

The Development of Nationalist Sentiment in Libya, 1908–1922

Lisa Anderson

Shortly after the Young Turk revolution of 1908, the Ottoman provinces now known as Libya embarked on more than a decade of political turbulence.[1] The particular character of this upheaval—the timing of events, the nature of the participants—was to profoundly influence subsequent Libyan conceptions of the country's place in modern Islamic and Arab identities. The importance of these years is not unique to Libya. On the contrary, much of the Ottoman elite was prompted by events between the Young Turk revolution and the end of World War I to reexamine and readjust their political identities, and many abandoned the Ottomanist and pan-Islamic sentiments they had earlier embraced in favor of Turkish, Arab, or regional loyalties. That Libya remained loyal to the pan-Islamic aspirations associated with the empire and did not, by and large, turn to Arab nationalism reflected the specific historical circumstances in which these issues were debated in the province.

In Libya, the Young Turk revolution was soon followed by Italy's invasion of the province in 1911. The Young Turks viewed the defense of the province as both a political necessity and a moral obligation and encouraged Ottoman officers from throughout the empire to converge on Libya to aid in repulsing European encroachment. Thus, by the time World War I began, several years of Ottoman-led provincewide resistance to the

Italians in Libya had encouraged transcendence of the policy disputes that plagued the Young Turk administration elsewhere. Continued Ottoman confrontation of the major European powers, including Italy, during the war cemented the fidelity of most of LIbya's elite to the failing empire and its pan-Islamic rationale. Moreover, Islam provided the most persuasive ideological rationale by which to rally local opposition to continued Italian occupation.

In the wake of the defeat of the empire, a segment of the Libyan elite attempted to constitute an independent political administration on secular "republican" grounds, but the effort foundered in internecine disputes, and its organizers were required to look once again to religiously inspired leadership to carry the banner of resistance to European rule. Thus, the most widely embraced political identity in Libya during this period was provided by Islamic rather than Arabic symbols and attachments. Both the wider loyalty to the Ottoman empire and the narrower provincial patriotism were expressed in the idiom of Islam.

Libyan adherence to Islamic rather than Arabic formulae for cultural expression and political identity was by no means a foregone conclusion at the turn of the century. Just as the local experience of the Ottoman empire's final days was the crucible in which new nationalist identities were forged in the Arab East, so, too, the definition of nationalism in Libya was born in the specific experience of the events that followed the Young Turk revolution.

The Young Turk Revolution. At the turn of the century, contemporary European observers believed Libya to be merely a backwater of the Ottoman empire, neglected and stagnant. Although it was not among the most cosmopolitan of the empire's provinces, it was in fact more closely attuned to events in Istanbul than was immediately apparent. The latter decades of the nineteenth century had been a time of relative prosperity in Libya as the province became the last remaining outpost of the trans-Saharan trade, and Libyan merchants maintained wide networks of commercial ties with the rest of the empire. Moreover, Sultan Abdülhamid II had often used the North African provinces as a sort of Saharan Siberia, exiling the more troublesome of his political opponents to prisons or minor posts in these distant reaches of empire, and the Libyan elite was therefore exposed to much of the intellectual ferment of the time.[2]

Among the best indications of intellectual sentiment among the Libyan elite are, here as elsewhere, in the newspapers that flourished with the lifting of press censorship after the Young Turk revolution. At least seven newspapers began publishing between 1908 and 1910, and they give useful indications of the political thought of the time. Well aware of the menace of European expansion, the press recalled the dangers of the commercial penetration that had preceded the English and French occupations of Egypt and Tunisia. Particularly sensitive to Italian activity—correctly, as it would turn out—local journalists exposed administrators who cooperated with Italians and led campaigns against those they considered insufficiently steadfast in the face of Italian pressures, calling for strikes to protest Italian activity.

The issues that preoccupied the Arabs elsewhere in the empire were also apparent in Tripoli. Turkification policies and neglect of Arabic in government schools raised openly expressed opposition, and religious reform was important; in the years following the revolution, for example, a local newspaper, *Taraqqi* [Progress], published a number of articles on Muhammad ʿAbduh. Social and economic reform was also advocated: *Taraqqi* and a sister weekly, *al-ʿAsr al-Jadid* [The New Era], called for the promotion of agriculture, expansion of industry, and the institution of compulsory education, linking internal reform with the defense of the province against European imperialism.[3]

At this stage, there is no hint of separatist sentiment. Many Europeans, who were quick to look for sources of local unhappiness with the Ottoman government, thought they had found such a cleavage in the Sanusi disputes with Istanbul over the stance to be adopted toward the French incursions into Chad. The leaders of the Sanusiyya, the religious brotherhood that provided the organizational background of the political administration—and the trans-Saharan trade—in eastern Libya (or Cyrenaica), advocated direct military confrontation; the Ottoman authorities preferred to temporize in the vain hope of gaining French support against Italian designs on the province. This was a serious difference of opinion, but it was a policy dispute and not the basis of a separatist movement.

Similarly, Sulayman al-Baruni, a prominent man of letters and who was leader of the 'Ibadi Berbers in Tripolitania (and also a deputy from Tripolitania to the newly reopened Ottoman parliament after 1908), was suspected of harboring ambitions for an autonomous 'Ibadi province in the western mountains. Although he was imprisoned for subversive activity during the reign of Abdülhamid, it appears that Baruni envisioned his province within the religious and political sovereignty of the Ottoman empire, not as a fully independent entity.[4]

If there was no separatism in Libya during this period, however, there was plenty of dissatisfaction. Despite the Young Turks' opposition to Italian penetration, local enthusiasm for the new regime in Istanbul was not unanimous. The new freedoms did not impress more than a small fraction of the population, and Turkification language policies were unpopular. For the most part, however, the opposition grew out of more immediate interests, as some of the newly appointed functionaries began a campaign to rid the local administration of "reactionary" supporters of Abdülhamid, who included a fair proportion of the upper class of Tripoli. Soon after the revolution was announced in Tripoli, for example, the mayor presided over a large meeting in a Tripoli mosque where it was charged that the liberty proclaimed by the Young Turks was a menace to Islam and the Arab people.

In Banghazi, an Arab-Ottoman club was established in opposition to the Committee of Union and Progress (CUP). This club was said to have been more sympathetic to pan-Arab ideas and to have represented general sentiment (including that of the Sanusiyya). The Arab-Ottoman conservatives, blackballed by Young Turk administrators who were fiercely opposed to Italian influence in the province, contacted the Italian consul in Banghazi and persuaded the shaykh of the Sanusi *zawiya* in the city to pay him a visit.[5]

The Italians interpreted these disputes as evidence that the Arab population would not support the Ottomans against an Italian invasion. In this they were mistaken. Although the differences between the Ottoman administration and the provincial notables might have grown more severe over the years, as they did elsewhere in the empire, in Libya the Italians themselves intervened to provide a cause that inspired Ottoman loyalists throughout the empire and united the local Ottoman authorities and the provincial notables in a common purpose: resistance to the Italian occupation.

The Italian-Ottoman War, 1911–1912. Italy sent an ultimatum to the Sublime Porte on September 26, 1911, announcing its intention to occupy Libya and demanding that within twenty-four hours the Ottoman government "give orders so [the invasion force] may meet with no opposition from the present Ottoman representatives" in the province. The Ottoman authorities refused, and Italy declared war on the empire. In November, Italy announced its annexation of the North African province, and the war for control of the territory was on. Greatly embarrassed by the sorry state of the provinces' defenses, the Ottomans soon began sending military officers to organize the resistance.[6]

By the close of 1911, an important group of Ottoman officers had arrived from Istanbul. The group, known as the teskilat-i mahsusa, or special organization, included, in addition to Enver Bey (Enver Paşa; later Ottoman minister of war), his brother Nuri, ʿAziz ʿAli Bey al-Misri (later chief of staff of the Egyptian army), Mustafa Kemal (later Atatürk), Nuri al-Saʿid and Jaʿafar al-ʿAskari (both later prime ministers of Iraq), as well as local notables such as Sulayman al-Baruni, and eventually the leader of Sanusiyya, Ahmad al-Sharif. It was a pan-Islamic secret intelligence unit developed to meet what Enver Bey viewed as the principal dangers to the Ottoman state-local separatist movements and European occupation.[7] These officers promptly took over military resistance to the Italians, and it was their enthusiasm for the defense of the province that helped bolster Libyan loyalty to pan-Islamic and Ottomanist ideologies. Indeed, it may even have been Ottoman officer Enver Bey who personally convinced Sanusi leader Ahmad al-Sharif to declare a *jihad* (holy war) against the Italians.[8]

In Tripolitania, two of the deputies who represented the province in the reopened Ottoman parliament, Sulayman al-Baruni and Farhat Bey al-Zawi, were instrumental in organizing the resistance. Farhat Bey spent his youth in Tunisia and France, spoke French, and on his return to Libya had been a judge in his hometown, Zawiya. Dismissed twice for political intrigue before the revolution, he joined Baruni in enthusiastically supporting the CUP and represented his native district in

Parliament.⁹ By the end of October 1911, they were both traveling throughout their districts preaching resistance and calling for volunteers. The provincial elite had been well aware of the precarious position of the Libyan provinces of the empire; it had long been common knowledge that Italy had laid claim to the territory in the councils of Europe and that the empire was going to be hard put to defend the province. Indeed, the likelihood that they would be left to their own devices had obviously occurred to the province's educated elite. As Farhat Bey was reported to have remarked to a French journalist who toured the Ottoman front during the war: "Holy war! Do not write this word... You will make us suspect in France. We are patriots in bare feet and rags, like your soldiers of the revolution, and not religious fanatics... If the Turkish government abandons us we will proclaim that it has forfeited its rights over our country. We will form the Republic of Tripolitania."¹⁰

Farhat Bey's prediction proved remarkably prescient, although at the time it reflected an opinion that was decidedly a minority view even among the elite. The willingness of the empire to throw its best officers into the battle against the Italians persuaded most of the skeptics of the legitimacy of Ottoman claims to their loyalties.

Of course, by midsummer 1912, the Ottoman government in Istanbul began having a change of heart about support for the Libyan resistance. As the situation in the Balkans deteriorated, the Sublime Porte opened negotiations to end the war with Italy, and the empire signed a treaty of peace shortly after the Balkan war broke out in October. While the Ottomans did not cede sovereignty over the North African province to Italy, the sultan did issue a declaration to his Libyan subjects granting them "full and complete autonomy," reserving the right to appoint an agent charged with "protecting Ottoman interest in your country," and agreeing to withdraw the Ottoman "officers, troops, and civil officials." The Italians reaffirmed their annexation of the province, an act that was not recognized by international law until after the Allied peace settlement with Turkey in 1924.¹¹

The teskilat-i mahsusa officers were disappointed, and it was not until the news of the empire's difficulties in the Balkans reached Libya that they decided to join their compatriots there. Leaving several of the number (including ʿAziz ʿAli Bey al-Misri) to advise the local combatants, they departed at the end of 1912. By then, however, the local resistance was well organized and enthusiastic. The employment of local notables in the provincial administration meant that the sultan's promise to withdraw Ottoman officials could only be an empty one. The provincial administrators stayed, the annexation of the province by Italy was not recognized by the insurgents, and the war would go on.

The First Local "Governments". On the morrow of the signing of the peace treaty, a number of provincial notables and administrators met in what became known as the Congress of ʿAziziyya to decide on their stance in light of Italy's declared annexation of the province and the empire's grant of autonomy. In what appears to have been an acrimonious meeting, two positions took shape-to negotiate with the Italians or to continue of armed resistance. The major proponent of the first position was Farhat Bey al-Zawi; the second was urged by Sulayman al-Baruni. Baruni appears to have felt that the autonomy accorded the province by the Ottomans offered a better chance of realizing his goal of an autonomous 'Ibadi province. Farhat Bey, by contrast, was familiar with the French Protectorate in Tunisia and may have hoped to gain what then appeared to be the advantages of European tutelage through cooperation.[12]

The meeting broke up without an agreement, and Farhat Bey met with the Italian governor outside Tripoli to sound out Italian intentions. The new governor, appointed in September 1912, was unaware of the dispute within the Libyan elite and mistakenly interpreted Farhat Bey's overture as a reflection of general opinion. Nonetheless, the Italians were aware of the competition posed by the Ottomans. They reported, soon after the peace treaty was signed, that the Ottoman governor of the province had conferred with the local leader in Tripolitania. He had told them that although the imperial government could no longer aid the resistance formally, the ruling CUP would do so, and he offered to leave twenty thousand Turkish lira and the government provisions in their custody. Although some of the Tripolitanian notables judged the support insufficient to continue the resistance, Sulayman al-Baruni did not, and he distributed the money and twelve thousand sacks of wheat, rice, beans, and sugar to his supporters in the Jabal.[13]

Both Baruni in Tripolitania and Ahmad al-Sharif in Cyrenaica attempted to use Ottoman support to win autonomy from the Italians. By the beginning of 1913 the Sanusiyya was stamping its correspondence *al-hukuma al-Sanusiyya* ["the Sanusi government"], and Baruni opened the new year with a telegram to the foreign ministries of the European powers announcing that: "I have the honor to designate myself head of the provisional independent Government we have formed [and] I ask that... I be addressed in all affairs concerning the following regions: Warfalla and the south of Tripolitania, the inhabitants of the coast, [from] the Ajilat littoral to the Tunisian frontier, and all the mountain residents."[14]

Although the Italians reported that Baruni had received no replies to his announcement, they soon opened negotiations with him themselves. Discussions conducted with his representative in Tunis and Paris led to apparent agreements to establish a "Berber province," but failure of the governments in Rome and Tripoli to coordinate their policies led to the collapse of the understanding. By the end of March 1913, Italian troops occupied the Jabal town of Yaffran after the defeat of Baruni's forces. Baruni himself escaped to Tunisia and then went on to Istanbul.

The Italians also pursued negotiations in Cyrenaica with the Sanusiyya through the intermediary of Mansur al-Kikhiya and his son 'Umar, a former deputy to the Ottoman parliament. Ahmad al-Sharif demanded, in return for the cessation of hostilities, internal autonomy under the Sanusiyya for all parts of Cyrenaica not occupied by the Italians by June 1913–that is, the entire province except for a few coastal towns. The Italians refused, although they did offer to "recognize and respect the privileges already accorded by Constantinople" to the Order and to provide annual stipends to the Sanusi family. These discussions came to naught, however, and the fighting continued as the Italians made slow but fairly steady progress into the interior.[15]

By the fall of 1913 the Libyan side of the battle appeared to be in trouble. Sometime late that year the commander in Cyrenaica, 'Aziz Bey al-Misri, allegedly deserted the cause and fled to Egypt, with the money and artillery destined for the resistance, after a battle at the border with the Sanusi shaykh 'Umar al-Mukhtar.[16] During the summer, Italian columns reached

Sabhah in the Fazzan, as two years of failed crops were beginning to take their toll on the resistance.

Nonetheless, Italian strength was not as real as it appeared. In November 1914 the garrison at Sabhah was sacked and destroyed by Libyan forces. A general revolt broke out and by April 1915 the Italian loss of control was nearly complete: a battle in Sirt turned into a rout when the Italians' "friendlies," led by Ramadan al-Suwayhli of Misratah, joined the forces attacking the Italians. This battle, known as Gardabiyya or Qasr Bu Hadi, marked the end of any semblance of Italian control in the hinterland. For the duration of World War I, which Italy entered in My of that year, the Italian occupation of Libya would be limited to a few coastal cities.

World War I: The Rise of Ramadan al-Suwayhli and Idris al-Sanusi. World War I saw the reappearance of Ottoman influence in Libya, but the failure of Ottoman efforts to dislodge the European powers occupying Libya and Egypt—efforts that would reveal the continuing importance of pan-Islamic loyalties in Libya—left the province with political leaders who were more concerned with retaining local authority than with developing or maintaining wider loyalties. These local leaders gladly accepted aid from outside powers, including Britain and Germany as well as the Ottoman empire, but by the end of the war they had given up any hope or desire for reincorporation into a larger Ottoman or Islamic political union.

Although the Ottoman government had formally withdrawn from the Libyan province, the authorities in Istanbul had continued to encourage resistance to the Italians. With the Italian entry into the war on the side of the Entente powers, the Ottoman empire and its German allies saw an opportunity to use what Ottoman troops remained in Libya to spark a revolt against the British and French, as well as Italian, presence in North Africa. Although Sulayman al-Baruni had left Libya in the spring of 1913, he had by no means abandoned the struggle against the Italians. In October he had gone to Istanbul, where he was named a senator in the Ottoman parliament, and by the end of that year the Italians were hearing reports that Baruni was in Cyrenaica conferring with Ahmad al-Sharif.[17] The Ottoman officer Nuri Bey and a number of other teskilat-i mahsusa officers all returned to Libya at the outbreak of the war, charged with winning Ahmad al-Sharif's agreement to an attack on British positions in Egypt in the fall of 1915. This they did—not without great difficulty—and well supplied with German arms, Ottoman-Sanusi forces took the British garrison at al-Sallum in November. By March of the following year, however, the British had regained their positions, routing the Sanusi forces.

This "reverse Arab revolt"—a local revolt supported by the Ottomans to undermine the British position in the war—had obviously failed. What is most striking about this effort, however, is the contrast it presents to the virtually simultaneous Arab revolt in the Hijaz, for the Libyan revolt was not in fact "Arab" at all but Islamic. At the same time as the British capitalized on Arab resentment against Turkish rule in the Arab East, the Ottomans had persuaded their coreligionists in Libya to cooperate against the Christian occupiers of Egypt. In the aftermath of his defeat, Ahmad al-Sharif, apparently realizing that the Sanusiyya would have to enter into negotiations with the British, turned over the Order's leadership to his cousin, Idris.[18] Nuri Bey, unable to convince Idris to take up the banner of the Ottoman cause, left Cyrenaica for Misratah.

In Misratah, and under the protection of Ottoman-German forces, Ramadan al-Suwayhli's star was rising. Ramadan had taken the field against the Italians during the Ottoman-Italian war; after the signing of the peace treaty, he briefly cooperated with the Italians before leading the revolt against the Italian column in Sirt. The withdrawal of the Italians from Misratah with the outbreak of World War I left Ramadan, then in his early thirties and well known for his exploits at Qasr Bu Hadi, among the most prominent figures in the town. The Ottoman-German forces used Misratah as one of their most important supply ports (German submarines landed men and supplies there throughout the war), and Ramadan shortly became their favored local contact.

Like most of the Libyan notables at the time, Ramadan was as concerned to extend his own political influence as to serve the Ottoman cause. For several years, however, he and Nuri Bey cooperated in strengthening Misratah as a safe haven for the Ottoman forces and as a de facto autonomous political district. Early in 1916 the Sanusiyya made an effort to extend its influence and, as importantly, its taxing powers, into Tripolitania. Safi al-Din, cousin of Idris, was sent into western Sirt to collect tribute from the population there, and his troops were met and defeated by those of Ramadan. Nuri Bey had been dismayed with Sanusi policies under Idris and probably did not discourage Ramadan's action against the Order, but Ramadan was acting on his own account as well: western Sirt had been paying taxes to his government in Misratah.[19] The scarcity of resources was taking its toll on the erstwhile united front against the Italians. By July 1916, Idris entered negotiations with the British and Italians, and the Ottomans put their remaining hopes in Ramadan al-Suwayhli and Sulayman al-Baruni.

By the end of the war the situation in Libya was confused. The autonomy of the Sanusiyya in Cyrenaica was formally recognized by the Italians in the agreement of 'Akramah signed in April 1917 (negotiated through the good, and by no means disinterested, offices of the British). Concerned that further upheaval in Cyrenaica would undermine the security of their position in Egypt's Western Desert, the British arranged a modus vivendi in Cyrenaica by which hostilities were to cease at the same time confirming that the responsibility for security in the regions then controlled by the Italians and the Sanusiyya rested with Italian administration and Idris, respectively. The Italians, as Britain's junior partner in the allied war effort, were obliged to acquiesce in the arrangement despite serious misgivings; Idris agreed on order to win the lifting of a British blockade and resumption of commerce with the coast.[20]

The autonomy of Tripolitania was not recognized by the Italians but it was no less real. In fact, the leaders of the west Libyan province were cooperating with no one. During the early months of 1918, Nuri Bey was recalled to Istanbul and replaced first by Ishaq Pasha, a military commander who had distinguished himself in the Libyan war of 1911–1912, and, later in the summer, by Ottoman prince 'Uthman Fu'ad (Osman Fuat). Neither of these men proved any more able than Nuri to unite the various political factions in Tripolitania. According to the British, by the end of the war:

The Turks did not even figure in the eyes of the local population as the Government, much less in those of the leader. They were there to help fight the Italians; they sometimes provided arms and money and were always very encouraging.

There was never any chance of Tripoli becoming once again a Turkish province. Even Ramadan, the most Turcophil [sic] Arab in the country, was at the same time the most bitter opponent of Turkish rule, which could only mean a diminuation of his influence.[21]

In October 1918 the Ottoman empire signed the armistice agreement that ended its involvement in World War I. The Libyan elite would make one last effort in the aftermath of the Ottoman defeat to win political recognition. Tellingly, despite the presence of one of the future leaders of Arab nationalism in Libya, the effort was a decidedly local one.

The Tripoli Republic and the Period of Accord: Local Patriotism. Toward the end of World War I, ʿAbd al-Rahman ʿAzzam Bey, a young Egyptian who would become the first secretary-general of the Arab League after World War II, arrived in Misratah. He had studied medicine in England, traveled in the nationalist circles of Tunisia and Egypt, and upon his arrival in Libya took up the cause of unity and resistance as adviser to Ramadan al-Suwayhli. He was as close as Libya would get to a genuine Arab nationalist.

President Woodrow Wilson's declaration of support for national self-determination in January 1918 was warmly received in Libya, as elsewhere in the Arab world. The modus vivendi of ʿAkramah, signed in April 1917, which accorded the Sanusiyya local autonomy, had also been welcomed in Tripolitania as a suitable starting point from which to obtain self-determination. What was needed was a broadly based organization to represent Tripolitanians; so a meeting of the region's notables was held in Misallatah. At the conclusion of the meeting, the birth of al-jumhuriyya al-tarablusiyya, or the Tripoli Republic, was announced.[22]

The name of the new organization was proposed before the form of government had been agreed upon—this was the first formally republican government in the Arab world—and although such ideas had clearly been in the air for some time in Libya, the choice appears to have been less a reflection of the republican sentiments of its founders than of their inability to agree on a single individual to serve as amir. The position was offered to ʿUthman Fuʿad Pasha, the Ottoman prince who resided in Misratah, but he declined it. A Council of Four was therefore created to act as the ruling body, composed of Ramadan al-Suwayhli, Sulayman al-Baruni, Ahmad al-Murayyid of Tarhuna, and ʿAbd al-Nabi Bilkhayr of Warfalla. ʿAzzam Bey was the council's secretary, and a twenty-four-member advisory group was established, its members carefully selected to represent most of the regions and interests of the province.

The republic's announcement of Tripolitania's independence and its leaders' attempt to plead their case at the Paris Peace Conference after the war met the same chilly reception from the European powers as had Baruni's similar earlier proclamation.[23] As with Baruni, however, the Italians agreed to meet with the Republican leaders, hoping to negotiate an arrangement similar to the one they enjoyed with Idris. The two sides met in April 1919, each operating under a fundamental misapprehension of the other's intentions. The republic's leaders were negotiating, or so they thought, as equals of the Italians: two independent governments discussing disputed territory. The Italians, by contrast, viewed their talks with the Tripolitania leaders as the inauguration of a system by which they would rule undisputed through the native chiefs.

The misunderstanding was never resolved, but the negotiations laid the groundwork for the Legge Fondamentale of June 1919 and its October 1919 extension in a comparable statute for Cyrenaica. These laws provided for a special Italian-Libyan citizenship and accorded all such citizens the right to vote in elections for local parliaments. The Parliament of Cyrenaica met five times before it was abolished in 1923; in Tripolitania, the elections were never held. In Cyrenaica, the Italians had been required by British intervention to work through the Sanusiyya, which they did only ill-humoredly; in Tripolitania, they simply stalled.

Dissatisfaction with the modus vivendi of ʿAkramah led the Italians to reopen discussions with the Sanusiyya in 1920, and by October they reached a new agreement with Idris, known as the Accord of al-Rajma. Under the terms of the new arrangement, Idris was granted what the Italians viewed as the ceremonial title of Amir of Cyrenaica and was permitted to organize the autonomous administration of the oases of the interior. In return, Idris agreed to cooperate in the application of the Legge Fondamentale of Cyrenaica, to disband his Cyrenaican military units, and to levy no taxes above the Sanusi religious tithe. The most important of these concessions—the disbanding of the military units—was not carried out.

The willingness of the Italians to recognize formally the Sanusiyya enhanced the Order's standing in Cyrenaica, and it was able to maintain a semblance of regional administration and unified action. In Tripolitania, however, the republic never won formal recognition from the Italians. Although the membership of the council that oversaw administrative appointments under the Legge Fondamentale was nearly identical with that of the founders of the republic, the republic itself was not recognized, and the Italians did not acknowledge its authority to administer the hinterlands. As a consequence, there was more competition than coordination among the republic's policymakers.

During the fall of 1919, for example, a quarrel between Ramadan al-Suwayhli and ʿAbd al-Nabi Bilkhayr broke out because Ramadan refused to confirm several of ʿAbd al-Nabi's family members in administrative positions in Warfalla, and ʿAbd Al-Nabi disapproved of Ramadan's hostility toward the Sanusiyya, They also traded accusations about accounting for the large sums of money sent from Istanbul during the war. The Italian efforts at mediation appeared successful—both Ramadan and ʿAbd al-Nabi were counselors of the Italian government under the terms of the Legge Fondamentale at the time—but by the spring of 1920, Ramadan had expelled the Italian adviser in Misratah, and he shortly found himself the object of local and Italian intrigues to unseat him. In June the Italians sent several truckloads of arms and ammunition to their local allies and to ʿAbd al-Nabi Bilkhayr, and by August Ramadan felt obliged to launch a campaign against his opponents. His forces were defeated and Ramadan was killed as his captors attempted, or so it was said, to take him prisoner.[24]

The republican leadership, reduced by one, but with the still active support of ʿAzzam Bey, called a general meeting in Gharyan shortly after the Accord of al-Rajma was announced in the fall of 1920. Recognizing that internal discord was weakening the republic's united front, the Gharyan conference resolved that a single Muslim ruler be designated to govern the country, established a fourteen-member Council of the Association for National Reform and arranged to send a delegation under the leadership of Khalid al-Qarqani—known to the British as a dangerous "political agitator"—to Rome to inform the Italian government of its new position.[25]

Sulayman al-Baruni, who had rallied to the Italian cause after the promulgation of the Legge Fondamentale and visited Rome—as did Idris—to join the celebration of its announcement had refused to attend the Gharyan conference. The Italians believed he still harbored ambitions for an autonomous 'Ibadi province, and they considered his adherence to the Tripoli Republic merely tactical. For their part, the Italians had long entertained hopes of dividing the Berbers of the Jabal from their Arab compatriots. Their perhaps deliberately arbitrary and divisive administration of Berber areas soon precipitated fighting that developed into a full-scale civil war during the first several months of 1921. By that summer most of the Berber population had taken refuge on the coast under the Italian flag. Baruni was blamed for the disorder by many of the Berbers, according to Italian reports, and he ended his career in Libya despised by the other republican leaders, who held men responsible for Italian gains. In November 1921 he left the country for the last time.[26]

In Cyrenaica at about the same time, the Italians concluded the agreement of Bu Maryam, in what proved to be their last attempt to negotiate control of the eastern province. Under the agreement, "mixed camps" of Sanusi and Italian troops were organized and made jointly responsible for the security of the countryside. In light of the deep-seated animosity of the two sides, the arrangement was destined to be short-lived. At the end of that year, representatives of the Gharyan conference met in Sirt with delegates from the Sanusiyyah.

With Ramadan al-Suwayhli dead and Sulayman al-Baruni out of the country, the major opponents to Sanusi influence in Tripolitania were gone, and the conferees at Sirt were able to agree on a proclamation announcing their intention to elect a Muslim amir to represent the entire country.[27] When the Tripolitanian delegates returned to Misratah, they found the city in flames. A new Italian governor had lost patience with attempts to cooperate with the Libyans and made known the new policy by attacking the town.

Renewed negotiation with the Italians in March 1922 broke down after the National Reform Association refused to discuss Tripolitanian issued separately from Cyrenaican, arguing that the regions had been ruled as a single province by the Ottomans. Once again under siege from the Italians, the Reform Association leaders sent a delegation to Cyrenaica to request that Idris assume the amirate of all Libya.[28] Idris as first balked, fearful of giving the Italians an excuse to renege on their agreements with him. By October 1922, however, it was apparent that conflict with Italy was unavoidable; the Sanusiyya was going to lose its special prerogative no matter what position Idris took. He therefore accepted a second request that he become the country's amir and promptly fled to Egypt, where he would remain until 1943. This was precisely the excuse the Italians were looking for to justify a military offensive, and by the spring of 1923, as the Fascists consolidated their power at home, they abrogated all accords and agreements with the Libyans and began what they were to call the riconquista.

Although military resistance to the Italians would continue for another decade—its end formally marked by the capture and hanging of the Sanusi shaykh ʿUmar al-Mukhtar in 1931—the efforts to create and win recognition for political autonomy had ended in failure. By 1923 the Sanusi leadership was in exile and the Tripoli Republic was but a memory. ʿAbd al-Rahman ʿAzzam Bey left Libya for Egypt, where he won a seat in parliament in 1924. Ramadan al-Suwayhli was dead. Sulayman al-Baruni, who had left Libya in 1921, was expelled from Tunisia as an undesirable agitator, traveled to France, Egypt, Turkey, and Mecca before settling, in 1924, in Oman, where he was appointed finance minister. ʿAbd al-Nabi Bilkhayr continued armed resistance in southern Tripolitania and the Fazzan and was reported to have died of thirst in Chad in 1930. Ahmad Murayyid left for Egypt before 1924 and settled in Fayyum, buying land with Ahmad al-Suwayhli, Ramadan's brother. Khalid al-Qarqani, who had traveled to Moscow for a Muslim Revolutionary Congress as well; by the mid-1930s he was in government service in Saudi Arabia.[29]

In the decade and a half that followed the Young Turk revolution, Libya had gone from being the symbol of the Ottoman and pan-Islamic struggle against European encroachment to a forsaken corner of a vanished empire. At first encouraged and aided by the moral and material support of the leading lights of the Ottoman elite, the Libyan resistance died a mere ten years later, abandoned even by its founders, while in the meantime

Arab nationalism had hardly appeared on the scene. The pan-Islamic underpinnings of Ottoman solidarity had served admirably to justify and rally resistance to the Italians. By the time loyalty to the empire had become pointless, Libyans had already begun to turn inward and see the resistance in particularistic terms. The secular "republicans" of Tripolitania soon found themselves required to make common cause with the leader of the Sanusiyya. From this point on, nationalism, anti-imperialism, and pan-Islamic loyalties would be clearly and closely associated in Libya.

Notes

1. The name "Libya" was not formally adopted for the three Ottoman provinces of Tripolitania, Fazzan, and Cyrenaica until 1929. Parts of this essay are based on the discussion in my book *The State and Social Tranformation in Tunisia and Libya, 1830–1980*.
2. See Lisa Anderson, "Nineteenth-Century Reform in Ottoman Libya."
3. Ahmad Sidqi Dajani, *Libya qubayl al-ihtilal al-itali aw tarablus al-gharb fi akhir al-ʿahd al-ʿuthmani al-thani* [Libya before the Italian occupation, or Tripoli at the end of the second ottoman era], pp. 276–95. Also see Christiane Souriau-Hoebrechts, *La presse maghrebine*.
4. According to Idris al-Horeir (personal communication, April 21, 1979), Baruni appears to have envisioned an autonomous province in the western mountains of Tripolitania as a revival of the medieval ʿIbadi Rustamiyya state, which had once existed there. The Italians viewed his motives as ethnic. See ASMAI (Archivo Storico del Ministero dell'Africa Italiana, Minstero degli Affari Esteri) 150/4.
5. See D. D. Cumming, "Modern History," *Handbook on Cyrenaica*.
6. Francesco Malgeri, *La guerra Libica*, p. 335ff.
7. Phillip Hendrick Stoddard, "The Ottoman Government and the Arabs, 1911–1918," p. 3.
8. Certainly that is what the Italians believed: see Sergio Romano, *La quarta sponda*, p. 156. Stoddard, "The Ottoman Government and the Arabs," p. 83, says it was at Farhat Bey's urging that Ahmad al-Sharif decided on resistance.
9. ASMAI 150/16.
10. Quoted in Stoddard, "The Ottoman Government and the Arabs," p. 84.
11. Texts in Malgeri, *La guerra Libica*, pp. 399ff.

12. Tahir Ahmad al-Zawi, *Jihad al-abtal fi tarabus al-gharb* [The holy war of the heroes of Tripoli], p. 61. Soon thereafter Farhat Bey quit public affairs altogether to take up private commercial pursuits.
13. ASMAI 150/4, January 1913.
14. Reproduced in ibid.
15. Enrico de Leone, *La colonizzazione dell'Africa del Nord* (Padua, 1960), pp. 399–400.
16. ʿAziz Bey al-Misri was later court-martialed for his action, and he refused until his death in 1962 to discuss it (See Stoddard, "The Ottoman Government and the Arabs"). A different verison of these events can be found in Majid Khadduri, "ʿAziz al-Misri and the Arab National Movement," pp. 143–45.
17. ASMAI 150/4, December 1916.
18. E. E. Evans-Pritchard, *The Sanusi of Cyrenaica*, p. 126.
19. This incident is treated from the Sanusi perspective by Evans-Pritchard in *The Sanusi*, and from Ramadan's point of view in Zawi, *Jihad al-abtal.*
20. Evans-Pritchard, *The Sanusi*, pp. 141–44.
21. Evans-Pritchard Office [PRO], FO 371: 3806, June 1920.
22. See Lisa Anderson, "The Tripoli Republic, 1918–1922," pp. 43–66. I prefer the convenience of the translation "Tripoli Republic" to "Republic of Tripolitania," but it should be kept in mind that the representation was provincewide and the republic extended throughout Tripolitania, not only to Tripoli.
23. P. D'Agostino, *Espansionism italiano odierno*, vol. 1, *La nostra economica coloniale* (Salerno, 1923), p. 43.
24. PRO, FO 371: 3805, November 19, 1919; 371: 3806, April 15, 1920; and 371: 4888, September 2, 1920.
25. Zawi, *Jihad al-abtal*, pp. 404, 417, 422–29; and PRO, FO 371: 3805, 1919–1920.
26. ASMAI 150/4, November 17, 1921.
27. Zawi, *Jihad al-abtal*, p. 430.
28. Ibid., pp. 485ff; and Evans-Pritchard, *The Sanusi*, p. 153.
29. Anderson, "The Tripoli Republic," p. 61.

TWELVE

Egypt and Early Arab Nationalism, 1908–1922

James Jankowski

"Arab nationalism" is not a monolithic construct. The early Arab nationalism discussed in this volume refers to the aspirations and activities directed toward autonomy and/or independence that developed among the Arab population in the Ottoman provinces of western Asia in the few decades immediately prior to World War I. Because it has since been viewed by Arabs themselves as the direct forerunner of the later movement of Arab unity in the mid-twentieth century, this period has often been regarded as at time of Arab nationalism par excellence.

But this particular variety of nationalist sentiment and activism was not the only one to emerge among Arabs before World War I. In the same milieu of the late nineteenth and early twentieth centuries, other nationalist or protonationalist tendencies—a Maronite Christian focus on the unique geography and demography of Lebanon, a wider identification with the land of "Syria" by some writers of the late-nineteenth-century *nahda*, and a similar regional affiliation with Tunisia by the "Young Tunisians" of the immediate pre-World War I period—had manifested themselves among the Arabic-speaking population of western Asia and northern Africa.[1]

This essay examines the relationship of the best known and perhaps the most important of these other Arab nationalist movements—Egyptian nationalism—to early Arab nationalism. Egyptian nationalism antedated early Arab nationalism by a generation. It also was a distinct and separate phenomenon whose adherents saw little similarity and even less connection between their nationalism and that emerging among Arabs.

Modern Egyptian nationalism had its inception in the late nineteenth century.[2] Thus it was a clearly articulated concept with a generation of literary and political expression by the time similar nationalist manifestations became important in the Ottoman Arab provinces. In its initial formulation by Egyptian intellectuals and political leaders from the 1870s onward, early Egyptian nationalism combined two potentially conflicting loyalties in uneasy symbiosis. One was a vivid sense of the historical as well as the contemporary uniqueness of the land and the people of Egypt. It was the territorial factor that received primary emphasis from early Egyptian nationalists: the historical, geographical, and political distinctiveness of the Nile Valley and its inhabitants. The other was the external loyalty to Egypt's formal sovereign, the Ottoman Empire. The centuries-old Ottoman link remained important on the symbolic level for many Egyptians even as its substance eroded over the course of the century. In addition, a continuing connection with the still independent Ottoman state came to be perceived as a useful instrument for resisting European imperialism as the latter first menaced and eventually engulfed Egypt. Thus, while some late-nineteenth-century Egyptian nationalists wrote in terms of Egypt as a distinct geographical entity whose people had had a separate historical existence since the pharaonic era, others (particularly many of the Muslims among them) asserted a powerful sense of allegiance to the Ottoman Empire as both the embodiment of the historic Islamic *umma* and a bulwark against European domination.

What is most significant in the context of this volume is the absence of an *Arab* component in early Egyptian nationalism. The thrust of Egyptian political, economic, and cultural development throughout the nineteenth century worked against, rather than for, an "Arab" orientation on the part of educated Egyptians. Economically, Egypt's early integration into the world economy centered on Europe linked the country to the industrial nations of Europe at the same time that it reduced the importance of Egypt's economic relationship with its immediate neighbors. Socially, the influx of a European middle class and the emergence of new landholding and bureaucratic strata, whose position was rooted in the local economy and polity, served to replace the previous Arab/Muslim associations and sympathies of the Egyptian elite with local or European linkages and loyalties. Culturally, the introduction of European ideas—including European nationalist doctrines—and the rediscovery of Egypt's massive pharaonic legacy both worked to diminish the appeal of traditional religious concepts of identity and to reinforce the alternative idea of Egypt as a territorially defined community.

But nationalism is above all a political phenomenon, and it is particularly the course of Egyptian political evolution over the nineteenth century that explains the autochthonous quality of early Egyptian nationalism. Before 1882, the all-but-formally independent Egyptian state created by Muhammad ʿAli and his successors placed Egypt on a course of political development that was very different from that of its neighbors. In its autonomous bureaucratic structure, its early struggles with the Ottoman Empire, and its state-supported educational system (which consciously promoted a sense of Egyptian distinctiveness), the nineteenth-century Egyptian state operated in a manner such as to replace older Ottoman institutions and affiliations with new Egyptian ones. After 1882, Egypt's occupation by Great Britain accentuated its political separation from its neighbors; while the Arab lands of western Asia were coming under increasingly effective Ottoman control, the dominant political issue facing Egyptians was their relationship with their European occupier. Paradoxically, the British occupation of Egypt reinforced an Egyptian orientation toward the Ottoman Empire at precisely the same time when other Arabs were becoming alienated from the Ottoman polity.

This situation—that of divergent political trajectories for Egyptians and Arabs—if anything increased after 1900. The seedtime for early Arab nationalism was particularly the years from 1908 to 1914, when first the constitutional revolution and later the ascendancy of the Committee of Union and Progress (CUP) in the Ottoman Empire presented the Arabs of western Asia with both new opportunities and new threats. At precisely the same time, the catalyst of the Dinshawai incident of 1906 (see the second section of Beth Baron's essay, in this volume), the temporary loosening of British control after the departure of Lord Cromer in 1907, and the establishment of formal political parties from 1907 onward, led to a surge in Egyptian nationalist expression and activism in the years prior to World War I. The years 1908 to 1914 were thus the first time that a significant relationship between Egyptian and Arab nationalism was a possibility.

The gulf that existed between the two nationalist movements in the immediate prewar period is most obvious in the noninvolvement of Egyptians in Ottoman Arab political activity before World War I. The sizable Syro-Palestinian community by then resident in Egypt was definitely involved in Arab politics at the time, articulating Arab grievances against the current Ottoman regime in their publications and organizing one of the leading Arab political bodies of the period, the Ottoman Administrative Decentralization party.[3] But other than the two exceptions discussed below, there is no evidence of Egyptians playing a significant role in prewar Arab political life.

The two exceptions to this generalization are however, important ones. One relates to the "Arabist" activities of the Khedive of Egypt, ʿAbbas Hilmi II, whose political involvement in the affairs of Arab Asia centered on the idea of the creation of an Arab caliphate. Perhaps as a result of a meeting with Jamal al-Din al-Afghani (al-Asadabadi) in Constantinople in 1895, early in his reign, the Khedive conceived of the idea of himself as ruler of the largest Arab country, replacing the Ottoman sultan as the symbolic religious leader of the Muslim world. He actively pursued this aim from the late 1890s, dispatching agents to various parts of the Muslim world—to Syria and Arabia in particular—to promote his claims to the office.[4] The relevance of his activities for Arab nationalism per se comes from his probable sponsorship of the famous proto-Arabist tract *Umm al-Qura* of ʿAbd al-Rahman al-Kawakibi, which in its praise of the Arabs as against the Turks was a stimulus to the gradually developing sense of Arab distinctiveness within the Ottoman Empire.[5]

From then until World War I, there are numerous indications that ʿAbbas Hilmi and those associated with him promoted the idea of an Arab caliphate. The khedival-backed journal *al-Mu-'ayyad* of Shaykh ʿAli Yusuf published articles asserting Egypt's claims to leadership of the Arab world and maintaining its suitability as the seat of a revived Arab caliphate.[6] Little specific information concerning the precise nature of the Khedive's contacts with Arabs outside Egypt in the years before World War I is available. But it was the common assumption among the British, the Egyptian nationalists, and the Ottoman authorities that he was actively promoting, through the use of agents and the sponsorship of propaganda, the idea of an Arab alternative to the existing Ottoman caliphate.[7] He was reportedly in secret contact with various Arab notables—Sharif Husayn in the Hijaz (Hejaz), the Sanusis in Libya, the Idrisids in ʿAsir—before the war, and several Egyptians arrested in Syria by the Ottoman authorities for advocating an Arab caliphate may have been his agents.[8] When Ottoman involvement in the Balkan wars placed the empire in a vulnerable position militarily, the Khedive was rumored to have encouraged Arabs in the Ottoman garrison in Syria to revolt and establish the independence of Syria.[9]

But ʿAbbas Hilmi's involvement in the politics of the Arab world before World War I needs to be put in perspective. From the limited evidence available, the Khedive's motives in encouraging Arab separatism appear to have been personal and dynastic in nature. His intermittent promotion of the idea of an Arab caliphate was clearly related to the enhancement of his political position. His involvement in the Italo-Ottoman war in Libya in the prewar period was, if anything, anti-Arab nationalist in character; according to the memoirs of the knowledgeable Muhammad Farid, the Khedive's contacts with the Arab and Ottoman military forces in 1913 were undertaken in exchange for financial considerations from the Italians, and were directed at splitting the anti-Italian resistance and thereby forcing it into an agreement with the Italians.[10] Thus, while the Khedive may have involved himself in prewar Arab politics and fostered Arab separatism from the Ottomans, he did so in the pursuit of personal advantage.

The other Egyptian involved in pre-World War I Arab politics is ʿAziz ʿAli al-Misri.[11] A third-generation Egyptian of Circassian descent, Misri was educated at the Ottoman Military College. After 1908 he involved himself in the activities of the Arab societies that emerged in the Ottoman capital in the wake of the constitutional revolution. He was one of the Ottoman officers sent to lead the struggle against the Italians in Libya in 1911, and was the officer left in command of Ottoman forces in Cyrenaica when the bulk of the Turkish military was withdrawn. Despite his abrupt and later controversial departure from Libya with his troops in 1913, his service against the Italians earned him a reputation, in Egypt, as the "hero of Cyrenaica."[12] His most noteworthy participation in Arab nationalist activities came in 1913–1914, when he is credited with organizing al-ʿAhd, the secret society of Arab Ottoman army officers. In February 1914 he was arrested, placed on trial, and sentenced to death (later commuted to fifteen years hard labor); by April a combination of Arab-Egyptian protests and British diplomatic pressure secured his pardon, release, and departure for Egypt.[13] (See Lisa Anderson's account of this episode in her essay in this volume.)

The above activities gained ʿAziz ʿAli al-Misri a reputation among Arab nationalists in the pre-World War I period as "the father of the Arab idea and the bearer of its standard."[14] But his prewar relationship to the Arab nationalist movement was more ambiguous than this implies. Emotionally, he appears to have shared the resentment felt by most Arabs against their supercilious treatment by the Turks, and he accused the Turks of having despised and insulted their Arab compatriots.[15] His substantive thoughts about the Ottoman-Arab relationship were less than completely Arab nationalist in content: al-ʿAhd originally appealed to both Turks and Arabs and advocated Ottoman decentralization rather than full Arab independence; and Misri himself acknowledged the historical role of the Turks as "the foremost guardians against the West" and the need for discontented Arabs to avoid doing anything that would weaken Ottoman capabilities in that respect.[16]

There was a considerable personal dimension to his politics, contemporary sources both pro and con crediting much of his discontent to his having been eclipsed in CUP circles by his rival, Enver Pasha (Enver Bey).[17] Misri was also closely associated with Khedive ʿAbbas Hilmi. When he was in Libya, Misri reported regularly to the Khedive on the military situation there and requested the Khedive's financial support.[18] However, Misri's abrupt retreat from Cyrenaica in 1913—fighting Arab tribal forces along the way—was reportedly encouraged by the Khedive as part of an effort to produce the capitulation to the Italians. According to the same source, the Khedive also urged Misri to proceed from Libya to Syria in order to work for Syrian separation from the Ottoman Empire.[19] The basis of his arrest and trial in 1914 are still somewhat uncertain; while the formal charges brought against him were those of embezzling funds and deserting the Ottoman cause in Libya, a contemporary communication to the Khedive from one of his agents in Constantinople reported (on the authority of the Ottoman grand vizier) that the real reason for his arrest was because of his recent activities relating to Arab dissension within the empire.[20]

Besides ʿAbbas Hilmi's personal ambitions for an Arab caliphate with himself as caliph and ʿAziz ʿAli al-Misri's complicated relationship to the emerging Arab movement, the available sources contain only incidental references to Egyptian participation in Ottoman Arab politics prior to World War I. Egyptian notable Khalil Himada, serving in the Ottoman Ministry of Awqaf in the prewar period, provided peripheral assistance to Arab nationalists in Constantinople through advising the founders of al-Muntada al-ʿadabi in 1909 and later by allowing Arabs living in the Ottoman capital to use his residence for meetings.[21] Princes ʿUmar Tusan and Yusuf Kamal of the Egyptian ruling house were both rumored as possible candidates for the governorship of Syria in the immediate prewar period; but their role in Syria would have been as Ottoman surrogates rather than as Arab nationalists.[22] When Dr. Saʿid Kamil, an Egyptian observer at the First Arab Congress in Paris in 1913, requested permission to participate in the deliberations, his request was rejected by the chair.[23] The best indication of the uninvolvement of Egyptians in early Arab nationalist activities comes from the tabulation of prewar Arab nationalists made by C. Ernest Dawn; of the 126 spokesmen for Arab nationalism and/or members of Arab nationalist societies identified by Dawn, only one (presumably ʿAziz ʿAli al-Misri) was an Egyptian.[24]

When we turn from the subject of Egyptian participation in prewar Arab politics to that of Egyptian opinion about the emerging Arab nationalist movement, the evidence indicates a prevailing Egyptian attitude of unconcern mingled with suspicion toward Arab nationalism. Egyptian publicists of the 1908–1914 period appear to have addressed the subject of Arab nationalism only occasionally; when they did so, their views were usually either noncommittal or hostile.

A convenient barometer of Egyptian political opinion is the work of Egyptian poets, much of which has traditionally been political in content. Egypt's leading poets of the early twentieth century often discussed developments in the Ottoman empire in their poetry. Other than the anti-Ottoman poet Wali al-Din Yakan, their position was invariably pro-Ottoman: praise of the Ottoman sultan/caliph as defender of the faith, support for the empire in its current travails (particularly the Italo-Ottoman war and the subsequent Balkan wars), and summons to Muslims in general and Egyptians in particular to support the empire against its enemies.[25] Conversely, Egyptian poets criticized Arab anti-Ottoman activities in the pre-World War I period, with Arab unrest in the Hijaz and Sharif Husayn's rumored toying with the idea of an Arab as opposed to an Ottoman caliphate drawing particular criticism.[26] In the eyes of Egypt's poets, the circumstances of the early twentieth century called for Arab-Turkish solidarity under the Ottoman sultan/caliph:

O people of 'Uthman, Turks and Arabs (and what people is equal to the Turks and the Arabs?)
    Protect the Crescent and increase its glory, for no glory will remain after its loss or disappearance.[27]

The most significant manifestations of political opinion in prewar Egypt were the views expressed by the spokesmen of Egypt's new political parties. Of the several parties that emerged in Egypt before the war, the pro-Ottoman yet fervently Egyptianist Watani party, led first by Mustafa Kamil and later by Muhammad Farid, and the exclusively Egyptian territorial nationalist Umma party, whose leading ideologue was Ahmad Lutfi al-Sayyid, were the most influential. Although the spokesmen of these two organizations differed radically in their attitudes toward the Ottoman empire, their views on the Arab question emerging within the empire were similar.

Mustafa Kamil died in 1908, before the question of the Arabs' position within the Ottoman empire became a significant public issue. But the views he occasionally expressed on the Arab-Ottoman relationship were solidly pro-Ottoman. His 1898 work on "The Eastern Question" (*al-Mas'ala al-sharqiyya*) was a staunch defense of the Ottomans vis-à-vis their European rivals; more importantly in this context, it attacked contemporary rumors of a movement for the establishment of an Arab caliphate as a British-inspired scheme for breaking up the empire and bringing its Arab territories under British domination.[28] Although he sometimes referred to Egyptians as "the heirs of two great civilizations—the Pharaonic and the Arabic,"[29] it was clearly the land and the people of Egypt that were the object of his nationalist rhetoric and the focus of his political activity. Like many other Egyptian nationalists of the prewar era, he also expressed a personal resentment over the privileged position and the pro-British attitude of the Syrian community residents in Egypt, characterizing them as intruders (*dukhala'*) in Egypt.[30]

The pro-Ottoman and at least implicitly non-Arabist position of Mustafa Kamil became more explicit in the attitudes and actions of his disciples from 1907 onward. Watani party leaders attempted, without much success, to make common cause with the new regime in the empire after the constitutional revolution of 1908. After their departure from Egypt in 1911–1912, the Watani spokesman, Muhammad Farid, and Shaykh ʿAbd al-ʿAziz Jawish spent much of their time in Constantinople, supporting the Ottomans in their struggles in Libya and the Balkans and collaborating in Ottoman anti-imperialist propaganda efforts.[31] Given this pro-Ottoman orientation, Watani party leaders can hardly be expected to have been sympathetic to the Arab discontent with Ottoman rule that surfaced during the 1908–1914 period. They were not. Muhammad Farid himself shared Mustafa Kamil's attitude of hostility toward the Syrian Arab community living in Egypt.[32] Debates at the party's annual congresses ignored the emerging Arab question in Ottoman Asia, focusing solely on Egyptian national issues.[33] The party press publicly criticized Muhammad Rashid Rida and other Syrians for their efforts aimed at Ottoman decentralization; in the Watanist view, by weakening and dividing the Ottoman empire such efforts would only serve British desires to extend their dominion over the bulk of the Muslim world.[34] The most revealing Watanist action concerning Arab nationalism in the prewar period was its explicit rejection of a suggestion from ʿAziz ʿAli al-Misri that the party support Arab aspirations for greater autonomy; according to Muhammad Farid, the Administrative Council of the party discussed but rejected the idea because of the dangers of encouraging Arab-Turkish tension at a time of great international pressure on the empire.[35] Watani leaders continued to differ from their Arab nationalist counterparts right up to World War I; in Constantinople just before the war, both Farid and Jawish are reported to have debated with Arab nationalist activists in the Ottoman capital, accusing the latter of treason to the empire.[36]

Ahmad Lutfi al-Sayyid of the Umma party took quite a different approach to the Ottoman empire. In his predominantly secular and thoroughly Egypt-oriented concept of nationalism, religion was an anachronistic principle of solidarity. Egypt was a nation unto itself, its various population groups over time having fused into one unique national community all of whom owed political allegiance to Egypt and Egypt alone. Lutfi was vehement in opposing an Ottoman—or any other external—sense of allegiance on the part of Egyptians, calling on his countrymen to "absolutely reject any attachment to any other homeland but Egypt, whatever our origin—Hijazi, Nubian, Turkish, Circassian, Syrian, or Greek."[37]

With this perspective on the Egyptian nation, Lutfi found little to approve of in early Arab nationalism. In a discussion of rumored Arab discontent with their underrepresentation in the Ottoman parliament, he acknowledged the reality of the Arab grievance but nonetheless maintained that it was a temporary aberration that could be resolved through Arab-Turkish reconciliation and cooperation. Thus his counsel to the Arab activists was that "[i]t is better for those who are trying to form a party to broadcast and publicize the complaints of the Arabs that they instruct the Arabs in the meaning of the constitution."[38] Lutfi was the most outspoken opponent of Egyptians offering assistance to the Ottoman-Arab struggle against Italian imperialism in Libya in 1911–1912; his editorials in *al-Jarida* repeatedly argued that Egypt had no national interests at stake in that conflict, and that the country should remain uninvolved in it.[39] Lutfi's disregard for an Egyptian-Arab connection comes out most vividly in an incident of 1911. When two Syrian notables visiting Egypt suggested Syrian annexation to Egypt if the Ottoman empire should collapse, Lutfi recalls his response as being that "I did not agree with this idea, not only because of the impossibility of the request, but because I did not see it as being in the interest of Egypt."[40]

With one exception, the more ephemeral political parties that emerged in Egypt in the years before the war also lacked any Arab orientation.[41] The exception was the pro-khedival Islah party of Shaykh ʿAli Yusuf. In the post-1907 period, as khedival-Ottoman relations cooled and the Khedive's interest in the politics of Ottoman Asia increased, 'Ali Yusuf's journal *al-Mu'ayyad* began to promote both the concept of an Arab caliphate and the suitability of Egypt as the leader of the Arab lands.[42] The journal appears to have been the only party organ in Egypt to express Arab anti-Ottoman views during this period; it published contributions by Arab spokesmen such as Muhibb al-Din al-Khatib accusing the Turks of discriminating against the Arabs, and 'Ali Yusuf himself wrote sympathetically of Arab grievances against the Ottomans.[43] But again an appreciation of the political context is necessary: this openness to the Arab position appears to have been only temporary, and was probably linked to the Khedive's ambitions in Arab Asia.

The aloofness of prewar Egyptian nationalists from political currents in the neighboring Arab world is evident in a consideration of Egyptian reaction to the idea of closer Egyptian-Syrian ties. Ottoman defeats in Libya and the Balkans in the immediate prewar years produced considerable sentiment in Syria in favor of Syrian political linkage with Egypt as an alternative to an apparently disintegrating Ottoman polity.[44] What is relevant for our discussion is that this sentiment was unreciprocated by Egyptian nationalist spokesmen. While the idea found some support in the Syrian-run press of Egypt, the leaders of Egypt's new political parties were unmoved by it.[45] There is no evidence of Watanist spokesmen favoring the possibility of an Egyptian-Syrian linkage, and we have already noted that Ahmad Lutfi al-Sayyid explicitly rejected the idea when it was broached to him. For Egyptian nationalists of the prewar era, Egypt was either a national unit completely separate from its neighbors (the perspective of Lutfi al-Sayyid and the Umma) or it was one of several national units within a larger Muslim community currently represented by the Ottoman empire (the Watanist approach); but it was not involved in the Arab nationalist movement then emerging in Ottoman Asia, and its problems had no connection with the current problems of the Arabs.

Much the same Egyptian diffidence toward the Arab nationalist movement obtained during World War I. The overall Egyptian attitude toward the war and its participants appears to have been one of sympathy with the Ottoman-German rather than the Allied cause. Both contemporary reports and later evaluations of the Egyptian scene during the early years of the war speak of a considerable anticipation within Egypt of an Ottoman-German victory that would entail Egyptian liberation from the British occupation; there are vague reports of some Egyptian nationalists having considered an anti-British uprising in conjunction with an anticipated Ottoman invasion across the Suez Canal. Leading anti-British Egyptian political figures —ʿAbbas Hilmi, deposed as khedive in December 1914; Muhammad Farid of the Watani party; and younger national enthusiasts such as ʿAbd al-Rahman ʿAzzam—attempted to make common cause with the Ottoman war effort.[46] British security measures in the early years of the war prevented either pro-Ottoman sentiment or the pro-Ottoman activism of these individuals from becoming a factor of significance. Nonetheless, as late as the fall of 1918, when the Ottoman war effort had collapsed, a British evaluation was still speaking of "the well-known sympathy of the masses of the [Egyptian] people to the Turkish Khalifate."[47]

This attitude of Egyptian sympathy with the Ottoman cause during World War I was paralleled by a reserved and sometimes hostile Egyptian attitude toward the wartime Arab revolt. The Egyptian press was at first reluctant to publish news of the revolt when it began in June 1916; it did so only after proddings from the censor's office that "events of such importance should be commented upon *in the proper sense.*"[48] In their initial reports which followed this directive, Egyptian newspapers were careful to adhere to a clearly pro-Allied position on the Arab revolt, consistently presenting it as justified in view of the oppressive policies of the Unionist regime in control in the Ottoman empire. By its prewar measures of Turkification, its recent repression of Arab sentiment in Syria, and particularly its irreligious and anti-Islamic attitude, the Ottoman government had made rebellion the only recourse for the oppressed Arabs of its Asian provinces.[49] The Arab revolt was thus the inevitable outcome of Unionist policies of "destruction, division, and expulsion"; it was "the natural result of the evil Turkish rule . . . and their desire to kill the Arab spirit and to Turkify the Arabs."[50]

But the views expressed in the British-manipulated Egyptian press are of limited value in assessing the Egyptian response to the revolt. A better indication of Egyptian attitudes comes from the contemporary assessments of the Egyptian scene made by

British officials. Initial British evaluations of the Egyptian reaction to the revolt were cautious, noting Egyptian surprise at its outbreak, claiming some but far from general sympathy for the Sharifian movement in Egypt, and on the whole discerning "little interest or comment" by Egyptians about the revolt.[51] Later British reports were consistent in minimizing the impact of the Arab revolt upon wartime Egypt. When apprehensive about the possible collapse of the revolt in the fall of 1916, the British concluded that such an eventuality would have no significant repercussions in Egypt.[52] A detailed appreciation of the Egyptian attitude toward the revolt a year after it had begun emphasized its marginality in wartime Egypt and indicated that Egyptian public opinion largely saw it as a peninsular phenomenon whose impact would be ephemeral:

Moslem opinion in Egypt as a whole continues to be entirely apathetic to the Arab movement for independence. The King of the Hedjaz has a few ardent supporters, chiefly Ottoman Arabs, but no party of sufficient importance to influence public opinion and to gain powerful adherents. An influential minority of Egyptians of Turkish extraction are bitterly opposed to the Sherifial Government of the Hedjaz.[53]

Egyptian indifference to the revolt apparently changed little by 1918; at a meeting of British officials in March of that year, Sir Reginald Wingate's view was that "the Sherifian movement had gained little sympathy" in Egypt in the two years since it began.[54] By the closing months of the war, it was virtually a truism among British officials concerned with the Middle East that "hostility toward the Arab movement" prevailed in Egypt.[55]

Given this general attitude of indifference and/or hostility toward the Arab revolt within Egypt, it is not surprising that there is little evidence of Egyptian involvement in the Arab movement between the beginning of the revolt in 1916 and the end of the war two years later. Immediately upon the outbreak of the revolt, Sharif Husayn requested the dispatch of Egyptian artillery to bolster his military position vis-à-vis the remaining Ottoman forces in the Hijaz.[56] Sultan Husayn Kamil of Egypt resisted this, at first recommending the dispatch of Sudanese rather than Egyptian troops, later suggesting that any Egyptian forces sent to aid the Sharifians be disguised as volunteers and compelled to wear "native clothes" rather than their Egyptian uniforms.[57] The British themselves were apprehensive over "pro-

Turkish feeling among the native officers" of the Egyptian army, convinced that "the idea of sending Egyptians to cooperate with Arabs . . . was certain to be unpopular" within Egypt.⁵⁸

Two Egyptian mountain batteries were sent to the Hijaz in June 1916, where they participated in several military engagements.⁵⁹ The Egyptian troops in the Hijaz, on their part, were critical of the "want of organization among the Arabs"; on the other side, the Hijazis are reported to have disliked the idea of Egyptians being sent to aid them and to have opposed the landing of the Egyptian forces at Rabigh.⁶⁰ T. E. Lawrence summarized the attitude of the Egyptian troops towards Sharif Husayn's tribal forces as follows: "[t]hey were fighting the Turks, for whom they had a sentimental regard, on behalf of the Arabs, an alien people speaking a language kindred to their own, but appearing therefore all the more unlike in character, and crude in life."⁶¹

The only Egyptian of note associated with the Arab revolt during World War I was ʿAziz ʿAli al-Misri. Living in Egypt from 1914 until 1916, Misri was only indirectly involved in the genesis of the revolt. Immediately upon the outbreak of the war in Europe, he is reported to have approached the British on behalf of an otherwise-unidentified "Central Committee" at Baghdad to seek British support for the creation of an independent Arab state under the tutelage of Great Britain; the British ignored the approach at the time.⁶² In October 1914 he offered the British an uprising of Arab Ottoman forces in Iraq if the British would provide assistance; again, the British declined to pursue the gambit.⁶³ In 1915, Misri was tangentially involved in the exchanges between Sharif Husayn and Sir Henry McMahon, being consulted by the British concerning the credentials of the Sharif's emissary Muhammad Sharif al-Faruqi and reportedly concurring in the terms eventually offered to the Sharif by McMahon.⁶⁴ The British in Cairo wished to send Misri, along with Faruqi, to Iraq in the spring of 1916 to promote dissension among the Ottoman forces in the field, but opposition from the military killed the idea.⁶⁵

It was only with the beginning of the Arab revolt in mid-1916 that Misri again became involved in the Arab movement. In September 1916, after a trip to Arabia and a meeting with Sharif Husayn, Misri was appointed chief of staff of the Arab army. Friction soon developed between him and the Sharif. In

October he argued against an attack on Medina, and by his own later recollection contemplated secret negotiations with the Ottoman forces located there in order to end the revolt in exchange for Ottoman recognition of Arab autonomy within the empire.[66] Neither the attack on Medina nor secret contacts with the Ottomans ever occurred. But Misri made his discontent with the disorganized and poorly led state of the Arab forces known to the British, and threatened to resign from his position.[67] Themselves disillusioned with the Arab military effort, the British in turn pressured Sharif Husayn to give Misri, a well-trained and proven regular officer, a more active role in military operations. Although Sharif Husayn initially promised to appoint Misri to the position of minister of war and to entrust him with field operations, the combination of Misri's putative contact with the Ottomans and the threat of his emerging as a potential rival to the sharifian family's leadership of the revolt apparently were enough to turn Sharif Husayn against him.[68] For his part, by the beginning of 1917, Misri had become thoroughly disillusioned with the organization of the revolt, at one point speaking of "the impossibility of doing anything serious with the Shereef and his sons."[69] In March 1917 he left the Hijaz, returning to Egypt and thereafter proceeding to Spain where he remained until 1922. His participation in the Arab nationalist movement—at least this phase of it—was over.

The evidence available leaves Misri's substantive position on the wartime Arab revolt somewhat ambiguous. According to one British report, in 1914 he had been talking in terms of "a united Arabian state, independent of Turkey."[70] Yet in conversations with Sir Ronald Storrs in 1916 he expressed grave reservations concerning the possible expansion of sharifian operations to the Fertile Crescent, and in later interviews he maintained that his wartime position had been the attaining of Arab autonomy within a reformed Ottoman polity rather than outright Arab independence.[71] Misri's personal views on the capability and potential of the different "Arab races" as expressed during his brief sojourn in the Hijaz in 1916 provide an insight into how even an important figure in the early Arab nationalist movement distinguished between different Arab groups and sometimes portrayed his compatriots in less-than-flattering terms: "the people of Baghdad are really the most intelligent and advanced of all. . . . Syrians have more education and polish, but less brain and character. Closely following these come the Tripolitanians, of whom he thinks a great deal might, but certainly will not, be made.... After the Tripolitanians he placed the people of the Yemen whom he finds greatly superior to that of the Hijaz, generations of a better diet being the possible reason." Despite their preeminent advantages, the Egyptians, nevertheless, come last: "Aziz Aly [sic] has indeed such a horror of their deft thankless corrupting nature that he would vote with all his strength against the inclusion of Egypt in any Arab empire or Confederation."[72]

Besides ʿAziz ʿAli al-Misri, there seems to have been no other significant Egyptian involvement in the wartime Arab revolt. From his exile in Istanbul and later Europe, the deposed khedive ʿAbbas Hilmi attempted to maintain personal contacts with at least the sharifian family in the Hijaz during the early years of the war.[73] Perhaps in an effort at reconciliation as well as an attempt to convince them of his potential utility for their war effort, the ex-khedive boasted to the British of his influence among the Arabs of western Asia.[74] He played the Ottomans in a similar fashion, at one point attempting to persuade them to make him their instrument in weaning the sharifians away from the British by appointing him as an Ottoman "viceroy" in Syria in competition with the sharifian movement.[75]

Nothing substantial came from the ex-khedive's wartime efforts to offer himself as an Ottoman surrogate or British agent in the Arab East. There is no evidence of his having played a role in the inception of the Arab revolt. It occurred as a result of Arab-British negotiations from which the ex-Khedive was excluded, and the memoirs of his fellow-exile Muhammad Farid explicitly state that ʿAbbas had had "no hand" in it when it broke out in mid-1916.[76] Paradoxically, his most significant impact upon wartime developments in western Asia may have been upon the British. His prewar activities aimed at promoting an Arab caliphate were a factor in Lord Herbert Kitchener's unexpectedly raising the issue of the caliphate with Sharif Husayn late in 1914, as well as serving as a more indirect stimulus to those British officials in Egypt who periodically advocated the extension of Egyptian control over Syria-Palestine as a solution to the question of how to dispose of these regions after the war.[77]

Any other Egyptian connection with Arab politics during the

war was incidental. The Watanist leader Shaykh ʿAbd al-ʿAziz Jawish was reported to have been in Mecca in late 1914, but his presence there was to rally Arab support for the Ottoman *jihad* rather than to encourage Arab revolt.[78] Jawish's colleague Muhammad Farid sympathized with wartime Arab grievances against the Unionist government, at one point noting how the Turks despised the Arabs and treated them "like dogs."[79] His wartime memoirs, however, make no mention of any direct connection of Farid with the Arab movement. An expression of support for the Arab revolt was made by Saʿd Zaghlul, who, in a meeting with the young Nuri al-Saʿid shortly after the outbreak of the revolt, reportedly encouraged the latter to participate in the sharifian movement which he viewed as an opportunity to realize Arab national aspirations.[80] But Zaghlul's encouragement was that of a disinterested external observer rather than that of a participant in the Arab movement.

Egypt's separation from early Arab nationalism was most apparent in the years immediately following World War I, when the postwar settlement in the Middle East was being arranged. The elimination of a meaningful Ottoman option for Egyptian loyalties due to the defeat of the empire did not lead to a more positive Egyptian relationship with the Arab world. Rather, it left the territorial Egyptian nationalist orientation that had coexisted with Ottomanism in the prewar period at least temporarily unchallenged for the national loyalties of articulate Egyptians. The Egyptian nationalist revolution that occurred immediately after World War I was thoroughly Egyptianist in its goals and activities; as such, it neither had any links with, nor desired any connection with, the parallel Arab nationalist movement in Arab Asia.

The goal of Egyptian nationalists of whatever party through the hectic years from 1919 until 1922 was the "complete independence" of Egypt. This meant in the first instance liberation from the British Protectorate which had been declared in 1914. But it also meant the elimination of all vestiges of Ottoman sovereignty as well as the avoidance of any alternative external affiliations in place of the Ottoman connection. The political forces active in the revolution (most notably the Wafd formed in 1918–1919 to seek Egyptian representation in the postwar peace conference) in their manifestos and declarations both rejected any Ottoman connection for Egypt and made no mention of alternative regional solidarities.[81] Popular opinion during the revolution was equally non-Arabist; other than one demonstration in Asyût in which the demonstrators reportedly claimed Amir Faysal (Faisal) as "king of the Arabs," there is no evidence of those involved in the massive protests and demonstrations of the spring of 1919 being concerned with developments in the Ottoman Arab provinces.[82] Similarly, the scores of public letters and pamphlets put out by Egyptians during the visit of the Milner Mission in late 1919 addressed Egyptian issues and ignored the Arab question.[83]

Nor does there appear to have been any practical connection between the postwar Egyptian and Arab nationalist movements. There is no evidence of any meaningful contact or collaboration between Egyptian nationalist leaders and their Arab counterparts in the immediate postwar period. In Paris in 1919, Wafdist leaders are reported to have rejected an invitation to collaborate with other "Eastern" nationalists present at the peace conference; while they approved of such cooperation in the abstract, in their own case the specifically Egyptianist mandate of their movement prevented them from involving themselves in broader Eastern issues.[84] In London a year later, Saʿd Zaghlul declined to comment on the situation in Syria and Palestine on the grounds that his own political focus was Egypt alone.[85] Zaghlul's personal opinion of Arab nationalism after World War I had frequently been summarized by the remark he made to his associate, ʿAbd al-Rahman ʿAzzam, at the time of the Syrian revolt in 1925: when asked his views on the political movements in the various Arab countries of western Asia, his response was the contemptuous statement "[i]f you add a zero and a zero and a zero, what is the result?"[86]

The only exception to this Egyptian lack of involvement in postwar Arab affairs was the exiled ex-khedive ʿAbbas Hilmi. In the early 1920s, the ex-khedive made several attempts to establish a personal sphere of influence in the Arab East. At Constantinople in 1920, ʿAbbas Hilmi is reported to have advocated sending an Ottoman mission to the Arab government at Damascus in the hope of establishing a common Ottoman-Arab anti-imperialist front.[87] A year later he was in contact with Syrian groups promoting the idea of his own candidavy for the throne of Syria under French suzerainty.[88] In 1921 he presented a proposal to the British advocating a network of British-Egyptian-Arab alliances as a way of linking the Arab lands to Great Britain through Egypt; the proposal not disinterestedly suggested the replacement of the "detested" King Husayn of the Hijaz by "an Egyptian prince."[89] He promoted a similar idea with both Arab nationalists and the new Turkish government, and at Lausanne during the peace conference of 1922–1923 he worked assiduously to create a "Supreme Oriental Revolutionary Council" under his own leadership.[90]

As had been the case with ʿAbbas Hilmi's wartime maneuvers, nothing came of these postwar schemes. Indeed, rather than leading to an enhancement of his political position, they may have damaged his reputation—if not among Arabs, at least with his former Egyptian subjects. His efforts of 1921–1922 to obtain the Syrian throne were criticized within Egyptian nationalist circles in Europe on the grounds that the ex-khedive should have been devoting his political energies to Egyptian issues rather than pursuing non-Egyptian goals.[91] ʿAbbas's activities at Lausanne drew similar Egyptian criticism. Although many of the Arab activists and even the small Watanist delegation present in Lausanne are reported to have approved of his concept of an Eastern anti-imperialist front, the Wafdist delegation that was attempting to obtain a hearing at the conference largely opposed his efforts at Eastern "revolutionary" coordination.[92] Thus ʿAbbas Hilmi's attempt to involve himself in Arab politics after World War I was a personal endeavor of the ex-khedive unreflective of the position of politically active Egyptians.

British reports on Egyptian public opinion when the peace settlement in the Fertile Crescent was being arranged in 1920 indicate that the fate of the Ottoman Arab provinces was an issue of major concern only to the Syrian community in Egypt. The decisions taken at the San Remo Conference in April 1920 did draw Egyptian nationalist criticism for their disregard of the principle of self-determination, but it was particularly the strictly Egyptian issue of continuing tribute to the Ottomans that produced Egyptian press commentary, with "native opinion" within Egypt being evaluated as having been "almost apathetic" on the broader issue of the fate of the Ottoman empire.[93] Egyptian disapproval of the terms of the postwar peace settlement in the Middle East was "frequent" but it was also "rarely passionate."[94] Even the crisis between the Arab government at Damascus and the French in the summer of 1920 is reported to have generated "little excitement outside local Syrian circles" in Egypt.[95] Egyptian newspapers decried the French use of force in Syria, complaining that "the policy of self-determination does not apply to Eastern nations" and that "freedom has geographical and racial limits"; but the overall treatment of the destruction of the Arab state in 1920 in the Egyptian press was as an external issue peripheral to Egyptian nationalist concerns.[96]

The abstract sympathy with Arab self-determination sometimes expressed by Egyptians after World War I was also overlaid by another, considerably less favorable, attitude. This was a definite sense of resentment over what Egyptians perceived to be the preferential Allied treatment of the Arab nationalist movement immediately after the war. Upon the issuance of the Anglo-French Declaration of November 7, 1918, which promised application of the principle of self-determination in Ottoman territories conquered by the Allies, High Commissioner Wingate reported his apprehensions that the Declaration would produce unfavorable repercussions "among Egyptian nationalists who will, no doubt, desire similar treatment for Egypt."[97] Wingate's prediction was soon borne out. At the famous meeting of November 13, 1918, where an Egyptian delegation requested Egyptian attendance at the peace conference, one of their arguments was that "they consider themselves far more capable of conducting a well-ordered government than the Arabs, Syrians, and Mesopotamians to whom the Anglo-French Governments have granted self-determination."[98] Other Egyptian leaders voiced the same complaint; as Wingate summarized the Egyptian position in late 1918, "the Arab Emir Faisal was allowed to go to Paris. Were Egyptians less loyal? Why not Egypt?"[99]

An appreciable tone of anti-Arab resentment marked Egyptian nationalist manifestos in 1919. The official Wafdist declaration addressed to the Paris Peace Conference early in 1919 referred to Egypt as "infinitely more advanced" than the Arab countries attending the conference, and as such suited to be heard as well.[100] Similarly, a letter to President Woodrow Wilson maintained that "from all points of view, Egypt is much more superior than the Hijaz, Arabia, Syria, Lebanon, Armenia, and the states of the Caucasus," and thus deserved representation in Paris.[101] Reports from Egypt during the uprising in the spring of 1919 made the same point about Egyptian sentiment: as Sir Ronald Graham put it, "[t]here is no doubt that Egyptian amour-propre has been wounded by the absence of Egyptian representation at the Peace Conference, when India and, still worse, the disliked and despised Bedouin of the Hedjaz have been represented."[102] Egyptians themselves presented the issue of Arab representation and Egyptian exclusion from the peace conference as a cause of the postwar Egyptian revolution:

> Another cause of encouragement to use was the recognition of the independence of our brothers of the Hedjaz, who speak the same language as ourselves and are of the same religion as most of us. The Arabs of the Hedjaz did not have before a separate political existence like [sic] ourselves. In fact, within a century, they were under our political control.... Was it illogical for us to expect from the British Government, in view of the oft-repeated assertions of its members, treatment at least as generous as that accorded the Arabs of the Hedjaz?[103]

Despite the reference to "our brothers," the assertion of Egyptian-Arab brotherhood clearly is not the central message of this petition.

A consideration of three official documents of the mid-1920s may serve to summarize the Egyptian relationship to Arab nationalism at the close of the postwar settlement. The first is the Egyptian Constitution promulgated in April 1923. The constitution's thrust was solidly Egyptian territorial nationalist, proclaiming that "Egypt is a sovereign state, free and independent"; save for Article 149, which declared Arabic to be the official language of the state, it was devoid of any Arab dimension.[104] This exclusively Egyptian orientation was borne out diplomatically in the position of the newly established Egyptian state toward the British and French mandates in the Fertile Crescent. Both the French position of dominance in Syria and that of the British in Iraq and Palestine were given official acknowledgment by the government of Egypt—the French indirectly in an exchange of notes of 1925, which defined legal jurisdiction over Syro-Lebanese in Egypt and Egyptians in Syria and Lebanon,[105] the British directly in a note of 1926 "recognizing the special position of His Majesty's Government in relation to the territories of Palestine and Irak."[106] The only reservation in the latter document was the thoroughly Egyptianist one that the ongoing definition of the boundaries of the Palestine Mandate should in no way affect the Ottoman-Egyptian boundary agreement of 1906, which had placed the Sinai peninsula under Egyptian authority.[107] Thus the new Egyptian regime, created in the same postwar settlement that had resulted in the elimination of an independent Arab regime in greater Syria, soon acquiesced in European domination over the birthplace of Arab nationalism.

Notes

1. For an overview of these trends, see Albert Hourani, *Arabic Thought*, pp. 273–79, 362–63.
2. There are numerous studies in depth dealing with Egyptian nationalism in the late nineteenth and early twentieth centuries. The following are perhaps the most useful on the subject: Muhammad Muhammad Husayn, *al-Ittijahat al-wataniyya fil-adab al-muʿasir* [Nationalist orientations in contemporary literature]; Fritz Steppat, "Nationalismus und Islam bei Mustafa Kamil," *Die Welt des Islams* 4 (1955–1956): 241–341; Anis Sayigh, *al-Fikra al-ʿarabiyya fi misr* [The Arab idea in Egypt]; Jamal Mohammed Ahmed, *The Intellectual Origins of Egyptian Nationalism;* Hourani, *Arabic Thought;* Arthur Goldschmidt, Jr., "The Egyptian Nationalist Party, 1892–1919," pp. 308–33; Robert L. Tignor, *Modernization and British Colonial Rule in Egypt, 1882–1914* (Princeton: Princeton University Press, 1966); Muhammad ʿImara, *al-ʿUruba fil-ʿasr al-hadith* [Arabism in the modern era]; Afaf Lutfi al-Sayyid [Marsot], *Egypt and Cromer;* P. J. Vatikiotis, *The Modern History of Egypt* (New York, 1969); Dhuqan Qarqut, *Tatawwur al-fikra al-ʿarabiyya fi misr, 1805–1936* [The Development of the Arab idea in Egypt, 1805–1936]; Jacques Berque, *Egypt: Imperialism and Revolution;* Charles Wendell, *The Evolution of the Egyptian National Image;* Faruq Abu Zayd, *Azmat al-fikr al-qawmi fil-sihafa al-misriyya* [The crisis of nationalist thought in the Egyptian press]; James Jankowski, "Ottomanism and Arabism in Egypt," pp. 226–59; Dennis Walker, "Mustafa Kamil's Party: Islam, Pan-Islamism, and Nationalism," *Islam and the Modern Age* 11 (1980): 329–88, and 12 (1981): 1–43, 79–113; Alexander Schölch, *Egypt for the Egyptians!;* Israel Gershoni and James Jankowski, *Egypt, Islam, and the Arabs.*
3. See Rashid Khalidi's essay in this volume for more on this topic.

4. Elie Kedourie, "The Politics of Political Literature: Kawakibi, Azoury, and Jung," in his *Arabic Political Memoirs*, pp. 108–10.
5. See Sylvia G. Haim, ed. *Arab Nationalism*, pp. 27–28.
6. Abu Zayd, *Azmat al-fikr*, pp. 115–17.
7. For such speculation, see Husayn, *al-Ittijahat*, 1:91; Wilfred Scawen Blunt, *My Diaries*, 2 vols. (New York, 1921), 2:251; Vatikiotis, *Modern History of Egypt*, p. 206; Rashid Khalidi, *British Policy*, pp. 226, 274–75; Elie Kedourie, *In the Anglo-Arab Labyrinth*, pp. 10–14; and Markaz watha'iq wa ta'rikh misr al-mu'asir, *Awraq Muhammad Farid* [The papers of Muhammad Farid], 1:105, 116, 122, 202.
8. Markaz watha'iq, *Awraq Muhammad Farid*, 1:99–100, 112, 235; Blunt, *My Diaries*, 2:390; Kedourie, *Anglo-Arab Labyrinth*, pp. 10–14; and Khalidi, *British Policy*, p. 239.
9. Markaz watha'iq, *Awraq Muhammad Farid*, 1:99–100; see also Khalidi, *British Policy*, p. 234.
10. Markaz watha'iq, *Awraq Muhammad Farid*, 1:99–100, 116.
11. For discussions of Misri's prewar career, see George Antonius, *The Arab Awakening*, pp. 110–11, 118–21; As'ad Daghir, *Mudhakkirati 'ala hamish al-qadiyya al-'arabiyya* [My memoirs on the margins of the Arab cause], pp. 37–42; Majid Khadduri, "'Aziz 'Ali al-Misri and the Arab Nationalist Movement," pp. 140–63, especially 140–51; Muhammad Subayh, *Batal la nansahu* [A hero we will not forget], pp. 42–62.
12. The phrase of the poet Ahmad Shawqi as quoted in Khadduri, "'Aziz 'Ali al-Misri," p. 143. For accounts of Misri's activities in Libya, see also Subayh, *Batal la nansahu*, pp. 47–49; Muhammad 'Abd al-Rahman Burj, *'Aziz al-Misri wal-haraka al-'arabiyya, 1908–1916* [Aziz al-Misri and the Arab movement, 1908–1916], pp. 58–73; and Lisa Anderson, *The State and Social Transformation*, pp. 128–30.
13. Discussed in Antonius, *The Arab Awakening*, pp. 118–21; Khadduri, "'Aziz 'Ali al-Misri," pp. 144–45, 150; Subayh, *Batal la nansahu*, pp. 57–61; and Djamal Pasha, *Memories of a Turkish Statesman, 1913–1919*, pp. 63–64.
14. Daghir, *Mudhakkirati*, p. 37.
15. See Djamal Pasha, *Memories*, p. 61.
16. Quotation from remarks of 1913 as quoted in Ahmad Shafiq, *Mudhakkirati fi nisf qarn* [My memories of half a century], 3:82; see also Khadduri, "'Aziz 'Ali al-Misri," pp. 149–50 (based on later interviews with Misri).
17. Emphasized by Misri's opponent Djamal Pasha, *Memories*, p. 62, and also reported by the Egyptian nationalist leader Muhammad Farid (Markaz watha'iq, *Awraq Muhammad Farid*, 1:165–66); see also Khadduri, "'Aziz 'Ali al-Misri," in Hourani, pp. 148–50.

18. ʿAbbas Hilmi II Papers (Sudan Archive, Oriental Section, Durham University Library), file 112.
19. Markaz watha'iq, *Awraq Muhammad Farid*, 1:99–100; see also ʿAbbas Hilmi II Papers, file 116. The report receives partial confirmation in a French source of 1913, which evaluated Misri's organizing activities among Arab army officers as being "evidently associated with Egypt" (Khalidi, *British Policy*, p. 343).
20. ʿAbbas Hilmi II Papers, file 112, pp. 1–4; see also Antonius, *The Arab Awakening*, p. 120; Khadduri, "ʿAziz ʿAli al-Misri," p. 144; and Anderson, *The State and Social Transformation*, pp. 191–92.
21. Subayh, *Batal la nansahu*, p. 62; Akram Zuʿaytir, "al-ʿUruba fi Misr," *al-ʿArabi*, no. 244 (March 1979): 8.
22. Djamal Pasha, *Memories*, pp. 231–32; Abu Khaldum Satiʿ al-Husari, *Muhadarat fi nushu'al-fikra al-qawmiyya* [Lectures on the growth of the national idea] (Cairo, 1951), pp. 270–75.
23. Reported in ʿImara, *al-ʿUraba fi al-ʿasr*, p. 331, no. 1.
24. C. Ernest Dawn, *From Ottomanism to Arabism*, pp. 152–53.
25. For numerous examples, see Husayn, *al-Ittijahat*, 1:23–40; see also Mounah A. Khouri, *Poetry and the Making of Modern Egypt, 1882–1922*, pp. 103–16.
26. See especially Husayn, *al-Ittijahat*, 1:23–29; and Khouri, *Poetry*, pp. 106–8.
27. Ahmad Muharram as quoted in Khouri, *Poetry*, pp. 103–4.
28. Discussed in Husayn, *al-Ittijahat*, 1:8–10; Jack A. Crabbs, Jr., *The Writing of History in Nineteenth-Century Egypt*, pp. 156–61; Hourani, *Arabic Thought*, p. 203; and Abu Zayd, *Azmat al-fikr*, pp. 121–22.
29. Quoted in Wendell, *Egyptian National Image*, p. 248.
30. Discussed in Steppat, "Nationalismus und Islam," pp. 258–61; Ahmed, *Intellectual Origins*, p. 82; Wendell, *Egyptian National Image*, p. 249; and Goldschmidt, "The Egyptian Nationalist Party," p. 315.
31. Details in ibid., pp. 323–29.
32. See Rifʿat Saʿid, *Muhammad Farid*, pp. 143–45.
33. Sayigh, *al-Fikra al-ʿarabiyya*, p. 54.
34. Ibid., p. 55; see also Haim, *Arab Nationalism*, p. 47.
35. Reported in Markaz watha'iq, *Awraq Muhammad Farid*, pp. 100–1.
36. Daghir, *Mudhakkirati*, pp. 47–48.
37. Quoted in Wendell, *Egyptian National Image*, p. 259.
38. Quoted in Sayigh, *al-Fikra al-ʿarabiyya*, p. 55.
39. See Abu Zayd, *Azmat al-fikr*, pp. 155–57; Ahmad Lutfi al-Sayyid, *Qissat hayati* [The story of my life], pp. 129–30; Muhammad Husayn Haykal, *Mudhakkirat fil-siyasa al-misriyya* [Memoirs of Egyptian politics], 1:50–51; and Ahmad Zakariyya al-Shaliq, *Hizb al-*

umma wa dawruhu fil-siyasa al-misriyya [The Umma party and its role in Egyptian politics], pp. 229–30.
40. al-Sayyid, *Qissat hayati*, p. 137.
41. Discussed in Sayigh, *al-Fikra al-ʿarabiyya*, pp. 59–61.
42. Abu Zayd, *Azmat al-fikr*, pp. 114–17.
43. Ibid., pp. 117–20.
44. See Khalidi, *British Policy*, pp, 260–79.
45. al-Sayyid, *Qissat hayati*, p. 137.
46. Discussed in detail in Gershoni and Jankowski, *Egypt, Islam, and the Arabs*, pp. 23–28.
47. Wingate to Hardinge, November 24, 1918, FO 371/3204: reproduced in Mu'assasat al-Ahram, *Khamsun ʿaman ʿala thawrat 1919* [Fifty years since the 1919 revolution] (Cairo, 1969), document 14.
48. Memo from the Adviser's Office, Ministry of the Interior, June 25 1916, FO 141/461, 1198/146 (emphasis added).
49. For examples of this theme of recent Ottoman oppression of the Arabs, see *al-Ahram*, June 25, 1916, p. 1, and July 8, 1916, p. 1; *Misr*, June 27, 1916, p. 2, and July 10, 1916, p. 2; *al-Muqattam*, June 23, 1916, p. 5, and June 27, 1916, p. 1, and July 7, 1916, pp. 1–2, and July 25, 1916, pp. 1–2; and *al-Watan*, July 11, 1916, p. 3.
50. *al-Ahram*, June 25, 1916, p. 1; and *al-Muqattam*, July 7, 1916, p. 1.
51. Sir Ronald Storrs to the High Commissioner, July 30, 1916, FO 141/461, 1198/169a; telegram from the High Commissioner, July 3, 1916, FO 141/461, 119/188; and "Second Note: Effect in Egypt of the Hijaz News," Sir Ronald Storrs, July 4, 1916, FO 141/641 1198/190.
52. Note by General Clayton, received September 29, 1916, FO 141/461, 1198/463; telegram from the High Commissioner, September 29, 1916, FO 141/461, 1198/468.
53. "Egypt and the Arab Movement," August 14, 1917, FO 141/783, 5317/1.
54. "Account of a Meeting Held at the Residency," March 23, 1918, FO 141/430, 5411/17.
55. From a report of August 22, 1918 by W. Ormsby-Gore as reprinted in Kenneth Bourne and D. Cameron Watt, eds., *Documents on British Foreign Affairs: Reports and Papers from the Foreign Office Confidential Print. Part II: From the First to the Second World War, Series B: Turkey, Iran, and the Middle East, 1918–1939* 13 vols. (Washington, D.C., 1986), 1:5.
56. See the material in FO 141/461, 141/461, 141/825.
57. Telegram from the High Commissioner's Office, June 25, 1916, FO 141/461, 1198/143. See also Elie Kedourie, "Egypt and the Caliphate, 1915–52," in his *Chatham House Version*, pp. 181–82.

58. Quotations from telegrams from the Sirdar, June 20, 1916 (FO 141/461, 1198/126) and June 26, 1916 (FO 141/461, 1198/152).
59. See Sir George MacMunn and Cyril Falls, *Military Operations, Egypt and Palestine: From the Outbreak of War with Germany to June 1917* (London, 1928), pp. 221, 226–37.
60. Telegram from the Sirdar, June 24, 1916, FO 141/461, 1198/142; telegram from the Arab Bureau, July 3, 1916, FO 141/461, 1198/186.
61. T. E. Lawrence, *Seven Pillars of Wisdom: A Triumph* (London, 1935), p. 93.
62. Report on a conversation with Misri by Captain R. E. M. Russell, August 16, 1914, FO 371/2140, W44/46261/14.
63. See A. L. Tibawi, *Anglo-Arab Relations*, pp. 36–37.
64. Antonius, *The Arab Awakening*, p. 212; and Kedourie, *Anglo-Arab Labyrinth*, pp. 74, 96, 106–7.
65. Ibid., pp. 126–29.
66. Khadduri, "ʿAziz ʿAli al-Misri" p. 154.
67. The unofficial diary of Sir Ronald Storrs on a trip to the Hijaz, October 1916, FO 141/462, 1198/613; abbreviated version in Sir Ronald Storrs, *Memoirs*, p. 194.
68. Sir Ronald Storrs at one point speculated that Sharif Husayn's reserve about Misri was due to "fear that Aziz Bey had not changed his Committee spots and might set himself up as Enver (or even betray them to the Turks)"; unofficial diary, December 1916, FO 141/825, 1198/769.
69. In a conversation with the naval commander in the Red Sea, January 25, 1917, FO 141/825, 1198/807.
70. Report on a conversation with Misri by Captain R. E. M. Russell, August 16, 1914, FO 371/2140, W44/46261/14.
71. The unofficial diary of Sir Robert Storrs on a trip to the Hijaz, October 1916, FO 141/462, 1198/613; see also Storrs, *Memoirs*, p. 194; and Khadduri, "ʿAziz ʿAli al-Misri," pp. 152–53.
72. The unofficial diary of Sir Ronald Storrs on a trip to the Hijaz, October 1916, FO 141/462, 1198/613.
73. See Markaz watha'iq, *Awraq Muhammad Farid*, pp. 202, 235; and Shafiq, *Mudhakkirati fi nisf qarn*, 3:61.
74. See Thomas Mayer, "Dreamers and Opportunists: ʿAbbas Hilmi's Peace Initiative in Palestine, 1930–1931," in Amnon Cohen and Gabriel Baer, eds., *Egypt and Palestine: A Millennium of Association (868–1948)* (New York, 1984), pp. 285–86.
75. Report on the Journey of the Khedive to Constantinople, October 1917, FO 141/648, 232/154; see also Mayer, "Dreamers and Opportunists," in Cohen and Baer, eds., *Egypt and Palestine*, p. 286.
76. Markaz watha'iq, *Awraq Muhammad Farid*, p. 308.
77. See Kedourie, *Anglo-Arab Labyrinth*, pp. 18, 33, 41–42, 63–64.

78. Dispatch from Intelligence Department, War Office, Cairo, November 25, 1914, FO 371/1973, W16/81562/14.
79. Markaz watha'iq, *Awraq Muhammad Farid*, p. 308.
80. Cited in Zeine N. Zeine, *The Struggle for Arab Independence*, p. 214.
81. Discussed in detail in Gershoni and Jankowski, *Egypt, Islam and the Arabs*, pp. 40–54.
82. Quotation from Reinhart Schulze, *Die Rebellion der Agyptischen Fallahin 1919* (Berlin, 1981), p. 187; for copies of numerous British reports on the demonstrations of 1919 and the demands of the participants, see Mu'assasat al-Ahram, *Khamsun*, documents.
83. "Expressions of Egyptian Opinion," vol. 12 of the Milner Mission Report, FO 848/12.
84. Mahmud Abu al-Fath, *al-Mas'ala al-misriyya wa al-wafd* [The Egyptian question and the Wafd] (Cairo, 1921?), p. 199.
85. Thomas Mayer, *Egypt and the Palestine Question, 1936–1945* (Berlin, 1983), p. 9.
86. From ʿAzzam's later recollections as published in *al-Usbuʿ al-ʿarabi*, January 17, 1972, p. 43. Although ʿAzzam did not date this conversation in the above source, he did so in a private letter to a British official in 1933; see FO 141/744, 824/2/33.
87. Report from Constantinople, March 1920, FO 141/648, 232/181.
88. Reports from A. W. Courtney of March 22 and May 4, 1921, in FO 141/648, 232/231 and 232/233; see also FO 141/650, 232/269; FO 141/800, 14/66, 14/67, and 14/70; FO 371/6457, E12788/117/89.
89. "Brouillon d'une étude sans titre concernent les pays arabes et d'Angleterre," ʿAbbas Hilmi II Papers, file 99, pp. 83–92; for the British report on the presentation of these ideas, see FO 371/6343, E1393/1393/65.
90. See FO 141/430, 5411/89; and FO 141/650, 232/305, 232/319, 232/324a, 232/352, 232/353, 232/359, 232/381.
91. Report on the "activities of the ex-Khedive in Europe," December 19, 1921, FO 141/650, 232/248.
92. FO 141/650, 232/352, and 232/359.
93. "Note on Egyptian Press," April 24 to May 1, 1920, FO 371/4996, E4758/426/16.
94. "Note on Egyptian Press," May 23 to June 5, 1920, FO 371/4996, E6478/426/16.
95. "Note on Egyptian Press," July 28 to August 11, 1920, FO 371/4996, E10463/426/16.
96. Quotations from *al-Akhbar*, July 28, 1920, p. 1; see also "Note on Egyptian Press," September 1–12, 1920, FO 371/4996, E11648/426/16.
97. Wingate to Balfour, November 8, 1918, FO 407/183, no. 140. For similar warnings by Wingate, see Sir Ronald Wingate, *Wingate of*

the Sudan: The Life and Times of General Sir Reginald Wingate, Maker of the Anglo-Egyptian Sudan (London, 1955), pp. 228, 233.
98. Wingate to Hardinge, November 14, 1918, FO 141/773, 7819/3. Later Egyptian accounts of the meeting refer to this sentiment as well; see the memoirs of one of the Egyptian participants, ʿAbd al-ʿAziz Fahmi, *Hadhihi hayati* [This is my life], pp. 76–89, and ʿAbd al-Rahman al-Rafiʿi's *Thawrat sanat 1919* [The revolution of 1919], 1:93–97.
99. Wingate, *Wingate of the Sudan*, p. 235.
100. "Les Revendications Nationales Egyptiennes," found in FO 407/184, no. 66, and in ʿAbbas Hilmi II Papers, file 35.
101. Unsigned letter to President Wilson, contained in the ʿAbbas Hilmi II Papers, file 106.
102. "Memorandum by Sir R. Graham on the Unrest in Egypt," April 9, 1919, FO 407–184, no. 152 (reproduced in Mu'assasat al-Ahram, *Khamsun*, document 31).
103. "To the Members of the House of Commons," from the Egyptian Delegation, Paris, July 13, 1919, ʿAbbas Hilmi II Papers, file 35.
104. The text of the constitution is available in Marcel Colombe, *L'évolution de l'Egypte* (Paris, 1951), pp. 281–304.
105. Summarized in Allenby to Chamberlain, April 5, 1925, FO 371/10908, J1569/1069/16.
106. Henderson to Chamberlain, February 7, 1926, FO 371/11605, J397/397.
107. Ibid.

THIRTEEN

Mothers, Morality, and Nationalism in Pre-1919 Egypt

Beth Baron

"Do not reproach me for I am not a person of rhetoric and not among those who excel in the art of composition and writing," began a contributor to *al-Jins al-latif* [The Fair Sex] in 1911. "I do not have the right to write what I do because of my young age. But what inspires me to write is that I am an Egyptian girl who loves her nation."[1] Through protestations of patriotism, this young woman legitimized her literary activity, still a highly controversial undertaking for Egyptian women in the early 1900s. She used rhetoric to advantage to expand the perimeters of her activities at the same time that she served nationalism.

This article challenges the conventional boundaries of nationalism, moving beyond a study of nationalist activities in the streets, parliament, and general press to look for forms of nationalism in the home, schools, and women's press. Its purpose is to illuminate the cultural and social dimensions of nationalism in Egypt, to explore its gendering, and to find a new nexus of women's activities and nationalist expression.

Scholars have recently begun to examine the participation of women in nationalist movements in the Middle East. A picture emerges of women helping in revolts, revolutions, and wars in Iran, Yemen, Egypt, Algeria, Morocco, and elsewhere.[2] In moving from the home to the street, even to the battlefield, women have been transformed from passive spectators to active combatants, carrying placards, pamphlets, guns, and bombs. Mobilized and politicized, they have also developed raised expectations for improved women's rights when the battle is over. However, women are often disappointed, for they do not make the expected advances and sometimes return to earlier, constricted roles. Seen in this way, women have served nationalism, but nationalism, in some respects, has failed women.

In the case of modern Egypt, historians have highlighted the role of women in the 1919 revolution.[3] Prior to that, women are generally seen as uninvolved in the national struggle. Thomas Philipp notes the "total lack of political involvement and the almost complete absence of patriotic nationalist expression" before 1919.[4] The 1919 revolution is also seen as the pivotal point in the shift from nationalist to feminist activities.[5] Yet this stress has caused scholars to overlook antecedents for women's nationalist and feminist endeavors as well as bypass nonfeminist women and groups in the preceding decades.

Studies of women and nationalism in Egypt have also concentrated on the perspectives of the nationalists. Thus the "woman question" in the period prior to 1919 has been studied mostly through the writings of male proponents of reform such as Qasim Amin, or through the works of their male opponents, rather than through the eyes of women writers.[6] Yet starting from the late nineteenth century, middle- and upper-class women in Egypt began writing in greater numbers. With the exception of the essays of Malak Hifni Nasif, also known as Bahithat al-Badiya (Searcher in the Desert), the poems and prose of 'A'ysha al-Taymuriyya, and the works of a few others, the writings of these women are hardly known. The Arabic women's press—a series of magazines and newspapers started in Egypt in 1892—provides the most concentrated collection of literary material by Egyptian women from this period.[7] In these periodicals, writers tried various arguments in an attempt to link their concerns with other causes and overcome marginalization of the "woman question." Nationalist rhetoric succeeded in convincing men and women to support new literary, organizational, and educational ventures. In this way elite women used their commitment to nationalism to justify their own expanding array of activities.

Attitudes and activities of Egyptian women and their advocates during the early 1900s have often been pronounced "feminist," even when stemming from an Arabic original (*nisa'iyya*) more aptly translated in this context as "women's." The term "feminism" has been used to mean a variety of things. As a result some scholars have warned against labeling all of women's historical experiences as feminist.[8] Jill Conway distinguishes between enhanced-authority feminists (those who sought to expand women's roles within the home), and equal rights feminists (those who aimed to dismantle the boundaries of separation and press for equal social, political, and economic rights with men). She also emphasizes the need to study female opposition to feminism.[9] These categories are useful in understanding ideological positions in early-twentieth-century Egypt. At that time, women's advocates worked toward enhancing their authority within the home but did not push for equal rights. Moreover, not all of those who claimed to work for women's progress actually did; some endorsed programs that decreased rather than increased women's authority—for example, calling for heavier veiling or intensified seclusion. Yet antifeminists in Egypt have not received the same attention as feminists (however broadly defined) and have often been confused with them.

The temptation to see all of Egyptian women's activities as feminist is part of a larger tendency to see Egyptian women (or Arab, Middle Eastern, and Muslim women) as a monolith. The extent to which the "woman question" in early-twentieth-century Egypt meant lower-, middle-, and upper-class women, rural and urban, Muslim and minority, varied. Certain issues, such as veiling and seclusion, were class and region specific while others, such as marriage and divorce, transcended class and region but not religion. Nationalism was used as a rallying cry to obliterate some of the differences.

Several nationalist ideologies emerged in the decades following the British occupation of Egypt in 1882. The proponents of each debated the role women should play in society, thus linking the "Egyptian question" and the "woman question." Elite women actively participated in these debates. Challenged to contribute to the national effort while maintaining accepted female norms, they participated through new endeavors. This article looks at the nationalist camps, their positions on the "woman question," and women's special relationship to nationalism. It then focuses on elite women's literary, organizational, and educational activities and the channels that women found outside the traditional political arena for nationalist expression.

Nationalism in Egypt. Egypt's status at the beginning of the twentieth-century differed from that of Ottoman Arab provinces to the east. Occupied by the British, Egypt sought independence from European imperial rule, not only greater autonomy from Ottoman authority. As a result, nationalism in Egypt followed a unique course in the period until World War I. Three trends emerged: religiously inspired Egyptian Ottomanism, territorially grounded secular nationalism, and ethnic-linguistically based Arab nationalism.[10] The proponents of each vied for national preeminence and adopted varied postures toward the Khedive, the Sublime Porte, and the British.

Mustafa Kamil, an Egyptian lawyer, became the leading spokesman for Egyptian Ottomanism, which saw an Egyptian-Ottoman alliance as the best strategy for ending the British occupation. Kamil emphasized religious ties to the sultan/caliph in an effort to mobilize the masses. His position has been called "radical neotraditionalist" (as opposed to conservative traditionalist) because he used traditional rhetoric in the struggle to overthrow Western rule.[11] Kamil articulated his views in speeches and articles, many of which were printed in the paper *al-Liwa'*, which he edited from 1900 to 1907. In 1907 those clustered around the paper founded *al-Hizb al-watani* (the Nationalist Party). Egyptian Ottomanism attracted a large following: the pan-Islamic component drew the masses, the anti-Western portion appealed to the Western educated but alienated petite bourgeoisie, and the Turkish element attracted members of the upper class, particularly those of Turco-Circassian origin.

Egyptians showed anti-British, pro-Ottoman sentiments throughout the early 1900s. When British and Ottoman troops came close to clashing in the Taba territorial dispute of 1906, many Egyptians sided with the Ottomans against the British, preferring loss of land to acceptance of British negotiations on their behalf. National feeling swelled again against the British a few months later in reaction to the handling of the Dinshawai affair. In this incident, British army officers who had been pigeon hunting near the village of Dinshawai accidentally wounded a woman. In the ensuing confrontation with villagers, several officers were hurt and one died attempting to return to his camp on foot. Egyptians involved in the affray received harsh sentences, including flogging, imprisonment, and death, which were swiftly carried out and caused an outpouring of anti-British anger.[12] Five years later, Egyptians sided with Ottoman forces in the Turkish-Italian war in Tripoli. They also backed the Ottomans against secession in the Balkan wars of 1912–1913. In short, many Egyptians continued to show allegiance to the Ottoman Empire until its defeat in World War I.

Other Egyptians saw in the increasing dismemberment of the Ottoman Empire decreasing chances of help from Istanbul in the struggle for independence. They turned instead to secular territorial nationalism, founding *Hizb al-umma* (the Party of the Nation) in 1907 around the newspaper *al-Jarida* (1907–1915). Led by Ahmad Lutfi al-Sayyid, the theorist of the party and editor of the paper, the liberal nationalists rejected alignment with the Ottoman Empire. Instead they sought social and political reform, and were willing to cooperate with the British toward this end. Though Egyptian territorial nationalism gained some supporters, it lacked a substantial following prior to World War I. Most Egyptians still preferred Islamic unity to a secular polity founded on principles associated with the British occupation. The liberal program only emerged as the basis of the nationalist movement in the wake of World War I.

Arab nationalism also found little expression in Egypt during the prewar period. Though Egypt was the center of an Arabic literary awakening, Egyptians did not yet identify themselves primarily as Arabs. Moreover, Ottomanism and Arab nationalism competed as ideologies. Whereas Arab nationalists sought greater autonomy from Ottoman rule, Egyptian Ottomanists solicited Ottoman aid in order to oust the British from Egypt and perceived Arab nationalism as a machination of the British to weaken the empire. In addition, Egyptians were sometimes excluded from the meetings of Arab nationalists. For example, the chairman of the First Arab Congress, which met in Paris in 1913, denied an Egyptian the right to address the assembly and later declared the Congress restricted to Arabs from Arab Ottoman provinces east of Egypt.[13]

Egyptian liberals and conservatives had conflicting views on the "explosive question of the emancipation of women," reflecting splits on the issue of Islam and modernism.[14] The conservatives and neotraditionalists never accepted more than minor reforms for Egyptian women, granting them educational rights but rejecting demands such as unveiling. In their view, women's current situation derived from the erosion of indigenous religious values and the spread of immorality caused by Western influence. Juan Cole suggests that men of the petite bourgeoisie felt threatened by feminism, fearing the loss of traditional status as guardians of family honor and the triumph of values of their European competitors and British occupiers. Men of the new upper middle class, on the other hand, were more likely to support women's emancipation in an effort to emulate those in power.[15]

Drawing their strength from the new upper middle class, liberal nationalists seemed eager to promote women's progress. For Lutfi al-Sayyid and his cohort, "feminism was an essential part of true nationalism."[16] The liberal newspaper *al-Jarida* published works by women writers and sponsored lectures by speakers such as Malak Hifni Nasif.[17] Salama Musa, a Coptic intellectual, confirmed this picture of liberal interest in the position of women. "In those years there were two subjects that we used to discuss more than anything else, as they concerned the whole of Egyptian society," wrote Musa. "They were the English occupation, and Qasim Amin's movement for the liberation of women."[18]

Qasim Amin, an Egyptian judge, argued for women's rights in his books *Tahrir al-mar'a* [The liberation of woman] and *al-Mar'a al-jadida* [The new woman].[19] He advocated increased education, unveiling, greater mixing, and limits to polygyny and divorce. Other liberals supported many of these reforms, linking national progress and women's progress. Founders of *al-Sufur* (Unveiling), a newspaper that followed in the footsteps of *al-Jarida*, spoke of "liberating the mind, delivering Egyptian nationalism from weak elements, and freeing women from the chains of ignorance and unsound traditions."[20] To these writers, the subordinated position of women was a measure of the backwardness of the nation.

Egyptian women supported the different nationalist parties, coupling their discussion of women's rights with national issues. Conservative women favored the Egyptian Ottomanists and attacked the spread of immorality and Western influence. For example, Fatima Rashid, editor of *Tarqiyat al-mar'a* (Woman's progress; 1908–1909) criticized blind imitation of European women and urged a return to Islamic law. She argued that Egyptian women "did not understand the full scope of religious law which has given them all the rights that they need."[21] Conservative women also showed their support for Egyptian Ottomanism in the journals al-'Afaf (Virtue; 1910–1922), and Fatat al-nil (Young Woman of the Nile; 1913–15), among others. Nonliterary women echoed this sentiment in demonstrations. In 1911 at a march honoring the third anniversary of Mustafa Kamil's death, one journalist noted, "in every window, balcony, and door that the procession passed stood Egyptian women joining with men in the commemoration."[22]

Conservative women's advocates shared a cultural vision with the Egyptian Ottomanists. They drew models from the Islamic past and pointed to the wives of the Prophet, poets, and fighters as guides. However, this meant that they often endorsed traditions (veiling and seclusion, for example) that contributed to their own subordination. In short, these women faced conflicting cultural and sexual identities, leading, in the words of Leila Ahmed, to the plight of Middle Eastern feminists "caught between those two opposing loyalties, forced almost to choose between betrayal and betrayal."[23] Rather than challenge the cultural prescriptions and religious interpretations of others, they attempted to reconcile their claims for women with the current ideology of cultural nationalism or they denied their separate concerns altogether. In juggling their loyalty to class, culture, and gender, conservative women remained bound to their strata, defended their traditions, and only argued for women's rights within this context.

Liberal women, on the other hand, pointed to the persistence of traditional attitudes and lack of education as causes of women's problems. They published their views in women's magazines such as Anis al-jalis (Intimate Companion; 1898–1908), Fatat al-sharq [Young Woman of the East; 1906–1939), and al-Jins al-latif (The Fair Sex; 1908–1924). Liberals turned to indigenous models from the pharaonic past to prove that women's models need not come from the West. "Egyptian women used to study science, speak from pulpits, and govern the empire when women in other countries were still in a state of slavery and misery," wrote one woman in al-Jins al-latif in 1908.[24] Both liberal and conservative women exploited nationalist arguments, sometimes using them at cross-purposes. For example, one writer maintained that the light, white veil (*yashmak*) was a symbol of the nationalist woman.[25] At the same time, another called for unveiling on the grounds that "we are the heads of the family and child-raisers of the people, and the basis for building nationalism."[26] Writers agreed, however, on the necessity for girls' education, domestic improvement, and, of course, strengthening the nation.

Women could not join the national struggle as equals; they had to enter it in a special capacity that conformed with approved roles for women. Motherhood was singled out for a number of reasons. First, mothers had the potential to shape a generation and reshape society because of their moral influence on their children.[27] Also, motherhood unified across religious lines and transcended liberal and conservative debates. Finally, motherhood touched a sensitive chord in a country that idealized the childbearer. As a result women argued that their responsibilities as mothers of the nation necessitated their ventures out of their homes to schools, hospitals, and meetings. Aided by nationalist rhetoric, they expanded their realm of activities. It is to these activities that we now turn.

Literary Activities. Egyptian nationalism found expression in newspapers like Shaykh ʿAli Yusuf's *al-Muʾayyad* (1889), Kamil's *al-Liwaʾ*, and Lutfi al-Sayyid's *al-Jarida*. Though the British authorities sometimes censored or banned the nationalist newspapers, especially after reviving the 1881 Press Law in 1909, the women's press enjoyed relative freedom and became a forum for ideas and instruction. Starting in 1892, numerous Arabic magazines and newspapers for women began to appear in Egypt. In its first decade, the women's press was guided by Syrians; yet Egyptians also wrote and soon started editing their own magazines. By 1919 over thirty different women's Arabic weeklies and monthlies had been circulated in Egypt, some appearing briefly, others running for years. The creators of the new literary form consciously called them *al-majallat al-nisaʾiyya* (women's magazines), and they developed a canon that included articles on health, marriage, housekeeping, dress, romance, rights, and responsibilities.

The women's press grew out of an effort to improve the situation of women and help the nation advance. Malaka Saʿd, owner and editor of *al-Jins al-latif*, started her magazine "to raise the status of Egyptian women in particular and Eastern women in general."[28] Writers in the magazines often used nationalist loyalties to justify their entry into the literary arena.[29] Others did not sign their names; yet their pseudonyms—"daughter of the Nile," "one loyal to her nation," or a "Muslim Egyptian Ottoman woman"—show patriotic sentiment. Writers denied that they engaged in politics or had political aspirations.[30] They dissociated themselves from Western suffragettes who were struggling for the right to vote. European women "are in a worse situation now," wrote Sarah al-Mihiyya, editor of *Fatat al-nil*, "having striven to attain political rights alone."[31] These Egyptian women opted for enhanced authority in the home and moral influence, not political power. Given these constraints, writers contemplated women's special relationship to the nation.

Fatima Rashid described women's patriotic duty in an article entitled "Nationalism and Woman." She began by explaining the need to develop a nationalist spirit, especially in an occupied country like Egypt. Some men and enlightened women felt it, but they had to spread it to all levels of society. Therefore, it was incumbent upon "every educated woman who senses the critical situation of her country" to "inspire all she meets with the essence of this honorable sentiment."[32] In their unique capacity as "mothers of the world and child-raisers," women were given the imperative of imbuing their children with love for the nation, teaching them national songs and stories. "It is upon you, tenderhearted mother, to impart to your son respect for his beloved nation, which has no dignity without him. The glory of this nation and its misery are in your hands."[33] Mothers were seen as particularly well-suited to be inculcators of moral values and patriotic virtues.

By demonstrating their loyalty to the nation, women hoped in turn that their demands would receive redress. Thus after defining their special responsibilities, they voiced their own concerns. For example, they protested against the growing number of marriages of Egyptian men and foreign women.[34] Egyptian writers used nationalist arguments to condemn these marriages, claiming that Egyptian women would copy foreigners to compete with them and that children of mixed marriages would also follow European customs.[35] The "theft" of husbands by foreign women, or threat of it, harmed Egyptian women in the same way that foreign competition in jobs and trade hurt Egyptian men. Literate women joined the nationalist debate in the press, carving out a special role for themselves and articulating their own grievances.

Organizational Activities. Three nationalist parties emerged around newspapers in Egypt in 1907: *Hizb al-umma, al-Hizb al-watani,* and *Hizb al-islah al-dusturi* (the Party of Constitutional Reform). The following year, a group of Muslim women founded the organization *Jam'iyyat tarqiyat al-mar'a* (the society for woman's progress) and began publishing a journal by the same name. They did not call their organization a party (hizb) nor did they meet in public halls. Like other women's groups of that time, they called themselves a society (*jam'iyya*) and met in private homes.

The members of *Jam'iyyat tarqiyat al-mar'a,* some of whom were of Turkish origin, remained loyal to the empire. When the Young Turks revolted in 1908 and forced Sultan Abdülhamid to restore the constitution suspended thirty years earlier, members celebrated. "The entire Egyptian nation welcomes this constitution that was granted to the Ottoman nation," wrote Fatima Rashid, arguing that it protected their honor and defended their rights.[36] Writers praised those veiled Turkish women who marched in front of the caliph's palace and compared their activities to those of women in the Prophet's time.[37]

Members also called for an Egyptian constitution. "We do not have a remedy for our present situation except through work and reform, and this will never be accomplished as long as the nation is not granted a constitution like that of the Ottoman Empire," wrote Munira 'Abd al-Ghaffar, a member of *Jam'iyyat tarqiyat al-mar'a.* "What does that constitution mean? That our men will formulate their own policy, and foreigners will not prevent reform."[38] Munira called upon women to persuade their male relatives to fight for an Egyptian constitution. She also sought economic sanctions against foreigners and urged all Egyptians to make their own goods, buy Egyptian products, and develop the indigenous economy.[39] These women tried to use persuasion as a weapon.

In emergencies, some women acted as fund-raisers or as donors. When Italy invaded Tripoli in 1911, Egyptian Ottomanists quickly responded. The pages of al-ʿAfaf carried stories of aid collected for Ottoman troops. A "Muslim Egyptian Ottoman woman" called on her compatriots for donations: "Awake! Awake! Hurry! Hurry! Take off your ornaments and jewelry!! Leave behind your silk and brocades! Give up coquetry and amusement! Listen to the voice of duty that calls you!!" She told of one woman who had given over seven hundred Egyptian pounds to the cause.[40] Princess Shivekiar gave six thousand pounds to the Ottoman navy.[41] And Zubaydan Falhi collected over four thousand dollars for the Ottoman War Ministry.[42] Meanwhile, women in ʿAbbasiyya organized a committee to raise money for the war effort. They held parties and gave speeches, meeting at the home of ʿAziza ʿAli Fawzi, wife of the editor of the nationalist paper al-ʿIlm.[43] Another committee member, Amina Nimazi, rallied women by pointing to the precedents of women helping men in the early Islamic wars.[44] A female "nationalist in the countryside" reported the formation of committees in Asyût and Bani Suwayf that collected hundreds of pounds.[45]

During this period, middle- and upper-class women also developed a network of charities. They faced less resistance to volunteer work than they would have to paid work, for they claimed that they were working for national renewal, not themselves. They transferred services typically performed for the family to the community, distributing food, sewing clothes, and setting up clinics. The motives of these women varied. A charity founded in 1908 to care for orphans attracted over fifty patrons who hoped through their efforts to contribute to the "vitality of the nation."[46] Others attempted to wrest control of the country's welfare agencies from foreigners. Huda Shaʿarawi refused to take part in the Lady Cromer dispensary, named after the first wife of the British consul general Lord Cromer and headed by a British woman, but later helped to found the Mabarrat Muhammad ʿAli, a royal Egyptian project.[47] These associations were considered respectable outlets for the energies of middle- and upper-class women and served working-class and peasant women. By starting organizations, orphanages, and clinics, elite women established power bases outside the home and developed new skills. At the same time, they provided social services that the nation desperately needed.

Education. The nationalist papers and parties debated a number of issues, including the government's education policy. The bureaucracy had limited the development of schools, neglecting girls' education in particular, which writers in the women's press protested. "We have seen that the men of the government have devoted all their energy to boys, opening government schools for them. They have not given girls' schools the least attention and have not put any effort into teaching girls, who are half the nation," wrote Alexandra Avierino, owner of *Anis al-jalis*, in 1898.[48]

Girls' education was presented as the path to women's progress. Arguing that girls would be mothers, and mothers were responsible for the physical and moral well-being of their families, advocates asserted that girls' education was crucial for the sake of the nation.[49] "If we say teach and refine girls, we do so because they are the mothers of tomorrow," wrote an essayist in *al-Saʿada*.[50] Mothers had to be well educated so they could care for their children, socialize them, and lay the foundation for their formal education. Ignorant women were considered even more dangerous than ignorant men, according to one advocate, for they could never have educated children.[51] By endowing mothers with a special moral mission, women gained greater authority within the home and greater access to education.

Glorified as "mothers of tomorrow," women's impact extended beyond the home. Mothers were considered integral to maintaining the moral well-being of the family, the building block of society. "When mothers have improved, families improve. When families have improved, the nation improves," wrote one reformer.[52] In sum, the happiness not only of a single family but of the entire nation depended upon them. "The girl of today is the woman of tomorrow, and the woman of tomorrow is the mother who rocks the cradle of her child by her right hand and the world by her left hand," wrote Malaka Saʿd.[53]

Women were given the mission to cultivate and inculcate moral values, a job that became increasingly more important in the struggle for national renewal. "It is evident that the woman's job in the social body is to build the moral character of the nation," wrote Qasim Amin. "The moral character has a greater influence on society from the point of view of the nations' progress and regression than does the influence of governmental systems, laws, and religions."[54] This moral realm became increasingly more significant to Egyptians as they claimed moral superiority over Europeans in the face of a growing sense of material inferiority.[55] The push for girls' education resulted in rising enrollments and new schools as women promised to fulfill their moral mission. Yet, they soon became trapped by their own arguments, which could be turned around to limit their years in school and circumscribe their roles. Thus while moral authority initially empowered women, it eventually restricted them.

The proposed national university, for example, had no plan to include women, for whom university education was considered unnecessary. As a result, some women debated whether or not they should contribute to the project. "If it were for women, I would help them with all that I possess," said one woman who had been approached for funds. As it was for men only, she felt that it was "their responsibility to give what they can to complete their plan."[56] The university was opened in 1908 and later received a large grant from a royal woman, but women did not start degree programs there until the late 1920s.

While women contributed to the national effort, male nationalists often showed little sustained interest in improving the situation of women. Malak Hifni Nasif complained about those men who visited Europe and saw "with their own eyes how European men respect their women." They returned "calling for the need to teach women, claiming that they are women's patrons and that women deserve respect." Yet she noted, "It does not take long until their words fly with the wind."[57] Elite women carved out a place for themselves in the national struggle in part in order to overcome apathy about their plight. Participation enriched them, but many of their separate concerns remained unaddressed and unresolved.

Conclusion. Until World War I, Egyptian Ottomanism was the predominant nationalist ideology in Egypt; most Egyptians preferred Ottoman suzerainty to prolonged British rule. The debate on nationalism in newspapers and parties found echoes in the women's press and women's organizations. Women's advocates were intent on enhancing their authority within the home and rejected calls for the vote or other political rights. They legitimized their demands by linking their cause with nationalism and emphasizing their moral influence as mothers. In so doing, however, they set limits, defining themselves in their relationships to men rather than as autonomous human beings and appealing to men for reform and change rather than trying to implement more of their own ideas. They criticized the foreign occupation and Western ways, claiming that these contributed to the nation's and women's plights; but they rarely condemned Egyptian men for their role in subordinating women or explored women's own recreation of the social system. They reinforced strict standards of morality and purity that could then be used to confine them. Nonetheless, these women did manage to win a number of concessions and generated a greater awareness of the "woman question."

Elite women served nationalism in special roles, using their writings, meetings, and classrooms as forums to promote the national spirit and to link women's concerns with the national struggle. Thus these women expanded the basis of their authority within the home and gained greater legitimacy for literary, philanthropic, and educational activities outside the home. In this light, women's participation in the 1919 revolution represents less a break in Egyptian women's history, or the start of it, than further evidence of the increasing involvement of some women in a wider range of activities.

These women's activities helped them in their fight to expand their own roles. Yet how valuable were they to the national struggle? The answer depends upon where we locate the struggle. I have suggested that the women's press, schools, societies, and even their homes were important forums for the dissemination of nationalist ideologies and strategic battlefields in the contest for cultural hegemony. As such, women's contributions in these realms were significant. Elite women and men carved out roles for themselves in the national struggle in Egypt in the early 1900s. Women opted for moral influence, while men tried to gain political power.

Most Egyptians continued to show allegiance to the Ottoman Empire and the sultan/caliph through World War I. At the outbreak of the war in 1914, the British imposed martial law and declared Egypt a protectorate, thus cutting the country's ties to the empire. The British deposed Khedive ʿAbbas Hilmi II, then visiting Istanbul, and replaced him with Husayn Kamil, who was subsequently named sultan. Although nationalist activity was suppressed during the war years, Egyptian desires for independence grew. At the end of the war, the defeat and dismemberment of the Ottoman empire spelled the end of the Ottoman option as a means of throwing off the British occupation. This cleared the way for other nationalist ideologies. Egyptians then turned toward the territorial nationalism of the liberals. Many women's advocates welcomed the shift from a conservative nationalist ideology to a liberal one, hoping that it would be a further step forward in their struggle for greater integration into Egyptian society.

Notes

1. Munira 'Atiyya Suriyal, "al-Mar'a al-misriyya," *al-Jins al-latif* 3, no. 10 (April 1911): 279.
2. A sampling of this literature includes Mangol Bayat-Philipp, "Women and Revolution in Iran, 1905–1911," in Lois Beck and Nikki Keddie, eds., *Women in the Muslim World* (Cambridge: 1978), pp. 295–308; Maxine Molyneux, "Women and Revolution in the People's Democratic Republic of Yemen," *Feminist Review* 1 (1979); Soraya Antonius, "Fighting on Two Fronts: Conversations with Palestinian Women," *Journal of Palestinian Studies* (Spring 1979): 26–45; Franz Fanon, *A Dying Colonialism* (New York: Grove Press, 1965); C. R. Pennell, "Women and Resistance to Colonialism in Morocco: The Rif 1916–1926," *Journal of African History* 28, no. 1 (1987): 107–18.
3. Muhammad Kamal Yahya looks at women's "partnership" with men in the nineteenth century in *al-Judhur al-ta'rikhiyya li-tahrir al-mar'a al-misriyya fi al-ʿasr al-hadith* [The historical roots of the liberation of women in the modern era] (Cairo: 1983), pp. 93–118); Latifa Muhammad Salim, *al-Mar'a al-misriyya wa al-taghir al-ijtimaʿi, 1919–1945* [The Egyptian woman and social change, 1919–1945] (Cairo: 1984), pp. 26–29; and Afaf Lutfi al-Sayyid Marsot, "The Revolutionary Gentlewomen in Egypt," in Beck and Keddie, eds., *Women in the Muslim World*, pp. 268–269. Philipp finds the reports on women's participation in the 1919 revolution idealized and exaggerated (Philipp, "Feminism and Nationalist Politics," p. 289).
4. Philipp, "Feminism and Nationalist Politics in Egypt," p. 284.
5. See, for example, Huda Shaarawi, *Harem Years*, p. 20.
6. Byron D. Cannon, "Nineteenth-Century Arabic Writings on Women and Society," pp. 463–84; Juan Cole, "Feminisim, Class and Islam

in Turn-of-the-Century Egypt," *International Journal of Middle Eastern Studies* 13, no. 4 (November 1981): 387–407.
7. On the women's press, see Ijlal Khalifa, "al-Sihafa al-nisa'iyya fi misr, 1919–1939" [The women's press in Egypt, 1919–1939] (Master's thesis, University of Cairo, 1966); Ijlal Khalifa, *al-Haraka al-nisa'iyya al-haditha* [The modern women's movement]; Beth Ann Baron, "The Rise of a New Literary Culture: The Women's Press of Egypt, 1892–1919" (Ph.D. diss., UCLA, 1988).
8. See Gerda Lerner, *The Creation of Patriarchy* (New York: 1986), appendix.
9. Jill Conway, *The Female Experience in 18th- and 19th-Century America* (Princeton: 1985), pp. 198–200. The plurality of feminism is now quite accepted; different schools include maternalists, Marxists, and liberals, among others.
10. Israel Gershoni and James P. Jankowski, *Egypt, Islam, and the Arabs*, introduction and chapter 1.
11. Nikki R. Keddie, "Western Rule Versus Western Values: Suggestions for Comparative Study of Asian Intellectual History," *Diogenes* 26 (Summer 1959): 71–96.
12. P. J. Vatikiotis, *The History of Egypt*, 3rd ed. (London: Weidenfeld 1985), pp. 204–6.
13. Gershoni and Jankowski, *Egypt, Islam, and the Arabs*, p. 17.
14. Vatikiotis, *History of Egypt*, p. 231.
15. Cole, "Feminism, Class and Islam," pp. 387–407.
16. Albert Hourani, *Arabic Thought*, p. 182.
17. Malak Hifni Nasif [Bahithat al-Badiya], *al-Nisa'iyyat* (Cairo: Matbaʿat al-jarida, 1910).
18. Salama Musa, *The Education of Salamah Musa*, trans. L. O. S. Schuman (Leiden: 1961), p. 29.
19. Qasim Amin, *Tahrir al-mar'a* [The liberation of woman] and *al-Mar'a al-jadida* [The new woman] (Cairo: 1984).
20. ʿAbd al-Hamid Hamdi, *al-Sufur* [Unveiling] 5, no. 202 (May 22, 1919): 1.
21. Fatima Rashid, "al-Mar'a wa huququha fi al-Islam," *Tarqiyat al-mar'a* [Woman's progress] 1, no. 10 (1908): 150.
22. Jacques Dufour, "ʿAla ʿatiq al-ummahat," *al-ʿAfaf* 1, no. 15 (February 17, 1911): 4.
23. Leila Ahmed, "Early Feminist Movements in the Middle East," in Freda Hussain, ed., *Muslim Women* (New York: 1984), p. 122.
24. Malaka Saʿd, "al-Mar'a fi misr," *al-Jins al-latif* 1, no. 2 (August 1908): 38–39.
25. "Al-mar'a wa al-wataniyya," *al-Sufur* 3, no. 140 (January 24, 1918): 2–3.
26. A writer using the pseudonym "al-Mar'a al-Safira" ("Unveiled

Woman") in "al-Mar'a wa al-sufur," *al-Jins al-latif* 10, no. 9 (March 1918): 232.
27. For another view of this, see Timothy Mitchell, *Colonising Egypt* (Cambridge: 1988), pp. 111–13. Mitchell briefly examines the rhetoric on mothers as part of his argument about the ordering of Egyptian society.
28. Malaka Sa'd, "Fatihat al-'amm al-sadis," *al-Jins al-latif* 6, no. 1 (May 1913): 2.
29. Suriyal, "al-Mar'a al-misriyya," *al-Jins al-latif,* p. 279.
30. See for example Layla al-Shamakhiyya, "al-Mar'a wa safsatat al-kitab," *Tarqiyat al-mar'a* 1, no. 12 (1908): 179–82.
31. Sarah al-Mihiyya, "Tahrir al-mar'a fi Europe," *Fatat al-nil* 1, no. 6 (Jumada II 1332, April 1914) 239.
32. Fatima Rashid, "al-Wataniyya wa al-mar'a," *Tarqiyat al-mar'a,* 1 no. 2 (1908): 28.
33. Ibid., p. 29.
34. See, for example, Fatima Munib, "Ila mata wa antum la hun," *Tarqiyat al-mar'a* 1, no. 9 (1908): 134.
35. See, for example, Nasif, *Nisa'iyyat,* p. 14.
36. Fatima Rashid, "Farah al-sayyidat misr," *Tarqiyat al-mar'a* 1, no. 8 (1908): 81.
37. Najiyya Rashid, "Khutba," *Tarqiyat al-mar'a* 1, no. 8 (1908): 119–22.
38. Munira 'Abd al-Ghaffar, "La tuqulu al-nisa'," *Tarqiyat al-mar'a* 1, no. 6 (1908): 127.
39. Ibid., pp. 126–28.
40. A writer calling herself "Muslim Egyptian Ottoman woman," in "Istayqizna ayyatuha al-sayyidat," *al-'Afaf* 1, no. 35 (October 13, 1911): 6.
41. Sulayman al-Salimi, "Tabarra'u amira," *al-'Afaf* 1, no. 13 (February 3, 1912): 4.
42. Saint Nihal Singh, "The New Woman in the Mohammedan World," *The American Review of Reviews* 46 (December 1912): 719.
43. 'Aziza 'Ali Fawzi, "Lajnat al-sayyidat bi al-'abbasiyya," *al-'Afaf* 1, no. 37 (October 21, 1911): 5–7.
44. Amina Nimazi, "Khutba," *al-'Afaf* 1, no. 38 (October 27, 1911): 5–6.
45. A writer using the pseudonym "Wataniyya bi al-rif" (Female patriot in the Countryside), in "Nahdat al-sayyidat," *al-'Afaf* 1, no. 38 (October 27, 1911): 7.
46. Z. Anis, "Jam'iyyat al-shafaqa bi al-atfal," *al-Rihana* 1, no. 1 (March 20, 1908): 6–7.
47. Shaarawi, *Harem Years,* p. 94.
48. Alexandra Avierino, "al-Mar'a wa ta'thiruha 'ala al-rajul," *Anis al-jalis* 1, no. 10 (October 1898): 327.

49. See for example Selma Muhammad Ridawiyya, "Ta'lim al-banat," *Fatat al-nil* 1, no. 2 (Safar 1332): 66–67.
50. Regina 'Awwad, "'Allimu al-banat," *al-Sa'ada* 1, no. 4 (1902): 73.
51. "al-Mar'a fi al-sharq," *Anis al-jalis* 1, no. 1 (January 1898): 11.
52. "Islah wa al-hukuma," *Anis al-jalis* 1, no. 7 (July 1898): 214.
53. Sa'd, "Ta'lim al-banat," *al-Jins al-latif* 11, no. 5 (November 1918): 70.
54. Amin, *al-Mar'a al-jadida*, p. 122; Mary Arnett, trans., *The New Woman* in "Qasim Amin and the Beginnings of the Feminist Movement in Egypt," (Ph.D. diss., Dropsie College, 1965), p. 86.
55. Amin, *al-Mar'a al-jadida*, pp. 188–91; Arnett tran., pp. 131–32.
56. M. Y. Hanim Sabri, "Muhadatha," *al-Rihana* 1, no. 3 (Rabi'a I 1325): 76.
57. Nasif, *Nisa'iyyat*, p. 74.

Glossary of Turkish and Arabic Terms

agha (A and T): lord, master; esp., title of a Kurdish tribal chief
al-ʿAhd (A): "The Covenant"; a secret Arab nationalist society formed shortly before World War I, and led largely by Ottoman army officers from Iraq
aʿyan (A and T; sing. ʿayn): people of distinction or importance; notables
Baʿth (A): lit., "resurrection"; the Arab Socialist Resurrection party, a secular, socialist, and pan-Arab nationalist party founded in the early 1940s
bilad al-sham (A): geographical Syria; region encompassing present-day Syria, Lebanon, Jordan, Israel, and the Occupied Territories
chalabi (A; originally from Turkish, celebi): honorific title of a high-status Muslim merchant; used chiefly in Iraq
çiftlik (T): a farm; rural land; form of state-owned land in the Ottoman Empire
hizb al-lamarkaziyya al-idariyya al-ʿuthmani: the Ottoman Administrative Decentralization party, an Arab nationalist party formed in 1913 largely by Syrians living in Cairo
al-hukm (A): authority; government; regime
idadiye (T): secondary school
iltizam (A): tax concession; tax farm
al-jamʿiyya al-ʿarabiyya al-fatat (A): lit., "The Young Arab Society"; a secret Arab nationalist society composed mainly of students and intellectuals, active during the Young Turk period (1908–1918) in Istanbul, Damascus, Beirut, and Paris
mamluk (A): lit., "owned"; Turkish and Circassian slaves, soldiers; the military rulers of Egypt and Syria between 1250–1517
mashriq (A): lit., "east"; the eastern regions of the Arab world: Egypt, Sudan, and southwest Asia
mecelle (T): Ottoman Civil Code compiled by Cevdet Pasa between 1869 and 1878

miri (A): state property in the Ottoman Empire

mudawwara (A): land transferred to the state from the private holdings of Sultan Abdülhamid II after his abdication in 1909

muhafaza (A): Ottoman administrative unit subordinate to *wilaya* or province; governorate

muhafiz (A): subgovernor; head of a *muhafaza*

mujtahid (A): religious legal or theological authority, especially among the Shi'a

multazim (A and T): holder of an *iltizam* (q.v.)

al-muntada al-adabi (A): lit., "the Literary Club"; a literary society formed in 1909 in Istanbul to revive the appreciation of Arabic language and literature among the Arab students studying in the Ottoman capital

al-nahda (A): lit., "awakening, renaissance"; the Arab cultural and political awakening of the last several decades of the Ottoman Empire

naqib al-ashraf (A): title used in Ottoman Iraq and elsewhere to designate chief of the descendants of the Prophet

nizami (A): state courts established as an outgrowth of the *tanzimat* reforms, used in contrast to *sharica* (q.v) courts

al-Qahtaniyya (A): lit., "descendants of Qahtan"; an Arab nationalist group composed of military officers and civilians, founded in 1909 in Istanbul

rüşdiye (T): higher level of state primary school

salafi (A): from the Arabic *salaf*, forebearers, the companions of the Prophet; a modernist Islamic intellectual movement of the late nineteenth and early twentieth centuries that attempted to reconcile fundamental Islamic beliefs with modern Western concepts

sayyid (A, pl. sadah): descendant of the Prophet

shari'a (A): lit., "the path"; Islamic religious law

sharif (A, pl. ashraf): descendant of the Prophet

shaykh (A): elder; dignitary; tribal or religious leader

sufi (A): pertaining to Muslim mystic orders or sects

al-sulta (A): power; authority; sovereignty

tanizimat (A and T): "reorginzation"; Ottoman administrative and economic reforms of the mid-nineteenth century

'ulama' (A; sing. 'alim); ulema (T): the learned, particularly in religious sciences; religious scholars and jurists

umma (A): the political, cultural, and religious community of Muslims; the community of the faithful

wali (A); vali (T): Ottoman provincial governor

waqf (A: pl. awqaf): Islamic foundation or endowment in perpetuity of real property, dedicated to religious purposes sometimes offering benefit to the descendant of the founders

watan (A); vatan (T): homeland; fatherland

wataniyya (A): patriotism; local nationalism

wilaya (A); vilayet (T): Ottoman administrative unit; province

Bibliography

Reference Tools (Bibliographies, Encyclopedias, Handbooks)

Alsberg, P. A. *Guide to the Archives in Israel.* Jerusalem, 1973.

Cannon, Byron D. "Nineteenth-Century Arabic Writings on Women and Society: The Interim Role of the Masonic Press in Cairo *al-Lata'if,* 1885–1895." *International Journal of Middle East Studies* 17 (1985): 463–84.

Clements, Frank. *The Emergence of Arab Nationalism from the 19th Century to 1921: A Bibliography.* London, 1976.

Cleveland, William L. "Sources of Arab Nationalism: An Overview," *Middle East Review* 11 (1979): 25–33.

Dajani, Ahmad Sidqi and ʿAbd al-Salam Adham, eds. *Watha'iq tarikh Libya al-hadith: al-watha'iq al-ʿuthmaniyya* [Documents of modern Libyan history: Ottoman documents]. Benghazi, 1974.

al-Dalil al-ʿIraqi al-rasmi li-sanat 1936. [The Iraqi official guide for 1936]. Baghdad, 1936.

Hopwood, D. and D. Grimwood-Jones. *The Middle East and Islam: A Bibliographical Introduction.* Zug, 1972.

McCarthy, Justin. *The Arab World, Turkey, and the Balkans 1878–1914: A Handbook of Historical Statistics.* Boston, 1983.

al-Mawsuʿa al-Filastiniyya [The Palestinian encyclopedia]. 4 vols. Damascus, 1984.

Ochsenwald, William. "Ottoman Sources for the History of the Hijaz," In Abdelgadir Abdullah et al., eds., *Sources for the History of Arabia.* Riyadh, 1979.

Qudama, Ahmad. *Maʿalim wa-aʿlam fi bilad al-ʿarab* [Places and eminent personalities in the Arab lands]. Damascus, 1965.

Simon, Reeva S. *The Modern Middle East: A Guide to Research Tools in the Social Sciences.* Boulder, 1978.

Souriau-Hoebrechts, Christiane. *La presse maghrebine: Libye, Tunisie, Maroc, Algerie.* Paris, 1975.

Tamimi, Rafiq and Muhammad Bahjat. *Wilayat Bayrut* [Beirut vilayet]. 2 vols. Beirut, 1916. Reprint. Beirut, 1979.

Tarazi, Philippe de. *Tarikh al-sahafa al-ʿarabiyya* [History of the Arabic press]. 4 vols. Beirut, 1913–1944.
Tunaya, Tarik Z. *Turkiye'de Siyasi Partiler, 1859–1952* [Turkish political parties 1859–1952]. Istanbul, 1952.
Yehoshua, Jacob. *Ta'rikh al-sahafah al-ʿarabiya fi Filastin fi al-ʿahd al-ʿuthmani* [History of the Arabic press in Palestine during the Ottoman period]. Jerusalem, 1974.
al-Zirikki, Khayr al-Din. *al-Aʿlam: Qamus tarajim li-ashhar al-rijal wa al-nisa' min al-ʿArab wa al-mustaʿaribin wa al-mustashriqin*. (Eminent personalities: Biographical dictionary of noted men and women among the Arabs, the Arabists, and the Orientalists). 10 vols. Cairo, 1954–1957.

Primary Sources

Official Government Publications and Document Collections
ʿAbd al-Hadi, Awni. *Awraq khassa* [Private papers], prepared by Khayriyya Qasmiyya. Beirut, 1964.
'Allush, Naji, comp. *Mukhtarat al-Mufid li ʿAbd al-Ghani al-ʿUraisi* [Selections from *al-Mufid* by ʿAbd al-Ghani al-ʿUraisi]. Beirut, 1981.
France. Ministère des affaires étrangères. *Documents diplomatiques françaises, 1871–1914*. 2e serie, XII-XIV (1953–1955); 3e serie, II-III, VI-IX (1931–1936) Paris, 1861–.
Germany. *Die grosse politik der europaischen kabinette 1871–1914*. Berlin, 1922–1927. Selections are available in English: *German Diplomatic Documents, 1871–1914*. London: Methuen, 1928–1931.
Great Britain, Foreign Office. G. P. Gooch and H. Temperley eds., *British Documents on the Origins of the War 1898–1914*. London, 1926–1938.
Great Britain. *Parliamentary Papers, 1938–1939* (xxvii); *Correspondence between Sir Henry McMahon ... and the Sherif of Mecca, July 1915–March 1916*, Cmd. 5957, London, 1939.
Great Britain. *Parliamentary Papers, 1938–1939* (xiv); *Report of a Committee set up to consider certain Correspondence between Sir Henry McMahon and the Sherif of Mecca in 1915 and 1916*, Cmd 5974. London, 1939.
Haim, Sylvia, ed. *Arab Nationalism: An Anthology*. 2d ed. Berkeley, 1976.
Hanioğlu, M. Şükrü. *Bir Siyasal Örgüt: Olarak Osmanli Ittihad ve Terakki Cemiyeti ve Jön Türklük (1889–1902)* [A political organization: The Ottoman society of Union and Progress and the Young Turks, 1889–1902]. Istanbul, 1985.
Hurewitz, J. C., ed. *The Middle East and North Africa in World Politics: A Documentary Record*. Vol. 1, *European Expansion, 1535–1914*. New Haven, 1975.

Italy. Ministero degli Affari Esteri. *I Documenti diplomatici Italiani: 1861–*. Rome, 1952–.
al-Khatib, M., ed. *al-Mu'tamar al-'arabi al-awwal [The first Arab congress]*. Cairo, 1913.
Musa, Suleiman, ed. *al-Thawra al-'arabiyya al-kubra: watha'iq wa asanid* [The great Arab revolt: Documents and records]. Amman, 1970.
Turkey. Fourth Army Command. *La Verité sur la Question Syriènne*. Istanbul, 1916.
Turkey. *Dustur tertib-i sani*. 11 vols. Istanbul, 1911–1928.
Turkey. *Salname* [Annual reports for the central government and the provinces].
Young, George. *Corps de droit Ottoman: recueil des codes, lois, réglements, ordonnances et actes les plus importants du droit interieur et d'études sur le droit contumier de l'Empire Ottomane*. 7 vols. Oxford, 1905–1906.

Newspapers

al-Ahram (Cairo), 1876 -.
Filastin (Jaffa), 1911–.
al-Hadara (Istanbul). 1909–1916; reopens as *al-Madaniya* (to 1912), reappears as *al-Idara*.
al-Haqiqa (Beirut), 1909–.
al-Hilal (Cairo), 1892–.
al-Ittihad al-'uthmani (Beirut), 1908–.
al-Karmil (Haifa), 1909 -
Lisan al-Hal (Beirut), 1877–.
al-Manar (Cairo), 1898–.
al-Mu'ayyad (Cairo), 1889–.
al-Mufid (Beirut), 1909–1914.
al-Muqattam (Cairo), 1889–1952.
al-Muqtabas (newspaper) (Damascus), 1906–.
al-Muqtabas (journal) (Cairo and Damascus), 1906–1916.
al-Taqaddum (Aleppo), 1909–.

Memoirs, Biographies, Works by Arab Nationalists and Contemporaries
'Abdullah ibn-al-Husayn. *Mudhakkirati* [My memoirs]. Jerusalem, 1945. English version: *Memoirs*. London, 1950.
'Ali Jawdat. *Dhikriyat 'Ali Jawdat, 1900–1958* [Memoirs of 'Ali Jawdat, 1900–1958]. Beirut, 1967.
Alusi, L. *Muhammad Kurd 'Ali*. Baghdad, 1966.
Antonius, George. *The Arab Awakening*. Philadelphia, 1939.
Arslan, al-Amir Shakib. *al-Sayyid Rashid Rida aw ikha' arba'in sana* [Sayyid Rashid Rida, or the friendship of forty years]. Damascus, 1937.

al-Asad, Nasir al-Din. *Muhammad Ruhi al-Khalidi: Ra'id al-bahth al-tarikhi al-hadith fi filastin* [Muhammmad Ruhi al-Khalidi: Pioneer of modern historical research in Palestine]. Cairo, 1970.

al-A'zami, Ahmad Izzat. *al-Qadiyya al-'arabiyya* [The Arab cause]. Vol 1. Baghdad, 1931.

al-'Azm, 'Abd al-Qadir. *al-Usra al-'Azmiya* [The 'Azm family]. Damascus, 1960.

al-'Azm, Khalid. *Mudhakkirat Khalid al-'Azm* [Memoirs of Khalid al-'Azm]. Beirut, 1973.

Azoury, Negib. *Le Réveil de la nation arabe dans l'Asie Turque*. Paris, 1905.

al-Baruni, Za'ima. *Safahatun khalidah min al-jihad* [Pages from the holy war]. 2 vols. Cairo, 1964.

Birdwood, Lord. *Nuri As-Said: A Study in Arab Leadership*. London, 1959.

Daghir, As'ad. *Mudhakkirati 'ala hamish al-qadiyya al-'arabiyya* [My memoirs on the margins of the Arab cause] Cairo, n.d.

Daghir, As'ad. *Thawrat al-'arab* [The revolt of the Arabs]. Cairo, 1916.

Daghir, Yusuf. *Masadir al-dirasai al-adabiyya: al-fikr al-'arabi al-hadith min sayr a'lamhi* [Sources of literary studies: Modern Arab thought]. Vol. 2, part 1: 1800-1955. Beirut, 1955.

al-Dahhan, S. *Muhammad Kurd 'Ali: hayatuhu wa atharuhu* [Muhammad Kurd 'Ali: His life and works]. Damascus, 1955.

Darwaza, Muhammad 'Izzat. *Durus al-ta'rikh al-'arabi min aqdam al-azminah ila ilan* [The lessons of Arab history from the earliest times until now]. Cairo, 1929 and subsequent editions.

Darwaza, Muhammad 'Izzat. *Hawla al-haraka al-'arabiyya al-haditha* [Regarding the modern Arab movement]. 6 vols. Sidon, 1949–1952.

Darwaza, Muhammad 'Izzat. *Nash'at al-haraka al-'arabiyya al-haditha* [The birth of the modern Arab movement]. Sidon, 1971.

Darwaza, Muhammad 'Izzat. *al-Qadiyya al-filastiniyya fi mukhtalaf marahiliha* [The Palestine question in its different phases]. 2 vols. Sidon, 1951.

Djemal Pasha. *Memoires of a Turkish Statesman, 1913–1919*. New York, 1922.

Erskine, Mrs. Stewart. *King Faisal of Iraq*. London, 1933.

Fahmi, 'Abd al-'Aziz. *Hadhihi hayati* [This is my life]. Cairo, 1963.

al-Hakim, Yusuf. *Dhikrayat al-Hakim* [Memoirs of al-Hakim]. Vol. I, *Suriyyah wal-'ahd al-'uthmani* [Syria and the Ottoman period]. Beirut, 1966.

al-Hashimi, Taha. *Mudhakkirat Taha al-Hashimi, 1919–1943* [Memoirs of Taha al-Hashimi], ed. Khaldun al-Husri. Beirut, 1967.

Haykal, Muhammad Husayn. *Mudhakkirat fil-siyasa al-misriyya*. [Memoirs of Egyptian politics]. 3 vols. Cairo, 1951, 1953, 1978.

al-Husri, Sati'. *Abhath mukhtara fil-qawmiyya al-'arabiyya* [Selected Studies in Arab Nationalism]. Cairo, 1967.

al-Husri, Sati'. *al-Bilad al-'arabiyya wal-dawla al-'uthmaniyya* [The Arab countries and the Ottoman state]. Beirut, 1960.

al-Husri, Sati'. *Yawm maysalun: safha min tarikh al-'Arab al-hadith.* Beirut, n.d. English version: *The Day of Maysalun.* Translated by Sidney Glazer. Washington, DC, 1966.

al-Husri, Sati'. *Mudhakkirati fil-'Iraq* [My memoirs in Iraq]. 2 vols. Beirut, 1966–1968.

al-Husri, Sati'. *Nushu' al-fikra al-qawmiyya* [The birth of the nationalist idea]. Beirut, 1956.

Ibish, Y., ed. *Rihlat al-Imam Muhammad Rashid Rida* [Journeys of al-Imam Rashid Rida]. Beirut, 1971.

al-Khalidi, Anbara Salam. *Jawla fi al-dhikrayat bayna Lubnan wa Filastin* [Memoirs of Lebanon and Palestine]. Beirut, 1978.

al-Khalidi, Muhammad Ruhi. *al-Inqilab al-'uthmani wa turkiya al-fatat* [The Ottoman revolution and young Turkey]. Cairo, 1909.

Kurd 'Ali, Muhammad. *al-Mudhakkirat* [Memoirs]. 3 vols. Damascus, 1948.

Lutfi al-Sayyid, Ahmad. *Qissat hayati.* [The story of my life]. Cairo, 1962.

Markaz watha'iq wa ta'rikh misr al-mu'asir. *Awraq Muhammad Farid.* Vol.I: *Mudhakkirati ba'da al-hijra, 1904–1919.* [The papers of Muhammad Farid, vol I: Memoirs after the migration]. Cairo, 1978.

Mushtaq, Talib. *Awraq ayyami 1908–1958* [The papers of my days 1908–1958]. Beirut, 1968.

Nassar, Najib. *al-Sahyuniyya* [Zionism]. Haifa, 1911.

Qadri, Ahmad. *Mudhakkirati 'an al-thawra al-'arabiyya al-kubra* [My memoirs of the great Arab revolt]. Damascus, 1956.

al-Qaysi, Sami 'Abd al-Hafidh. *Yasin al-Hashimi.* 2 vols. Basra, 1975.

al-Rawi, Ibrahim. *Min al-thawra al-'arabiyya al-kubra ila al-'Iraq al-hadith: dhikriyat* [From the great Arab revolt to modern Iraq: Memoirs]. Beirut, 1969

al-Rikabi, Jawdat and Jamil Sultan. *al-Irth al-fikri li al-muslih al-ijtima'i 'Abd al-Hamid al-Zahrawi* [The intellectual patrimony of the social reformer 'Abd al-Hamid al-Zahrawi]. Damascus, 1963.

Sa'id, Amin. *Asrar al-thawra al-'Arabiyya al-kubra wa ma'sat al-Sharif Husayn* [Secrets of the first Arab revolt and the tragedy of Sharif Husayn]. Beirut, [1935].

Sa'id, Amin. *al-Thawra al-'Arabiyya al-Kubra* [The Great Arab Revolt]. 3 vols. Cairo, 1934.

Sakakini, Hala, ed. *Kadha ana ya dunya: yawmiyat Khalil al-Sakakini* [I am thus, oh world: Diaries of Khalil al-Sakakini]. 2d ed. Beirut, 1982.

Sha'rawi, Huda. *Harem Years: Memoirs of An Egyptian Feminist (1879–1924)*. Translated with an introduction by Margot Badran. New York, 1987.
Shafiq, Ahmad. *Mudhakkirati fi nisf qarn* [My memories of half a century]. 3 vols. Cairo, 1931–1937.
Shahbandar, 'Abd al-Rahman. *Mudhakkirat 'Abd al-Rahman Shahbandar* [Memoirs of 'Abd al-Rahman Shahbandar]. Beirut, 1967.
Storrs, Sir Ronald. *The Memoirs of Sir Ronald Storrs*. New York, 1937.
al-Suwaydi, Tawfiq. *Mudhakkirati: nisf qarn min tarikh al-'Iraq wal-qadiyya al-'Arabiyya* [My memoirs: A half century of the history of Iraq and the Arab cause]. Beirut, 1969.
Vambery, Arminius. "Personal Recollections of Abdülhamid and his Court," *Nineteenth Century* 66(1909):69–88.
Wilson, A.T. *Loyalties: Mesopotamia 1914–1917*. London, 1930.
al-Zirkili, Khayr al-Din. *Ma Ra'aytu wa ma sami'tu* [What I saw and what I heard]. Cairo, 1923.
Zu'aytir, Akram. *Watha'iq al-haraka al-wataniyya al-Filastiniyya* [Documents of the Palestinian national movement]. Beirut, 1979.

Secondary Sources

Abir, M. "Local Leadership and Early Reforms in Palestine, 1800–1914." In Moshe Ma'oz, ed. *Studies on Palestine in the Ottoman Period*. Jerusalem, 1975.
Abu-Ghazaleh, Adnan. *Arab Cultural Nationalism in Palestine During the British Mandate*. Beirut, 1973.
Abu-Lughod, Ibrahim. *Arab Rediscovery of Europe: A Study in Cultural Encounters*. Princeton, 1963.
Abu-Lughod, Ibrahim, ed. *The Transformation of Palestine: Essays on the Origin and Development of the Arab-Israeli Conflict*. Evanston, 1971.
Abu-Manneh, Butrus. "The Christians Between Ottomanism and Syrian Nationalism: The Ideas of Butrus al-Bustani." *International Journal of Middle East Studies*, 11 (1980):287–304.
Abu-Manneh, Butrus. "The Rise of the Sanjak of Jerusalem in the Late 19th Century." In Gabriel Ben-Dor, ed. *The Palestinians and the Middle East Conflict*. Ramat Gan, 1978.
Abu-Manneh, Butrus. "Sultan Abdülhamid II and the Sharifs of Mecca (1880–1900)." *Asian and African Studies* 9 (1973): 1–21.
Abu Zayd, Faruq. *Azmat al-fikr al-qawmi fil-sihafa al-misriyya* [The Crisis of nationalist thought in the Egyptian press]. Cairo, 1976.
Ahmad, Feroz. *The Young Turks: The Committee of Union and Progress in Turkish Politics, 1908–1914*. Oxford, 1969.
Ahmed, Jamal Mohammad. *The Intellectual Origins of Egyptian Nationalism*. London, 1960.

Ajay, Nicholas, Jr. "Political Intrigue and Suppression in Lebanon during World War I." *International Journal of Middle East Studies* 5 (1974): 140–160.

Akarli, Engin D. "Abdulhamid II's Attempts to Integrate Arabs into the Ottoman System." In David Kushner, ed. *Palestine in the Late Ottoman Period: Political, Social, and Economic Transformation.* Jerusalem, 1986.

Akarli, Engin D. "The Problems of External Pressures, Power Struggles, and Budgetary Deficits in Ottoman Politics Under Abdulhamid II." Ph.D. Diss. Princeton University, 1976.

Akrawi, Matta. *Curriculum Construction in the Public Primary Schools of Iraq.* New York, 1943.

al-ʿAllaf, Ahmad Hilmi. *Dimashq fi matlaʿ al-qarn al-ʿashrin* [Damascus at the beginning of the twentieth century]. Edited by ʿAli Jamil Nu'iysa. Damascus, 1976.

Allush, Naji. "al-Haraka al-ʿarabiyya baʿd al-harb al-ʿalamiyya al-ula" [The Arab movement after the first World War]. *Dirasat ʿArabiyya* (December 1965): 44–75.

Allush, Naji. *al-Muqawama al-ʿarabiyya fi Filastin 1914–1948.* [The Arab resistance in Palestine, 1914–1948]. Beirut, 1967.

al-ʿAmr, Saleh. "The Hijaz under Ottoman Rule 1869–1914: The Ottoman Vali, the Sherif of Mecca, and the Growth of British Influence." Ph.D. Diss., Leeds University, 1974.

Anderson, Lisa. "Nineteenth-Century Reform in Ottoman Libya." *International Journal of Middle East Studies* 16 (1984): 325–348.

Anderson, Lisa. *The State and Social Transformation in Tunisia and Libya, 1830–1980.* Princeton, 1986.

Anderson, Lisa. "The Tripoli Republic, 1918–1922," In E. G. H. Joffe and K. S. Maclachlan, eds. *Social and Economic Development of Libya.* London, 1982.

Ansari, Zafar Ishaq. "Egyptian Nationalism vis a vis Islam." *Pakistan Horizon* 13(1960): 21–47.

al-Arhayyam, Faysal Muhammad. *Tatuwwur al-ʿIraq taht hukm al-ittihadiyya* [The development of Iraq under the rule of the Unionists]. Mosul, 1975.

Attiyah, Ghassan R. *Iraq, 1908–1921: A Political Study.* Beirut, 1973.

ʿAttiyah, Naʿim. "Maʿalim al-fikr al-tarbawi fil-bilad al-ʿarabiyyah fil-miʾat al-sana al-akhira" [Landmarks of educational thought in the Arab countries during the past hundred years]. In Fuʾad Sarruf and Nabih Amin Faris, eds. *al-Fikr al-ʿarabi fi miʾat sanah* [Arab thought over a hundred years]. Beirut, 1967.

'Awad, ʿAbd al-ʿAziz Muhammad. *Al-Idara al-ʿuthmaniyya fi wilayat suriyya, 1864–1914* The Ottoman administration in the Province of Syria, 1864–1914]. Cairo, 1969.

Baer, Gabriel. "Village and City in Egypt and Syria: 1500–1914." In A. L. Udovitch, ed. *The Islamic Middle East, 700–1900: Studies in Economic and Social History.* Princeton, 1981.

Baker, Randall. *King Husain and the Kingdom of the Hijaz.* Cambridge, 1979.

Barber, Aghil Mohammed. "The Tarablus (Libyan) Resistance to the Italian Invasion: 1911–1920." Ph.D. Diss., University of Wisconsin, 1980.

Batatu, Hanna. *The Old Social Classes and the Revolutionary Movements of Iraq: A Study of Iraq's Old Landed and Commercial Classes and of its Communists, Ba'thists, and Free Officers.* Princeton, 1978.

Be'eri, Eliezer. *Reishit Ha-sichsuch Yisrael-Arav, 1882–1911* [The Genesis of the Arab Israeli Conflict, 1882–1911]. Haifa, 1986.

Berkes, Niyazi. *The Development of Secularism in Turkey.* Montreal, 1964.

Berque, Jacques. *L'Egypte: Imperialisme et Revolution.* Paris, 1968; English version: *Egypt: Imperialism and Revolution.* Translated by J. Stewart. New York, 1972.

Bessis, Juliette. "Chekib Arslan et les mouvements nationalistes au Maghreb." *Revue Historique* 259 (1978): 467–489.

Birru, Tawfiq. *al-'Arab wa al-turk fi al-'ahd al-dusturi al-'uthmani 1908–1914* [The Arabs and the Turks during the Ottoman constitutional era 1908–1914]. Cairo, 1960.

Birru, Tawfiq. "al-Muntada al-adabi [The literary club]." *al-Ma'rifa* (Damascus): 1965.

Buheiry, Marwan R. "Colonial Scholarship and Muslim Revivalism in 1900." *Arab Studies Quarterly* 4 (1982): 1–16.

Buheiry, Marwan R., ed. *Intellectual Life in the Arab East 1890–1939.* Beirut, 1981.

Buheiry, Marwan R. "Al-Sadirat al-zira'iya li-mutasarafiyyat al-Quds al-Sharif, 1885–1914." *Samid al-Iqtisadi* 3 (November, 1980): 3–22. Published in French as "Exportations agricoles de la Palestine meridionale 1885–1914." *Revue détudes Palestiniennes* 20 (Summer 1986): 49–70.

Burke, Edmund III. "A Comparative View of French Native Policy in Morocco and Syria." *Middle Eastern Studies* 9 (1973): 175–186.

Busch, B. C. *Britain, India, and the Arabs, 1914–1921.* Berkeley, 1971.

Busch, B. C. *Britain and the Persian Gulf 1894–1914.* Berkeley, 1967.

Burj, 'Abd al-Rahman. *'Aziz al-Misri wal-haraka al-'arabiyya, 1908–1916.* [Aziz al-Misri and the Arab movement, 1908–1916]. Cairo, 1979.

al-Bustani, Sulayman. *'Ibra wa dhikra: al-dawla al-'uthmaniya qabl al-dustur wa ba'dahu* [A lesson and a reminder: The Ottoman state

before and after the constitution]. Beirut, 1908. Reprint. Beirut, 1978.
Caplan, Neil. *Futile Diplomacy: Early Arab-Zionist Negotiation Attempts, 1913–1931.* vol. 1, London, 1983.
Caplan, Neil. *Palestinian Jewry and the Palestine Question, 1917–1925.* London, 1978.
Carmel, Alex. "The German Settlers in Palestine and Their Relations with the Local Arab Population and the Jewish Community, 1868–1918." In Moshe Ma'oz, ed. *Studies on Palestine During the Ottoman Period.* Jerusalem, 1975.
Chejne, Anwar G. *The Arabic Language: Its Role in History.* Minneapolis, 1968.
Chejne, Anwar G. "The Use of History by Modern Arab Writers." *Middle East Journal* 14 (1960): 382–396.
Chevallier, D. *La Société du Mont Liban a l'époque de la révolution industrielle en Europe.* Paris, 1971.
Cleveland, William L. "Ataturk Viewed by His Arab Contemporaries: The Opinions of Sati' al-Husri and Shakib Arslan." *International Journal of Turkish Studies* 2 (1983): 15–23.
Cleveland, William L. *Islam Against the West: Shakib Arslan and the Campaign for Islamic Nationalism.* Austin, 1985.
Cleveland, William L. *The Making of an Arab Nationalist: Ottomanism and Arabism in the Life and Thought of Sati' al-Husri.* Princeton, 1971.
Cleveland, William L. "The Role of Islam as Political Ideology in the First World War." In Edward Ingram, ed. *National and International Politics in the Middle East.* London, 1986.
Cohen, Stuart A. *British Policy in Mesopotamia 1903–1914.* London, 1976.
Commins, David. "Religious Reformers and Arabists in Damascus 1885–1914." *International Journal of Middle East Studies* 18 (1986): 405–425.
Conrad, Lawrence I., ed. *The Formation and Perception of the Modern Arab World: Studies by Marwan R. Buheiry.* Princeton, 1989.
Crabbs, Jack A., Jr. *The Writing of History in Nineteenth Century Egypt: A Study in National Transformation.* Detroit, 1984.
Cumming, D. D. (Sir Duncan). "Modern History." In *Handbook on Cyrenaica.* Cairo, 1947.
al-Dajani, Ahmad Sidqi. *Libya qubayl al-ihtilal al-itali aw tarablus al-gharb fi akhir al-'ahd al-'uthmani al-thani* [Libya before the Italian occupation or Tripoli at the end of the second Ottoman era]., 1971.
al-Darraji, Abdul Razzaq. *Ja'far Abu al-Timman wa dawruhu fil-haraka al-wataniyya fil-'Iraq* [Ja'far Abu al-Timman and his role in the national movement in Iraq]. Baghdad, 1978.

Davico, Rosalba. "La guerilla libyenne, 1911–1932." In *Abd al-Krim et la République du Rif: Actes du colloque international d'études historiques et sociologiques, 18–20 janvier 1973*. Paris, 1976.
Davison, Roderic. *Reform in the Ottoman Empire 1856–1876*. Princeton, 1963.
Davison, Roderic. "Westernized Education in Ottoman Turkey." *Middle East Journal* 15 (1961): 289–301.
Dawn, C. Ernest. "The Development of Nationalism in Syria." In Abdeen Jabara and Janice Terry, eds., *The Arab World from Nationalism to Revolution*. Wilmette, 1971.
Dawn, C. Ernest. *From Ottomanism to Arabism: Essays on the Origins of Arab Nationalism*. Urbana, Ill., 1973.
Dawn, C. Ernest. "Ottoman Affinities of 20th Century Regimes in Syria." In David Kushner, ed., *Palestine in the Late Ottoman Period: Political, Social, and Economic Transformation*. Jerusalem, 1986.
Dawn, C. Ernest. "The Rise of Arabism in Syria." *The Middle East Journal* 16 (1962): 145–168.
Desparmet, J. "Afrique du Nord et le pan-arabisme: L'Afrique du Nord vue de Damas" *L'Afrique Française* 48 (1938): 56–58.
Eliraz, David. "Markiviah shel ha-leumiyut ha-ʿaravit behaguto shel Satiʿ al-Husri" [The components of Arab nationalism in Satiʿ al-Husri's philosophy], *Hamizrah Hehadash* 22 (1972): 152–169.
Escovitz, Joseph. "He Was the Muhammad ʿAbduh of Syria: A Study of Tahir al-Jazaʾiri and His Influence." *International Journal of Middle East Studies* 18 (1986): 293–310.
Evans-Pritchard, E. E. *The Sanusi of Cyrenaica*. Oxford, 1949
Fall, Cyril Bentham. *Military Operations: Egypt and Palestine from June 1917 to the End of the War*. London, 1930.
Farah, Caesar. "Censorship and Freedom of Expression in Ottoman Syria and Egypt." In William W. Haddad and William L. Ochsenwald, eds. *Nationalism in a Non-National State: The Dissolution of the Ottoman Empire*. Columbus, 1977.
Farah, Caesar E. "The Dilemma of Arab Nationalism." *Die Welt des Islam* 8 (1963): 140–164.
Farhi, David. "Documents on the Attitude of the Ottoman Government towards the Jewish Settlements in Palestine after the Revolution of the Turks (1908–1909)." In Moshe Maʿoz, eds. *Studies on Palestine During the Ottoman Priod*. Jerusalem, 1975.
Farman, T. F. "French Claims on Syria." *Contemporary Review* (1915): 343–383.
Fawaz, Leila Tarazi. *Merchants and Migrants in Nineteenth Century Beirut*. Cambridge, 1982.
Frey, Frederick W. *The Turkish Political Elite*. Cambridge, 1965.
Friedman, I. "The McMahon Correspondence and the Question of Palestine." *Journal of Contemporary History* 5 (1970): 83–122.

Friedman, I. *The Question of Palestine, 1914–1918: British-Jewish-Arab Relations*. London, 1973
al-Gari, Emil. *The Struggle of the Arab Nationalist against Colonialism.* Cairo, 1957.
Gendzier, Irene L. *The Practical Visions of Yaʿqub Sanuʿ.* Cambridge, 1966.
Gerber, Haim. *Ottoman Rule in Jerusalem 1890–1914.* Berlin, 1985.
Gershoni, Israel. "Arabization of Islam: The Egyptian Salafiyya and the Rise of Arabism in Pre-Revolutionary Egypt." *Asian and African Studies* 13 (1979): 22–57.
Gershoni, Israel. *The Emergence of Pan-Arabism in Egypt.* Tel Aviv, 1981.
Gershoni, Israel. "The Emergence of Pan-Nationalism in Egypt: Pan-Islamism and Pan-Arabism in the 1930s."*Asian and African Studies* 16 (1982): 59–94.
Gershoni, Israel and James P. Jankowski. *Egypt, Islam, and the Arabs: The Search for Egyptian Nationhood. 1900–1930.* New York, 1986.
Ghali, Ibrahim Amin. *L'Egypte nationaliste et liberale de Moustapha Kamel à Saad Zaghloul* (1892–1927). The Hague, 1969.
Goldschmidt, Arthur, Jr. "The Egyptian Nationalist Party, 1892–1919." In P. M. Holt, ed. *Political and Change in Modern Egypt.* London, 1965.
Griffiths, Merwin A. The Reorganization of the Ottoman Army under Abdulhamid II, 1880–1897. Ph.D. Diss., University of California, Los Angeles, 1966.
Gross, Max. "Ottoman Rule in the Province of Damascus 1860–1909" Ph.D. Diss., Georgetown University, 1979.
Hadawi, Sami. *Bitter Harvest: Palestine Between 1914–1967.* New York, 1967.
Haddad, Elias N. "Political Parties in Syria and Palestine (Qaisi and Yemeni)."*Journal of the Palestine Oriental Society* 1 (1921).
Haddad, Robert. *Syrian Christians in Muslim Society: An Interpretation.* Princeton, 1970.
Haddad, William. "Nationalism in the Ottoman Empire." In William W. Haddad and William Ochsenwald, eds., *Nationalism in a non-National State: The Dissolution of the Ottoman Empire.* Columbus, 1977.
Haim, Sylvia. "Islam and the Theory of Arab Nationalism." In W. Z. Laqueur, ed., *The Middle East in Transition.* New York, 1958.
al-Hakim, Yusuf. *Bayrut wa lubnan fi ʿahd al-ʿuthman* [Beirut and Lebanon during the Ottoman era]. Beirut, 1964.
al-Hakim, Yusuf. *Suriyya wal-ʿahd al-faysali* [Syria and the Faysal era]. Beirut, 1966.
al-Hakim, Yusuf. *Suriyya wal-ʿahd al-ʿuthmani* [Syria and the Ottoman era]. Beirut, 1966.

Hallaq, ʿAli Hassan. *Mawqif al-dawla al-ʿuthmaniyya min al-haraka al-sahuniyya, 1897–1909* [The Stand of the Ottoman State Towards the Zionist movement 1897–1909]. Beirut, 1978
Harran, Tag Mohammad. "Turkish-Syrian Relations in the Ottoman Constitutional Period, 1908–1914." Ph.D. Diss., University of London, 1969.
Heyd, Uriel. *Foundations of Turkish Nationalism: The Life and Teachings of Ziya Gökalp.* London, 1950.
al-Hilali, ʿAbd al-Razzaq. *Tarikh al-taʿlim fil-ʿIraq fil-ʿahd al-ʿuthmani, 1638–1917* [History of Education in Iraq in the Ottoman era 1638–1917]. Baghdad, 1959.
Holt, P. M. *Egypt and the Fertile Crescent 1516–1922: A Political History.* Ithaca, 1966.
Holt, P. M., ed. *Political and Social Change in Modern Egypt: Historical Studies from the Ottoman Conquest to the United Arab Republic.* London, 1968.
Hopwood, D. *The Russian Presence in Syria and Palestine 1843–1914: Church and Politics in the Near East.* Oxford, 1969.
el-Horeir, Abdulmola S. "Social and Economic Transformation in the Libyan Hinterlands during the Second Half of the Nineteenth Century: The Role of Sayyid Ahmad al-Sharif al-Sanusi." Ph.D. Diss., University of California, Los Angeles, 1981.
Hourani, Albert. "The *Arab Awakening* Forty Years After." In Albert Hourani, *The Emergence of the Modern Middle East.* Berkeley, 1981.
Hourani, Albert. *Arabic Thought in the Liberal Age, 1798–1939.* Cambridge, 1983.
Hourani, Albert. *The Emergence of the Modern Middle East.* Berkeley, 1981.
Hourani, Albert. *Europe and the Middle East.* Berkelely, 1980.
Hourani, Albert. *Minorities in the Arab World.* London, 1947.
Hourani, Albert. "The Ottoman Background of the Modern Middle East." In Kemal Karpat, ed., *The Ottoman State and its Place in World History.* Leiden, 1974.
Hourani, Albert. "Ottoman Reform and the Politics of the Notables." In W. R. Polk and R. L. Chambers, eds., *Beginnings of Modernization in the Middle East.* Chicago, 1968.
Hurewitz, J. C. *The Struggle for Palestine.* New York, 1976.
Husayn, Muhammad Muhammad. *al-Ittijahat al-wataniyya fil-adab al-muʿasir* [Nationalist orientations in contemporary literature]. 2 vols. Cairo, 1954.
al-Husni, Muhammad. *Kitab muntakhabat al-tawarikh li dimashq* [Book of selections from the histories of Damascus]. 3 vols. Beirut, 1979.
al-Husry, Khaldun S. *Three Reformers: A Study in Modern Arab Political Thought.* Beirut, 1966.
al-Hut, Bayan Nuwayhid. *Al-Qiyadat wal-muʾassasat al-siyasiyya fi filas-*

tin 1917–1948 [Political leadership and institutions in Palestine 1917–1948]. Beirut, 1986.
ʿImara, Muhammad. *al-ʿUruba fil-ʿasr al-hadith* [Arabism in the modern era]. Cairo, 1967.
Islamoglu, H. and C. Keyder. "Agenda for Ottoman History." *Review* 1 (1974): 31–55.
Issawi, Charles. "British Trade and the Rise of Beirut 1830–1860." *International Journal of Middle East Studies* 8 (1977): 91–101.
Issawi, Charles. *An Economic History of the Middle East and North Africa*. New York, 1982.
Issawi, Charles. *The Economic History of the Middle East, 1800–1914*. Chicago, 1966.
Issawi, Charles. *The Fertile Crescent, 1800–1914: A Documentary Economic History*. New York, 1988.
al-Jabbar, ʿAbdullah. *Al-Tayyarat al-adabiyya al-haditha fi qalb al-jazira al-ʿarabiyya*. [Trends in modern literature in the heart of the Arabian peninsula]. Cairo, 1959.
Jankowski, James. "Ottomanism and Arabism in Egypt 1860–1914." *Muslim World* 70 (1980): 226–259.
al-Jundi, Adham. *Shuhada' al-harb al-ʿalamiyya al-kubra* [Martyrs of the Great World War]. Damascus, 1960.
Jung, Eugene. *La Révolte Arabe*. 2 vols. Paris, 1924–1925.
Kalaycioğlu, Ersin, ed. *Türk Siyasal Hayatinin Gelisimi* [Development of Turkish political life]. Istanbul, 1986.
Karpat, Kemal. "Ottoman Population Records and the Census of 1881/2–1893." *International Journal of Middle East Studies* 9 (1978): 262–271.
Karpat, Kemal. "Reinterpreting Ottoman History: A Note on the Condition of Education in 1874." *International Journal of Turkish Studies* 2 (1981–1982): 93–100.
Karpat, Kemal. "The Transformation of the Ottoman State 1789–1908." *International Journal of Middle East Studies* 3 (1972): 243–281.
Kassimy, Zafer (al-Qasimi, Zafir). "La participation des classes populaires aux mouvements nationaux d'independence aux XIXe et XXe siecles: Syrie." In *Mouvements nationaux d'indépendance et classes populaires aux XIXe et XXe siecles en Occident et en Orient*, Edited by the Commission Internationale d'Histoire des Mouvements Sociaux et des Structures Sociales. Paris, 1971.
Kawtharani, Wajih. *Bilad al-sham, al-sukkan, al-iqtisad wal-siyasa al-faransiyya fi matlaʿ al-qarn al-ʿishrin: qira'a fil-watha'iq* [Bilad al-Sham, population, economy, and French policy at the beginning of the twentieth century: a reading of the documents]. Beirut, 1980.
Kawtharani, Wajih. *al-Ittijahat al-ijtimaʿiyya wal-siyasiyya fi jabal lubnan wal-mashriq al-ʿarabi 1860–1920* [Social and political trends in Jabal Lubnan and the Arab East 1860–1920]. Beirut, 1978.

al-Kayyali, ʿAbd al-Wahhab. *Palestine: A Modern History*. London, 1973.

Kazamias, Andraes M. *Education and the Quest for Modernity in Turkey*. Chicago, 1966.

Kedourie, Elie. *Arabic Political Memoirs and Other Studies*. London, 1974.

Kedourie, Elie. "Cairo and Khartoum on the Arab Question." *The Historical Journal* 7 (1964): 280–297.

Kedourie, Elie. *The Chatham House Version and Other Middle Eastern Studies*. London, 1970.

Kedourie, Elie. *England and the Middle East: The Destruction of the Ottoman Empire 1914–1921*. London, 1956.

Kedourie, Elie. "The Impact of the Young Turk Revolution on the Arabic-Speaking Provinces of the Ottoman Empire." In Elie Kedourie, *Arabic Political Memoirs and Other Studies*. London, 1974.

Kedourie, Elie. *In the Anglo-Arab Labyrinth: The Hussein-McMahon Correspondence and Its Interpretations 1914–1939*. Cambridge, 1976.

Kenny, L. M. "Satiʿ al-Husri's Views on Arab Nationalism." *Middle East Journal* 17 (1963): 231–256.

Khadduri, Majid. *Arab Contemporaries, The Role of Personalities in Politics*. Baltimore, 1973.

Khadduri, Majid. "Aziz ʿAli al-Misri and the Arab Nationalist Movement." In Albert Hourani, ed., *St. Antony's Papers* 17 (Oxford, 1965): 140–163.

Khadduri, Walid. "Social Background of Modern Iraqi Politics." Ph.D. Diss., Johns Hopkins University, 1970.

Khalid, ʿAbdallah. "Maktab ʿAnbar: Suwar min safhat al-butula fi dimashq al-ʿuruba [Maktab ʿAnbar: Scenes from the pages of heroism in Arab Damascus]." *al-Manabir* 8 (October 1986): 110–118.

Khalidi, Rashid I. "ʿAbd al-Ghani al-ʿUraysi and *al-Mufid:* The Press and Arab Nationalism before 1914." In M. Buheiry, ed., *Intellectual Life in the Arab East 1890–1939*. Beirut, 1981.

Khalidi, Rashid I. "Arab Nationalism in Syria: The Formative Years 1908–1914." In William Haddad and William Ochsenwald, eds., *Nationalism in a non-National State: The Dissolution of the Ottoman Empire*. Columbus, 1977.

Khalidi, Rashid I. *British Policy Towards Syria and Palestine 1906–1914*. London, 1980.

Khalidi, Rashid I. "Palestinian Peasant Reactions to Zionism before World War I." In E. Said and Christopher Hitchens, eds., *Blaming the Victims: Spurious Scholarship and the Palestine Question*. New York, 1987.

Khalidi, Rashid I. "The Role of the Press in the Early Arab Reaction to Zionism." *Peuples Méditerranéens* [Mediterranean Peoples] 20 (July-September 1982): 105–123.

Khalidi, Rashid I. "Social Factors in the Rise of the Arab Movement in Syria." In Said Arjomand, ed. *From Nationalism to Revolutionary Islam*. Albany, 1984.

Khalidi, Rashid I. "The 1912 Election Campaign in the Cities of *bilad al-sham*." *International Journal of Middle East Studies* 16 (1984): 461–474.

Khalifa, Ijlal. *al-Haraka al-nisa'iyya al-haditha* [The Modern women's movement]. Cairo, 1966.

al-Khatib, ʿAdnan. *al-Shaykh Tahir al-Jaza'iri: ra'id al-nahda al-ʿilmiyya fi bilad al-sham wa aʿlam min khirriji madrasatihi* [Shaykh Tahir al-Jaza'iri: Pioneer of the intellectual awakening in bilad al-sham and eminent graduates of his school]. Cairo, 1971.

Khouri, Mounah A. *Poetry and the Making of Modern Egypt, 1882–1922*. Leiden, 1971.

Khoury, Philip S. "Factionalism Among Syrian Nationalists During the French Mandate." *International Journal of Middle East Studies* 13 (1981): 441–469.

Khoury, Philip S. *Syria and the French Mandate: The Politics of Arab Nationalism 1920–1945*. Princeton, 1987.

Khoury, Philip S. *Urban Notables and Arab Nationalism: The Politics of Damascus 1880–1920*. Cambridge, 1983.

Khuddur, Adib. *al-Sihafah al-suriyyah* [The Syrian press]. Damascus, 1972.

Khuri, Yusuf. *al-Sihafa al-ʿarabiyya fi filastin 1876–1948* [The Arab press in Palestine 1876–1948]. Beirut, 1976.

Klieman, Aaron S. "Britain's War Aims in the Middle East in 1915." *Journal of Contemporary History* 3 (1968): 237–252.

Kohn, Hans. *A History of Nationalism in the East*. Translated by Margaret N. Green. New York, 1939.

Kramer, Martin. *Islam Assembled: The Advent of the Muslim Congresses*. New York, 1985.

Kürkcuoğlu, Omer. *Osmanli Devleti'ne Karsi Arap Bagimsizlik Hareketi (1908–1918)*. [Arab independence movements against the Ottoman state, 1908–1918]. Ankara, 1982.

Kushner, David. *The Rise of Turkish Nationalism, 1876–1908*. London, 1977.

Kushner, David, ed. *Palestine in the Late Ottoman Period: Political, Social and Economic Transformation*. Jerusalem, 1986.

Landau, Jacob M. "An Arab Anti-Turk Handbill, 1881." *Turcica* 9 (1977): 215–270.

Landau, Jacob M. *The Hejaz Railway and the Mecca Pilgrimage: A Case of Ottoman Political Propaganda* Detroit, 1971

Laoust, Henri. "L'Evolution politique et culturelle de l'Egypte contemporaine." *Entrentiens sur l'Evolution des Pays de Civilisation Arabe* 3 (1937): 68–94.

Lesch, Ann Mosely. *Arab Politics in Palestine, 1917–1939: The Frustration of a Nationalist Movement.* Ithaca, 1979.
Lesch, Ann Mosely. "The Origins of Palestinian Arab Nationalism." In William W. Haddad and William Ochsenwald, eds., *Nationalism in a non-National State: The Dissolution of the Ottoman Empire.* Columbus, 1977.
Lewis, Bernard. *The Emergence of Modern Turkey* London, 1979.
Luqa, A. *al-Haraka al-adabiyya fi dimashq, 1800–1900* [The literary movement in Damascus 1800–1900]. Damascus, 1976.
Lutfi al-Sayyid [Marsot], Afaf. *Egypt and Cromer: A Study in Anglo-Egyptian Relations.* London: John Murray, 1968.
Malgeri, Francesco. *La guerra Libica (1911–1912).* Rome, 1970.
Mandel, Neville J. *The Arabs and Zionism before World War I.* Berkeley, 1976.
Mandel, Neville J. "Attempts of Arab-Zionist Entente 1913–1914." *Middle Eastern Studies* 1 (1965): 238–267.
Mandel, Neville J. "Turks, Arabs and Jewish Immigration into Palestine, 1880–1914." In Albert Hourani, ed., *St Antony's Papers* 17 (1965).
Ma'oz, Moshe. *Ottoman Reform in Syria and Palestine, 1840–1861: The Impact of the Tanzimat on Politics and Society.* Oxford, 1968.
Ma'oz, Moshe, ed. *Studies in Palestine During the Ottoman Period.* Jerusalem, 1975.
Mardin, Serif. *The Genesis of Young Ottoman Thought.* Princeton, 1962.
Marmorstein, Emile. "A Note on Damascus, Homs, Hama and Aleppo'." In Albert Hourani, ed., *St Antony's Papers* 11 (1961): 161–165.
Marr, Phebe A. *The Modern History of Iraq.* Boulder, 1985.
Marr, Phebe A. "Yasin al-Hashimi: The Rise and Fall of a Nationalist." Ph.D. Diss., Harvard University, 1966.
Mattar, Philip. *The Mufti of Jerusalem: Muhammad Amin al-Husayni, a Founder of Palestinian Nationalism.* New York, 1988.
McCarthy, Justin. "The Population of Ottoman Syria and Iraq 1878–1914." *Asian and African Studies* 15 (1981): 7-25.
McCarthy, Justin. *The Population of Palestine: Population Statistics of the Late Ottoman Period and the Mandate.* New York, 1990.
Mori, Renato. "La penetrazione pacifica italiana in Libia dal 1907 al 1911 e il Banco di Roma." *Rivista di studi politici internationali* 24 (1957).
Musa, Suleiman. *al-Haraka al-ʿarabiyya: sirat al-marhala al-ula li al-nahda al-ʿarabiyya al-haditha* [The Arab movement: The story of the first period of the modern Arab awakening, 1908–1924]. Beirut, 1970.
Musa, Suleiman. "Jamʿiyyat al-ʿarabiyya al-fatat," [The Young Arab movement]. *al-ʿArabi* 101 (1971): 52–54.
Musa, Suleiman. "The Role of Syrians and Iraqis in the Arab Revolt." *Middle East Forum* 43 (1967): 5–18.

Muslih, Muhammad. *The Origins of Palestinian Nationalism*. New York, 1988.

al-Nasuli, Anis Zakariya. *Asbab al-nahda al-ʿarabiya fi al-qarn al-tasiʿ ʿashr* [Reasons for the Arab awakening in the nineteenth century]. Beirut, 1926.

Ochsenwald, William. *The Hijaz Railroad*. Charlottesville, 1980.

Ochsenwald, William. "Opposition to Political Centralization in South Jordan and the Hijaz, 1900–1914." *The Muslim World*. 62 (1973): 297–306.

Ochsenwald, William. *The Middle East in the World Economy. 1800–1914*. London, 1981.

Ochsenwald, William. *Religion, Society and the State in Arabia: The Hijaz under Ottoman Control, 1840–1908*. Columbus, 1984.

Owen, Roger, ed. *Studies in the Economic and Social History of Palestine in the Nineteenth and Twentieth Centuries* London, 1982.

Parla, Taha. "The Social and Political Thought of Ziya Gokalp." Ph.D. Diss., Columbia University, 1980.

Philipp, Thomas. "Feminism and Nationalist Politics in Egypt." In Lois Beck and Nikki Keddie, ed. *Women in the Muslim World*. Cambridge, 1978.

Philipp, Thomas. *The Syrians in Egypt 1725–1975*. Sttutgart, 1985.

Polk, W. R. and R. L. Chambers, eds. *Beginnings of Modernization in the Middle East*. Chicago, 1968.

Porath, Yehoshua. *The Emergence of the Palestinian-Arab National Movement 1918–1929* 2 vols. London, 1974–1977.

Porath, Yehoshua. "The Political Awakening of the Palestinian Arabs and Their Leadership Towards the End of the Ottoman Period." In Moshe Ma'oz, ed., *Studies on Palestine During the Ottoman Period*. Jerusalem, 1975.

Qarqut, Dhuqan. *Tatawwur al-fikra al-ʿarabiyya fi misr, 1805–1936* [The development of the Arab idea in Egypt 1805–1936]. Beirut, 1972.

Qasimiyya, Khayriyya. *al-Hukuma al-ʿarabiyya fi dimashq bayna 1918–1920* [The Arab government in Damascus between 1918 and 1920]. Cairo, 1971.

Qasimiyya, Khayriyya. "Najib Nassar wa jaridat *al-Karmil*, ahad al-aʿdaʾ al-ruwwad lil-sahyuniya." [Najib Nassar and the newspaper *al-Karmil:* One of the pioneer opponents of Zionism] *Shu'un Filastiniyya* (1973): 110–115.

al-Qaysi, Abdul Wahhab Abbas. "The Impact of Modernization on Iraqi Society During the Ottoman Era: A Study of Intellectual Development in Iraq, 1869–1917." Ph.D. Diss., University of Michigan, 1958.

al-Rafiʿi, ʿAbd al-Rahman. *Thawrat sanat 1919* [The revolution of 1919]. 2 vols. Cairo, 1946.

Rafiq, Abdulkarim. *al-ʿArab wa-al-ʿuthmaniyyun, 1516–1916* [The Arabs and the Ottomans 1516–1916]. Damascus, 1974.

Ramsaur, Ernest Edmonson. *The Young Turks: Prelude to the Revolution of 1908*. Princeton, 1957.

Reid, Donald M. *The Odyssey of Farah Antun: A Syrian Christian's Quest for Secularism*. Minneapolis and Chicago, 1975.

Remond, Georges. *Aux campes Turco-Arabes: Notes de route et de guerre en Cyrenaique et en Tripolitaine*. Paris, 1913.

Roded, Ruth. "Ottoman Service as a Vehicle for the Rise of New Upstarts among the Urban Elite Families of Syria in the Last Decades of Ottoman Rule." In Gabriel R. Warburg and Gad G. Gilbar, eds., *Studies in Islamic Society: Contributions in Memory of Gabriel Baer*. Haifa, 1984.

Roded, Ruth. "Social Patterns among the Urban Elite of Syria during the Late Ottoman Period 1876–1918." In David Kushner, ed., *Palestine in the Late Ottoman Period: Political, Social and EConomic Transformation*. Jerusalem, 1986.

Ro'i, Yaacov. "The Zionist Attitude to the Arabs 1908–1914." *Middle Eastern Studies* 4 (1968): 198–242.

Romano, Sergio. *La quarta sponda: La guerra di Libia, 1911/1912*. Milan, 1977.

Roumani, Jacques. "From Republic to Jamahiriya: Libya's Search for Political Community." *The Middle East Journal* 37 (1983): 151–168.

Saab, Hassan. *The Arab Federalists of the Ottoman Empire*. Amsterdam, 1958.

Saʿdun, Fawwaz."al-Haraka al-islahiyya fi bayrut fi awakhir al-ʿasr al-ʿuthmani" [The reform movement in Beirut at the end of the Ottoman period]. Master's thesis, Lebanese University, 1978.

Safran, Nadav. *Egypt in Search of Political Community: An Analysis of the Intellectual and Political Evolution of Egypt, 1804–1952*. Cambridge, 1961.

Saʿid, Rifʿat. *Muhammad Farid: al-Mawqif wal-maʿsa*. Cairo, 1978.

Salem, Salaheddin Hassan. "The Genesis of Political Leadership in Libya, 1952–1969." Ph.D. Diss., George Washington University, 1973.

Salibi, Kamal. "Beirut Under the Young Turks: As Depicted in the Political Memoirs of Salim ʿAli Salam (1868–1938)." In Jacques Berques and Dominique Chevalier, eds., *Les Arabes par leurs Archives xvi-XX Siècles*. Paris, 1976.

Sayigh, Anis. *al-Fikra al-ʿarabiyya fi misr* [The Arab idea in Egypt]. Beirut, 1959.

Sayigh, Anis. *al-Hashimiyyun wa-qadiyat filastin* [The Hashimites and the Palestine question]. Sidon, 1966.

Schilcher, Linda Schatkowski. *Families in Politics: Damascus Factions and Estates in the 18th and 19th Centuries*. Stuttgart, 1985.

Schölch, Alexander. *Egypt for the Egyptians: The Socio-Political Crises of 1878–1882*. London, 1982.

Schölch, Alexander. "European Economic Penetration and the Economic Development of Palestine, 1856–82." In Roger Owen, ed., *Studies in the Economic and Social History of Palestine in the Nineteenth and Twentieth Centuries.* London, 1982.

Seikaly, Samir M. "Damascene Intellectual Life in the Opening Years of the 20th Century: Muhammad Kurd ʿAli and *al-Muqtabas.*" In M. Buheiry, ed., *Intellectual Life in the Arab East 1890–1939.* Beirut, 1981.

Shabikah, Makki. *al-ʿArab wal-siyasah al-baritaniyya fi al-harb al-ʿalamiyyah al-ula* [The Arabs and British policy during the first world war]. Cairo, 1975.

al-Shaliq, Ahmad Zakariyy. *Hizb al-umma wa dawruhu fil-siyasa al-misriyya* [The Umma party and its role in Egyptian politics]. Cairo, 1979.

al-Shamikh, Muhammad 'Abd al-Rahman. *al-Sihafa fil-hijaz 1908–1941* [The Press in the Hijaz 1908–1941]. Beirut, 1959.

Shamir, Shimon. "Midhat Pasha and the anti-Turkish Agitation in Syria." *Middle Eastern Studies* 10 (1974): 115–141.

Sharabi, Hisham. *Arab Intellectuals and the West: The Formative Years 1875–1914.* Baltimore, 1972.

Shaw, Stanford. "The Ottoman Census System and Population 1831–1914." *International Journal of Middle East Studies* 9 (1978): 325–338.

Shaw, Stanford J. and Ezel Kural Shaw. *History of the Ottoman Empire and Modern Turkey: Vol. 2: Reform, Revolution, and Republic: The Rise of Modern Turkey, 1808–1975.* Cambridge, 1977.

al-Shihabi, Mustafa. *al-Qawmiyya al-ʿarabiyya* [Arab nationalism]. Cairo, 1958.

Shorrock, W. *French Imperialism in the Middle East: The Failure of Policy in Syria and Lebanon 1900–1914.* Madison, 1976.

Shorrock, W. "The Origins of the French Mandate in Syria and Lebanon: The Railroad Question 1901–1914." *International Journal of Middle East Studies* 1 (1970): 133–153.

Shukri, Muhammad Fuʿad. *Milad dawlal libiya al-haditha: watha'iq tahrirha wa istiqlalha* [Birth of the modern Libyan state: Documents of its liberation and independence]. Cairo, 1957.

Sidqi, Najati. "al-Haraka al-wataniyya al-ʿarabiyya min al-inqilab al-ittihadi ila ʿahd al-kutla al-wataniyya" [The Arab nationalist movement from the Unionist coup d'etat until the era of the National bloc]. *al-Taliʿa* 4 (1938): part 5, pp. 318–328; part 6, pp. 413–424.

al-Sifri, 'Isa. *Filastin al-ʿarabiyya bayna al-intidab wal-sahyuniyya* [Arab Palestine between the mandate and Zionism]. Jaffa: Maktabat Filastin al-Jadida, 1933.

Simon, Rachel. *Libya Between Ottomanism and Nationalism: The Ottoman Involvement in Libya during the War with Italy (1911–1919).* Berlin, 1987.

Simon, Reeva S. *Iraq Between the Two World Wars: The Creation and Implementation of a Nationalist Ideology.* New York, 1986.
Simon, Reeva S. "The Teaching of History in Iraq before the Rashid Ali Coup of 1941." *Middle Eastern Studies* 22 (1986): 37–51.
Slousch, N. "Le nouveau regime turc en Tripoli." *Revue du monde musulman* (1908).
Slousch, N. "Les Senoussiya en Tripolitaine." *Revue du monde musulman* (1907).
Slousch, N. "Les Turcs et les indigenes en Tripolitaine." *Revue du monde musulman.* (1907).
Steppat, Fritz. "Eine Bewegung unter den Notabeln Syriens, 1877–78: Neues Licht auf die Entstehung des arabischen nationalismus." *Zeitschrift der Deutschen Morgenlandischen Gesellschaft.* (Supplementa I) 17 (1969): 631–649.
Stoddard, Phillip H. "The Ottoman Government and the Arabs 1911–1918: A Preliminary Study of the Teskilat-i Mahsusa." Ph.D. Diss., Princeton University, 1963.
Subayh, Muhammad. *Batal la nansahu: ʿAziz al-Misri wa ʿasruhu* [A hero we will not forget: ʿAziz al-Misri and his era]. Sidon, 1973.
Tibawi, A. L. *Anglo-Arab Relations and the Question of Palestine, 1914–1921.* London, 1921.
Tibawi, A. L. *Islamic Education: Its Traditions and Modernization into the Arab National System.* London, 1972.
Tibawi, A. L. *A Modern History of Syria including Lebanon and Palestine.* London, 1969.
Tibawi, A. L. "Syria in the McMahon Correspondence: Fresh Evidence from the British Foreign Office Records." *Middle East Forum* 42 (1966): 5–32.
Tibi, Bassam. *Arab Nationalism: A Critical Enquiry.* Edited and translated by Marion Farouk Sluglett and Peter Sluglett. New York, 1981.
Vinogradov, Amal. "The 1920 Revolt in Iraq reconsidered: The Role of the Tribes in National Politics." *International Journal of Middle East Studies.* 3 (1972): 123–139.
Warburg, Gabriel R. and Gad G. Gilbar. *Studies in Islamic Society: Contributions in Memory of Gabriel Baer.* Haifa, 1984.
Wendell, Charles. *The Evolution of the Egyptian National Image: From Its Origins to Ahmad Lutfi al-Sayyid.* Berkeley, 1972.
Wild, Stefan. "Negib Azoury and His Book 'Le Réveil de la Nation Arabe." In M. Buheiry, ed., *Intellectual Life in the Arab East 1890–1913.* Beirut, 1981.
Wilson, Mary C. "A Passage to Independence: King Abdullah and Transjordan, 1920–1950." In Edward Ingram, ed., *National and International Politics in the Middle East.* London, 1986.

al-Zawi, Tahir Ahmad. *Jihad al-abtal fi tarabus al-gharb* [The holy war of the heroes of Tripoli]. Beirut, 1970.

al-Zawi, Tahir Ahmad. ʿ*Umar al-Mukhtar: al-khalifat al-akhirah min al-jihad al-watani fi Libya* [Umar al-Mukhtar: The last leader of the national holy war in Libya]. Tripoli, n.d.

al-Zawi, Tahir Ahmad. *Wulat tarablus al-gharb min bidayat al-fath al-ʿarabi ila nihayat al-ʿahd al-turki* [The governors of Tripoli from the beginning of the Arab conquest until the end of the Turkish era]. Beirut, 1970.

Zeine, Zeine N. *Arab Turkish Relations and the Emergence of Arab Nationalism.* Beirut, 1958.

Zeine, Zeine N. *The Emergence of Arab Nationalism, with a Background Study of Arab-Turkish Relations in the Near East.* 3d ed. New York, 1973.

Zeine, Zeine N. *The Struggle for Arab Independence: Western Diplomacy and the Rise and Fall of Faisal's Kingdom in Syria.* Beirut, 1960.

Ziadeh, Nicola A. *Origins of Nationalism in Tunisia.* Beirut, 1962.

Index

'Abbas al-Azhari, Shaykh Ahmad, 61
'Abbas Hilmi II, Khedive, 209, 210, 246-47, 248-49, 253, 254, 258, 260, 261, 284
Abbasids, 169
'Abd al-Faqar, Munira, 280
'Abd al-Hadi, 'Awni, 177, 178, 179
'Abdallah (Abdullah), xv-xvi, 175, 206, 207-9, 210, 211-12, 213, 214, 215-17, 218, 219
'Abduh, Muhammad, 6, 7, 8-9, 10, 61, 193, 227
Abdülhamid II, Sultan, 16, 21, 32, 79, 109, 124, 129-30, 154-55, 158, 191, 192, 194, 207, 226, 228, 280
Abdülkerim Bedran ('Abd al-Karim Badran), 40
Abu Bakr, 169
Abu al-Timman, Ja'far, 124, 141-42
al-'Afaf (Virtue), 277, 281
al-Afghani, Jamal al-Din (al-Asadabadi), 6, 193, 198, 246
'Aflaq, Mishal, 11
al-'Ahd (secret society), 13, 60, 161, 162, 248
Ahmad, Feroz, 14

Ahmad Mukhtar Pasha, 101
Ahmed, Leila, 277
al-Ahram, 61
Akçura, Yusuf, 111
'Akramah, agreement of, 235, 236, 237
Aleppo, 39, 41, 42, 56, 180
'Ali (brother of 'Abdullah), 209, 213
'Ali, Muhammad, 245
'Ali (orthodox caliph), 169
Allan Brothers of Aberdeen, 124; see also Iraq; "Lynch Affair"
Allenby, General Sir Edmund, 170, 172
American University of Beirut, ix, 153
Amin, Qasim, 272, 276, 282
'Ammun, Iskander, 102
Anderson, Lisa, viii, ix, xi, xvi
Anglo-French Declaration (November 7, 1918), 262
Anglo-German-Ottoman draft convention (1914), 137
Anis al-jalis (Intimate Companion), 277, 282
Antonius, George, x, 3, 11, 13, 50, 51, 52, 53, 73, 168, 204, 206, 208, 212
Antun, Farah, 7

314 Index

Arab Caliphate *(al-khilafa al-'arabiyya)*, 83
Arab Club, The (al-Nadi al-'arabi), 178, 181
Arabia, 211, 215, 216, 219
Arab Independence *(istiqlal al-'Arab)*, al-'Asali on, 83-84, 91
Arab Independence party (Hizb al-istiqal al-'arabi), 175-76
Arabism, xvi-xvii, 8, 9, 11, 12, 14, 17, 54-55, 207; Ba'thist, 58; defined, viii-ix, 9-10, 51, 62; Hashemites, xv, 209, 214; indicators of, 12-14; *see also* Arab nationalism; self-view; Syria
Arab League, 236
Arab nationalism, viii, x-xii, 50-66, 205, 206; defined, vii, Egypt (1908-1922), 243-264, 275; Iraq, 120-42; Hijaz (1882-1914), 189-201; Palestine, 176-82; self-view, 169; strength of (1914), 12-13; Syria, 167-82; *see also* Arabism, Arab revolt; proto-Arab nationalism
Arab nationalists, post-1918, 16; pre-1918, 15-16
Arab Ottoman club, 228
Arab party (al-Hizb al-'Arabi), 86-87
Arab Reform Committees, repression of (1913), 102
Arab Revolt, xv, 189-90, 200-1, 204-5, 217, 219, 254-55, 256-59; *see also* Husayn, Sharif
Arabs, x, 51-52, 60, 61-62, 63; *see also* Christian Arabs; Iraqi Arabs
Armistice of Mudros, 215
Arslan, 'Adil, 174-75, 176
Arslan, Emir (Amir Amin Arslan), 34, 35, 36-38
Arslan, Shakib, 10, 61
al-As'ad, Kamil, 15, 59, 101

al-'Asali, Shukri, xi, xiii, 59, 74, 78, 82, 89, 90, 91-92, 101, 105; on Arab independence, 83-84, 91; and Arab party, 86-87; and CUP, 77, 84-85, 88-89; early life and education, 75-76, 92*n*7; on education, 79-81; execution of, 91; *Faja'i' al-ba'isin*, 78-79; on language, 81-82, 84-85; *mustarrif* of Latakia, 89-90; and Ottoman parliament, 76-77, 82-83, 85-89; women, attitude towards, 79-80; on Zionism, 83, 88
'Asir, Idrisids of, 210, 216, 247
al-'Askari, Ja'afar, 157, 229
al-'Asr al-Jadid (The New Era), 227
Ataturk, Kemal (Mustafa Kemal), 159, 162, 229
al-Ausi, Mahmud Shukri, 9, 10
Avierno, Alexandra, 282
Azimzâdes ('Azms) family, 40
'Aziza 'Ali Fawzi, 281
al-'Azm, Haqqi, 74
al-'Azm, Rafiq, 107
al-'Azm, Shafiq Mu'ayyad, 86, 128
'Azuri, Najib, 11, 74, 199
'Azzam, 'Abd al-Rahman ('Azzam Bey), 236, 237, 238, 254, 260

Baban, Isma'il Haqqi, 129, 147*n*83
Baghdad, 151-52, 155; *see also* Iraq
Baghdad (newspaper), 161
Baghdad Law College, 153
Baghdad Railway, 133
al-Bakri family, 208
al-Bakri Bey, Nasib, 172, 173
al-Bakri, Tawfiq, *naqib al-ashraf*, 98
Balfour Declaration, 170

Balkans, and CUP, 37, 38, 43, 101, 102
Balkan wars, 43, 230, 247, 250, 275
Banghazi, 228
al-Barazi, Khalid, 59, 101
al-Barghuthi, 'Umar Salih, 11
Baron, Beth, xvii
al-Baruni, Sulayman, 228, 229-30, 231-32, 233, 235, 237, 239, 240
Basra, 133, 135-37, 140-41
Basra Reform Committee, 133-34, 136, 137-38, 146n66, 146n75, 161
Batatu, Hanna, 125, 139, 140-41
Bayna al-Nahrayn (Mesopotamia), 161
Beirut, 33, 35, 41, 54-58, 205
Beirut Reform Committee, 168
Berbers, xvi, 228, 239
Berkes, Niyazi, 16
Bilkhayr, 'Abd al-Nabi, 237, 238, 240
Birdwood, G. C. M., 198
Bismarck, Count von, 155
Blunt, Wilfrid Scawen, 198
British Lynch Brothers Company, *see* "Lynch Affair"; Lynch Brothers Company; Navigation
Buheiry, Marwan, 51, 57, 60
Bu Maryam, agreement of, 239
al-Bustani, Butrus, 7
al-Bustani, Sulayman, 7, 8

Cairo, 58, 60-61, 196
Caliphs: Islamic, 135; orthodox, 169
Cemal Pasa, 91, 108
Central Committee, *see* Committee of Union and Progress (CUP)
Chad, 227
Chamber of Deputies *(majlis al-mab'uthan)*, *see* Ottoman Parliament
Christian Arabs, 3-4, 7-8, 11
Christian Armenian Committees, 34
Christians, 3, 43, 115, 191, 213; Syrian, 51; *see also* Christian Arabs; Lebanese Christians; Religion
Cleveland, William L., 19, 51, 52, 214
Cole, Juan, 276
College of Political and Administrative Sciences (Mulkiye Shahana), 153
Committee of Union and Progress (CUP), ix-x, xiii, 12, 14-15, 16, 19, 32-34, 37, 41, 54, 57-58, 63, 84-85, 99-102, 104, 106-108, 111, 112, 114, 160-61, 177, 198, 208, 214, 228, 231, 245, 248; Adana branch, 41; Baghdad branch, 122-24; Central Committee, x, xii, 31, 22, 42, 43-44; Hijaz, 194, 195-96, 201; Iraq, xi, 120, 122; Istanbul, 132-33, 195; Mosul branch, 123, Nazareth branch, 77, Paris agreement, 107-8; Syrian branch, 38-42; Syrian Parliament, 15, 58-59; Turanists, 161, Turkish-Syrian Committee, 34, 36-38; Unionists, 100-1, 106; *see also* Decentralization party; al-Zahrawi
Congress of 'Aziziyya, 231
Constantinople, 134, 135, 249, 251-52
Conway, Jill, 273
Cromer, Lord, 245
Crow, British Consul, 134, 146n75
Crown Lands, 129-30, 136; *see also mudawwara* lands
Cudizâde Sabit Hoca, 41

Çürüksulu Ahmed Bey, 37
Cyrenaica, 232, 235, 237-38, 239-40, 247-48

Daghir, As'ad, 50, 52, 54, 175
al-Dajani Pasha, 'Arif, 180
Damascus, viii, xiii, 55, 56, 171, 173, 174, 178, 180, 205, 208, 217, 218-19; *see also* Syria
Darwaza, Muhammad 'Izzat, 11, 13, 50, 175, 177, 178-79
Dawn, C. Ernest, vii-ix, x, xii, 31, 50, 51-52, 54-55, 58, 204, 209-10, 249
Decentralization party, 61, 73, 102-3, 104, 105-6, 107, 108, 168, 246; *see also* al-Zahrawi
al-Dia, 87
Dinshawai incident (1906), 245, 274-75
al-Durrah, Mahmud, 162

Eastern and Western Review, 34
"Eastern Question," 102, 110, 250-251
Ebu Nadarra, Shaykh ('Abu Natharra), 36
Edhem Pasa, 39
Education, 4, 20, 153, 163n4; al-'Asali on, 79-81; Hijaz, 192-93, 197-98; Iraq, 151-63; military schools, xiv, 152-63, 163n10; "Turkification" process, 158-63; Western missionary schools, 3-4; women, 79-80, 282-83; *see also* Ottoman Empire
Education Law of 1868 (Maarif-i Umumiye Nizamnamesi), 152, 163n4
Egypt: and Arab nationalism (1908-1922), 243-64; Arab Revolt, attitude towards, 254; British Protectorate, 259; Christians in, 234; European imperialism, 244; Hijaz, 250, 255-58; Islam, xvi, 275, 277; Ottoman-Egyptian boundary agreement (1906), 264; and Ottomanism, xvi-xvii, 274; poets, 249-50; political parties, 250-54; publications, 278-80; Sharifian movement, 255-56; socioeconomics, 244-45; Syro-Palestinian community, 246; Taba territorial dispute (1906), 274; and World War I, 253-54; *see also* Egyptian women; Ottoman Empire
Egyptian Expeditionary Force, 170
Egyptian nationalism, 243-45; 274-78; *see also* Egypt; Egyptian women; Ottoman Empire
Egyptian women: Arabic women's press, 272; charities, 281; conservative, 276-78; education, 282-83; elites, 272, 273, 283, 284; emancipation of, 275-76; liberal, 277-78; literary activities, 278-80; middle and upper-class, 281; motherhood, 278, 279, 282; and nationalism, xvii, 272-85; organizational activities, 280-82; Revolution (1919), 272, 284
Elhac, Yusuf (Yusuf al-Hajj), 35
England, *see* Great Britain
Entente Liberale party (Hürriyet ve Itilaf), 14-15, 17, 62, 89, 100, 132
Ententists, *see* Entente Liberale party
Enver Bey (Enver Paşa), 108, 229, 248
Esad Bey, 41
Euphrates River, *see* "Lynch Affair"; Navigation

Fa'ad Pasha, 'Uthman, 236
Fahmi Bey, 158
Faja'i' al-ba'isin, 78-79
Falhi, Zubaydan, 281
Farid, Muhammad, 247, 250, 252-52, 254, 258, 259
Faris, Selim (Salim Faris), 32-33, 34, 38
Faruq (Farouk), King, 9
al-Faruqi, Muhammad Sharif, 256
al-Fatat, 13, 55, 208, 167; origins and factions, 168-71; Palestinian agenda, 176-82; Syrian agenda, 171-76
Fatat al-nil (Young Woman of the Nile), 277
Fatat alsharq (Young Woman of the East), 277
Faysal (Faisal), King, 161, 162, 163, 167, 174, 175, 206, 209, 213; Arab revolt, 214-15, 217-19, 260; Damascus, viii, xiv-xvi, 171, 181, 212; al-Fatat, 168, 172, 208
Faysal-Clemenceau agreement, 176, 184n38
Fehmi Bey, Ahmad, 54
"Feminism" (misa'iyya), 272-73, 276; *see also* women
Fertile Crescent, xi, 205, 207, 208, 209, 215, 257, 261
Fikri, Lutfi, 101
Filastin, 57
First Arab Congress, 13, 55, 90, 103-4, 116, 249, 275
France, 154, 169-71, 172, 173, 174, 182, 205, 217, 227
Franks, the, 5
French Protectorate (Tunisia), 231
Fuad Efendi, 149n100
Fu'ud, 'Uthman (Osman Fuat), 235, 236

Ganem, Halil (Khalil Ghanim), 35, 36, 37
Gardabiyya (Qasr Bu Hadi), 233, 234
Germany, 154-56, 159, 170, 233, 234
Geylani family, 39
Geylanizâdes (Kaylanis) family, 40
Gharyan conference, Council of the Association for National Reform, 238-40
Gökalp, Ziya, 18, 159
Goltz, Colmar Freiherr von der, 42, 155, 156, 159, 160
Graham, Sir Ronald, 263
Great Britain, 169-71, 189, 199; and 'Abdallah, 211-12, 213, 215-16, 217, 219; Anglo-Ottoman agreement (1913), 133; and Egypt, 245, 254-55, 256, 260-61; and Faysal, 217-18; Hashemites, alliance with, 205-7, 214; Husayn-McMahon correspondence, 212-13; and Iraq, 121, 124, 125-29, 132-38, 140-41, 170, 218; and Libya, 233, 234, 235-36; Red Sea embargo, 213; Transjordan, 219; Zionism, 177-81; *see also* "Lynch Affair"; Lynch Brothers Company; Navigation; Zionism
Grey, Sir Edward, 133

al-Hadara (Civilization), 60, 108
Haddad, Mahmoud, xi, xiii
Haim, Sylvia G., 9-10, 50
al-Hakim, Yusuf, 19-20
Halil Efendi, 40
Halim, Sa'id, 18
Hamid, 'Abd al-Haqq, 160
Hamidiyya Steamship Company, 124-25

318   *Index*

Hanioğlu, M. Šükrü, x, xii, 53-54
Hanotaux, Gabriel, 34
al-Haqiqa, 56
Haqqi Pasha, 89, 132-33, 135-36, 138
Hariri, Adib Daud, 197
Hashemites, xi, xii, xv, 189, 204-19; *see also* Hijaz (Hejaz)
al-Hashimi, Taha, 162-63
al-Hashimi, Yasin, 161-62, 163
Hasqail, Sasson, 129, 138, 144n38
Hazim Bey, 89
Hijaz (Hejaz): 'Abdallah, 209, 211-12, 213, 217; culture and ideology (1908-1914), 196-201; in 1881-1908, 190-94; Husayn, xv, 194-96, 199, 206-13, 216, 219; Muslims, 198; politics in (1908-1914), 194-96; *see also* Egypt; Hijaz Railroad
al-Hijaz, 197
Hijaz Railroad, 192, 195-96, 201, 207, 211, 212
Hilmi Pasha, Hüseyin, 128
Himada, Khalil, 249
Hizb al-islah al-dusturi *see* Party of Constitutional Reform
Hizb al-lamarkaziyya al-idariyya al-'uthmani, *see* Decentralization party
Hizb al-umma, *see* Party of the Nation
al-Hizb al-watani, 280
Hürriyet (Liberty), 32-33
Hürriyet ve Itilaf, *see* Entente Liberale party
Husayn, Sharif: Arab Revolt, 19, 189, 190, 201, 202n10; Egypt, 247, 250, 255-58, 261; Hijaz, xv, 194-96, 199, 206-13, 216, 219; Syria, 172, 175; *al-Islah al-Hijazi*, 197
Husayn, Tawfiq, 162
al-Husayni, al-Hajj Amin, 163

al-Husayni Pasha, Musa Kazim, 180
al-Husayni, Rushdi al-Imam, 177
al-Husayni, Sa'id, 59
Husayn-McMahon correspondence, 212-13
Husayn-Young Turk alliance, 206-7
al-Husri, Sati, 50, 159

Ibha, 210
ibn 'Abdallah, 'Ali, 192
ibn Ghalib, 'Abd al Muttalib, 191
ibn Muhammad, Amir 'Awn al-Rafiq, 191-92
Ibn Sa'ud, Shaykh, 216, 217
Ibrahim, Shaykh ("Khurasani" of Kazimayn), 128
Idrisids, of 'Asir, 210, 216, 247
al-'ilm, 281
Imperial Military College (Istanbul), 153, 154, 156-58
Inchape, Lord, 133, 146n74
India, 126-27, 170
Indian Muslims, 193
al-Inklizi, 'Abd al-Whahhab, 105
al-Iqbal, 56
Iraq, xi-xiv, 151, 204; anti-European Arab Ottomanism, 121-42; British interests in, 170-71, 217-18, 219; education, 151, 158, 161-63; General Staff, 157-58, 160; Imperial 6th Army Corps, 151, 153, 155; Irrigation, 121, 125-27; "Lynch Affair," xiii-xiv, 121-29; navigation rights, 121-23, 140-41, 150n102; Ottoman officers corps, 154-61, socioeconomics, 140
Iraqi Arabs, 138
Iraqi Military College, 158, 162
Iraqi Sunnis, 160

Irrigation, *see* Iraq; Willcocks, William
Ishaq Pasha, 235
Ishaqi Adib, 7, 8
al-Islah al-Hijazi, 197
Islam, xi-xii, xvi, 7, 8-9, 169, 192, 217, 226, 275-77; modernism, 6-7, 8-9, 10, 11, 23; Sunni, 200
Isma'il Pasha, 158
Istanbul, 58, 134, 151, 12, 155, 205, 207, 211, 228, 233; Crown lands, auction of, 136; CUP, xvi, 128, 132, 138-39; Hijaz, 191-92, 195; Military College, 154, 158; Sanusi, disputes with, 227, Syria, trade with, 227; *see also* Istanbul-Mecca axis
Istanbul-Mecca axis, 209, 210, 212, 214
Italy, xvi, 226, 228-29, 231-33; Gardabiyya (Qasr Bu Hadi), 233, 234; Italian-Ottoman war, 229-31, 234, 247, 250
al-Ittihad al-'uthmani, 56, 63
Izzet Bey, 131

al-Jabiri, Ihsan, 174
al-Jabiri, Nafi', 59
Jaffa, 60
Jahid, Husayn (Cahit), 131, 144n49
Jamal Pasha, 168
al-Jam'iyyat al-'arabiyya al-fatat, *see* al-Fatat
Jam'iyyat tarqiyat al-mar'a (the society for women's progress), 280
Japan, 76
al-Jarida, 252, 275, 276, 278
Jawdat, 'Ali, 154, 160, 163
Jawish, Shaykh 'Abd al'Aziz, 259
al-Jaza'iri, 'Abd al-Qadir, 198

al-Jaza'iri, Colonel Salim, 107
al-Jaza'iri, Tahir, 10, 75
Jews, 17-18; immigration of, 130, 170
Jidda, 191, 194, 195, 217
al-Jins al latif (the fair sex), 277, 279
Journal des Debats, 35

Kadri Efendi, 40
Kamal, Prince Yusuf, 249
Kamil, Husayn (Sultan), 255, 284
Kamil, Mustafa, 250, 251, 274, 277, 278
Kamil Pasha, Grand Vizier, 207
Kamil, Dr. Sa'id, 249
al-Karmil, 57
Kateb, Alexis (Alexis Katib), 35, 36, 37-38
al-Kawakibi, 'Abd al-Rahman, 9, 10, 21, 74, 198-99, 246
Kayali, Hasan, 53
Kazim Bey, 40
Kedourie, Elie, 9, 50, 204
Kemal, Namik, 160
Kesf-ül-nikab (Kashf al-niqab), 35
Khadija (the Mother of Believers), 99
Khaiyatzadah, Abdul-Jabbar, 122
Khalidi, Rashid, ix, xiii, 12, 13-15, 17, 74
al-Khalidi, Ruhi, 59
al-Khalil, 'Abd al-Karim, 90-91, 104, 105, 106-7
Khalil, Sa'd al-Din, 59
Khammash, Ahmad, 59
al-Khatib, Muhibb al-Din, 10, 174-75, 253
Khedival family (Egypt), 18
Khilafat, 33
Khoury, Philip, 51, 52, 55, 61, 65
al-Khudayri, 'Abd al-Qadir, 123-24, 128, 129, 132, 141

Khurma, 216-17
al-Kikhiya, Mansur, 232
Kitchener, Lord Herbert, 61, 211, 258
Kramer, Martin, the "Beirut school," ix
Kurd 'Ali, Muhammad, 4, 21, 22, 65, 77, 81, 90, 174

La Jeune Turquie-Türkiya el-Fettat, 36
Language: Arabic, 4, 20, 99, 103, 104, 161, 169, 198, 263; al-Asali on, 81-82, 84-85; French, 154; Islam, 213-14; Ottoman, 19-20, 43; Turkish, 19-20, 159-60
Lausanne peace conference, 261
Law and Civil Service Academies (Mekteb-i Mülkiye), 153
Law of the *Vilayets*, 211
Lawrence, T. E., 213, 215, 216, 256
Lebanese Christians, 4, 10
Lebanese nationalism, 8
Lebanon, 169, 170
Le Croissant-Hilal, 35
Legge Fondamental, 237, 238, 239
Le Temps, 102
Levant, the, 169-70, 171
Libya: 'Akramah agreement, 235, 236, 237; Congress of 'Aziziyya, 231; elites, 226, 227; Gharyan conference, 238-40; governments (local), 231-33; Islam, 226; Italian imperialism, vii, xi, xvi, 112, 225-26, 229-31, 234; publications, 227; al-Rajma, accord of, 237, 238; Sanusiyya, 227, 232, 234, 235, 236, 237-38, 239-40; Tripoli Republic, 236-41; World War I, 231-36; Young Turk revolution, 226-29

al-Liwa', 274, 278
Lutfi, Khudr (deputy of Dayr al Zur), 128
"Lynch Affair," 121-29
Lynch Brothers Company, 121, 124, 127, 141, 148n84; concession of, xiii, 127, 128, 209

Mabarrat Muhammad 'Ali, 281
McMahon, Sir Henry, 212, 213, 256
al-Madi, Mu'in, 177
Mahmud II, Sultan, 151, 155
al-Majali, Tawfiq, 59
al-Majallat al-ni-sa'iyya (women's magazines), 278
Majlis al-mab'uthan, see Ottoman Parliament
Mallet, Sir Louis, 137
Malumat, 98
al-Manar, 61, 98, 99
Mandel, Neville, 74
al-Mar'a al-jadida (The New Woman), 276
Marling, Sir Charles, 138
Marwani Umayyads, 169
Maryud, Ahmad, 176
Mecca, 190-91, 197, 215; 'Abdallah, 208, 209; amirs of, 191, 194; Hijaz Railroad, 195, 196, 211; Husayn, 196, 206-7; Islamic language, 213-14
Medina, xv, 190, 195, 198, 207, 211, 215, 216, 217, 257
Mekteb-i Harbiye, see Military Academy
Mesveret, 33, 36
Midhat Pasha, 152
al-Mihiyya, Sarah, 279
Military Academy (Mekteb-i Harbiye), 153, 156-57, 158
Military College, see Imperial Military College
Milner Mission, the, 260
al-Miqdadi, Darwish, 11

Mir'at al-gharb (Mirror of the West), 116
Misallatah, 236
Misratah, 234, 236, 238, 239
al-Misri Bey, 'Aziz 'Ali, 229, 230, 232, 247-49, 251, 256-58
Mongols, 18
Mousa, Suleiman (Sulayman Musa), 50, 206
Mu'ayyad, Shafiq, 59, 99-100
al-Mu'ayyad 98, 246, 253, 278
Mudawwara lands, 130-31, 132, 133-34, 137
al-Mufid, 55-56, 62, 130
Muhammad, the Prophet, 169, 199, 215
al-Mukhtar, 'Umar, 232, 240
Multazimi al-a'ashar (tax farmers), 78
al-Munir, 40, 98
al-Muntada al-'adabi (Arabist society), 60, 73, 90-91, 249
al-Muqattam, 61, 98
al-Muqtabas, 55, 77, 90-91
al-Muqtataf, 61
Murad Bey, 34, 36-37, 40
Murad Bey, Mizanci, 37
al-Murasalat al-tarikhiyya (Historical Correspondence), 206
al-Murayyid, Ahmad, 237, 240
Musa, Salama, 276
Mushtaq, Talib, 19, 153-54
Muslih, Muhammad, viii, xiv
Muslims, 3, 4, 5, 7, 8, 51, 91, 191, 200, 213
Muslim Young Turkish party, 34

Nahriyya Company, 121, 141; *see also* Iraq; "Lynch Affair"; Navigation
Naim, Ahmed, 18-19
Najd (Nejd), 210
al-Naqib, Sayyid Talib, 128, 131, 133-37, 139-40, 146*n*66, 146*n*70, 161
al-Nashashibi family, 178
Nasif, Malak Hifni (Bahithat al-Badiya), 272, 276, 283
Nassar, Najib, 22, 65
National Scientific Club, 132
Navigation: Euphrates, 121, 122, 123, 133, 135-36, 140-41; Port of Basra, 133; Shatt al-'Arab waterway, 133, 136; Tigris, 121, 122, 123, 124, 133, 135-36, 140-41; *see also* Iraq; "Lynch Affair"; Lynch Brothers Company
Nâzim Bey, Dr., 31
Nazim Pasha, 98, 122
Nile Valley, 244
Nimazi, Amina, 281
Nuri Bey, 233-34, 235
Nuri, Osman, 191, 192
Nusuli, Anis, 4

Occupied Enemy Territory (OET), 170, 172; *see also* Syria
Ochsenwald, William, x, xi, xv, 51
Oil, Kirkuk-Tripoli pipeline, 169
Osman Efendi, 40
Ottoman Administrative Decentralization party, *see* Decentralization party
Ottoman-British Commission, 136
Ottoman-Egyptian boundary agreement (1906), 264
Ottoman Empire, xvi-xvii, 35, 108; and Arab nationalism, 14-16, 23, 51, 62-63, 189-90, 275; Arab provinces, xv, 101-2, 109, 169, 189-90, 200-1; Arab Revolt against, xiv, 189-90, 200-1; centralization, 63, 192, 207, 212; decentralization, 63, 102-3, 110, 139, 251; demise of, xi, 23, 169, 205, 226; and Egyptian nationalism, xvi-

322 Index

Ottoman Empire (*Continued*) xvii, 244, 250-52, 274-75; elites, 23, 51-52, 209, 225, 228; government, xiii-xiv, x-xi, 32-33, 58-59, 129, 132-33; intellectuals of, 5-8; military, xiv, 41-42, 128, 154-58, 193-94, 229; opposition parties, 12, 14, 35, 100, 228; state schools of, 4, 20-21, 152, 158-59, 193, 198; World War I, 108, 196, 233-36; *see also* Ottomanism

Ottoman Islamic College, 61

Ottomanism, xi, xiii, 63, 100, 138; defined, 61-63

Ottoman Parliament, xiii, 13, 15, 99; Chamber of Deputies (*majlis al-mab'utham*), 121-22, 128-29

Ottoman River Navigation Company, 133

Ottoman Turks, 23

Palestine: British-Zionist alliance, 177; Mandate system, 181, 264; "Palestine First,"179-80; Palestinian Youth Society, 181; pan-Arabism, 178, 179, 180-81; Zionism, 22, 57-58, 176-82, 209

pan-Arabism, 9, 159, 162, 171, 178, 179, 180-81, 218, 228

pan-Islam, 192, 226, 229, 233, 240-41, 274

pan-Syrian unity, 177, 178

Paris Peace Conference, 12, 237, 262-63

Parti Constitutional en Turqui, 32

Party of Constitutional Reform (Hizb al-islah al dusturi), 280

Party of the Nation (Hizb al-umma), 275, 280

Patriotism (wataniyya), 4-5, 8

Persian Gulf, 135-36

Phillip, Thomas, 272

Porte, the, 31-32, 125, 129, 132, 151, 152, 210, 212, 229, 230

Press Law (1881), 278

proto-Arab nationalism, 120, 129; *see also* Arab nationalism

al-Qabas, 90, 91

al-Qahtaniyya (Arabist society), 60

al-Qarqani, Khalid, 238-39, 240

al-Qassab, al-Shaykh Kamil, 176

al-Qibla, 214

al-Quwwatli, Shukri, 175

el-Raca (al-Raja'), 35

al-Rajma, accord of, 237, 238

Rashid, Fatima, 276-77, 279

al-Rawi, Ibrahim, 154, 163

Red Sea, 211, 213

Reform Committee of Beirut, 106

Religion, xv, 5, 190, 192, 199, 200

Reshid Pasha, Mustafa, 6

Rida, Rashid, 9, 21, 65, 74, 98, 105, 107, 108, 117n1, 193, 251

al-Rihani, Ammin, 11

al-Rikabi Pasha, 'Ali Rida, 172, 173, 174

Riza, Ahmad, 33, 34, 36, 37, 100

Roded, Ruth, 75

al-Rusafi, Ma'ruf, 160

Russian Revolution (1905), 76

Russo-Turkish War (1877-1878), 154

Rustow, Dankwart, 14

al-Sa'ada, 282

al-Sabbagh, Salah al-Din, 162

Sabbah, 233

Sa'd, Malaka, 278-79, 282

Safi-al-Din, 234-35

Sa'id, Amin, 13, 50, 52

Sa'id, Hafiz, 59
al-Sa'id, Nuri, 157, 161-62, 163, 229, 259
salafi, 193
Salam, Salim 'Ali, 55
Salih, Manahim, 122
Salmoné, Habib Antony, 34, 35, 37-38
Saman Bey, 39-40
San Remo conference, 261
al-Sanusi, Idris, 233, 234-35, 237, 239
Sanusis, 237, 239, 247
al-Sa'ud, 'Abd al-'Aziz ibn 'Abd al-Rahman, xv, 210
al-Sayyid, Ahmad Lutfi, 98, 250, 252, 253, 275, 276, 278
Schölch, Alexander, xvi
Second Congress of Ottoman Liberals, 42
Secret societies, 31, 55, 161, 248; *see also* al-'Ahd; al-Fatat
Seikaly, Samir, ix, xi, xiii, 51
Sefik Bey (Colonel), 37
Self-view, 4-7, 8, 11, 21, 22, 169, 172
Selim III, Sultan, 155
Sem'azâde Ahmad Refik Pasa, 29
Senia property, 131
Sha'arawi, Huda, 281
Shahbandar, 'Abd al-Rahman, 87, 123-24, 128, 143n10, 174-76
Sham'a, Rushdi, 59
Shams al Haqiqa, 197
Shantub, Yusuf, 122
Sharabi, Hisham, 3, 7, 10, 11, 12
al-Sharif, Ahmad, 229, 232, 234
Sharifian family, 172, 172; *see also* Egypt
Shatt al-'Arab waterway, *see* Navigation
Shawkat, Mahmud, 128, 160, 161

Shawkat Pasha (deputy of Diwaniyya),128
al-Shidyaq, Ahmad Faris, 7, 8
al-Shihabi, Mustafa, 76
Shirazi, Mirza 'Ali Aqa, 199
Shivekiar, Princess, 281
Shumayyil, Shibli, 7
Shuqayr, As'ad, 59
Simon, Reeva, viii, xiv
Sinai peninsula, 170, 264
Steppat, Fritz, 19
Storrs, Sir Ronald, 211, 257
Suavi, Ali, 41
Sublime Porte, *see* Porte, the
Suez Canal, 170, 254
Sufi sects, 39, 40
al-Sufur (Unveiling), 276
Sufyani, 169
Sükûti, Ishak, xii, 31, 33
Sulayman Pasha, 210
al-Sulh, Rida, 59, 86, 87
Supreme Oriental Revolutionary Council, 261
al-Suwaydi, Tawfiq, 153
al-Suwayhli, Ramadan, 233, 234-35, 236, 237, 238, 239, 240
Sykes-Picot agreement, 170
Syria, xi, xv, 13, 15-16, 37, 38, 189, 196, 249, 262; Arab Club, 178, 181; Arab Independence party, 175-76; Beirut influence on, 56-58; civil servants, 40; Egypt, 253-61; al-Fatat, 167, 168-82; Occupied Enemy Territory (OET), 170, 172; Ottomanism and Arabism (pre-1914), 8, 50-65; Syrian National party, 174, 175
Syrian Arabs, 15-16, 34
Syrian Christians, 51
Syrian National party (Hizb al-watani al-suri), 174, 175

Tabbara, Shaykh Ahmad Hasan, 63, 65

324   Index

Tahrir al-mar'a (The Liberation of Woman), 276
al-Tahtawi, Rifa'ah Rafi', 4-6, 7-8, 21, 22
Talât Paşa (Talât Bey), 108, 132, 195-96
al-Tamimi, Rafiq, 178
Tanin, 87, 88, 130-31
Tanzimat, 6, 151
Tarabein, Ahmed, xi, xiii
Taraqqin (Progress), 227
Tarqiyat al-mar'a (Woman's Progress), 276-77
Tawakkul, Raghib Mustafa, 197
Tax-farmers *(multazimi al-a'ashar)*, 78
al-Taymuriyya, 'A'ysha, 272
Teachers Training College, 153
Teskilat-i mahsusa, 229-31, 233-34
Tibawi, Abdel Latif, 12, 50
Tibi, Bassam, 3, 7, 10, 12
Tigris River, *see* "Lynch Affair"; Navigation
Transjordan, xv-xvi, 208, 218, 219
Tribes, 128, 132, 137, 191, 195, 205, 210, 216
Tripoli, 227, 228, 238, 235-41; Italian invasion of, 99-100, 114, 275, 280; *see also* Tripoli Republic; Tripolitania
Tripoli Republic (al-jumhuriyya al-tarablusiyya), 236-41; Council of Four, 236-38; Gharyan conference, 238-39; *see also* Libya
Tripolitania, 228, 229, 234, 235, 236, 237, 238
al-Tunisi, Khayr al-Din, 6
Turanists, 161
Turco-Circasians, 274
Turco-Tartars, 21
"Turkification," x, xi, xii, 17, 18, 54, 113, 158-61, 177; *see also*, Turkish nationalism
Turkish Anarchist Committee, 42
Turkish Islamists, 18
Turkish-Italian war, 275
Turkish nationalism, ix, x-xii, 18, 53-54, 111, 214
Turkish-Syrian Committee, 33, 34, 35, 36, 37, 38
Türkiya-el-Fettat, 37
Tusan, Prince 'Umar, 249
Tuta (Tota), Khalil, 11

Ulema *('ulama')*, 19, 39-40
'Umar (orthodox caliph), 169
Umm al-Qura, 246
Umma party, 250, 252, 253
Union Liberale, 89
Unionists, 14, 15, 16, 17-18, 19, 22, 100, 105-6, 254, 259
al-Uraisi, Abd al-Ghani, 9, 55, 62-63, 65
al-'Urwa al-wathqa, 193
al-Uskubi, Ibrahim ibn Hasan, 196
'Uthman (orthodox caliph), 169

Vasfi Efendi, 40
Vehib Bey, 195

Wafd, 259-60, 261, 262
Wafik Bey, 122
War College, 154
Watani party, 250, 251, 253, 254, 261
Wataniyya, *see* Patriotism
Weizmann, Chaim, 181
Wilhelm II, Kaiser, 154-55
Willcocks, William, irrigation, 125-27
Wilson, Mary C., xi, xv
Wilson, President Woodrow, 236, 262-63

Wingate, Sir Reginald, 255, 262
Women, 36, 79-80, 280; *see also* Egyptian women
World War I, viii, 107, 205, 212, 225; *see also* Libya; Ottoman Empire

Yakan, Wali al-Din, 250
al-Yaziji, Ibrahim, 8
Yemen, Imam of, 216
Young Arab Society, *see* al-Fatat
Young Ottomans, 6
Young Turk party, 37
Young Turk revolution, 11, 16, 76, 206, 208, 226-29
Young Turks, 12, 14-15, 16, 17, 19, 20-22, 31, 37, 39, 42, 120-21, 159-61, 206-7, 280
Yusuf, Abd al-Rahman, 59, 76, 80-81, 86, 208

Yusuf, Shaykh 'Ali, 246, 252-53, 278

Zaghul, Sa'd, 259, 260
al-Zahawi, Jamil, 160
al-Zahrawi, Shaykh 'Abd al-Hamid (Abdülhamid el-Zehravi), xi, xiii, 9, 40, 59, 60, 74, 86; and Arab nationalist thought (1911-1914), 109-17; and CUP, 99-103; and decentralization, 108, 110; early life and education, 97-98; inaugural speech, 116, publications, 98-99; on "Turkification," 113
Zaluf, Yahuda, 122
al-Zawi Bey, Farhat, 229-30, 231
Zeine, Zeine N., 11, 12, 50
Zionism, 12, 17, 18, 57, 74, 83, 88, 170, 176-78, 181, 209
Zohrab, James, 198